THE PRISONER OF DURAZZO

Being a History of Six Months
in a Phantom Kingdom

and of

Armageddon Postponed

ROBERT A. LANIER

Zenda Press

Zenda Press
P. O. Box 41156
Memphis, Tennessee 38174

Printed and bound in the United States of America

Lanier, Robert A., 1938-

Includes bibliographical references and index.

ISBN 978-0-615-32523-1

Dedicated to the lovely Linda,
without whom this book would have never been printed.

The Kingdom of Albania now has an official existence. The Powers have wrought a miracle the like of which has not been seen since Mr. Anthony Hope invented Ruritania. It was done in Downing Street.

--*The Times* (London), March 4, 1914, p. 5

In this peculiar land there has never been any united nation under one ruler and one dynasty. In valleys, encircled and cut off by high mountain ranges, the Albanian tribes live separated to a considerable degree from one another. Their political system is not unlike the clan system of the Scotch. Christians and Mohammedans are represented in equal numbers.

The custom of "vendetta" is an ancient one, sanctified by tradition, which is no less true of robbery and cattle stealing. Agriculture is still in a backward stage of development, farming is in its infancy, the implements used therein date from before the flood... The head man of the clan dispenses justice in the open, under the village tree... Every man is armed and most are excellent shots. Whenever the head man of the clan turns up while on horseback tour through his territory in some hamlet, the inhabitants expect a blessing from him in the form of jingling coins, which sometimes are scattered about him from the saddle... Great is the dissatisfaction when it does not happen... Up to the time of the Balkan War, many Albanians entered the Turkish service, Young Albanian nobles [served in the] palace guards of the Sultan... These were partly relatives of the Sultan... Thus the Sultan was enabled to keep the usually turbulent Albanians quiet and loyal by means of "family ties."

---ex-Kaiser Wilhelm II of Germany, on Albania (1920)

History owes its excellence more to the writer's manner than to the materials of which it is composed. The intrigues of courts, or the devotion of armies, are regarded by the remote spectator with as little attention as the squabbles of a village, or the fate of a malefactor that falls under his own observation. The great and the little, as they have the same senses, and the same affections, generally present the same picture to the hand of the draughtsman; and whether the hero or the clown be the subject of the memoir, it is only man that appears with all his native minuteness about him, for nothing very great was ever formed from the little material of humanity.

---Oliver Goldsmith, in *Beau Nash*

Uneasy lies the head that wears a crown.

---William Shakespeare---*Henry IV*, Part III

TABLE OF CONTENTS

FOREWORD

When I first read about the peculiar incident which is the subject of this book, some thirty-five years ago, I only considered writing a book about it because the subject is so unknown to the average person. I was certain that I would have a virtual monopoly on informing the world about it. Through the years I collected information and obscure books on the subject with a view towards pulling it all together when I retired. However, upon settling down to work, I discovered that I was not entirely alone in my interest in the matter. In recent years, Albanian history has attracted the attention of some Western historians. I learned that there are archives on the subject available even to those of us not able to understand the Albanian language. Historians in the English language who have dealt with the part of Twentieth Century Albanian history in this book include Joseph Swire, who wrote a definitive account, *Albania: The Rise of a Kingdom* (1929), Gervase Belfield, who has edited and brilliantly introduced the invaluable memoir, *The Six Month Kingdom*, by Duncan Heaton-Armstrong (2005), and Jason Tomes, and Owen Pearson, who have produced *Zog, Europe's Self-Made Monarch* (2003) and *Albania, From Republic to Kingdom* (2004), respectively. However, these talented writers have not quite co-opted the field of my subject.

I believe that I have consulted most of the major sources of information available to me. It has been my hope to write an account of a fascinating event in a way which will appeal to the general reader, although everything in this book is founded on the historical record, and the sources are carefully supplied.

INTRODUCTION

Who Were the Kings?

"Once upon a time, in a kingdom far away…" Are there still children's stories which begin with those lines? In my childhood there were. Kingdoms always had to have a king, of course. But when I neared adulthood, and put away childish things, I put kingdoms and kings out of my mind. They were consigned to the fantasy world with Santa Claus and the Tooth Fairy. Certainly, I assumed that they were something in the far, distant past. What a surprise, then, when in 1951, when I was about 13, I saw a photograph in the newspaper of a handsome man in a naval officer's cap who, upon, closer investigation, was found to be a king! He was King George VI of Great Britain, father of the present Queen Elizabeth II. I soon became aware that there were many more kings in the world, still on their thrones. In Europe, there was King Haakon VII of Norway, Queen Juliana of the Netherlands, King Frederick IX of Denmark, King Gustav Adolf VI of Sweden, King Paul of Greece, and King Baudoin of Belgium. This is not to mention the reigning Prince Rainier II of Monaco (before he married Grace Kelly) and the reigning grand duke and duchess, respectively, of Liechtenstein and Luxembourg. And of course, the "third world" countries of Thailand (Siam that was), Egypt, Libya, Jordan, Iraq, and Saudi Arabia, also had kings. Japan and Ethiopia had emperors, and Morocco had a sultan who did not yet call himself a king. I will not even mention the living, exiled monarchs of Spain, Bulgaria, Romania, Albania, Germany, Italy, Austria, Hungary, and even France, which had at least two royal and one imperial families. All of this during my young life, in the bleak, communist-threatened post World War II world! Things have changed only slightly since then. Most of the incumbents have died of course, but Spain has gained a monarchy, while Greece has lost one.

This institution of monarchy piqued my interest because of the anachronism of it. How did it come to still exist in the modern world of republics, people's republics, and presidents? Monarchs are obviously still fascinating to the popular mind, as evidenced by everything from American carnival "royalty", to the obsession with Princess Diana, to newspapers and periodicals devoted to current royal peccadilloes. In the Twentieth Century, or the last part of the Nineteenth Century, royalty were the stuff of immensely popular books and plays, although their private lives were somewhat less open to scrutiny than today.

Even staunchly republican America has long fixed a fascinated gaze upon all things royal and imperial. We need go back no farther than the charming novel, *The Prisoner of Zenda*, published in 1894, which became an instant success and a classic of the type. Written by an Englishman calling himself Anthony Hope, the book told the story of another Englishman with an amazing resemblance to the young king of the mythical European country of Ruritania. This resemblance results in his temporary impersonation of the king, until the king, who has been secretly imprisoned in a hunting lodge by his evil half brother, can be rescued. The Englishman's masquerade fools almost everyone except the villains, (no explanation being given for his ability to speak fluent Ruritanian).[1] That best-selling novel led to numerous stage versions, as well as at least three Hollywood film productions (once that medium was invented). Of the latter, the most memorable, perhaps, was the 1937 version with Ronald Colman, which capitalized upon the coronation that year of King George VI. Countless inferior novels by other authors, set in mythical European kingdoms, came to be called, "Ruritanian romances," or, based upon an imitator, "Graustarkian romances." Another timeless popular success was the operetta, *The Merry Widow*, (*Die Lustige Witwe*) by the Hungarian Franz Lehar, which made its debut in Vienna in 1905. It was soon a huge hit throughout Europe, Britain, and the United States. So wealthy did Lehar become from his operetta that he acquired a baronial chalet in the Austrian lake district of Salzburg at Bad Ischl, where the Emperor Franz Josef summered.[2] A satire on royalty and especially Balkan[3] politics, it was set in what was then modern day. It told the story of a plot by the fictitious bankrupt kingdom of Pontevedro to prevent its richest citizen (the widow of the title) from marrying a foreigner and thus exporting her wealth. A handsome Pontevedran diplomat and nephew of the king, Count Danilo, is ordered to woo her—and succeeds. Some changes were made in the operetta to soothe Balkan sensibilities, notably those of tiny Montenegro, which had a crown prince named Danilo.[4] The popularity of the musical play, and especially "The Merry Widow Waltz," led to spin-offs of merchandise including, most notably, large feathered ladies' hats and a style of corset.[5]

Like plays based upon *The Prisoner of Zenda*, performances of the operetta usually included elaborate costumes and uniforms on the men, similar to those still worn then by European soldiers outside of actual combat. These uniforms were copied by military men in other nations, including even the United States and Japan. European and British soldiers in peacetime still wore elaborate and colorful uniforms patterned after famous fighting units of the past. Hussar regiments, based on traditional Hungarian cavalry, wore tunics covered with decorative loops of braid, round fur hats with plumes, and tight trousers tucked into shiny, knee-length boots. Over the shoulder was slung a short, fur-trimmed jacket called a dolman. And, of course, a sword or saber hung by the side of the officers. Other cavalrymen might wear pseudo-Roman metal helmets with horsehair plumes, or, emulating medieval Poles, helmets with little square "mortar-board"-like platforms on top, called *czapkas*. They might also wear shiny metal breast plates called cuirasses, and be called "Cuirassiers." Foot soldiers, called Grenadiers or Jägers or Chasseurs, depending on the country, might wear tall bearskin hats or pointed headgear like the Eighteenth Century Hessian troops we see in illustrations of the American Revolution. They might emulate Algerians and call themselves Zouaves, wearing fezzes with tassels, red baggy pants and gaiters, and short embroidered vests. Whether the uniforms were somber, like the dark green of the British 60th rifles, or bright, like the British red-coated infantry regiments, the uniforms of these soldiers were elaborate, well-tailored, handsome, and completely unsuited for anything but peacock-like display. Even ostensibly egalitarian American officers got themselves up in these operetta-like outfits for gala occasions such as presidential inaugurations. The sartorial influence of European military aristocrats was popular worldwide.

So, my fascination with the seeming anachronism of royalty and its trappings was not unique. Even in the late Nineteenth Century royal doings in Europe were a constant source of articles in newspapers and magazines and books of gossip, as well as fact. Perhaps the most dramatic incident, and no doubt one of the inspirations for writers like Anthony Hope, was the death of Crown Prince Rudolf of Austria-Hungary in 1889. He was the handsome young heir to the ancient throne of the Habsburgs. Like many royal sons awaiting their chance at the throne, Rudolf was something of a rebel against much that his father Emperor Franz Josef stood for. Though married, he was a ladies' man and a carouser, and something of a political rebel. He espoused the cause of Hungary (a partner country in the Empire) over that of the Austrians. It is thought that he suffered from mental instability, either as a result of depression or venereal disease of the brain, or both. In 1889, he took his 17-year old mistress to his hunting lodge, or "shooting box" at Mayerling, in the Vienna Woods. There he shot her to death before blowing his own brains out. The government, as may be imagined, was hard put to explain this to the public. They released absurd explanations ("heart attack", etc.) before they settled on suicide "while the balance of his mind was disturbed." The latter explanation was necessitated by photos of the Prince lying in state, with the top of his head covered with bandages. The murder of the girl was hushed up.[6]

Bear in mind that France and Switzerland were the only two significant countries in Europe in the early Twentieth Century which were republics. France had a brush with a royalist restoration in 1898, but the *coup* failed to materialize when the Pretender to the throne, the Duc d'Orleans, hesitated to leave Austria, where he was engaged in the "urgent business" of hunting.[7] It is hard now to realize the real political and moral authority held then by monarchs.

Investigation of the subject of modern monarchy plunged me into the arcane world of titles and forms of address, which I shall now share with the reader, whether ready or not.

Kings and Queens are now addressed as "Your Majesty," and are usually the sovereigns of major countries, while the royal heads of state of smaller countries are usually called Princes or Grand Dukes, and are addressed by some form of "Your Highness."[8] As readers of Shakespeare and other older writers will note, those exact titles were not always used in the past. But they have become rather standardized for the last 200 years or so, at least in English. Sometimes, in more formal address, modifiers were added, such as "His Britannic Majesty," (Britain) or, "His Most Catholic Majesty," (France), or "His Apostolic Majesty," (Austria), etc. Emperors were generally those royal persons who ruled over a more diverse kingdom or "Empire," and were referred to as "His (or Her) Imperial Majesty," to distinguish them from the rabble of mere kings. For example, the Austrian Empire contained many nationalities other than Austrian Germans as, to a lesser extent, did the German Empire of 1871-1918. The same could be said for Russia, whose emperor was called Czar by most, although knowledgeable Russians referred to him as "*Gosudar Imperator*," using either or both words.[9] The Emperor of Germany was referred to (even by English speakers) as "the Kaiser," even though Franz Josef of Austria and all other Germanic Emperors were "Kaisers." Like "Czar," the word "Kaiser" is another variation on the name Caesar (as in Julius). And, as all classical scholars will know, this emulation of the Roman Empire derived its vocabulary either from the famous Roman general and consul, or from the later Roman rulers who adopted the (originally military) title of Imperator. We simply call them emperors, and let it go at that.

Persons who were ranked above the commoners, but were less than royal, were called nobility. This always seems to be a matter of confusion to Americans, who confuse nobility with royalty. Nobles were originally the henchmen of the kings and ruling princes, and were given titles to suit their ranks in the pecking order. Unfortunately for uniformity and simplicity, these titles and ranks are somewhat different in each European country, and different still in Great Britain. Let us take the British system for a standard (leaving out the confusing question of the peerages of Scotland and Ireland) by which to illustrate and compare. The ranks of nobility in Britain, starting at the top (with some foreign equivalents) are as follows:

British:	European:
Royal Duke	*Duc* (French), *Erherzog* (Austrian)
Duke	*Duc* (French), *Duque* (Spanish), *Herzog* (German-Austrian)
Marquess	*Marquis* (French), *Marchese* (Italian) (note: the wife of a British Marquess is a Countess!)
Earl	*Comte* (French), *Graf* (German-Austrian), *Conte* (Italian)
Viscount	*Vicomte* (French)
Baron	*Baron* (German-Austrian), *Barone* (Italian)
Knight ("Sir") (not hereditary and not strictly noble)	*Freiherr* or *Reiter* (German)[10] (Note: The "Red Baron" Manfred von Richthofen, World War I German flying ace, was not a Baron, but a *Freiherr*.

Until recently, these British titles were hereditary and passed on to the eldest male heir. But now, by law, no new hereditary titles may be created in Britain.

These titles of nobility were conferred by the sovereign (i.e., the reigning emperor, king, queen, or prince), and the title holders never ruled a country. On the continent, however, things were not always so orderly. Enclosed in the German and Austrian Empires were former rulers of lesser states, who might be kings, grand dukes, dukes, or princes. In Austria there were also royal and imperial *arch*dukes, while in Russia there were imperial *grand* dukes. To make things more confusing, the rulers of Austria, Germany and Russia created some commoners "prince" or "baron" in return for services of varying kinds and degrees. In Austria and Germany, a duke ranked higher than a prince.[11] A *Fürst*, (to be explained later), ranked between a duke and a count.[12] In the newly-united Kingdom of Italy, both the king and the Vatican created titles, often for financial considerations. These titles passed not only to the eldest son, as in most countries, but to all the sons, resulting in a plethora of Italian counts, barons, marcheses, etc.[13]

In central Europe, the titles of nobility were not confined to the eldest son. A "Pocketbook of Counts" was published, listing the counts of Austria, Germany, and Hungary. It showed the close relations between the noble families of those countries. All the sons of counts were counts. In Hungary, for example, there were about 70 Counts Szecheny and about 70 Counts Zichy. It is said that, among the seven million Magyars of Hungary, there were 800,000 nobles of higher or lower degree.[14] After receiving a title, an Austrian had to pay for the registration thereof. For the rank of *Fürst* (prince), one had to pay 3,240 kronen (about $11,664 today); for *G raf* or Count 550 kronen; for *Freiherr* or *Baron* 440 kronen; for *Reiter* 400 kronen; for the simple ennobling "*von,*" 330 kronen.[15] The German suffix, "*von,*" ("of" or "from") means that a person is a noble (either born or created) of some degree, no matter how humble. The suffix "*zu*" ("of" or "to") means a somewhat higher rank.[16] As we shall see, some nobles had both suffixes after their names. By custom, a "von" was allowed to call himself a baron when he went abroad![17]

If the reader has not yet fallen asleep, it might be well to discuss here the two dominant central European empires which will play a major part in our story. The oldest was Austria-Hungary. It was the successor, in 1867, to the Austrian Empire, which in turn was the successor to the "Holy Roman Empire." The 1867 union *(ausgleich)* of Austria and Hungary resulted from the semi-secession of Hungary from the old empire. It was only a semi-secession because Hungary eventually agreed to be an equal part of a government which would have a joint ruler: the Emperor of Austria (who would also be king of Hungary and commander-in-chief of the armed forces). There were also some joint governmental institutions, such as a foreign ministry and a finance ministry. Austria and Hungary would continue to rule their own internal affairs (and those of the various other nationalities whom they controlled) with their own parliaments and prime ministers. Since 1867, the joint Austro-Hungarian sovereign was Emperor (Kaiser) Franz Josef of Habsburg and his capital was Vienna, although he also had palaces in the Hungarian capital of Budapest.

Let us back up a bit farther for some information which may be useful later on in this book. Austria, or rather its Habsburg rulers, had, for hundreds of years before the Nineteenth Century, dominated the loose central European confederation called, pretentiously, the Holy Roman Empire (famously described as neither holy nor Roman). The emperors of that empire were theoretically not born to rule, but elected by the member states. Invariably, however, only the Habsburg emperors had been elected. The conquests of Napoleon stirred up everything in Europe, and the then Austrian Emperor Franz was worried that Napoleon, newly self-proclaimed "Emperor of the French," would, with the help of the German rulers of Bavaria and Württemberg (called "electors," because they got to vote on candidates for Holy Roman Emperor) have himself elected Holy Roman Emperor. Franz then quickly converted his holdings into an "Austrian Empire," and two years later, abolished the title of Holy Roman Emperor altogether.[18] So, after 1867, Franz Josef was not only Imperial (Austrian Empire) but also Royal (Kingdom of Hungary). Franz Josef's acts were referred to as "K. u. K." That is, *Kaiserliche und Königliche* = "Imperial and Royal". His empire, because of its diverse and polyglot nature held together only by the Habsburgs, was often referred to as simply "the Monarchy." To avoid undue effort, Austria-Hungary will usually be referred to hereinafter simply as "Austria."

The German Empire was in a somewhat different condition. Whereas previously Prussia had been one of the German states subordinate to the Holy Roman Emperor, by 1871, it had conquered not only Austria and Bavaria, but also France. Thereupon, in 1871, it declared the creation of the German Empire (or *Reich*), with the King of Prussia embodied in the new imperial constitution as the emperor (*Kaiser*) of the Empire. In this empire, there was an imperial parliament (*Reichstag*) in the Prussian capital of Berlin, heavily weighted in favor of the throne, representing four kingdoms, six grand duchies, six duchies, and eight principalities.

With forty million of the Empire's sixty million population, Prussia naturally dominated. One of the German principalities had less than three thousand subjects, while some of the larger and more important states, like Bavaria, retained considerable internal control in matters such as posts, telegraph and railways, and military administration, as well as a separate diplomatic service, with ambassadors not only to foreign countries, but to Berlin itself! In the German Empire also resided the little German statelet of Wied-Neuwied in the Rhineland, which is important to our story.[19] Real control in Germany largely rested with the Emperor, or Kaiser, who could choose any prime minister (*Kanzler*, or Chancellor) he wanted, despite the wishes of the *Reichstag*, and could declare war and command the military forces. There was no German Imperial nobility; only the nobility of the member states.

Russia, of course, was a huge land empire with millions of peasants and relatively few city dwellers or middle-class subjects. Until 1905 there was no pretense of any representation of the people in government and no thought of restrictions on the rule of the Emperor (Czar). Even after a revolt that year, and the creation of a parliament *(Duma)* that could do nothing more than talk, the Czar kept control of government.

Becoming a Modern King

Although the written Norwegian and Danish languages are practically the same, Norway and Denmark are now two separate Scandinavian countries. By 1814, Norway had been ruled by Denmark for 400 years. In that year the Treaty of Kiel, approved by the Great Powers of the day, united Norway and Sweden to compensate Sweden for the loss of Finland to Russia. Similarly, Sweden and Norway were under the same king from 1814 until 1905. By 1905, unrest in Norway, sparked by a demand for a separate consular service, led to an overwhelming vote by Norway for independence. Sweden did not resist. Norway elected Prince Karl of Denmark to be their king, and he took the title King Haakon VII to honor the ancient Norwegian kings. There are no nobles in Norway. The old ones died out and no new ones were created.

Why discuss that episode? The idea of a foreign prince being installed as a country's ruler, like some heart transplant, was no longer unusual in 1905. In ancient times, kings got their power by simply taking it by brute force. Since the advent of the Enlightenment in the Eighteenth Century, the idea that the people to be governed (or someone) should be consulted, came to be accepted, more or less. Thus, although Napoleon and his nephew, Napoleon III, came to power through military *coups*, they pretended later to consult the people through plebiscites to ratify their governments. By the Nineteenth Century, new opportunities for creating kingdoms in Europe were arising. The Turkish Ottoman Empire, which had reached the gates of Vienna in the Seventeenth Century, was losing its grip on Europe. As late as 1800 it still ruled what is now Greece, Serbia, Romania, Bulgaria, Croatia, Montenegro, Bosnia-Herzegovina, and Albania. These countries are in that part of south-central Europe collectively known as the Balkans. In 1832, with the help of

Russia and foreign volunteers, Greece won its independence from Turkey. Setting the pattern for future events, including the major subject of this book, the Kingdom of Greece was created by a conference of the Great Powers in London, and was declared to be a monarchy. After some controversy, a Bavarian prince was chosen for the Greeks, and he was installed with the help of foreign troops, carrying with him a force of Bavarian soldiers to maintain his throne. In a few years he proved unsatisfactory to all concerned and was replaced by a Danish prince. The ordinary Greek people had little to say about the matter, but the new Danish king proved to be popular. A similar situation had occurred in Spain in 1870, when Amadeo, the ugly son of the ugly King of Italy was "called" to the turbulent throne of that Iberian country. Unpopular, he took the first opportunity of resigning in 1873, telling relatives that he had never found out why he had been "called," nor why he was rejected.[20]

Next came Romania. Long a puppet province of the Turks, it was strongly influenced by its neighbor, Russia. In 1864 it "elected" a German Catholic prince of the Hohenzollern family, who was recognized as a king (rather than a prince) in 1881. This followed a war with Turkey and the subsequent summit conference of great powers at the Congress of Berlin in 1878.[21]

Then came Bulgaria, which threw off the Turks and in 1879 "elected" a German prince who proved too popular and independent to suit the Russians. Because of the latter, he was replaced after only a few years by an Austro-German of the Coburg family, selected by a delegation from the Bulgarian parliament and approved by the European Great Powers. In 1908 this "Prince of Bulgaria" declared the nation free of even symbolic ties to Turkey, and gave himself the grandiose title of "Czar," to the dismay of other European royalty. Strangely, Bulgaria had no titled nobility.[22]

Serbia, by fits and starts from 1815 onward, gradually won its independence from Turkey by 1882, despite two murderous rival Serb dynasties.

By the terms of the 1878 Congress of Berlin, which dealt with the Russo-Turkish War and the ancillary problems thereof, the Turkish provinces of Bosnia and Herzegovina, resting on the northern Adriatic Sea, were to be administered by Austria-Hungary.

Montenegro ("Black Mountain"), a tiny country of a few thousand people south of Bosnia and Herzegovina and north of Albania, may be said to have always kept its *de facto* independence from the Turks by its population retreating to their mountains until the world recognized them as a country in 1878.

Calling foreign princes to a new throne could have tragic consequences. Prince Alexander of Battenberg was able to flee Bulgaria safely in 1886, but Maximilian von Habsburg, brother of Emperor Franz Josef of Austria, was not so lucky. Deceiving himself that he had been elected by the people of Mexico to be their emperor, he and his wife moved there in 1864, protected by French troops and a small contingent of foreign volunteers, as well as by the Mexican conservatives who had summoned them. In 1867, after the French were forced by the U.S. to withdraw, he was captured and executed by the Mexican republicans. Some other implantations worked out better. One of Napoleon's marshals, Bernadotte, was chosen King of Sweden. As noted, Greece eventually worked out well, and another Danish prince was chosen to be King Haakon VII of Norway when it gained its independence in 1905.

In the Nineteenth and early Twentieth Centuries, the life of a king was fraught with danger from anarchists and various malcontents. Anarchists seemed to think they could kill off governments permanently by killing all the leaders. Beautiful, harmless Empress Elizabeth of Austria was stabbed to death in 1898 while on vacation in Switzerland. King Umberto of Italy, who boasted a moustache like elephant tusks, was murdered in 1900 at a public event. The liberal Czar of Russia, Alexander II, was ungratefully blown up in 1882. Kings who went crazy, like Ludwig II and Otto of Bavaria could be deposed, the latter being removed peacefully because of his "grievous illness" in 1913.[23] But the King of Portugal and his son, the Crown Prince, were murdered simultaneously in 1908, while the popular King George of Greece was shot walking down the street in 1913.

The murder of the King and Queen of Serbia in 1903 was particularly brutal, and committed by their own officers. King Alexander Obrenovich, a rather unstable man, had adopted many unpopular foreign and domestic policies, and had married an unpopular commoner.

The evening of June 10, 1903, was hot and muggy in Belgrade, the capital of Serbia. At the royal palace complex where King Alexander, aged twenty-six, and his queen, Draga, aged thirty-six, lived, the captain of the guard, P. Panayotovich, was bored. He was easily plied with drink by a fellow officer, Lieutenant Peter Zivkovich. He soon fell asleep on a sofa. Within the palace, by midnight the King and Queen had retired to bed, the King reading a French novel through his pince-nez. Because of at least one previous attempt on their lives (by insinuating a poisoner into the royal kitchen), the pair had insured that there would be a hiding place within the palace, where, in case of another attempt, they could take refuge until help could come. This refuge consisted of an alcove, behind a false wall, which was virtually undetectable because of its iron door and close-fitting outline. Unknown to the royal pair, a group of army officers, led by the Queen's former brother-in-law Alexander Mashin, and the bull-necked Captain Dragutin Dimitrijevich, were intent upon their deaths that very night. By 11:45 p.m., these men and several others had donned their uniforms and surrounded the palace. The Police Commissioner happened to notice this unusual late night activity, and telephoned the Prefect of Police to report it. Angered at being awakened, that worthy official referred the Commissioner to the police duty officer for that hour. That gentleman, however, had absented himself on some personal business, leaving his post in the feeble hands of a young clerk, who did not know what to do. By now, it was a half hour after midnight and the disloyal Lieutenant Zivkovich opened the palace gates to the intruders, who raced up the paved carriage drive. The sergeant of the Palace Guard ordered the Guard to turn out, but he was shot dead on the spot, and Lieutenant Zivkovich ordered the rest of the Guard not to move. The conspirators then rushed into the quarters of the King's *aide de camp*, General Laza Petrovich, who was still awake and dressed, and wounded him in the left arm when he questioned their business.

There were then two palaces in the royal enclave; the old palace and the new palace, which was twenty yards away in the same courtyard. The traitors headed for the old palace, where they expected to find the King and Queen, but found the entrance locked. Having procured some dynamite, they blew open the doors, but thereby made a noise heard all over Belgrade. Unfortunately for the conspirators, it also shorted out the palace wiring, plunging the entire building into darkness. By now, police and soldiers were around and firing at each other in the confusion. The enraged intruders ran through the darkened palace, cursing and swearing as they searched for the King and Queen without success. They obtained candles and finally found the royal bedroom on the second floor, but it was empty. Still, the royal bed had obviously recently been occupied. The conspirators knew that, if the King escaped, their lives were forfeit. General Petrovich was collared and told that he would be spared if he told where the royal couple could be found. When he protested that he had no idea, they struck him with their swords. Fending off the blows, he ventured, "Perhaps they are at the new palace." They dragged him along as they crossed the courtyard. He protested that he needed to get his hat, as he might catch cold if he went outside bare-headed! Unimpressed by this argument from a man almost murdered a few minutes earlier, a lieutenant dropped his own cap upon the general's head.

Nothing having turned up in the new palace, the party returned to the old palace. One can imagine the horror felt by the King and Queen who, at the first sounds of danger, had hidden in the secret room. Several hours of darkness, explosions, gunshots, and screams had passed. The searchers had thumped the walls, looking for secret doors, without success. The front of the old palace faced a narrow street lined with horse chestnut trees. Directly across the street from the palace was the Russian legation and the Russian minister, Tcharikoff, was at that moment looking at the palace. He had been warned three days earlier that something was afoot, and the noise no doubt alerted him that night. The royal hiding place had a window facing the street and the Russian legation, and Queen Draga leaned her head against the window, looking for help. She saw a member of the Royal Guard, Captain Luba Kostich, walking below. She opened the window and shouted to him, "Soldiers! Your king is in danger! For God's sake, to the rescue! To the rescue!" Instead of rescue, the captain sent a bullet from his pistol in her direction. She hastily retreated into the alcove and drew the blinds, but Kostich immediately ran up the palace stairs to alert the other searchers. Despite this, they still could not locate the secret door. Frantically, they procured an axe and began chopping at the bedroom wall. General Petrovich then said, "Gentlemen, will you give me your word of honor that you will spare the life of the King?" They promptly lied in the affirmative, whereupon the general knocked on the iron door and called out, "Sire! Sire! Open! Open! I am your Laza. Here are your officers!" The King opened the door slowly. He was in his dressing gown, trembling from fear, and the Queen was in her petticoat, white silk stays, and one yellow stocking. The brave invaders then shot General Petrovich dead.[24] The King stepped in front of the Queen and asked, "What is it you want? What of your oath of fidelity to me?" He then fell to his knees and offered to do anything they wished, including banish the hated Queen, if they would spare him. A lieutenant addressed the other officers, who had hesitated, "What are you standing gaping at? Here is your oath of fidelity to him!" He then shot the King. The Queen then knelt and prayed for mercy. They called her insulting and obscene names and one officer cut her thigh with his sword. They then pumped both victims full of bullets and began slashing them with their swords. One of the patriots cut a strip of skin from Queen Draga's breast as a souvenir. Another drove his sword up to the hilt in her vagina. They continued to stab the prostrate bodies in order that the complicity of all should be established. The King, still living, groaned. Lieutenant Colonel

Mischich suggested throwing their bodies into the flower garden below so that the loyal soldiers could see what had transpired. They hoisted the Queen's body over the balcony rail so that it thudded to the ground. The King, however, was still groaning, and his fingers grasped the railing. At least one of his fingers was then cut off with a sword. He was pitched into the garden below, one eye falling from its socket as he hit the ground. Still living, his undamaged hand clutched the grass. The two lay among the grass and flowers for two hours, until at 4 a.m., it began to rain. The Russian minister crossed the street and looked more closely at the gruesome sight The proud assassins saluted him, certain, no doubt, that he would be pleased that Serbia's hitherto pro-Austrian policies would now favor Russia. To show their loyalty to the new dynasty, they shouted, "*Ziveo Kralji Petar!*" ("long live King Peter!" of the rival dynasty) as they dumped the bodies into the yard. With a sudden burst of sensitivity, the Russian envoy turned to them and said, "For God's sake, gentlemen, carry the bodies into the palace. Do not leave them here in the rain, exposed to the gaze of the public." A few minutes later, bed sheets were used to shroud the mangled corpses, and they were carried inside the palace.

Having presumably considered that they had done a good night's work, they ran through the palace like a pack of monkeys, screaming, dancing with joy, and firing their pistols at paintings, mirrors, and light fixtures. They smashed the royal bed and the Queen's personal effects, and then ordered the palace servants to bring wine from the cellar and set it up on tables in the courtyard. Any monies kept in the palace disappeared into patriotic pockets. After the Balkan War of 1912-13, each murderer proudly wore his decoration for the war low on his tunic to identify him as a regicide.

In such auspicious circumstances did the reign of King Petar Karageorgevich begin.[25] The details of the murders were quickly known to the world. The British King, Edward VII, was revolted and considered the rejoicings in Belgrade "in the worst possible taste." In a rare royal initiative, (still possible at that time), he persuaded his government to promptly sever diplomatic relations with Serbia and to recall their minister. He said that "There [is] no need for England to recognize a government consisting of assassins." When the new Serbian King, old Petar, telegraphed directly to King Edward for recognition, Edward replied, expressing the frosty hope that Petar would "succeed in restoring the good repute of your country upon which recent events have left so regrettable a stain." Edward refused to be represented at Petar's coronation. When Petar told Prince Danilo of Montenegro that he had known all along of the plot to murder Alexander and Draga, and cared nothing for England's attitude, Edward learned of it and noted, "What a man King Petar must be, worthy of a sensational novel." Was Edward, perhaps, thinking of *The Prisoner of Zenda*? Two years later, the Russian and Italian ministers jointly approached Edward at Windsor, Serbia now being Russia's "little brother" and its king the brother-in-law of Italy's queen. They sought to soothe King Edward's hostility toward renewing diplomatic relations. He rebuffed them, saying that British public opinion would not allow it. "And besides this reason," he said,

> I have another, and, so to say, a personal reason. *Mon métier à moi est d'être Roi.* [My profession is to be a king]. King Alexander was also by his *métier 'un roi.'* As you see, we belonged to the same guild, as labourers or professional men. I cannot be indifferent to assassination of a member of my profession, or, if you like, a member of my guild. We should be obliged to shut up our businesses if we, the kings, were to consider the assassination of kings as of no consequence at all. I regret, but you see that I cannot do what you wish me to do.[26]

This fraternal attitude would have a more portentous echo when expressed by Kaiser Wilhelm in 1914.

The methods of coming to a throne, even if not violent, were sometimes peculiar. King Ferdinand VII of Spain was paralyzed and dying in 1833. The existing Salic Law, common to most monarchies, would have required the nearest male relative, his brother Carlos, to become king after him. Instead, the King's sister grabbed his failing hand and made it sign a decree abolishing the Salic Law so that the infant Isabella became queen. The prime minister, seeing what she was up to, put his hand on the sister's to stop the fraudulent act, whereupon she socked him so hard he was dazed. Recovering, the minister bowed to the royal sister, and quoted the Spanish proverb, "A fair hand can do no wrong." She is supposed to have replied, "No, but it can strike, eh?"[27]

Perhaps it now can be understood why, when I learned in passing that in 1913, only twenty-five years before my birth, in an era which was already becoming accustomed to airplanes, automobiles, motion pictures, and telephones, something like a Ruritanian or Graustarkian romance was being played out. A small kingdom was being created and a search begun for someone to be its king. Further dimension was added by the knowledge that the events in this story occurred in a still troubled area about which we have read and heard so much recently, and by the knowledge that they showed a means by which one of the worst wars in history could have been avoided. For, the events described herein postponed World War I by slightly more than one year.

A WORD ABOUT WORDS

As this book is about people and places with names foreign to the English-speaking reader, it may take some effort to keep up with them all. For that reason, maps and a list of the chief characters will be given. The list will be found on the following pages. The matter is complicated somewhat, however, by the fact that Albania, the scene of our story, has person and place names which are spelled various ways, depending on who was doing the spelling. This may be due to the fact that Albania had no written language until modern times, and to the difficulty in making the Albanian spelling intelligible to the English-speaker's ear. This book will adopt an arbitrary spelling, usually the one current in Europe at the time of the story, which will be easier for the English-speaking reader to pronounce.

There is the additional factor that most of the Albanian characters in this book had the courtesy titles of rank, "bey" or "pasha", (in the Ottoman Turkish tradition), firmly stuck to their real names. The last name of these Albanian notables was usually related to their home district, as in Vlora (Valona), Elbasani (Elbasan), or Konitsa (Konitza). There are other similar spellings to add to the confusion.

MONEY

Reference will often be made in this book to various moneys. By 1914, all of the major powers had adopted the gold standard for their currencies. Britain was the world financial leader, and its pound "sterling," (although backed by gold rather than silver) was the soundest monetary unit. It was worth about $4.85 in U.S. currency at the time. There were 25.22 French francs to the pound, making each worth about 19.2 cents, while there were 20.43 German Marks, worth about 23.7 cents each. The pound would bring about 24.02 Austro-Hungarian Kronen, or about 20 cents each. The Turkish piaster, which fluctuated in value through the years, was said to be worth about 4.4 cents around that time, and a Turkish pound was worth 100 piasters. An estimate of the present value of the sums to be discussed is difficult, due to the many social and financial changes since that time. However, an arbitrary multiplier of eighteen has been adopted in this book in an attempt to supply the reader with some idea of the purchasing power of the various currencies in today's money.[1]

QUICK REFERENCE FOR NAMES

To assist the reader in keeping up with the many minor players who will briefly appear in this book, they are identified below. The Albanian names are given an arbitrary spelling and arrangement, due to the diversity found in the various contemporary sources. Some first names are unknown to this writer and could not be found after diligent inquiry. The reader may skip this until needed:

Abdi Bey Toptani = Durazzo-based royal Agriculture Minister.
Abdullah Effendi = Royal gendarmerie officer.
Adamidis, Dr. Themosticles Bey Frasheri = Christian physician and first royal finance minister of Albania.
Ahmed Bey Zogu = Loyal Chief of Mati clan.
Akif (a.k.a. Arif) Hikmet (a.k.a. Hikmer) = Central Albanian rebel leader.
Akif Pasha Elbasani = Royal Interior and War Minister, 1914.
Aliotti, Baron = Italian Minister to Albania
Ayet Bey Libohova Arslan Pashali = Cousin of Essad Pasha.
Aziz Pasha Vrioni = Royal military commander in south-central Albania.
Bekir Aga Grebenaly = Turkish-Albanian rebel commander.
Berghausen, Dr. ? = German medical adviser to Wilhelm zu Wied.
Bilinski, Count Leon von = Austro-Hungarian Finance Minister.

Bilinski, M.C. = Austro-Hungarian member, Southern Albanian Border Commission.

Buchberger, Baron = Austro-Hungarian Vice Consul in Albania, 1914.

Burghele, ? = Romanian Minister to Albania, 1914.

Burhaneddin Efendi = Turkish prince mentioned for Albanian throne, 1914.

Burney, Admiral Cecil = British naval commander in Albanian waters,.

Castoldi, Fortunato = Italian member of Southern Albanian Boundary Commission.

Chinigo, Professor ? = Italian spy in Durazzo, 1914.

Constantine I = King of Greece in 1914.

Contoulis, Colonel ? = Greek Army officer in Greek-occupied Albania, 1914.

Danilo, Prince of Montenegro = Commander, Montenegrin forces, 1913.

Ded Zoku = A tribal leader in northeastern Albania.

Dimitrijevich, Dragutin = Serbian Military official and plotter.

Djemil Bey (or, Effendi) = Prominent Scutari figure and later Wied opponent

Doorman, Captain Jetzde = Dutch captain of theAlbanian gendarmerie.

Dopler, Professor ? = German designer of royal Albanian coat of arms

Doughty-Wylie, Charles = British Army officer on Southern Boundary Commission.

Durham, Edith = English writer, artist and Albanophile.

Ekrem Bey Libohova = young *aide de camp* to Wilhelm zu Wied as King.

Ekrem Bey Vlora = Nephew of first Albanian president Ismail Kemal.

Eshref Frasheri = Post-Wied notable.

Evangele, Pandele = Leader of loyal Albanian colony in Bucharest.

Fabius, Captain Jan = Dutch captain of the Albanian gendarmerie.

Faik Bey Konitza = Cultured south Albanian "Founding Father."

Feizi Bey Alizot = Pre-Wied provisional Internal Affairs minister.

Fontenay, ? = French Minister to Albania, 1914.

Francis, Captain S. = British Army administrator of Alessio pre-Wied.

George I = King of Greece until murdered March, 1913.

George of Serbia = Insane prince, son of Serbian King Petar.

Ghilardi, Captain Leon = Croatian-Albanian officer of the royal gendarmerie.

Gioni, Marco = Cousin of Bib Doda and later Isa Bolein lieutenant.

Groot de, Dr. F. = Volunteer civilian Dutch doctor to the gendarmerie.

Gumpenberg, Baron ? = German volunteer in Wied's forces.

Gurakuchi, Louis = Albanian Catholic educator and Wied's Education Minister.

Gurschner, William = Austrian designer of Wied's uniforms and medals.

Hamdi Rebeiki, Sheik = Rebel leader in attack on Durazzo.

Hamid Bey Toptani = Essad's cousin and pre-Wied governor of Durazzo.

Hassan Bey Prishtina = North Albanian (Kosovan) Post & Telegraph Minister in Wied's cabinet.

Haxhi, Qerim (a.k.a. Haxi Kerem) = Pro-Turk Albanian notable.

Heaton-Armstrong, Jack = Brother of Wied's secretary, Duncan.

Herbert, Aubrey = British Member of Parliament and Albanophile.

Hilmi Pasha = Turkish Prime Minister in 1909 under the Young Turks and later Turkish ambassador to Vienna.

Hohenloe, Prince Conrad = Austro-Hungarian Governor of Trieste, 1914.

Ionescu, Take = Prominent Romanian government minister.

Isa Boletin (a.k.a. Boletinatz) = Albanian chieftain from Kosovo.

Ismail Kemal Bey = First President of Albania (1913).

Ismet (Izzat) Pasha = Turkish politician and plotter.

Jong, Carol de = Dutch captain of Albanian gendarmerie.

Kamil Haxifesa = Anti-Wied Muslim agitator.

Kennedy, Phineas B. = U.S. missionary educator in Albania, 1913-14.

Klingspor, ? = Hungarian artillery instructor to Albanian gendarmrie.

Kokovtzev, Count Vladimir = Russian Prime Minister in 1913.

Krajewski, Leon Alphonse = French International Control Commission.

Kral, Auguste von = Austro-Hungarian member, International ControlCommission

Kroon, Major Henri J.L. = Dutch officer in the Albanian gendarmerie.

Kühlmann, Richard von = German *Chargé d'Affaires* in London, 1913.

Labia, S.N. = Italian delegate to Southern Boundary Commission.

Laffert, ? von = German member, Southern Boundary Commission.

Lallemand, Lt. Col. M.A = French member, Southern Boundary Commission.

Lamb, Harry = British member, International Control Commission.

Leatham, Captain Eustace L. = British naval squadron commander, Albania.

Leoni, *Commandatore* Alessandro =Italian member, International Control Commission.

Levkovitch, Boudine = Russian member, Southern Boundary Commission

Löwenthal, Dr. ? von = Austro-Hungarian Minister to Albania, 1914.

Lucius, Baron ? von = German Minister to Albania, 1914.

Maiorescu, Take = Romanian Conservative government minister

Mallinckrodt, Capt. Gerard A. = Dutch *aide de camp* to Col. Thomson.

Martinaj, Nicoló = Wied supporter from Durazzo.

Mehdi Bey Frasheri = Young first Albanian member, International Control Commission.

Mehmed Bey Konitza = Pro-Greek brother of Faik Bey Konitza.

Mehmet Pasha Dralla = Kosovan member first Albanian government, 1913.

Moltedo, Captain ? = Italian-Albanian artillery officer.

Moore, Arthur = Special Correspondent of "The Times" of London.

Muricchio, Colonel = Italian Spy

Nadolny, Dr. Rudolph = German member, International Control Commission.

Nogga, Philip = Young pro-Wied Catholic Albanian.

Papoulas, Gen. Anastasios = Royal Greek Army general.

Pasich, Nichola = Serbian Premier

Petrayev, Aleksandr = Russian consul and International Control Commission member.

Petrovich, ? = Austro-Hungarian consul and International Control Commission member.

Phillips, George F., Colonel = British commander of international troops at Scutari, 1914.

Pimodan, Count ? de = Aristocratic young French volunteer in Wied's forces.

Prenk Bib Doda = Chief of the northern Catholic Mirdites.

Ranette, M. = Member of Durazzo Romanian Legation staff.

Rappaport, Alfred (Ritter von Arbengau) = Austro-Hungarian Foreign Office chief for Albania, 1914.

Reddingius, Dr. Tiddo = Dutch army physician to the gendarmerie.

Reimers, Hendrik G.A. = Dutch captain of the gendarmerie.

Roelfsema, Major Lucas = Dutch cavalry officer in the gendarmerie.

Sami Bey Vrioni = *Aide de camp* to Wied and son-in-law of Essad.

Sar, Captain Jan H. = Dutch gendarmerie officer.

Schmidt, Captain ? = Commander, Austrian cruiser *Szigetvar*, 1914.

Schneider, Commander ? =German naval commander at Scutari, 1914.

Schönberg-Waldenburg, Prince Gunther = Queen Sophie's younger brother

Selim Bey Wassa = A leader of the loyal northern Catholic Kastrati clan.

Shefket Bey = Loyal Albanian gendarmerie officer.

Simon Doda =Loyal Malissor leader.

Sluys, Major Johan M. = Dutch officer of the gendarmerie.

Spencer, Harold Sherwood = American volunteer with royal forces.

Strandtmann, Vasili N. = Russian *Chargé d'Affaires* in Serbia, 1914.

Sturdza, Prince Michel = Romanian legation *attaché* in Durazzo.

Sureya Bey Vlora = Wealthy Albanian notable and royalist.

Thierry, *Commandant* C. = German army officer and Southern Boundary Commissioner.

Thomson, Colonel Ludovic = Dutch army officer, second in command of Dutch gendarmerie mission.

Tomjenovic, ? = Austro-Hungarian army artillery instructor to the Albanian gendarmerie.

Tortoulis, Dr. Michael = Monarchist Greek Christian supporter of Prince Fuad and, later, of Prince Wied.

Trotha, Major ? von = German officer and Controller of the Household for Wied.

Troubridge, Admiral Ernest A. = Commander of British naval forces in Albanian waters, 1914.

Turkhan Pasha = Elderly veteran statesman and Wied's Prime Minister

Varatassis, ? = Greek governor of Corfu and *chargé* in Durazzo.

Veer, General Willem J. H. de = Dutch commander of gendarmerie.

Vehid Bey Toptani = Ottoman-Albanian general and Essad's brother.

Venizelas, Eleutherios = Greek Premier

Vollenhoven, Major Joan van = Dutch gendarmerie officer.

Waal, Major Wouter de = Dutch gendarmerie officer.

Wat Marash = Albanian leader in Alessio area.

Wied, Prince Friedrich = Older brother of Wilhelm zu Wied.

Wildenfels, Countess Anna zu = Wied family friend.

Williams, George F. = U.S. Minister to Greece, 1914.

Winchei, ? = Later German delegate to the International Control Commission.

Winckel, ? = German consul at Trieste and International Control Commission member.

Zog (Ahmed Zogu Mati) = Chief of the loyal northeastern Muslim Mati tribe.

Zographos, George Christaki = Greek-Albanian statesman and president of Albanian Epirus.

SOME VOCABULARY

The following are some Albanian-Turkish words which will be encountered from time to time.[2]

baraiktar = petty tribal chief

bey = governor of province; respected official

cadi = magistrate

effendi = honorable gentleman

hodja = Muslim religious scholar

kavass = armed constable, servant or courier

kaza = district

kemal = perfect

komitaji = Balkan guerilla band

mbret = king

mbretresha = queen

mufti = Muslim Islamic law advisor and leader

mutassarif = civil administrator of a sanjak or region; a colonel

padishah = imperial sultan

pasha = high honorary title

redif = home guard, armed followers

sanjak = administrative region between a kaza and a vilayet

vali = governor

vilayet = province; chief administrative district

PRELUDE

The Background Story

All histories must have an arbitrary beginning somewhere, otherwise we should have to return to the beginning of time. Let us begin by selecting an event in 1911, which I believe set in motion the events which produced this story. The narrative of history moves in starts and stops, but to taste the full flavor of our story, the reader must be given a bit of background.

Once upon a time, a great Muslim empire ruled not only what is today's Turkey, and much of North Africa, but all the once Christian, and later Muslim, areas west of Iran, including Arabia and much of the southern part of east central Europe. That is to say, the Balkan countries of Romania, Bulgaria, Serbia, Greece, Croatia, Bosnia, and Herzegovina, and Albania were under its sway. The empire was called in English the Ottoman Empire, because one of its founders was a sultan named Osman, and that name apparently sounded like "Ottoman" to westerners. Most of the people of the countries just named being (at least nominally) Christians, unrest was inevitable in the empire. From the 1700s onward, these subject Europeans regularly agitated for relief from the Turkish yoke. Little by little, through one sort of war or another, these Christian peoples gained full or semi-independence from the sultans.

Today, a map will show that there is still a tiny bit of Turkey across the Bosporus at Istanbul (formerly Constantinople), which is actually a part of the European continent. That is what remains of the Turkish Ottoman Empire's holdings since the end of the World War of 1914-1918.

Our story is about the Balkans, but to begin our story we will first look to that part of the Ottoman Empire which was not in Europe at all, but which stretched across northern Africa, an area that had been conquered by the Muslims in the Eighth Century, long before the Crusades. Stretching from Arabia to Morocco, these lands had been forcibly converted to Islam, but they eventually developed into semi-independent provinces under the ultimate sovereignty of the Turkish Sultan, who was also the supreme Muslim religious leader, or "Caliph."

As Edith Durham, the hardy English Balkanophile, was to write in a nice turn of phrase, by the Nineteenth and Twentieth Centuries, "The Turks lived in terror of the Great Powers who squatted round the edge, waiting an opportunity to pounce..."[1] Only jealousy between the Great Powers or their fear of losing a useful and harmless buffer between rivals prevented them from seizing the Empire for themselves. Thus, whenever Russia looked as though it might beat up on Turkey so badly that Russia would gain control of the Dardanelles outlet to the Mediterranean Sea, and thereby become too powerful, powers like Britain and France would intervene. They did this in the Crimean War of 1854-1856, and at the Congress of Berlin of 1878, which snatched the fruits of victory from the Czar. It was to the interest of most of the Great Powers, Britain, France, and Austria-Hungary, to at least maintain the *status quo ante* in the Balkans. But in the 1860s a new, ambitious country of Italy was created. France showed her the way to take Turkey's colonies by seizing Algeria in 1830, Tunisia in 1831, and dominating Morocco more or less peacefully since 1905. Britain in 1882 took effective control of Egypt behind the throne of its "Khedive," who was still theoretically the Turkish governor, and was usually of Albanian ethnic origin. So, Italy looked with lustful eyes across the Mediterranean upon the African coast immediately to her south, known today as Libya. With dreams of emulating the Roman Empire, which the impoverished little peninsula kingdom fancied to be its predecessor, in 1911 Italy fabricated a war with Turkey in order to seize what was then called Tripolitania and Cyrenaica. Those provinces, although cut off from the rest of the Turkish Empire by British-dominated Egypt, were still ruled from the Ottoman capital, Constantinople.

When Italy unsuccessfully proposed that Turkey sell its poorly-run North African province to her, the Great Powers raised no objection. Italy then formally complained of a series of acts of discrimination and mistreatment of Italians in the Empire, both individuals and merchants, the most recent of which allegedly took place on August 21, 1911. On that date, Turks boarded a merchant ship commanded by an Italian captain, who was flogged and thrown into the sea. On September 28, 1911, Italy delivered an ultimatum to the Sultan's government in Constantinople, which was also known as "the Sublime Porte." Receiving (and expecting) no satisfaction, Italy's fleet attacked Tripoli on October 2, 1911 and blockaded, among other places, the coast of what is now southern Albania.[2] Turkey and Italy made peace on October 18, 1912, with Turkey yielding Libya to Italy. This attack upon the crumbling Ottoman Empire, in turn, encouraged the small Balkan states to carry out their ambition to fall upon the Turks, drive them from all of Europe, and split up their remaining European holdings, including Albania, Macedonia, and Thrace. By May of 1912, Bulgaria, Serbia, Greece, and tiny Montenegro had made a succession of treaties forming "The Balkan League" for the purpose of ganging up on the Turks.[3] Montenegro was fierce beyond its size. At the time of our story it boasted of only about 282,000 people.[4]

Although Russia considered herself the champion of the Slavs, especially Serbia, she was not yet prepared for a general European war, which the eradication of the Turkish buffer might precipitate. Austria-Hungary would not permit Serbia to become a power on the Adriatic Sea, which would threaten its only maritime outlet to the Mediterranean, and provide a bad example for its subject Slav peoples. To understand why this issue was so important to Austria-Hungary, one must remember that among the many peoples included in its empire, the Slavs were perhaps the most restless, and many looked to Serbia as their spiritual homeland. Austria had already shared power with Hungary. Some then considered the possibility of giving the Slavs similar rights in the empire. But it seemed more likely that the Slavs would break away from the Monarchy. That is, of course, what did ultimately happen at the end of the First World War.

Russia and Austria-Hungary early in the Twentieth Century had joined in warning against a change in the *status quo*. The Balkan League ignored the warning and successfully attacked the outnumbered Turks in what became known as the First Balkan War. Tiny Montenegro was the first to declare war, on October 8, 1912.[5] Startling to all were the swift victories of the little Balkan countries over the Turks. The Greeks captured Salonika, the most important Ottoman harbor on the Aegean Sea, and most of Macedonia and the southern Albanian region, which they called "Northern Epirus." What the Greeks called Northern Epirus had two important towns; Koritsa and Argyrocastro. Manifestations of Greek sentiment in Koritsa after World War I were considered by some to be impressive.[6] Argyrocastro was dominated by a fortress. It was in the center of a region inhabited by the Bektashis, liberal and tolerant Albanian Muslim nationalists, who were happy to cooperate with northern Catholics and southern Orthodox Christians against Greeks and fanatical Muslims of the plains.[7] Argyrocastro was located almost in the south central-most portion of modern Albania.

By the beginning of November, 1912, the victorious Serb armies were channeled to the west, toward the Adriatic, and entered the coastal Albanian towns of Durazzo and Alessio toward the end of that month.[8] On April 16, 1913, Bulgaria and the Ottomans concluded an armistice shortly after that of the other belligerents. Negotiations by the belligerent ambassadors had been proceeding in London since December 17, 1912. Turkey's complete defeat led on May 30, 1913, to the Peace Treaty of London, leaving Turkey only a tiny bit of land on the European continent.[9]

Less than a month later, on June 29, 1913, Bulgaria suddenly and without warning attacked its former allies, Serbia and Greece, to increase its share of the loot.[10] Romania, like a jackal, watched for its opportunity, and on July 10, 1913, declared war on Bulgaria. Bulgaria was quickly defeated, resulting in the Peace of Bucharest on August 10, 1913. The London Peace Conference which followed will be discussed in detail in the next chapter.

The larger background to this story consists of the two rival groupings of Great Powers, usually called the Triple Alliance and the Triple Entente. The Triple Alliance consisted of

Germany, Austria-Hungary, and Italy. Stated simply, it resulted from the short-sighted abandonment in the 1890s by Germany of its alliance with Russia in order to make a close alliance with Austria-Hungary, its neighbor to the south. Italy was brought in as a third party, but its differences with Austria-Hungary made it an ever more doubtful ally. Russia, abandoned by Germany, formed an alliance with Germany's traditional enemy, republican France. By the early 1900s, Germany's aggressive foreign policy, the bombastic pronouncements of its emperor, and the creation of a large navy, led Britain to form an "understanding" (*entente*), if not a treaty, with France, and, thereby, with Russia.

These alliances were, in theory, defensive in nature. They did not commit the allies to go to war on the whim of one of the members. How this worked out in reality, however, we all know. Paranoia and fear of preemptive attack were to predominate. The interests of the Great Powers in the Balkan troubles varied from the almost total indifference of Britain and Germany, to life and death concern by Austria-Hungary.

1

ALBANIA

The Setting

As Albania will be the setting for our story, which is about what Queen Elisabeth of Romania hopefully imagined as a "fairyland kingdom,"[1] we must spend a while learning about it as it was in 1913 and 1914. Albania – or what became Albania – is located on the Adriatic Sea, opposite the "heel" of Italy. It is bounded on the north by Montenegro (whose tiny size makes little Albania look large in comparison), by Serbia on the East, and by Greece on the south. At the time of our story, the amorphous region then generally considered "Albania" was made up of the four Turkish provinces (*vilayets*) of Kosovo, Scutari, Monastir, and Janina. The first of these, as we have come to know, was given to Serbia in 1913, and has been a bone of contention ever since.[2] To an American, Albania's climate and vegetation might remind one of California. To a European it might seem typically Mediterranean. That is to say, warm and even hot in the southern coastal part (visitors often commenting on the "sweatiness" at times), while the abundance of mountains and highlands farther inland lead to more moderate climate. In the north, with its mountainous areas and heavier rainfall, there is forest, including pines and firs.[3] Here is a 1914 newspaper correspondent's description:

> There are no villages, only houses dotted at intervals of nearly a mile, high up or round wide valleys. Everyone has killed, and all have enemies who seek their blood. Many men have not left their homes for years, and food has to be brought to them by their friends…[Brigandage] carries no dishonor…Agriculture is despised.

1

Government comes to an end at Dibra. North of
that there is nothing.[4]

Albania by 1913 was by no means an unknown territory.
Epirus, the title given by the Greeks to areas of northwest Greece
and today's southern Albania, was inhabited since ancient times
by a non-Hellenic, "barbarous" people known to the ancient
Greeks, and who all spoke the same language. Today there is a
slight racial distinction between northern and southern
Albanians. By 1913, the northern men, referred to as *Ghegs*,
tended to be "tall, fair, and dour." They wore both short,
ballerina-like skirts (called *fustanellas*) or close-fitting white
trousers with a stripe of some sort running vertically, a similar
shirt and a short, open vest. Around the waist typically would
run a sash. The southern Albanian men were "*Tosks*," often
"dark, short, and animated," and more often wore the *fustanella*,
with trousers beneath, much like the ceremonial clothing worn
today by the Greek Evzone soldiers. Many men still wore the
white fez or "*plis*," which varied in appearance from a somewhat
pointed skullcap to a cylindrical style similar to the Turkish fez,
depending on the region and personal preference. The Ghegs
were grouped together in autonomous tribes under a hereditary
chief (*Baraiktar*) and inhabited the mountainous northern section
of the country, where the inaccessible nature of the ground sets
up an additional barrier to intercourse. The *Malissori*,[5] the
principal racial tribe of northern Albania, were divided into seven
clans, each of which was autonomous and had its own local
history. In the mountains there was a mixed population of
Catholics and Muslims, with the exception of *Mirdites*, who were
all Catholics. In the plains, the people were in the in main
Muslims, with small minorities of Christian Orthodox of Serb
descent.[6]

The women were heavily dressed, with head scarves, and
maintained modest distance from public affairs. They often
looked like nothing so much as our stereotype of a gypsy
woman.[7]

The Venetians had held areas along the Albanian coast, building stone fortresses at the seaports, but were driven out by the Turks in the Sixteenth Century. The northernmost Albanian tribes, of the districts of Mirdita, Mati, and Ljuma, retained their autonomy throughout the four-hundred years of Turkish rule, engaging in guerilla war with the Turks to such an extent that they were largely left alone. In the Nineteenth Century, Muslim Ottomans of Albanian ethnicity were appointed governors of Albania. Well into the Twentieth Century, Albanians, even northerners, continued to volunteer for the Turkish army, and made some of its best soldiers.[8] This is perhaps partly explained by their fear of Serbs and Montenegrins.[9]

The Turkish occupation led to conversion of two-thirds of the population to Islam during the Fifteenth and Seventeenth Centuries. The penalty for non-conversion was ineligibility for office, payment of a poll tax, discrimination or, sometimes, death. Many Islamic Albanians were influential. Over the centuries, at least thirty Grand Viziers (prime ministers) of Turkey were Albanians.[10] The balance of the population was Christian, either Greek Orthodox in the south, or Roman Catholic in the north. Many visitors to Albania commented on the religious tolerance of the Albanians, if not of the Turks. It was said that the nominally Catholic Malissors regarded the Cross as a kind of charm and thought Heaven was on top of a very high mountain.[11] In northern Albania, Catholics and Muslims lived side by side in relative harmony, with their quarrels seldom about religion. Even members of the same family might follow different religions.[12]

In the Fifteenth Century many Christian Albanians fled to Italy, and in the Nineteenth and Twentieth Centuries, a number came to the United States. There were also colonies of Albanians in Romania.[13]

It is important to note that the Turks had discouraged the use of the Albanian language. It had not even been fully reduced to writing until the end of the Nineteenth Century, and there was no Albanian literature. It was not until 1913 that the Albanians got a uniform alphabet. In southern Albania, Turkish governors issued their edicts in Greek, which was the language of official and commercial documents. This resulted in most southern Albanians (Tosks) speaking two languages in public: Turkish for Muslims and Greek for Orthodox Christians, although they usually spoke Albanian at home. The Albanian Christians were told, with the approval of the Greek patriarch, that Christ would not understand their prayers if they were said in Albanian.[14] The Austrians, who had forced the Turks to grant them privileges and a sort of residual protectorate over Albanian Catholics, founded schools in northern Albania beginning in 1870. Late in the Nineteenth Century, they agreed to use the newly-invented system of Albanian spelling in the schools.[15] They taught the Albanian and Italian languages, but not German for some reason.[16] Between 1880 and 1908 more than thirty periodicals and books were printed abroad in Albanian, mostly in Bulgaria, Italy, Egypt, Romania, Austria, the United States, and England.[17] In the far south, many Albanians traded their Albanian nationality for a good Greek education. There were many Greek schools in southern Albania, but no Albanian schools. Becoming Greek offered a possible escape from poverty.[18] The north of Albania remained largely tribal and undeveloped and unofficially semi-autonomous, while the south was composed both of semi-serfs of the great beys, and more educated merchants and officials.[19]

As previously mentioned, many of the characters in this story will bear the title "bey" in their names. It was an honorary title, much as a British Knight has the title, "Sir" before his name. It denoted a person entitled to special respect, usually an owner of large estates who was often a tax collector for the Turks. Persons who held higher authority, such as governors and generals, were given the title of Pasha.[20]

Peasants engaged only in subsistence farming because market towns were so distant that produce would have spoiled in transit. Lack of access also prevented exploitation of the forests which covered a third of the country. A clansman prided himself on being a good fighter rather than a good farmer. *Tosk* peasants were too poor to build up businesses, while their beys were too rich to bother. Sixty percent of arable land belonged to 150 individuals. There were forty-odd great Albanian landowning families, with names like Verlace, Vrioni, Libohova, and Vlora.

Most Albanians had to rely on traditional medicine. An example was the cure for typhus: place warm sugar and frog guts on the patient's head.[21]

In the Albanian mountains, as in Bosnia, Austria had been at work in its guise of protector of the Roman Catholic northern Albanians. Every Catholic tribe had its neat and usually well cared for church, whose priest lived nearby. Austria trained priests, built and maintained churches and hospices, built the Cathedral of Scutari, and protected the first Albanian schools of the north. An English visitor in 1901 observed that the standard of cleanliness in the Catholic quarter of the northern Albanian city of Scutari was higher than in the nearby capital of Montenegro. When Turkish authority broke down in Scutari in 1908 at the time of a Turkish Revolution, no disorders broke out, earning the admiration of foreign consuls.[22]

In the interior of Albania in 1914, great tracts of country remained uncultivated; there were practically no roads, and of course no railways. The few bridges that existed were in many cases unsafe, and rivers had to be forded on horseback or crossed in primitive boats. The country towns were still entirely Turkish in appearance, with their tall white minarets gleaming amid encircling trees but "hideous and appalling" within; the houses were dilapidated, and the narrow crooked streets stank from refuse. The streets were paved with mountainous boulders which, in time of rain, "formed islands in stagnant malodorous pools, the breeding grounds of mosquitoes and fever."

Around 1913, the Austrians built a school in the mid-coastal town of Durazzo with free books, clothes, and food, and the Italians did the same, even offering the parents three francs (about $10 today) for every child sent to the school.[23]

Austria's interest in Albania had begun in the Seventeenth Century. It was then that the Turks gave the Habsburgs a "religious protectorate" over the Catholics of the Ottoman Empire, including the *Malissori* tribesmen of northern

Albania. Later treaties and agreements in the Eighteenth Century renewed and expanded Austria's right to build and support churches, schools, and religious institutions. Until the middle of the Nineteenth Century, Austria took a rather casual interest in the affairs of the Albanians, but after her exclusion from Germany in 1866, and her expansion into the Balkans in 1878, Austria's interest in her "protectorate" became more animated.

Also toward the end of the Nineteenth Century, expansion-minded Italy instigated a challenge to Austria's influence in Albania by founding Italian schools there. Albanian was spoken in most of these, but in 1888 Italy established two elementary schools in Scutari, traditionally a center of Habsburg influence, with Italian as the language of instruction. Still, the Catholic mountaineers of northern Albania placed heavy reliance on Austria as their guardian.

Albanians continually raided Montenegrin lands, stole sheep for sport, ambushed unsuspecting Montenegrins, and used their neighbors' mountains for a firing range. Montenegrins retaliated in like fashion.[24]

The mountains which dominated the north of Albania ran south from Montenegro through most of Albania, somewhat east of the center of the country, although there were numbers of mountain ranges running east and west in the center, and generally north and south in the southwest part of the country. Albania was little more than sixty miles from its northernmost to its southernmost tip, and less than ninety miles from west to east at its widest point.[25] The mountain ranges were divided by narrow river valleys, and the snow from the mountains created narrow streams which flowed down over rocky bends.[26]

There were towns and small-scale commerce, to be sure, but by 1913, the only modern devices available were the telegraph lines, installed under the Turks. At one point in 1914, all telegrams from Durazzo to foreign recipients had to be sent through foreign warships in the harbor.[27]

Because of the historic Italian connection, dating from the Venetians, most of the Albanian towns near the sea coast were known to other Europeans by their Italian names.

That usage was current at the time of our story, so it will be used here as well. For reference sake, however, it may be mentioned that the places also had Albanian names as follows:

Italian or European:	Albanian:
Alessio	Lezhë, Lesh
Colonia	Ersek, Hersek
Debar, Dibra	Dibër[28]
Durazzo	Durrës
Koritsa, Koritza	Korçë
Kruja	Krugë
Premeti	Permët
San Giovanni di Medua	Shëngjin
Santi Quaranta	Sarendë
Saseno	Sazan
Scutari, Skutari	Shkodra, Shkodër
Shiak	Shjak
Valona, Avlona	Vlorë, Vlonë

Suffice it to say that the reader will not be called upon to master the arcane language of Albania, but will be furnished, as an English-speaking newspaper reader in 1913 would have been, with the traditional Italian names. Reports of names of persons who will appear in this story received so many variations that an arbitrary choice of the western European version has been adopted.

After the First World War, the League of Nations surveyed and found the population of Epirus (including southern Albania) to be 113,845 Muslims and 112,868 Christians, of which only seventeen percent were even Grecophones. The population of Albania as a whole in the early Twentieth Century was variously estimated at from 840,000[29] to one million (*circa* 260,000 Orthodox Christians, 140,000 Catholics, and 600,000 Muslims).[30] Nobody knows for sure.[31]

The tax system, where it existed, was inherited from the Turks and worked badly. There was a tithe, a tax on buildings, tobacco and oil and roads, and a cattle tax that oppressed the peasants. There was also a maximum six-percent income tax on earners who failed to bribe the tax collector. The government had only one practical means of raising cash: sale of commercial concessions in forests, tobacco, oil, and minerals, as well as historical artifacts.[32] Under the Turks, there were twenty-seven administrative districts or *kazas*, and ten *kazas* usually paid no taxes at all.[33]

In November of 1912, Hilmi Pasha, the Turkish ambassador to Vienna, told the British ambassador that the estimated revenues from Albania were five to ten million francs (perhaps eighteen to thirty-six million dollars today), which proved to be true, but he said ten thousand gendarmes at a cost of seven million French francs and more, were required to maintain order. Each Albanian district had a separate budget and collected its own taxes. In early 1914, taxes were being raised in only four districts: Valona, Durazzo, Elbasan, and Scutari. Epirus, the most prosperous, contributed nothing.[34] Gold napoleons, British gold sovereigns, and American dollars were mixed together and valued by weight in Albania, with change given in coinage of a half-dozen countries. Most Albanians resorted to barter.[35]

By 1914, the Turks had been forced to yield Albania to the keeping of the Great Powers. For reasons discussed hereafter, a Captain S. G. Francis of the British Army had been administering Alessio and San Giovanni di Madua in April of 1914, with a detachment of the West Yorkshire Regiment and Austrian and Italian troops. He had been obliged to try to collect Ottoman debt taxes, but had great difficulty. Albanians did not understand why the taxes continued after the Turks had been expelled. The fish tax had always been earmarked for the purpose of the debt, but now the fish market had to be surrounded by gendarmes before the tax could be collected. [36]

After the 1908 Turkish "Young Turk" revolution, northern Albanians (still legally Turkish subjects), talking to Edith Durham the British traveler, said: "When all is set in order…when we have [setting forth a utopian list of government services], then, if we are quite satisfied, it will be right for us to pay a little tax. But it would be silly to pay for a thing before we know how we liked it.　If Konstitutzioon [the new Turkish constitution] is not rich enough to do these things, it can go to the devil—the sooner the better."[37]

2

SOME ROYALTY AND CAST OF CHARACTERS

The Heads of State

As we have seen, by the dawn of the Twentieth Century all of the great European powers except France were headed by some sort of royal person and his or her ministers. These royal persons had markedly different powers.

Consider, first of all, King George V, of Great Britain, Ireland, and the Dominions Beyond the Seas, Emperor of India. This stolid, bug-eyed, bearded country squire and former naval officer, crowned in 1911, was heir to generations of constitutional change which had left the monarch with very little real power to actually govern. Should the monarch try to exercise his theoretical power to veto legislation, or to disobey the advice of the ministers selected by the majority in Parliament, British history taught that he (or she, for Britain was allowed to have female sovereigns) would be somehow removed from office. He was not helpless, however. He had the right to be consulted by his ministers, and to offer his advice. He gained considerable authority from the respect that his high social position commanded traditionally. It was the fact, observed in the early Twentieth Century by the German ambassador, Prince Lichnowsky, that a British king was "the apex of the social pyramid...An Englishman is either a member of Society or would like to be one. It is his constant endeavor to be a gentleman."[1] King George's no-nonsense character is epitomized in the report---apocryphal or not---of his comment after he recovered from a serious illness at the seaside town of Bognor. The city requested permission to change its name to the more dignified "Bognor Regis" (Bognor of the King) in honor of his stay. When told of the request, the King is supposed to have impatiently said, "Oh, bugger Bognor!"[2]

In 1912, the King's chief, or "prime" minister was a mild chap, Henry Herbert Asquith, whose name quite fit his kewpie-doll appearance. Foreign affairs were left chiefly in the experienced hands of Sir Edward Grey, whose hawk-like appearance resembled nothing so much as the drawings of Sherlock Holmes. Grey was the foreign minister, or, technically, "His Majesty's Principal Secretary of State for Foreign Affairs."

The Prime Minister's wife wrote of Grey that that his "reality, thoughtfulness, and freedom from pettiness, gave him true distinction. He is unchangeable and there is something lonely, lofty, and even pathetic about him which I could not easily explain."[3] The American ambassador described him as "a frank and fair man."[4] Even the German ambassador quite agreed.[5] Grey's characteristic pose with associates was with his elbows resting on the sides of his chair, his hands folded and placed beneath his chin, and leaning forward with his light blue eyes searching those of his visitor, with perhaps a confidential smile or a grim demeanor.[6] A widower, he was an avid outdoorsman with a passion for fishing, squirrel breeding (!), and bird watching. He hated spending time in London and was often bored when forced to attend sittings of the House of Commons. As all governmental ministers had to be members of Parliament, and had to answer questions regarding their departments from time to time, this tedious duty could not be avoided. As a very model of an English country gentleman, he was popular with the British public.[7] He was admired, but not entirely trusted, by the Austrian and German ambassadors.[8] Grey hated cities and had such a horror of modernity that he thought God might well destroy the world blighted by factories which "defiled the beautiful country, …ghastly competition and pressure [that] makes men swarm to gather and multiply horribly." His love of country pursuits was so serious that he even wrote a book on fly-fishing.[9] He was surprised to learn that foreign men, like the German ambassador, Prince Lichnowsky, preferred to have their clothes made by London tailors. He had seldom been abroad but spoke schoolboy French. Upon the visit of King George V to Paris in the spring of 1914, Grey was the minister in attendance, and "found the gift of tongues." Paul Cambon, ambassador to London from France, observed Grey in conversation with President Poincaré and exclaimed, "The Holy Ghost has descended upon Sir Edward Grey and he now talks French."[10] Grey's wife died in an accident in 1906, and by 1913 he was becoming tired. He had failing eyesight. In London, he roomed with the Winston Churchills in one of the fine, cream colored row houses in gated Eccleston Square, near Victoria Station,[11] Eccleston Square was considered not quite as smart as Belgravia as a residence for a minister of the Crown. There was a library on the second floor where Churchill spent much time with Grey as both were government ministers at the time. Grey was a paying lodger but during late night talks in the library the two men drank fine cognac and smoked expensive cigars and became close friends.[12]

Grey would arrive at work at the Foreign Office soon after 11 a.m. If there was no business left from the previous day, he would open a box with copies of deciphered telegrams. These he would read and presently the Under-Secretary would come to his room. If there was any urgent matter, he would discuss it and if needed, a private secretary would make appointments with ambassadors or ministers for the afternoon. The Assistant Under-Secretary would send papers to the Under-Secretary if they were important and they would then be sent up to Grey. They would arrive in red wooden boxes of various shapes. Each box had a label protruding from it on which was printed the official title or name of the foreign minister, and also the name of the official from whom it came. When Grey read the contents, he reversed the label, locked the box, and returned it to the official who sent it. In it he would have read telegrams and a copy of each would be affixed to a large sheet of thick paper on which "Minutes" (notes) were written. The Foreign Minister would simply add his initials in red ink to the last minute on the paper and write comments or instructions. About one-thirty in the afternoon he went to lunch and returned around three p.m. for appointments. When he could, he dealt with the red boxes that were reaching him. Between five and six p.m. he would have some tea brought in while he worked and read a newspaper, probably *The Times*. He stayed at the office until six or seven in the evening and unfinished papers were sent to his home. After dining at Eccleston Square, or out somewhere, he might work until bedtime, unless he had to attend the House of Commons (which met in the evening), or had a long discussion with Winston Churchill. Debate in the House of Commons might last from four to eleven p.m. In his room at the Commons he also had red boxes with labels: Red for urgent, white for ordinary, and green for intermediate. He would sort the papers and put them in one box to take home with him. A messenger would take the rest back to the Foreign Office. He would then dictate a summary to a shorthand clerk and proofread it in type.[13] Grey later ruminated,

> More and more, as the years went on, I chafed at the life of restraint. [If I left office I could have] life in a country home, with leisure for books, endless opportunities for observing the life of birds and bees, the beauty of trees, the delights of a garden, the ever-varying and ever-recurring seasons, leisure for sport and exercise...I longed to be free.[14]

His impatience with remote Albania can be imagined.

FRANZ JOSEF

The longest-reigning and oldest sovereign in Europe in 1912 was Emperor (*Kaiser*) Franz Josef von Habsburg, who was properly addressed as "His Imperial and Royal Apostolic Majesty, Emperor of Austria and King of Hungary." He had come to the throne amidst revolutions throughout Europe in the fateful year of 1848, but had somehow survived it all. Since his accession, his country had been in wars with France, Italy (Piedmont) and Prussia, always losing. Second only to Turkey, Austria-Hungary was regarded as "the sick man of Europe." But somehow, the Emperor was still there, a bald, mutton-chop-whiskered, somewhat stooped old man, venerated not only by most of his people, but sentimentally, by most of Europe. Perhaps it was partly because of the personal losses that he had suffered. His brother, Archduke Maximilian was made a fool of by the parvenu French emperor, Napoleon III, who cynically lured him to his death as "Emperor of Mexico" in 1867. Over twenty years later, Franz Josef's son, Rudolf, had blown his own brains out after murdering his 17 year-old mistress at their hunting lodge trysting place. His beautiful, melancholy, Bavarian empress, Elisabeth, had been stabbed to death in 1898 by some misfit. Although still alert and in ultimate control of the elaborate joint government of Austria-Hungary, the old emperor was now more withdrawn, relying heavily on his ministers. His routine never altered, however. Living in two simply furnished rooms in his palaces, he continued to sleep on an iron bed, or cot, rose each morning at 4 a.m. and took a cold water sponge bath, despite constant coughs. He almost always wore a uniform, no underwear, and wore an army overcoat as a dressing gown. He expected his aides to begin work by six, giving him a program for the day by seven. He never came near a typewriter or telephone in his quarters, and only rode in an automobile once. He ignored books and cared nothing for music or the arts. He had a simple lunch on a small table in his study, and dined at five p.m. with Austrian wine or beer.[15] After 1913, he usually remained invisible to the public, living in suburban Schönbrunn Palace and no longer going to his workroom in the Viennese city palace, the Hofburg. He held no general audiences as in the past. To "spare" him, access to him was limited to a few ministers, but he still read all diplomatic reports of importance and followed current events around the world.[16] On March 5, 1913, Franz Josef, sitting in the garden, received a friend. The old Emperor was holding a picture of Woodrow Wilson, who was being inaugurated as President of the United States. "He is a very great man," said the Emperor, "A very fortunate man, too. It is much to know that you have really been chosen as most fit to govern by such a vast number of people."[17]

The most important of his ministers, for the purposes of our story, are fifty-ish, balding, Count Leopold von Berchtold, the Foreign Minister, and General Baron Conrad von Hötzendorf, the Army Chief of Staff.

As usual, Winston Churchill's prose, describing Berchtold, cannot be surpassed:

> Berchtold was one of the smallest men who ever held a great position. His caliber and outlook were those of a clever Foreign Office clerk of junior rank, accustomed to move a great deal in fashionable society. Fop, dandy, la di-da; amiable, polite and curiously un-self-seeking; enormously rich; magnate of a noble house, habitué of the Turf and of the clubs; unproved in any grave political issue; yet equipped with the all-too-intensive training of a chess-board diplomatist; thus conditioned, Berchtold fell an easy prey. He was allured by the glamour and force of the military men, and fascinated by the rattle and glitter of their terrible machines. We gaze with mournful wonder upon his doubting eyes and his weak, half-constructed jaw...we are appalled that from such lips should have issued commands more fateful to the material fortunes of mankind than any spoken by the greatest sovereigns, warriors, jurists, philosophers, and statesmen of the past. Berchtold is the epitome of this age when the affairs of Brobdingnag are managed by Lilliputians.[18]

The Count's most notable quality, and chief virtue, seems to have been his manner. When visited in retirement in 1928 at his fairy-tale castle of Buchlau in what is now the Czech Republic, he was found to be as charming and hospitable as he had been considered when Foreign Minister.[19] His full name was Leopold Anton Johann Sigismund Josef Korsinius Ferdinand,

Count Berchtold, von und zu Ungarchitz Fratting und Pullwitz.[20] (Note the especially elevating *zu*.) He was a sportsman who preferred breeding horses for the race course or the army, to riding them.[21] Whenever confronted with a difficult question as Foreign Minister, Berchtold would press a button, calling the appropriate section chief to provide the right answer. He was also close to Archduke Franz Ferdinand, the heir to the throne (*Thronfolger*, not *Kronprinz*, because he was not the Emperor's son).[22] Berchtold's office was in the imposing yellowish-grey *Ballhaus*, a palace on the *Ballhausplatz* (place) in Vienna, and therefore, the Foreign Ministry itself (*Ministerium des Äussern*) was often referred to as "the *Ballplatz*" or "the *Ballhausplatz*."[23]

Chief of the Imperial and Royal General Staff, off and on, was General of Infantry Franz, Freiherr (later Baron) Conrad von Hötzendorf. In his sixties by now, he had the gruff, grey, brittle-haired, moustachioed appearance of a typical Germanic military officer. His chief study and claim to attention was his concern for the possible dissolution of the polyglot Empire by the gravitational pull and enmity of surrounding nation-states, chiefly Serbia and Italy. Like an angry bulldog on a leash, he constantly looked for opportunities to attack these enemies (and make a reputation for himself) before they could dismantle Austria-Hungary.[24]

ARCHDUKE FRANZ FERDINAND

In 1913 the heir to the Austro-Hungarian throne was 49 year-old Archduke Franz Ferdinand, a stout, pop-eyed nephew of Emperor Franz Josef. He wore a W-shaped moustache not unlike that of his friend, German Kaiser Wilhelm. He was a staunch believer in peace for the Empire, a hater of Hungarians, and hoped to keep the Empire from disintegrating. Some said that he favored giving the Empire's Slavs a share of self rule and government like that of Hungary, but this has been disputed.[25] He and the Emperor were not close, especially after Franz Ferdinand upset all tradition and protocol by marrying a non-royal lady, Countess Sophie Chotek. This was so distasteful to

16

Habsburg sensibilities that he was not only required to renounce for their children any claim to the throne, but to agree that his wife would not have any royal status or equality with himself at ceremonies. This indignity would rankle with him for the rest of his days. It made an additional bond between him and Kaiser Wilhelm, who made a point of treating Sophie as her husband's equal when they visited Germany. Another bond with the Kaiser was the two men's love of "hunting," which largely consisted of shooting literally thousands of helpless animals driven past them for the purpose of being killed. The Archduke's fairy tale estate and *Schloss* (Castle), at Konopischt was some twenty-five miles south of Prague, in what is now the Czech Republic. The walls of the onion-domed *Schloss* were black with the antlers of various sized beasts which had fallen victim to the Archduke (his lifetime score was 274,889[26]), but Konopischt was also noteworthy for its rose gardens. In Vienna, the Archduke lived in the beautiful and expansive Belvedere Palace.[27]

KAISER WILHELM of GERMANY

Without question the most colorful ruler of that day was Wilhelm (William) II von Hohenzollern, Emperor (*Kaiser*) of Germany, who came to be known in the English-speaking world as, simply, "the Kaiser." We will follow that example. He was both Emperor of the German Empire and King of Prussia, the largest and dominant state in that empire. Thus, he was, like Franz Josef of Austria-Hungary, both "imperial" and "royal," (*Kaiserliche und Königliche*: K. u. .K.). Even his impressive position, which made him "Supreme War Lord" of the armed forces and chief executive of the Empire, was overshadowed by his flamboyant, mercurial personality. For most of his reign, this stocky, strikingly handsome monarch with pale blue eyes and iron grey hair, sported a massive moustache, which was not allowed to droop, but aggressively groomed to resemble nothing so much as the letter "W." When he went to bed, its carefully waxed ends were held in place by a sort of custom-made moustache brassiere. This was especially needed, no doubt, because he followed the German custom of a two-hour nap after lunch.[28] He gloried in the countless colorful uniforms of his own and other nations' armies and navies, which he happily donned. In fact, he changed uniforms several times a day. His favorite uniform seems to have been the black uniform covered by white braided loops, of the German "Death's Head Hussars", so named because of their skull-and-crossbones headdress badge.[29] His love of military garb was never exceeded by the occasion in 1910 when he wore the full dress uniform of his Body Guard army regiment on the bridge of his imperial yacht at a regatta. No doubt he intended to make a splash, because, unlike the drab naval uniform which he usually wore on such nautical occasions, this uniform consisted of shiny black knee-length cavalier boots, white breeches and tunic, and silver cuirass, or breast plate, topped by a silver helmet, upon which perched a golden eagle with its wings outstretched.[30] To maintain his ability to firmly sit a horse, and because he claimed to find a saddle more conducive to clear, concise thinking than a conventional desk chair, he had the desks in his offices in his palaces elevated, and a saddle-mounted stool installed next to them. He could be found, studying documents while so mounted.[31]

When the Kaiser was driven in his automobile in Berlin or other German cities, a horn player sat beside the chauffeur and tooted a special series of notes, sounding to some ears like "celery salad," to warn of the Emperor's approach so that others would make way. Seated beside the driver would be a Jäger (huntsman), dressed in a rich, green hunting uniform of the Kaiser's design, complete with gilt hunting dagger and a homburg hat with a spray of grouse feathers in the hatband.[32] Wilhelm never stayed in one place more than a few days. His mind and spirit were restless. Germans jokingly called him the "*Reise-Kaiser*" (traveling emperor). His favorite vacation spot was the sunny Greek island of Corfu, off the northwest coast of Greece and Albania. He tried to go there every year, having bought a beautiful marble villa, called the "Achilleon" from Franz Josef of Austria. Franz Josef had built it for his restless melancholy Empress, Elisabeth, but she had been murdered in

1898 in Switzerland while on holiday. King George of Greece generally arranged to be at Corfu at about the same time as Wilhelm. He told Queen Olga, "If I don't, he will think he's the King of Greece." Wilhelm always described his stay in Corfu as "my favorite way of leading a simple life." However, he invariably brought with him a number of generals, equerries, and military aides. His entourage would drive over the narrow mountain roads to the villa in a procession of imperial cars with the Kaiser's car in the lead, of course. It was reported that the Kaiser was amused to hear screams from an elderly general in the last car, as it negotiated hairpin curves. Wilhelm loved such fun, but he did not encourage the officers on his yacht to indulge in undignified romping.[33]

Leaving the merits of their content aside, Wilhelm's writings and speeches were well done. He composed music and verses, and painted, but did so with mediocrity. He read widely, and tried to learn the customs, manners, industries, and public figures of other countries. He was very fond of the English humor magazine, *Punch*, especially when it contained a caricature of him. He had a robust, good natured sense of humor, often at the expense of a friend or underling. He had a hearty, infectious laugh, often stamped his foot violently to show his appreciation of a joke,[34] and wagged his finger for emphasis.[35] He drank very little alcohol, particularly because etiquette required that he return the many toasts made to him. To disguise his abstemiousness, he usually drank wine or juice from a metal goblet.[36] After breakfast, in good weather he usually went to work in the Palace courtyard, at a green iron table under a large garden umbrella, and his beloved daschunds made themselves comfortable under his chair in the gravel, the Kaiser sitting right on its edge so as not to disturb them.[37] More unusual for the period, however, was his compulsion for public statements and speeches. Unlike the bland, ribbon-cutting public remarks of most European monarchs of the day, he had a tendency to make bombastic, exaggerated, and even threatening pronouncements whenever the occasion presented itself—or didn't. It was, and is, well known that this son of Queen Victoria's daughter suffered a damaged arm at the time of his birth, so that it was deformed and of little use to him. He courageously overcame the physical handicap which this presented, laboriously learning to become an excellent horseman. He had a special one-piece knife and fork set. But it seems clear that the arm must have largely, if not entirely, accounted for his lifetime of aggressively eccentric behavior and emotional mood swings. He came to the throne in 1888 and, by 1897 one of his Chancellors (prime ministers) was asking the Foreign Minister whether the Kaiser was "quite normal." Prince Bülow's reply stands the test of history:

> ...Wilhelm II is perfectly sane. The parallel with Louis II [Bavaria's mad King Ludwig II] is not exact, because the unfortunate King of Bavaria was sexually abnormal, was devoted to alcohol, and was in a high degree unsociable. Our Kaiser is physically quite normal, absolutely healthy, and morally a pattern of purity. But he is neuras-thenic [neurotic] and so is always oscillating between excessive optimism and equally excessive pessimism. ...It is also clear that in marked contrast to his father, grandfather, and great grandfather, our young Kaiser is inclined to hybris [hubris], which has been a common and highly dangerous trait in princes for centuries, aye for millennia. In Wilhelm II hybris is shown in his passion for boastful talking which not only makes him unpopular but is politically dangerous. It arises simply from the desire to conceal his feeling of insecurity and of anxiety, a feeling which the Kaiser has much more than people think. Fundamentally, his nature is not bold but timorous. And finally, Wilhelm II is very tactless, and tact, as you know, is a quality that is born and cannot be acquired...[38]

A good example of the Kaiser's psyche was shown after he had, in a burst of personal diplomacy without consulting his ministers, wheedled foolish Russian Czar Nicholai into a secret treaty that was inconsistent with existing treaty obligations of both countries. Bülow, by then his Chancellor, was astounded and offered to resign. Wilhelm wrote Bülow a pathetic letter, concluding,

> After you receive this letter, send me a telegram saying, 'all's well;' then I will know that you're going to remain. For the morning after your request for resignation arrives your Emperor will no longer be among the living. Think of my poor wife and children!"[39]   [n.b. All of the children were grown by then.]

Virtually free of restrictions, both legal and practical, on his power, Wilhelm actively kept in touch with the daily business of his government, and was not hesitant to issue orders—some of which were ignored—and to himself ignore the advice of his ministers.   He famously maintained a paranoid love-hate relationship with Britain and the British Royal Family, especially his uncle, King Edward VII.   Edward's death in 1910 only minimally soothed Wilhelm's resentment.

Wilhelm's Chancellor in 1913, who had been chosen by him without the necessity of reference to the parliament (*Reichstag*), was a gentle, grey bear of a man, some six feet five inches tall, named Theobald von Bethmann-Hollweg.[40] He came of a Frankfurt banking family. He did not like to speak English, although he could do so. He was scholarly and respected.[41] Bethmann had been head of his school as a boy, and still read Kant and the Greek classics in the original for recreation. As a young man, he passed his law exams brilliantly, and he was much respected as a guest at country weekends. He even played Beethoven beautifully on the piano.[42] His personality included a desire always to find which side would win or be in the majority, and then take the middle ground.[43]

The Kaiser's Foreign Minister was Gottlieb von Jagow, urbane, witty, with a typical German university fencing scar on his left cheek, and a small moustache. He has been described as a "polished and benign" man and "pleasant but not forceful."[44] He had recently reluctantly given up his comfortable embassy in Rome to take charge of the Foreign Ministry (*Auswärtiges Amt*) on the Wilhelmstrasse in Berlin. He was described by the United States' ambassador as "in appearance and manners...the ideal old-style diplomat of the stage."[45] He had lived abroad and had met people from many countries and took pains to learn about them.[46] He was constantly frustrated by the difficulty of predicting French foreign policy due to "the unsettled state of French internal politics" during this period.[47] He was opposed to the unrestricted submarine warfare by Germany which directly lead to the entry of the United States into the World War against his country.[48]

CZAR NICHOLAI II

Probably best known in modern times because of best selling books and films is Czar Nicholai II (Nicholas) of Russia. A small, balding, bearded man, who resembled his cousin, Britain's King George V, he inherited in 1896 the most powerful throne in Europe, in terms of unfettered authority. However, his vacillating personality, ignorance, stubbornness, and general lack of capacity made what would have been a Herculean task of governance for anyone, impossible for him. Although forced by a revolt to accept an impotent "talk shop" parliament, or *Duma*, in 1905, by1912 he still held the ultimate reins of government, hiring and firing those of his ministers who survived assassination. He was generally peacefully inclined but felt that Russia must champion the Slavs of Europe, especially Serbia. When Austria outwitted Nicholai's foreign minister in 1908, formally annexing the Balkan provinces of Bosnia-Herzegovina and giving nothing of value in return, Nicholai was enraged, but forced to avoid war by a German ultimatum. He vowed, "German action toward us has simply been brutal and we won't

22

forget it." However, by 1911, he said to one of his ambassadors, "Listen to me,...do not for one instant lose sight of the fact that we cannot go to war. I do not wish for war; as a rule I shall do all in my power to preserve...peace...[War] would be out of the question for us... for five or six years...[and] not a moment sooner [than 1915] in any circumstances or under any pretext whatsoever."[49] He dealt directly with his ministers although he had a prime minister of sorts in Ivan Goremykin, a worn out old bureaucrat with long whiskers, who spent much time on a sofa, reading French novels and smoking cigarettes.[50] His foreign minister, Sergei Dimitrievich Sazanov, had served in the diplomatic service abroad and had become foreign minister in 1910, exercising considerable influence on foreign affairs, at least until 1911, when his brother-in-law, Prime Minister Stolypin, was assassinated.[51] Sazanov was rich, unambitious and amiable, deeply religious and highly moral, and an Anglophile. His health was weak and he tended to be timid.[52] He had a short, bristly beard and lizard-like eyes.

Vladimir Kokovstov, an intelligent, able former finance minister, had become prime minister in 1912 upon the assassination of the able Stolypin, but was fired February 12, 1914, at least partly because of the Czarina's animosity resulting from his exposure of Rasputin, the dissolute monk who seemed able to heal the Czar's son.[53]

KING CAROL I of ROMANIA

Romania's first and only king, at the time of our story, was Carol, a member of the German Catholic Hohenzollern-Sigmaringen branch of the royal family related to the Protestant Kaiser Wilhelm of Germany. In 1861, the Great Powers indicated their consent to Prince Karl of Hohenzollern-Sigmaringen becoming Prince of Romania. In order to present the Turkish Sultan (nominal overlord of Romania) with a *fait accompli*, twenty-seven year old Karl devised a plan to sneak into the country. He obtained a Swiss passport under an assumed name, bought a second class Danube riverboat ticket to Odessa,

Russia, and put on glasses and the clothing of "a servant" as a disguise. He then jumped ashore when he reached Romania, ignoring the captain's shouts for him to return.[54]

A Romanian plebiscite then voted to make him their prince.[55] With his own money he built a fairy-tale, pseudo-German castle in the pine-forested mountains north of Bucharest, at a place called Sinaia. There, he and the Royal Family of Romania often refreshed themselves and spent much time. Czar Nicholai said of the country, "Romania, bah! It is not a state, it is not a nation. It is a profession."[56] Carol certainly took his profession seriously. By the time of our story, Carol was in his seventies, with a long, square-shaped white beard and moustache. He, along with the oligarchs of his successive ministries, exercised considerable personal control over government. King Edward of England considered him a "queer fellow."[57] Unlike many other monarchs, he rarely changed his choice of uniform, preferring a black, red, and gold infantry dress uniform and white kepi with tall white aigrette feather. But he was sober, humorless, and a hard worker, managing to forge a country out of a former Turkish province.[58]

QUEEN ELISABETH OF ROMANIA

More remarkable, and certainly more colorful, was Carol's wife, Queen Elisabeth. She had been born a princess of Wied, a small Protestant principality in the western German area of the Rhineland, near Coblenz. In the Twelfth Century, the heads of the House of Wied were counts, and, in 1720, were created Princes of Wied, with vast possessions and feudal power on the banks of the Rhine. Their oldest known ancestral seat was the Burg Palace, Ober Alt Wied (Above Old Wied). Later they moved to the Palace Nieder Alt Wied (Below Old Wied). They could count among their number a long line of archbishops and statesmen, including Archbishop Count Hermann zu Wied of Cologne (1515-1547), who became a staunch champion of the (Protestant) Evangelical Church, and corresponded with Martin Luther. The famous Prince Alexander Philip Maximilian zu

Wied was an intrepid explorer of the American West in the early 1800s.[59] Queen Elisabeth was born at the canary-colored, simple palace of Neu Wied (New Wied) in 1843. If she became a neurotic, it may be explained by the many sorrows she experienced. Her scholarly father was tubercular and bedridden in her youth. Her little brother was born with some "incurable malady," underwent a painful operation, and was nursed by Elisabeth until he died at age twelve. Her mother became ill and lay paralyzed and in great pain for months.[60] All of this had happened by the time Elisabeth was twenty-three. Her mother turned to faith healing and encouraged Elisabeth to join in table tappings, hypnotism, and spirit writing. Elisabeth was what was once called highly-strung and sensitive. She was forced to observe inmates at the lunatic asylum and to kneel beside her stepmother's bed as the woman died.[61] Her only youthful companions were her brothers, the invalid Otto, and William.

She spent her time in the summer garden of the palace or climbing in the hills of Westerwald (West Forest) which surrounded "Castle" (*Schloss*) Neu Wied in "a chain of undulating heights." In the distance could be seen the Rhine River, and far away, against the horizon, the towers of the city of Coblenz. The valley is divided by the Wied River, which cuts through the forest, and to the west the extinct volcanoes of Maifeld and Eifel look down on the woods and vineyards of the Mosel, which were not far away.[62] She originally did not intend to marry, but accepted Carol in 1869, at age twenty-six. Her only child by the King died at age four, and, despite trying the most bizarre remedies, she could never conceive again. Typically, she adopted as her mourning garb white instead of black, and had a nervous breakdown. What she considered to be her artistic temperament led her to write both poetry and prose, including such stories as the allegorical "The Serpent's Isle," and the quasi-historical "The Siege of Widen" which were published in English women's magazines under the by-line of "Her Majesty, the Queen of Rumania."[63] Somewhat coyly, she adopted the *nom de plume* of "Carmen Sylva," meaning "song of the forest," or "song and nature," one supposes.[64] Noone was fooled. During the Romanian War of 1877-1878 with Turkey, she was indefatigable in nursing the wounded soldiers, spending her whole time in hospitals, and earning for herself the Romanian name of "*Muma Ranitilor*," or, "the mother of the wounded." In 1876 a Romanian poem she wrote was set to music and performed at the national theatre in Bucharest.[65] She collected and edited many Romanian legends, doing much of her work in collaboration with her lady-in-waiting. She wrote easily in English, French, German, and Romanian. The following letter, which she wrote in English to an English magazine editor in the 1890s, is somewhat revealing of her character:

> Here is a little poem that was written by me in English in the year '68; if it is too bad English don't make use of it but you might like to put it into its right place in relating the tale of my life. To the English [sic] authors I fed upon you must add: Kingsley MacAuley and Carlyle; I translated some part of "Hero worship" for a learned gentleman who didn't know English. If something comes up out of the shadow of the past I shall write it to you, if you pardon these horrid little scrawls!
>
> Elisabeth

[Her letter went on:]

> Through lifes [sic] deep anguish grief and pain
> Where none to me beloved remain
> I overheard the echoing strain
> Oh 'serve the Lord with gladness'
> In the many storms and anguish past
> When hope and joy away were cast
> It oft came sommry [?] in the blast
> Oh 'serve the Lord with gladness'
> But now I know the joy that stays

The ever bright and sunny rays.
And soft and low I try to praise
Oh 'serve the Lord with gladness.'

March 3, 1868

(More than a year and a half before I married).[66]

She founded numerous schools and institutions for women and children, and revived old Romanian industries, traditions, and customs. She always rose early, before her household was up, using the time for study or writing poetry and delighted in needlework. She was the stereotype of the romantic poet, "ardent, warm-hearted..." and impetuous, but naïve and easily exploited. She surrounded herself with young female courtiers, who often sat at her feet and attended her words of wisdom while sewing and embroidering native materials. Moon-faced like many of her family and royal Dutch relatives, her hair had begun to turn white at an early age. Like so many European royals, she had intensely blue eyes and displayed beautiful teeth when she laughed, as she did often. It was said that she "saw all things as tragedies and therefore dramatized even the simplest events of everyday life."[67]

KING PETAR I of SERBIA

The King of Serbia, was, by virtue of the brutal murder of his predecessor, described earlier, the elderly Petar I of the Karageorgevich dynasty. He might have refused to accept a throne obtained as a result of such disgusting means, but he did not. Before his accession, he had not lived in Serbia since he was fourteen years old.[68] He was an intelligent, well-read and generally courageous man, although he became somewhat a captive of the thugs who brought him to the throne. Unless the King played his cards right, he might suffer the same fate as King Alexander and Queen Draga. Even though he had grown up in Austria as an exile, he must have known that his country's policy had to lean toward its protector, Russia, and away from the rival of Serbia and Russia, Austria-Hungary. By 1913, Petar was almost 70 years old, an avuncular figure with imposing white handlebar moustaches. Arthritis had taken its toll on him, so that he looked forward to passing the cares of kingship to his younger son, Prince Alexander. His eldest son, George, had to be bypassed because George was, unfortunately, a lunatic who had killed his valet by kicking him down some stairs in a fit of rage. This was too much, apparently, even for the Serbs, and George had to renounce his claim to the throne to save his skin. He seems to have suffered no other punishment, however.

King Petar had led a cultured and adventurous life, attending the French Military Academy at Saint Cyr, and fighting for France in the Franco-Prussian War during his long exile. He fought for Bosnia in its 1875 revolt against Turkey. He sent his sons to live with the Russian Czar, while he had lived in poverty in Switzerland.[69]

His prime minister during the period we will be discussing was Nikola Pasich. Almost as old as his king, this tall old man with a very long grey beard and moustache had also spent time as a political refugee in Switzerland, where he had received part of his education. He had met King Petar as early as 1875, and was a supporter of his claim to the throne. He was a strong Russophile and one of the founders of the Radical Party, which he led for thirty years.[70] His views were in line with those of the Serbian nationalists, who wanted to unite all Serbs (and a number of non-Serbs) under Serbian rule, even if they were more or less content elsewhere: Austria-Hungary, for instance. Pasich had said that the sole purpose of Serbia's existence was to detach Austria-Hungary's southern Slav provinces.[71] In August 1913, after the second Balkan War, he said, "The first round is won; we must prepare the second against Austria." A few days later, he said:

> Already in the first Balkan Wars I could
> have let it come to an European war, in order to
> acquire Bosnia and Herzegovina; but, as I feared
> that we should then be forced to make large

concessions to Bulgaria in Macedonia, I wanted first of all to secure the possession of Macedonia for Serbia, and only then to proceed to the acquisition of Bosnia.[72]

But first he needed a period of peace to consolidate Serbia's gains.

KING NIKOLA OF MONTENEGRO

The King of Montenegro was the notorious Nikola (Nicholas, or Nikita) born in 1860, who had ruled over the tiny mountainous country of only about 282,000 people for fifty-two years by 1913. Montenegro (named for its "black" mountains) caused trouble on the world stage far out of proportion to its size.[73] It did not even dare call itself a kingdom until 1910. Before that, Nikola was a prince of the mountain entity which the Turks had not even bothered to occupy, but claimed as part of its Ottoman Empire. In 1908, its capital, Cetinje, had a population of only five thousand and consisted of little more than a monastery, a modest official residence, and a number of thatched houses. Many foreigners considered it a village.[74]

In 1913, King Nikola was seventy-two years old, but still a big bear of a man with a grizzled stubble of a beard. He was usually seen wearing the national dress of high leather boots, a sort of white, long shirt, a short embroidered vest, baggy pants, and a small round cap. Despite his rough appearance and pretense at being a buffoon, he had been educated in Paris, spoke French, German, Italian, Russian, and some English. His avarice was notorious. He once stole the proceeds of the sale of grain intended to feed his starving province.[75] He hoped to succeed to the Serbian throne, and successfully married his daughter, Elena, to the future King of Italy, Vittorio Emmanuelle III, and his daughter Zorka, to the King of Serbia, Petar I Karageorgevich. He was ambitious to take any of the spoils of the Turkish Empire which he could get, especially that northern part of Albania lying on Montenegro's southern border, which included the important

29

city of Scutari. Serbia was both his ally and a rival for Slav loyalty.

Nikola gave his little country a parliament in 1905, but made sure that he kept the power in his hands.[76] He enriched himself by playing the stock markets with his inside knowledge of impending war matters. He dropped in regularly at the Russian Czar's country palace of *Czarskoe Selo* to pick up a subsidy check for not less than 300,000 gold rubles (perhaps $2,763,000 today).[77] In 1910, he was the last of the former Ottoman Balkan princes to declare himself a king.[78] His prime minister, Janko Vukotich, and his foreign ministers, Dukan Vukorich, Petar Plamenc, and General Mitor Martinovich, (who also served as prime minister) were but instruments of the venal king. He took bribes from Turkey, Austria, Italy, and Russia, but was loyal to none.[79] He claimed at various times that his ancestors, the Petroviches, were buried in Bosnia-Herzegovina or Scutari, depending on which lands he claimed at the time.[80]

RAYMOND POINCARÉ

Raymond Poincaré of France was an unusual figure in the Third Republic, which had been formed in the ruins of the Franco-Prussian War of 1870-1871. The only non-royal head of state of a major European power at this time, he was unusual because he had been, first, prime minister in 1912, and then became President of the Republic on January 16, 1913.[81] The office of President of the French Republic was meant to be largely ceremonial, like that of a constitutional monarch. But Poincaré, by dint of his forceful personality and political skill, was able to exert considerable influence on the constantly-changing parliamentary ministries under him. An Alsatian by birth, with the face of a bulldog, he longed even more than most Frenchmen for the return of Alsace-Lorraine, which had to be ceded to Germany in 1871.

France generally pursued a pro-Greek foreign policy in the Balkans, and prime ministers came and went with considerable regularity, leaving Poincaré as the one fixed star in the political firmament. He did little to restrain Russia, and much to prod her, as the ally upon which France had to cling for protection from France's traditional enemy, Germany.[82]

WILHELM ZU WIED

Prince (*Fürst*) Wilhelm zu Wied, (the protagonist of our little story, which we shall get to, by and by) was born in Neuwied am Rhein, Germany, March 26, 1876, and his full name was Wilhelm Friedrich Heinrich (William Frederick Henry) zu Wied. He was the second son of General of Infantry Prince Wilhelm, Fifth Prince (*Fürst*) zu Wied, sometime president of the Prussian House of Lords and active member of the Imperial German Council for Colonial Affairs. Our Wilhelm's mother was Princess Wilhelmina of the Netherlands, who had brought a large dowry.[83] Our prince was commissioned as an officer in the *Garde du Corps* (royal bodyguard) in the Royal Prussian Army, and promoted a captain of the Third Guards *Uhlan* (cavalry) Regiment in 1912, of which he was adjutant for a time. He married Princess (*Fürstin*) Sophie of Schönburg-Waldenburg on November 30, 1906, and they had two children, a daughter born February 19, 1909, and a son born May 19, 1913. His younger brother Victor was a diplomat and, in 1913, a secretary of the German Legation in Christiana, Norway.[84]

Very tall and trim, but balding, Wilhelm sported a modestly Kaiseresque moustache. He was considered a bright, able soldier, had attended the Staff College and for two years held an appointment in the German Great General Staff, which was reserved for promising officers. He was one of those "mediatized" princes who had no kingdom or principality to rule, and usually little money, but was royal enough to marry royalty. This leads us to a curious, but not altogether important, discussion of this status. Because of it, his title was "*Fürst*" and not "*Prinz*." Instead of "*Hoheit*," ("Highness") he was addressed as "*Durchlaucht*", a word which seems untranslatable literally, but was a notch above the other form of address. Although he was not the reigning prince ("*Erbprinz*"), he had the title just the

31

same. His family had settled on the Rhine since the Eleventh Century, and gave its name to the "country" of Wied, which had been divided in the Eighteenth Century (for reasons best known by long-dead Germans) into Wied-Runkel and Wied-Neuwied. In 1806, the area of Wied became a Prussian "*Standeherrschaft*" ("lordship"). Wilhelm zu Wied had a famous great-uncle, *Fürst* Alexander Philip Maximilian, who explored the uncharted American West in 1832-34, and made detailed records of the trip, which were eventually returned to the Joslyn Art Museum in Omaha, Nebraska.[85]

Everyone mentioned Wilhelm zu Wied's tallness, and his forehead was high, even for a young man with a receding hairline. The later Queen Marie of Romania, English by birth, noted that all the Wieds were charming, spoke excellent English, had perfect manners and a sense of humor. Although they were tall and aristocratic, she found them not particularly handsome. She found their mouths large and well filled with strong white teeth, "but when they smiled or laughed, their skin had a special way of creasing over their bones [which] gave them something a little wizened, but for all that attractive."[86] Wied had a nervous laugh to which he often gave vent.[87] It was once said of him by a Hungarian woman who had met him at balls and hunts in Germany, Austria, and Hungary, that "He was not very bright. Not enough even for those who did not expect much…"[88]

Wied's wife, *Fürstin* Sophie, was from a similarly petty royal dynasty. By modern standards she was not ugly, but not particularly pretty either. She was considered to be a main force behind her husband's acceptance of the Albanian throne and some of his actions in that position.[89]

Our Wied's father, the Fifth Prince, had two brothers and two sisters, and they had all lived in a large white house on top of a hill near New Wied (*NeuWied*). It was a large, low building, standing out against a background of large beech woods, with a beautiful view over the Rhine Valley. Their house was sympathetic, old-fashioned even in the 1890s, and full of family pictures. As previously mentioned, the fifth Prince's sister, Elisabeth, married King Carol of Romania. Fürstin Sophie was one of Elisabeth's favorites. Sophie's grandmother had been a Romanian through whom the Schönburgs had inherited a fine estate, "Fantanele," near Bacau, Romania. Sophie had spent much of her childhood at Fantanele, and adored all that was Romanian. Her parents had died when she was quite young and Carmen Sylva (the *nom de plume* of Queen Elisabeth) had taken her under her care. She was clever, talented, and a great music lover. The Wieds' salon at Potsdam, near Berlin, was the resort of musical and artistic nobility; and Sophie was later credited with the desire to become the "Carmen Silva" of Albania, and to introduce her subjects to the charms of learning and art.[90] The romance of Albania "sank into her soul".[91] She was a trained singer, mastered five instruments, and composed.[92] Queen Elisabeth had brought about the match with her nephew, Wilhelm zu Wied, second son of her brother.

Sophie's Wied was a "fine, healthy, kindly fellow with a soft voice and wide smile," but not an artistic temperament, so that he was understandably occasionally somewhat bewildered by Queen Elisabeth's atmosphere. She could not bear Sophie out of her sight. Sophie and the Queen sang, painted, composed, wrote poetry, played the harp and piano together, and may also have spoken with spirits. They were inseparable.[93]

VITTORIO EMMANUELLE III of ITALY

The monarch of Italy since 1900 (when his father was publicly murdered by an Italian who had taken the trouble to return from the U.S. for the purpose) was tiny, bulldog-faced Vittorio Emmanuelle III of Savoy. He was married to Elena, the ugly daughter of the shifty Montenegrin king, Nikola. Barely five feet tall, with the congenital protruding lower jaw, Vittorio Emmanuelle meant well, but functioned primarily as a constitutional monarch, ruling through his ministers. Well-read, like many of his contemporary monarchs he was frugal and preferred a simple, retiring life. He commuted from his suburban villa to his office in the venerable Quirinale Palace in Rome.[94] However, he was always the spearhead of any anti-Church policy.[95] Until March of 1914, his prime minister was the liberal, Giovanni Giolitti. Giolitti was succeeded by Antonio Salandra, a conservative. Throughout the period of our story, however, the Italian Foreign Ministry, known as "the *Consulta*," (because it was in the equally venerable Palazzo di Consulta), was run by the elegant Antonio Paterno Castelli, *Marchese* (marquess) di San Guiliano. A polished diplomat, he was a sixtyish nobleman with thinning hair and a grey, pointed beard.[96]

KING CONSTANTINE I OF GREECE

On the morning of March 18, 1913, the King of Greece, a former member of the Danish royal house, was the long-reigning and popular George I. When he was murdered later that day, he was succeeded by his equally popular soldier son, Constantine. Constantine was married to Sophie, the sister of German Kaiser Wilhelm II, and was thought to be pro-German. Forty-five year old Constantine, balding, with handlebar moustaches, was popular as a victorious commander in the Balkan Wars and as a simple soldier with the common touch. But his prime minister, the popular and powerful politician Eleutherios Venizelos (1864-1936) was expansionist, pro-French, and pro-Serb. The two men would eventually come to a test of strength.[97]

SOME NON-ROYAL CHARACTERS
IN OUR DRAMA

The Albanians

PRENK BIB DODA

Prenk (Peter) Bib Doda was educated in Constantinople, and succeeded his father as chief, or prince, of some thirty thousand Roman Catholic Albanians in the northernmost mountains of Albania. They were called Mirdites, logically enough, because their region was named Mirdita. Under the Ottomans, they were suspected by the Turks of independent leanings, despite furnishing a large number of volunteers to the Turkish Army. This suspicion led to the exile of Prenk Bib Doda to Turkey in 1881. His capture was accomplished by the simple expedient of inviting him to inspect a Turkish warship, and then carrying him off to Turkey. The Turks had tried something like this before, in the 1870s, but had to return him, promoted to *pasha,* in order to get Mirdite volunteers for their army.[98]   By 1908, he had risen to Brigade Commander in the Sultan's elite guards.   In that year, following the reformist Young Turk revolution, the Mirdites refused to accept the new Constitution. The Turks ordered the Catholic Mirdite Abbot to make the Mirdites obey, but he replied that only their prince—Bib Doda— could do that.   Therefore, the Turks rushed Prenk back to the highlands of northern Albania.   There, flinching from the unfamiliar but customary celebratory rifle shots of his tribesmen whizzing into the sky, he arrived on a white horse. He was wearing his Turkish best: a red fez and the gold-embroidered official uniform of an *aide de camp* of the Sultan. He had been gone so long he knew almost none of his clansmen.[99] Although the Mirdites believed Prenk was sent by God, he disappointed their expectation that he could work miracles.[100]

In May of 1912, his Mirdites rebelled and beat the Turks, who thereafter left them alone. The Mirdites took no part in the ensuing Balkan Wars. Prenk planned a Mirdite principality of Mirdita under Serbian protection, and the Serbs gave him money to bribe his clansmen with the understanding that the Serbs would have a way to the sea through Mirdita. However, the formation of the Albanian principality in 1913 frustrated this plan.[101]

King Nikola of Montenegro called the Mirdites, "That infamous Albanian clan: they are really Serbs or Bosniaks who flinched [from Ottoman attacks] and fled to the highlands while we held our ground against the Turks."[102]

ISA BOLETIN

Isa Boletin (also known as Iso Boletinatz, Isa Boletini, etc.) was an important Albanian chieftain, born in 1864, in a place called Boletin. He spent much of his early life fighting the Turks for Albania, and especially for Kosovo *vilayet* (also known as Kosova), where he had supreme authority. In 1912 he was tall, lithe, with aquiline features in a handsome, "fierce" face. He was head of the Kosovo delegation to the Albanian Provisional Government in 1912 and was noted for always wearing the traditional Albanian white cap, or fez (the *plis*) and Albanian dress.

A visitor in 1912 found Boletin on the second floor of a house, surrounded by his wild Albanian mountaineers, armed to the teeth. On the landing were more guards, and the walls were hung with arms.[103]

ESSAD PASHA TOPTANI

Essad Pasha Toptani was a villain worthy of the most melodramatic Ruritanian romance, but one whom no modern writer would expect readers to accept as believable. He was of the wealthy Toptani landowning family in the region of the central Albanian city of Tirana. Centuries before this, his family had converted to Islam under Turkish duress.[104] He had obtained important positions under the Ottoman regime, getting a good start due to the influence of his brother, Ghani Toptani, who was an assassin for the Sultan until he, himself, was assassinated, presumably upon the order of the Sultan.[105] Essad thereby became the head of the Toptani family. He had held the position of commander of the Ottoman gendarmerie (a sort of semi-military police) at Janina, which is now part of Greece.

In every position of authority which he held, he made sure to enrich himself by bribes or otherwise. In 1908, he praised the Young Turk revolution of that year, and was given command of the gendarmerie in Scutari, the northern Albanian city and seaport.[106] In the December 1908 Turkish parliament, Essad represented the central Albanian seaport of Durazzo. On May 10, 1909, Essad was sent by the Young Turk rebels to advise the Sultan in Constantinople that he was deposed. That encounter is reported to have gone like this: Essad was accompanied by a Greek, a Jew, and an Armenian—all subjects of the Sultan. At the Sultan's palace they were kept waiting until the rat-faced ruler emerged from behind a screen with his seventeen year-old son. Essad saluted him:

> *Essad:* In conformity with the *fetva* that has been pronounced, the nation has deposed you. The National Assembly charges itself with your personal security and that of your family. You have nothing to fear from anybody...

> *Sultan:* This is kismet. Is my life to be spared?

> *Essad:* The Ottomans are magnanimous.[107]

In the First Balkan war with the Serbs and Montenegrins, he was second in command of the Turkish forces in Scutari.[108] By the time of our story, he was fiftyish, stout, with piercing eyes and black handlebar moustaches, but was described by the writer Joyce Carey as "a fat, fair man."[109] On January 30, 1913, Essad's chief agent, Osman Bali, (probably sent by Essad), killed Scutari's able Turkish commander, Hassan Riza Bey, as he left a dinner at Essad's house. Hassan had been offered £30,000 (about $2,700,000 today) by the Serbs to surrender Scutari, but he refused.[110] On April 23, 1913, for a bribe of only £10,000, (roughly $900,000 in today's money), Essad surrendered the city of Scutari to the Montenegrins. Four days later, he declared himself King of the Albanians, taking his still-armed Albanian (heretofore Turkish) troops back to his homeland at Tirana. By July 2, 1913, however, he had been persuaded to join the new Provisional Government of Albania as a mere Minister of the Interior.[111] Although the Prince of Wied later wrote that he believed Essad to be illiterate,[112] the American, Stephan Bonsal, who knew him in 1918, said that he wrote well in French, spoke fairly good Italian and poor French. A favorite joke of his, in Albanian, at the expense of his erstwhile Italian sponsors, was a riddle. Referring to soldiers of a famous Italian Army regiment, who wore cock feathers in their headgear, he asked, "What is it that sports feathers but is not a bird? That carries a rifle but is not a soldier? That wears trousers but is not a man? ---The Italian Bersaglieri!"[113]

ISMAIL KEMAL VLORA

Ismail Kemal Vlora was one of the founding fathers of the Albanian nation. He was sixty-eight by the time independence was declared in 1912. He was well educated and fluent in Albanian, Italian, French, Greek, and Turkish. He had been high in the councils of the Turkish sultan, Ismail's cousin Ferid Pasha Vlora having been Grand Vizier (Prime Minister) of Turkey in 1903. At one time Ismail was Turkish governor of Tripolitania (Libya) and Governor General of Syria. In 1900 Ismail angered the Sultan and was forced to flee to Europe.[114] In 1908, upon the institution of the Turkish Constitution, he returned to Albania and was elected to the Turkish parliament as a liberal.[115] From 1909 to 1911, he was the leader of the opposition. By May of 1912, he had retired to Nice, France, but kept in touch with Albanians and their affairs.[116] In November of 1912, he returned to Albania and presided over an assembly which produced the Albanian declaration of independence.

Greek Prime Minister Venizelos once claimed to have bribed Ismail.[117] After the Second Balkan War, as the scion of an old Albanian family, he was named President of the Provisional Albanian Government but soon made way for Prince Wied. After the outbreak of the First World War he lived in France and Switzerland. During that war, he was respected for his intervention on behalf of the persecuted Armenians and he recommended the formation of a separate Armenian state. The German political section of their foreign office during the war considered Ismail to be respectable and reliable. They felt, however, that his sympathy would more likely be on the side of the Entente than the Central Powers.[118]

TURKHAN PASHA PREMETI

By the time of our story, gentle, white-bearded Turkhan Pasha Premeti had concluded a brilliant career in the Turkish civil service, capped by his stint as the Ottoman Ambassador to Russia from 1908 right up to 1913. He then became Wilhelm zu Wied's only Prime Minister and served him loyally.[119]

KRISTO MEXI

Kristo Mexi was an Albanian who had lived in Romania for many years and was a retired banker whose social position was good in Romania but not in Albania. He had been a "senator" at Valona in the Albanian Provisional Government and attended an Albanian Convention in Trieste in 1913. He had acted as one of Wied's agents in summoning a delegation from Albania offer him the throne. Rumors of shady deals in his youth and the hostility of many of Wied's courtiers in Durazzo did not prevent his daily audience with the King in 1914. [120]

MUFID BEY LIBOHOVA

It was said of Mufid that, "His courtly manner and ostentatious extravagance were hallmarks of the last generation elite." He served as one of Prince Wied's cabinet ministers, latterly as his foreign minister. He was loyal and sometimes hot tempered. He had lived in Turkey for many years before Wied's arrival, and had been a well-known lawyer until the Young Turk reformers came to power in that country in 1908.[121]

HASSAN BEY PRISHTINA

Hassan's real surname was Berisha. He had represented his northeastern Albanian region of Kosovo in the Young Turk

Parliament, where he eloquently denounced Ottoman brutality. He led the successful Albanian revolt against the Turks in the spring of 1912. A fluent French speaker, he then served the Prince of Wied, while King, as Postmaster General and later raised volunteers for Austria in World War I. He hated Serbs. Having supported the losing side, he was expelled from Kosovo in 1918 and went to Rome.[122]

The Foreigners

DUNCAN HEATON-ARMSTRONG

Born in Velden, Austria to an Irish father, who was also born in Austria and had Austrian relatives, Duncan Heaton-Armstrong's mother was the daughter of an Austrian baron. Although a British subject, Heaton (as we shall usually call him for brevity's sake) referred to himself as "an Irishman." He studied at Eton, but left early. He couldn't pass the entrance exams at Cambridge and, having a good allowance, spent much of his time entertaining friends, living the good life of a young bachelor and fox hunting. He was a reserve British Army officer in the Lancashire Fusiliers, and was 27 at the time of our story.[123]

MAJOR LODEWIJK W. J. J. THOMSON

Major Thomson had been a Liberal member of the Netherlands Parliament for two terms, from 1905 until his defeat in 1913. In Parliament he had opposed the near monopoly of German firms in supplying the Dutch military with arms. He was an experienced colonial officer, having spent years in the Dutch East Indies (now Indonesia) and, as a major in the Dutch Twelfth Infantry Regiment. He had been a military observer at the Greek siege of Janina in 1913 and before that, of the Boer War of 1899-1902. He spoke fluent French.

The Dutch War Minister had sounded Thomson out for possible service in Albania even before Holland was formally solicited to provide officers for that country's gendarmerie. He

40

agreed to go, serving under Colonel Willem J. H. de Veer of the Third Field Artillery Regiment.

The two were sent to Albania to make a preliminary report on the situation, and they met with the important Albanians, including Essad and Prenk Bib Doda before Wilhelm zu Wied arrived to become King.

Their report to Holland encouraged a Dutch mission as (1) uplifting the Albanians "for the sake of civilization in this poor country," and as (2) helping the Muslims there, which would boost Dutch prestige in the Dutch Muslim colonies in the East Indies.

Thomson was a vigorous organizer and diplomat, although he was subject to fits of rage, with tears, which angered Colonel de Veer. De Veer was also irritated by Thomson's impertinence towards him, and what appeared to be his personal ambition. Thomson kept close contact with Dutch and Italian journalists (especially those from the *Corriere della Sera*) to protect his own image and play down de Veer's. But his courage was patent and he was helpful in drawing up the stillborn royal Albanian Constitution.[124]

COLONEL (GENERAL) WILLEM J. H. de VEER

The commander of the Dutch military mission to Albania, Colonel (later General) Willem J. H. de Veer was an officer of the Dutch Third Regiment of Field Artillery. He was fifty-six at the time of our story, had been born in the Dutch East Indies, and was relatively obscure at the time of his assignment to the Albanian mission[125] Photos show that he was trim, upright, with long "handlebar" moustaches.

BARON ALIOTTI

The Baron Aliotti, whose first name is lost in the mists of time, was Italian Minister to Albania during Prince Wilhelm zu Wied's brief reign. He had formerly been in the Italian embassies in Vienna, Paris, Washington, and Caracas. He was considered by some an astute diplomat, but King Carol I of Romania said that he had the reputation of a cheat at cards, for which he had been forced to leave London in haste. Wied came to consider him a bully, a liar, a collaborator with the rebels, and to expect from him "any kind of mean deed."[126] Even Aliotti's own foreign minister, Marquis di San Giuliano, considered him unsuitable and out of control, but feared his popularity in the Italian parliament, where he was considered a brave patriot for some reason.[127] He was not above trying to profit from stock market speculations through his "inside information status, as when, during the rebel attack on Durazzo in June of 1914, he reported falsely that the city had fallen.[128] San Giuliano said that Aliotti,

> A diplomat of quick intelligence and full of zealous energy, had eagerly thrown himself into a contest with his Austrian colleagues, occasionally exceeding our instructions as to ends and means… but at that moment we could contain but not disown him. We had continual requests for his recall from the Austrian government.

San Giuliano upheld friendship with Austria, but Aliotti won over the entire Italian press and parliament and there was no way to remove him. San Giuliano said jokingly, "Aliotti is regarded here as the new Garibaldi of Italy."[129]

EDITH DURHAM

Although she did little to shape events in Albania, Mary Edith Durham's deep and abiding affection and admiration for the Albanian people made her their permanent advocate to the British and to all who would listen to her, although her British Foreign Office file spoke of the "inadvisability of correspondence with [her]"[130] A mannish spinster in the sexist terms of the time, she was born into an upper middle class English family in 1863 and was well educated for a woman of that day, with training and considerable skill as an artist. In her late thirties she seems to have had an attack of depression, and was advised to travel. This she did, in 1900 making her first contact with the Balkans. Her travels included Montenegro, Albania, and Serbia, but her heart belonged to the Albanians. She met King Nikola of Montenegro in 1906 and became his confidante. She considered the Serbs to be 'vermin" and "shameless liars" for their treatment of the Albanians, about whom she wrote books, reports, and letters to newspapers and for whom she arranged and carried relief supplies.[131] On her 1908 tour of the Albanian mountains, it was said that she "must have cut a disarmingly unusual figure in her 'waterproof Burberry skirt' and 'Scotch plaid gold cap'."

She remained in Montenegro and Scutari during the two Balkan Wars, doing relief work, wearing, a fellow relief worker said, "short hair, no stays, very plain and stout---old filthy Tam-o-Shanter, and dirty dark green flannel blouse."[132]

3

OTTOMAN ALBANIA

> Albania: Amid inveterate tribal hatreds and religious feuds, surrounded by young scions of native aristocracy who are unscrupulous adventurers and by a pastoral people more vigorous than industrious, and handier with the gun than with either the plowshare or spade.
> ---Italian Prime Minister Antonio Salandra, March, 1914[1]

In 1878, when Britain and the European Great Powers met in Berlin to assemble the messy debris of the latest Balkan Wars against the senile Turkish Ottoman Empire, the Albanians of that empire sent one Abdul Bey Frasheri as unofficial representative of their interests. When he approached the German Chancellor Bismarck to plead for Albanian autonomy, the old statesman replied, "But you haven't even got an alphabet or a written language. How do you expect to create a state?"[2]

By the end of the Nineteenth Century, the Balkan provinces of the Ottoman Empire were miserable. The poor peasants barely subsisted on the land, mulcted by independent contractors who purchased the right to collect taxes and harried by half-starved regular soldiers, who had not been paid in months. There were few schools, and doctors were even rarer. For hundreds of years, the Turks had ruled their subject peoples of Europe – Serbs, Bulgars, Greeks, Albanians, Macedonians – on the principle of "divide and rule." Ottoman officials, who considered a Balkan assignment a punishment, stayed in their crumbling *konaks* (government buildings), dispensing uneven justice. The official maps showed roads and bridges where none existed. Turkish investigating commissions of inquiry toured devastated regions and returned to Constantinople flush with *bakshish* (bribes) which bought reports of great prosperity in the region.[3] An English traveler wrote:

Northern Albania [in 1908] was a hotbed of Austrian intrigue. The Austrian Consul-General even takes it upon himself to spy [on] the actions of tourists, as though the land were already under Austrian jurisdiction. Scutari swarms with foreign consuls, and the Albanian has acquired the bad habit of crying to one and the other for help. Austria by lavish expenditure, strives to buy up the tribes. Italy offers counter attractions [the Albanians] accept money upon occasion from each and all…this annoys the consuls.

The Turks lost Greece, Bulgaria, and Serbia when those nations developed schools in their own languages, so they would not let Albanians have them except when forced to in "church" or "religious" schools, run by Austrians or Italians.[4] Some areas, such as Mirdita, ruled by Prenk Bib Doda, never accepted Turkish rule or paid any tax.[5]

Northern Albanians told Edith Durham in 1908 that "Konstitutzioon" [i.e., the new Turkish Empire constitution] was a failure because it did not give them roads, railways, schools, order, and justice after two whole months. "We have given our *besa* [peace oath] until St. Dmitri, and if it has not done them by then – goodbye Konstitutzioon." As justification of their expectations, they said that they knew that a government could do as it liked, that foreign companies could build railroads and that schools were all paid for by governments in civilized lands.[6]

Those who lived for any time in Albania, rather than passing through the country, refuted the country's reputation as a land of lawless bandits and murderers. The people's characters, they said, whatever they were, were forged by centuries of repression, especially four hundred years under Ottoman Turks. The defenders of Albania's reputation maintained that resistance to occupation and feuding over matters of honor were mistaken for banditry. It was true however, that Albanians often killed each other in blood feuds, to uphold their ancient code of honor.

45

The death of one member of a family at the hands of a member of another family, for whatever reason, demanded revenge on some member of the killer's family. This led to a vicious cycle of killing which could only be stopped, temporarily, by the *besa* or truce of honor, which could not be violated without loss of honor and violent reprisal.[7]

The law governing feuds was known as "the law of Lek," named for its original promulgator in the fourteenth century, but ironically, it forbade killing. Only fines and burning of property were permitted as retaliation. In fact, it covered almost every aspect of "life" from accidental parricide to hair cutting.[8] But the killing persisted. No one was trusted to arbitrate the disputes. Highland Ghegs regarded Turks, Slavs, and lowlanders as "fair game" for robbery and other unpleasantness. If they opposed roads it was only to keep out enemies.[9]

Important Albanian families, especially in the south, derived their surnames from their town or district of origin, or some ancestor.[10] Under Ottoman rule, in the course of time, nearly three-quarters of Albania had opted to become Muslims. Most were Sunni like the Turks, but a minority belonged to the heterodox Bektashi sect. Islam was strongest in the central regions. The far north (outside Scutari) stayed nominally Roman Catholic, because all it ever saw of the Turks was an occasional ineffectual raid. The Northern Mirdite Clan numbered around 30,000 and were Roman Catholic.[11]

Turkified beys had bought their posts and milked them. Contrary to what had happened in other Balkan countries when the Christians took power there, the Albanian beys stayed in place in 1914.[12] This was a great source of discontent.

The Turkish military defeat in 1877 by Russia and the Balkan Christian nations rekindled (if it needed rekindling) the spark of Albanian nationalism, although complete independence from Turkey was not sought.[13] This spark was somewhat quashed when Prenk Bib Doda, the northern Albanian leader, was kidnapped.

As early as 1897, Austria and Russia made a secret agreement which, *inter alia*, set out rough borders of "an independent state under the name of the principality of Albania," to the exclusion of every foreign domination, but only if maintenance of the *status quo* became impossible.[14] France supported Greece's ambitions in Turkish Albania, as she regarded Italy as a rival in the Mediterranean.[15] In 1900, the Sultan of Turkey forced the Albanian, Ismail Kemal Bey, to seek refuge abroad, where he agitated for eventual Albanian autonomy. The Sultan tried to counter Ismail's activities by propaganda in Albania, assisted by Essad Pasha Toptani, his commander of the gendarmerie in Janina in what is now northwestern Greece.[16] Ismail Kemal Bey joined fellow expatriate Faik Bey Konitsa in Belgium, and took over the newspaper, *Albania*. The Konitsas owned much property around Konits and Faik Bey had been educated in France and at Harvard.[17] Following the Young Turk Revolution of 1908, Albanian clubs, newspapers, and schools sprang up throughout Albania. Exiles, such as Ismail Kemal, returned. He was elected a representative to the Turkish parliament. That same year, Bulgaria took the opportunity to declare herself independent of the Sultan in name as well as in reality. During the confusion, with Russia's confused consent, Austria illegally annexed the provinces of Bosnia-Herzegovina, which lay on the Adriatic just north of Montenegro.[18]

Every spring for four years after the Young Turk Revolution of 1908, another major Albanian clan or region rebelled and then suffered violent reprisals. The northern clans, Catholic Mirdites and Malissors, launched a fresh revolt in April, 1912, after which the Turks conceded them autonomy. Then the Albanians helped the Turks fight their common enemies, the Slavs and Greeks, in the Balkan Wars.[19] Influenced by Muslim fear of the Christians, many Albanians fought loyally for the Sultan. Montenegro mediated concessions by Turkey for these northern Albanians, but in 1912 Isa Boletin of Kosovo peacefully temporarily occupied Skopje (now in the country of Macedonia), with twenty-thousand men in return for concessions. Albanian notables met at Koritsa and Elbasan and decided in favor of preserving the Ottoman Empire. Albanian leaders, such as

Ismail Kemal (then in Trieste, Austria) felt that Albania was not quite ready for autonomy.[20] He refused Montenegrin Crown Prince Danilo's request for common action against the Ottoman Empire.[21]

The tolerant, pan-theistic Bektashi Muslims led Albanian nationalism. Their tolerance of all creeds eased their cooperation with northern Catholics and southern Orthodox other than Christian fanatics. Some of the pro-Greek Orthodox opposed them. But in 1913 and 1914 their principal adversaries were the fanatical Muslims of the Plains, who would rebel in alliance with the Serbs and Greeks in 1914 against the new Prince Wied and persecute the Bektashis, whose main protection was in the mountains.[22]

4

THE LONDON CONFERENCE

In the autumn of 1911, Italy's attack on Turkey in North Africa whetted the appetites of officials of the Balkan nations to attack the Turkish "sick man of Europe." No one was more agitated by this than Franz, *Freiherr* Conrad von Hötzendorff, Chief of Staff of the Austro-Hungarian Army. His upturned grey-blonde moustaches fairly bristled and his facial tic accelerated in anticipation of opportunities to be exploited. While Italy was distracted in Africa, Austria might take the opportunity to regain the Italian-populated provinces of Venetia and Lombardy, which the Italians had wrenched from them in the wars of fifty years earlier. What did he care if Italy was an ally in the Triple Alliance with Austria and Germany? Italy was the traditional enemy of Austria, and therefore, unreliable. War should be made on them before they were prepared. Yes, now was the time. He must convince his old Emperor. He dictated a letter to Franz Josef asserting that "Austria's opportunity has come, and it is suicidal to leave the opportunity unutilized." The Emperor simply sent word that Conrad should apologize to the Foreign Minister for butting into his sphere.[1] The Emperor said that year that "My policy is pacific, and against offensive war." He had often told his *aide de camp*, "If we must go under, we had better go under decently."[2] Also pacifically inclined was Franz Ferdinand, the heir to the throne and the Emperor's nephew.[3] When Conrad continued to bother the Emperor with his written pleas for war against Italy, the old ruler sent word that he would see the general personally. As Conrad was ushered into the Emperor's study at suburban Schönbrunn Palace, Franz Josef was uncharacteristically excited and very angry as he addressed Conrad:

These continual attacks on [the foreign minister], especially the reproaches regarding

Italy and the Balkans which go on being repeated are directed against me, the policy is made by me; it is my policy.

Conrad, somewhat subdued, replied that he had merely written his views. "Your Majesty can, of course, mark them 'wrong.' That is Your Majesty's power."

The Emperor then stated firmly:

My policy is the policy of peace. To this policy of mine all must accommodate themselves… It is indeed possible that this war may come, probable, too. But it will not be waged until Italy attacks us… We have never had a 'war policy' hitherto.

Two weeks later, Conrad was again summoned to Schönbrunn and politely dismissed as Army Chief of Staff, the Emperor telling him, "The reason is well known to you and it is not necessary to talk about it."[4] That was the end of Conrad's open obsession with Italy.

In 1908, a revolution in Turkey had set off another chain of events eventually important to our story. A group of reform-minded Turks, calling themselves the Committee of Union and Progress, deposed the incompetent but tyrannical Sultan Abdul Hamid, and replaced him with his more pliable younger brother, who became Muhammad V. The Committee, popularly known as "The Young Turks", became the real power behind the throne. They promised a constitution and greater unity for all Muslims of the Ottoman Empire. This sounded good to the Albanians until they learned that it meant that they must begin to pay taxes and be subject to army conscription, as opposed to voluntary enlistment.[5] Revolts broke out in the Albanian provinces, especially in the north, where the mischievous King Nikola of neighboring Montenegro had encouraged them, but offered no help. The Turks suspended the new constitution and sent troops to suppress the Albanians, with some success, thanks to the treacherous aid of King Nikola.[6] (This quick suppression, and the cautious policy of the Italian government, deprived the famous Garibaldi's son of an opportunity to lead an Italian "legion" of volunteers to fight for the Albanians.)[7] By 1912, the Young Turks were forced to resign the government as a result of a counter-coup.

In September of 1912, our old friend, the courageous murderer of his helpless king and queen, Serbian Colonel Dragutin Dimitrijevich, slipped into northern Albania to foment rebellion against the Turks by Isa Boletin, among others, promising him arms which were never delivered. Then on October 8, 1912, King Nikola, hoping to expand his little kingdom, attacked the Turks in Albania without a declaration of war. The Albanians, now wise to the ambitions of the Serbs and Montenegrins, resisted forcefully, not from love of the Turks, but to protect their land from their greedy neighbors.[8] Montenegro had begun the war by harassing Turkish frontier posts. The favorite trick was to send unsuspecting peasants to mow grass near a Turkish blockhouse, while the Montenegrin troops hid nearby. The Turks predictably fired upon what they considered border trespassers. A Montenegrin soldier would then set fire to the Turkish blockhouse and his comrades would shoot the Turkish soldiers as they ran out. They would then cut the noses off for souvenirs[9], a common Montenegrin practice.[10]

What had led up to this spurious cause for war was as follows:

Bulgaria, under the scheming, self-proclaimed "Czar" Ferdinand, had made a treaty with Serbia on March, 13, 1912, looking toward war with Turkey and a division of the resulting loot. A similar treaty was made with Greece on May 29, 1912. Although the Serbs were wary of the Montenegrin King's known hopes for the Serbian throne, a treaty between those two countries was signed in September of 1912. The Great Powers, especially Austria-Hungary, had reminded everyone that they were opposed to a change in the *status quo ante* in European Turkey but, on October 9, 1912, King Nikola stood on a hill and watched his men fire the first shot at the Turks in Albania.[11] On October 13, 1912, Serbia, Greece, and Bulgaria presented an ultimatum to Turkey, demanding autonomy for all the subject races of European Turkey.[12] (This, despite the fact that Albania had already virtually won its autonomy through multiple successful rebellions.) The Powers took no action, and war broke out October 18, 1912, between the Turks and the Serbs, Bulgars and Greeks.[13]

On October 21, 1912, Austrian Foreign Minister Count Berchtold and his assistant, Count Alexander Hoyos, traveled to Italy to discuss issues with King Vittorio Emmanuelle III and his Foreign Minister, Marquess di San Giulano. They agreed to champion the cause of an autonomous (if not entirely independent) Albania. A few days later, Austria hurriedly proposed in a memorandum a governmental structure for Albania, also delineating its borders. What was more important, Austria added that she would go to war rather than permit any power which succeeded Turkey in the region to gain an outlet on the Adriatic Sea. A Serbia with a seacoast would become too powerful. Albania would do nicely as a buffer to prevent this. Both the German Kaiser and his foreign minister thought this plan "moderate and very reasonable."[14]

On October 23, 1912, after only a few days of war, the Serbs decisively defeated the outnumbered and outclassed Turks, leaving all of northern Albania open to themselves and the Montenegrins, who burned, killed, and looted as they advanced.[15] The two allies occupied the Albanian Adriatic seaports of San Giovanni di Medua, Alessio and Durazzo, in mid-to-late November 1912. Only Scutari, in the north, held out.[16] In view of its previously stated policy, and its fear of Serbian access to the sea, Austria was naturally alarmed, as was Italy. Serbia ignored Berchtold's appeals to stop crossing the Albanian mountains, and headed for the coast of the Adriatic. Premier Poincaré of France, hoping to help the Serbs, suggested to all the Great Powers (France, Russia, Britain, Italy, and Germany), that they maintain a neutral stance and stay out of the matter. Since the matter touched on Austria's vital interests, Berchtold refused.

On October 28, 1912, Montenegro, Serbia's ally, had begun its siege of Scutari. The next day, the Austrian ministers met in Vienna and ordered an increase in the Austrian Army's strength in the three southernmost provinces of the Austro-Hungarian Empire which were nearest to Montenegro, Albania, and Serbia. On November 10, 1912, Berchtold advised King Nikola that "while he did not want to dictate Montenegrin military operations in any way," a lasting occupation of the Albanian coast would be inconsistent with Austria's plans for an autonomous Albanian entity of some sort. He persuaded Italian Foreign Minister San Giuliano to make similar representations to Nikola.[17] The grizzled old king insolently refused during an automobile drive on November 12 with Austrian Ambassador Baron Wladimir Giesl von Gieslingen. Nikola lied that his troops had not reached the Scutari area, and suggested that perhaps it was Albanians themselves, who were besieging the city! Besides, he said that Berchtold's message was only oral (via the ambassador) and "not in proper form." He said that it was "null and void." To make matters worse, Nikola gave Austria's message to the Montenegrin newspapers, which published it, thus insulting Austria publicly. The next day, however, he apologized to Giesl, pleading a fever and sore foot! He then blithely proposed the marriage of his youngest son to some Austrian Archduchess, and suggested that an Austrian warship carry him to Valona, Albania, to be crowned King of that country also. When Nikola asked Giesl to keep these bizarre proposals secret, Giesl suavely replied, "Rest assured, Sire, I will consider them as null and void."[18]

On November 27, 1912, however, the King sent an emissary to Giesl to press his qualifications to be King of Albania: (1) He was not an Albanian, (2) he was not from a Great Power, (3) he was flexible, and would be a "tool" of the Great Powers, and (4) he was an able administrator. Giesl patiently refuted all his points.[19]

Meanwhile, by the autumn of 1912, educated Albanians, chiefly residents in Italy, Romania, and America, as well as in Albania itself, after watching events in their homeland, began to appeal for more formal Albanian autonomy. On November 3, 1912, the Turks sued for peace in the first Balkan War, and asked the Great Powers to mediate. On November 5, British Foreign Secretary Sir Edward Grey agreed with the Austrian ambassador in London that there must be an autonomous Albania. On November 7, Kaiser Wilhelm, still in a pacific mood, telegraphed his foreign minister that he disapproved of Austria's hostile attitude against Serb occupation of Durazzo. He saw no danger in it for Austria. On November 9, 1912, he telegraphed his Chancellor, Bethmann-Hollweg, to propose an autonomous Albania under a Serb prince, if it could not be arranged for Serbia to take responsibility for keeping order in Albania. He thought an autonomous Albania would be short-lived, as did Serbian Prime Minister Pasich.[20]

Ismail Kemal Vlora was the elder statesman of the Albanians. He had made one last try to counsel the Turkish government to avoid the war, without success. He met with Albanian expatriates in Bucharest, Romania. He then traveled to Vienna, where he met Count Berchtold at a mutual friend's house on the evening of November 12, 1912. Berchtold expressed his approval of Ismail's views on the Albanian question and readily granted his request for an Austrian steamer to permit him to arrive at an Albanian port before the Serbians could capture it. Ismail telegraphed his son in Valona, "*avenir Albanie assuré*," ["Albania's future assured"], and to notify all parts of Albania that he was coming home, asking that delegates be sent to a national congress in Valona on the southwest coast.[21] The Greeks, one of the Balkan nations fighting the Turks, had blockaded the small Albanian port of Valona, (which was, of course, still part of the Ottoman Empire). Because of this, Ismail's ship was sent to the more northerly port of Durazzo, where he arrived November 21. Greek warships got there first, however, arriving the night before. A Greek officer searched the Austrian steamship but found only "a few arms" in the possession of Ismail's companions. Apparently this was not enough to concern the officer, and the vessel was allowed to proceed to Durazzo, where the people were largely ignorant of the identities of the new arrivals. Joined by the local delegates to the proposed national congress, Ismail's party then proceeded by horseback to Valona, where they were greeted with enthusiasm.

The eighty-three delegates to the Valona congress, beys and chieftains, both Muslim and Christian, met from November 15 until November 28, 1912, at which time they unanimously proclaimed Albania's independence. The delegates then retired to Ismail Kemal's ancestral house, where they hoisted the red Albania flag bearing the traditional two-headed black eagle. The name of Albania in Albanian translates as "Land of the Eagle." Ismail and a ministry were elected with Ismail as President, notified the Powers and Turkey of these events, and asked for recognition. They had already decided that Albania should be a monarchy, and that the monarch should be a European Christian, rather than a Muslim. Whether this idea was imposed upon Ismail by the Austrians or not is unclear. Count Berchtold had told the Italians on November 17 that Albania should be a principality under a non-Albanian, Protestant prince.[22] It does seem clear that the idea of a republic as the permanent form of government was never considered by anyone at the time. The reason is something of a mystery, especially as the provisional government which was formed in Valona was headed by a president. The explanation is perhaps found in the overwhelming preponderance of monarchies in the world at the time. They were simply the norm. Ismail did want a European prince, however, to cement Albanian ties to vibrant Europe. He thought that religion was not a factor, as the Albanians were reasonably tolerant on that subject.[23]

Understandably, Turkey did not agree to the Albanians' proposals, and the Grand Vizier immediately telegraphed Ismail, demanding that Albania take as its sovereign a prince of the Ottoman Imperial Family. The Grand Vizier rather presciently argued that no power would protect Albania and asserted that it could only survive as a vassal of the Turks, under a Turkish prince. He suggested three princes, one of whom was Ahmed Fuad Pasha of Egypt, a descendent of Albania's soldier-statesman, Mehmid Ali Pasha.[24] Ismail rejected this demand and later wrote that "so ended what I may call the first candidature to the Albanian throne, which was followed by others that had no weight at all with the Albanians, who placed their confidence in the Great Powers."[25] Meanwhile other Albanians, in the central Tirana area, appealed to Austria-Hungary on November 12, begging Franz Josef to help them attain either complete autonomy or the status of a kingdom like the other Balkan states.[26]

There was no reply by the Slavic countries to the Albanian declaration of independence other than further looting and pillaging of northern Albania by the Montenegrins, while the Serbs, on November 30, 1912, completed occupying Durazzo, riding their horses into the sea and crying, somewhat presumptuously, "Long live the Serbian Sea!"[27] Serb premier Pasich declared that "an independent Albania is neither desirable nor possible."[28]This was just the thing to upset both the Austrians, and the Italians, the latter of whom were only some fifty miles away, at Brindisi. The Greeks (still at war with Turkey) advanced in the south of Albania and neared Valona, bombarding the town on December 4, 1912.[29] They occupied Koritsa, locked up Albanian nationalists, and began literally "painting the town", painting shop fronts in the towns blue and white, the colors of the Greek flag.[30] Austria and Russia had called up troops, but Russia sought to pacify the situation despite Poincaré's encouragement of a more belligerent stand[31]

By the end of November 1912, the Balkan situation had begun to seriously threaten the peace of Europe. Russia tended to back Serbia's possession of northern Albania, while Austria and Italy were backing the autonomy of Albania to keep Serbia out. Russia had even extended the period of enlistment of its troops on October 12, 1912, and both Austria and Russia increased their troop strengths, stopping short of ordering a general mobilization of their entire armies.[32] When the Serbs reached the Adriatic, the Austrian Army, which had increased its annual intake of conscripts by 42,000 men in October, called up 200,000 reservists in its new southern provinces of Bosnia-Herzegovina. When Serbian troops entered the coastal city of

Durazzo on November 28, 1912, Austria mobilized 900,000 men and demanded that Serbia withdraw. In Russia, the Council of Ministers was divided. Both its chairman, Kokovtsov, and Foreign Minister Sazanov feared another humiliation like the 1908 Bosnian crisis, and privately urged Serbia to compromise. Publicly, however, Russia sprang to Serbia's support. The victories of the Balkan countries over the Turks boosted Pan-Slav sentiment in Russia, and this encouraged more bellicose Russian ministers, headed by the Minister of Agriculture, Krivoshein. Russia conducted a trial mobilization in Poland during October and November, and on 22 November 1912. The Czar refused the war party's advocacy of a partial mobilization against Germany as well as Austria, believing somewhat naively that Russia's quarrel could be limited to Vienna alone, and not include Austria's ally Germany.[33] Due to Serbia's success, Russian Foreign Minister Sazanov ceased his admonitions of caution and said, to the Serb envoy, "Now you will see, I will be your best lawyer!"[34] Russia was not happy when victorious Bulgaria neared Constantinople, as Russia coveted that prize.[35] Archduke Franz Ferdinand, wanting no part of a fight, looked upon the Balkan war and said, "Let those ruffians bash in one another's skulls. We will watch from the stage box."[36]

In this crisis, the old war dog Conrad von Hötzendorf was recalled as Chief of the Austro-Hungarian General Staff on December 7, 1912. On December 23, 1912, he wrote, "Sole means to a solution: overthrow Serbia by war, undismayed by consequences."[37] But the Kaiser *was* dismayed by consequences and laid on a restraining hand. He had written to his foreign minister on November 7, 1912:

> …Vienna's interests are partially imaginary. Seen from the standpoint of Austrian domestic policy…they cannot be denied a certain justification, but their advocacy and their possible consequences (war, etc.) are purely a matter for Austria and not for [Germany]. Such far-reaching commitment does not accord with the spirit of the Triple Alliance, which…was intended to

guarantee the existing possessions; and the vital necessities and conditions of life in the Austrian Monarchy should not require it. Certainly as a result of the [Balkan] war there are many changes in the Balkans that are inconvenient for Vienna and quite undesirable, but there is [sic] none so decisive that because of it we should run the danger of military involvement. That I could not justify to my conscience or my people.[38]

Austrian Finance Minister Leon von Bilinski reported that the November-December 1912 mobilization had cost 200 million kronen (about $40 million in 1912 and roughly $720 million today). He argued that war might be cheaper than repeated mobilizations, but he said war would cause financial collapse.[39] Emperor Franz Josef replied to Conrad's advice, "Even in politics one should stick to the rules of decency...that [Conrad's plan] would mean war [with Russia] and I am against war...we must do nothing without mature reflection."[40] By December, 1912, the Turks held only footholds in Europe: Constantinople and its immediate environs, the surrounded fortresses of Adrianople, Janina and Scutari. They had been forced to apply for mediation by the Great Powers.[41]

Following an armistice between Turkey and the warring Balkan powers on December 2, 1912, the belligerents chose London as their meeting place to discuss making peace. As Britain had no real stake in the fight, other than keeping a major war from breaking out, and humanitarian concerns for the suffering populations, Sir Edward Grey took no active part in the negotiations. However, delegates occasionally paid him visits in his spacious office in the massive Foreign Office Building, just across Downing Street from the Prime Minister's residence at Number 10.[42] Built in 1868 at Britain's zenith, the Foreign Office building was said to partake architecturally of a "Venetian Palace," and boasted a great double staircase from the main floor, columns, frescoes and enormous reception rooms, as befit a vital structure of the world's greatest empire.[43] Despite its dignified façade, the ambience in the British Foreign Office in those days could sometimes resemble the jolly atmosphere of the Drones Club of the P. G. Wodehouse stories. Young men in stiff white collars with regulation short black coats and striped trousers might be seen playing soccer in the marble corridors, or "desk cricket" at their desks, out of sight presumably, of their superiors, and unlike the elderly clerks who still wrote fastidiously with quill pens. Employees were required to wear black bowler (derby) hats or silk top hats "in season." Those officials meeting foreign guests or royalty would usually wear black, knee-length, silk-lapelled frock ("Prince Albert") coats and grey striped trousers.

The leisurely pace of this hub of the world's mightiest empire was equaled by the hours of work, which usually began at eleven a.m., followed by a lunch from around one-thirty to perhaps three p.m., with the day's labors ending between five and seven p.m.[44] To show that the institution was not wanting in a sense of humor or humility, framed on a wall of the Foreign Office was a cancelled check for fifteen million dollars. It was with this check, payable to the United States, that Great Britain paid the arbitration award resulting from the damage caused by the Confederate ship, "Alabama," which a British firm had built and allowed to "escape" during the American Civil War.[45]

The Balkan armistice of early December, 1912, was a mere cessation of hostilities with nothing settled, and not a peace treaty. The Great Powers ostensibly had no stakes in the peace treaty, but Austria and Italy were very concerned that Serbia not control Adriatic ports. Britain and France did not want Constantinople and the Dardanelles to somehow fall to the Russians. President Poincaré at first warned Sazanov, "Do not count on our military assistance in the Balkans, even if you are attacked by Austria," unless Germany became involved. But by November 1912, he had changed, and said, "Territorial gains by Austria would jeopardize the general equilibrium, and would so jeopardize France's own interests...[as that she might be] drawn into military operation."[46] Germany probably had the least interest in the matter, as the Kaiser often asserted.[47]

On November 9, 1912 the Kaiser wrote again that, on no account, would he, in a matter involving Albania and Durazzo, march against Paris and Moscow.[48] There seems to have been a real danger of general war at that time, as Poincaré encouraged Russia to be firm in support of Serbia, and the Austrians seemed serious.[49] The Kaiser derided the idea of a war for what he called "a few Albanian goat pastures."[50] Typical of Kaiser Wilhelm's inconsistent and mercurial nature, however, was his reckless admonition in mid-November to his friend, Archduke Franz Ferdinand, "to strike while the iron is hot," because of the troop activity of Russia and Austria. To him it was now the inevitable "final struggle" between Slavs, Anglo-Saxons, "Gauls", and Germans.[51]

The two conferences which convened in London in December 1912 ran more or less simultaneously. There was the Balkan War conference, and the conference to decide the fate of Albania. When there was no progress from the Albanian talks, the ambassadors of the Great Powers "busied themselves" with negotiating peace between Turkey and the smaller Balkan nations with whom she was at war.[52] The latter talks were referred to as the "Conference of St. James's" because of the palace where they were held.[53] Then there was the Albanian conference of the ambassadors of the Great Powers: Germany, France, Britain, Italy, Austria-Hungary, and Russia. This was often referred to simply as the "Ambassadors' Conference," or, the "London Conference." They met almost daily from December 17, 1912 until August of 1913 at the Foreign Office.[54]

Grey had foreseen the possible collision of interests over Albania. That is why he called for the parallel conference of Great Power ambassadors, as avoidance of a European War between them was an essential goal. He did not press for London as the meeting place, and thought Paris the best site, as they should thereby make the French happy, and he felt that he was overworked already anyway. However, London was chosen, and Grey became chairman by default.[55] The ambassadors were a remarkable group of men, all but one being nobility of some sort, and several were actually related to each other, although loyally representing different countries. Grey at fifty-one, a widower, with failing eyesight and energy, was a baronet, ranked just below the lowest level of British nobility, so that he was still a commoner entitled to sit in the House of Commons rather than the less powerful House of Lords.[56]

The German ambassador, Prince (*Fürst*) Karl Max Lichnowsky, aged fifty-three, was a landowner in both Prussia (Germany) and Austria, but he was a Prussian, and therefore a German subject. His family had been given its title in 1773 by King Frederick the Great. Strongly Anglophile, he ordered his clothes from a London tailor and relished English Society. He even hung his walking stick in his pocket in emulation of Winston Churchill. His speech was slow and rather nasal, giving him something of an Austrian accent. The English reciprocated his affection for them.[57]

The Russian ambassador Alexander Konstantinovich Benckendorff was Lichnowsky's cousin, having spent most of his youth in Germany. In fact he spelled Russian so poorly that he had to get permission to write his dispatches to the Russian foreign office in French, which was the language of diplomacy in any event. He was the son of a princess and of a political diplomat.

The Austro-Hungarian ambassador was Count (*Graf*) Albert Mensdorff-Pouilly-Dietrichstein. He was related to the British Royal Family because his grandmother was a Coburg, and the British Royal Family were of the House of Saxe-Coburg-Gotha. He was also distantly related to Lichnowsky and had known him since childhood.[58] He loved the British aristocracy, but was referred to by a British Foreign Office official as "a flabby tabby Anglophile but impotent." He was close to King George, who was actually a cousin. Mensdorff's grandmother was a sister to Queen Victoria's mother and Prince Albert's father. In Vienna, they called him "Royal Albert," and King George addressed him as "my dear Albert," in letters, which he concluded with "Your Affectionate Friend and Cousin." The King told him confidences, which he promptly betrayed to the Ballhausplatz.[59]

This cozy club of relatives was not universal, however. None of the men were related to the Italian ambassador, the Marquess Imperiali di Francavilla, but he and Lichnowsky knew each other from his service in Berlin, and he was a naturally friendly and helpful fellow.[60]

The only non-aristocrat at the ambassadors' conference was republican France's Paul Cambon. He did have an important relative however. His brother Jules was ambassador to Germany. Paul was a polished diplomat, but he was not fluent in English like the other men despite his fifteen years in London as ambassador.[61]

Grey's large room at the Foreign Office provided an excellent place for the purposely informal meetings these six men held starting December 17, 1912. It boasted high ceilings with octagonal reliefs, huge windows to admit daylight, a fireplace, a huge mirror, Grey's desk, a number of leather chairs, a round table and a square table, with green baize draped over it. The electric lights, two with green glass shades on the square table, one on Grey's desk, and a circular chandelier, made detailed study of documents after dark (if ever needed) somewhat less uncomfortable.[62] The meetings usually began in the afternoon around four o'clock. The men took a tea break in an adjoining room and then worked until six or seven in the evening. Although they all got along famously, the meetings began to seem "protracted" and "sometimes intolerably wearisome," in Grey's opinion. After the first few weeks, when Cambon was asked about their progress, he replied that it would continue until there were six skeletons sitting around the table.[63] Nevertheless, the conference of ambassadors had started off smoothly. The Austrian, Mensdorff, predictably contended that Albania must be an independent and substantial entity, but Austria was willing to let Serbia have commercial access to the Adriatic through the port of San Giovanni di Medua. This would be guaranteed by the Powers. Britain had no objection to this arrangement, and Grey had already learned that Russia, not ready for a war, had agreed to it. When the Russian, Benckendorff, immediately announced Russia's acceptance, Count Mensdorff seemed stunned, and asked for confirmation. Benckendorff assured him that Russia accepted without qualification.[64] Thus, by December 20, 1912, the principal issue was already decided.[65] Under the proposal, however, Albania would remain under the theoretical "suzerainty" of Turkey, meaning more or less that Turkey was to at least be consulted in any change of Albania's political status. Albanian Provisional President Ismail Kemal soon persuaded the conferees to eliminate that vestige of Turkish authority.[66] At the first session Mensdorff proposed that the Powers agree to draw Albania's borders along strict ethnographic lines. Russia, with Lichnowsky's backing, proposed that the northern city of Scutari go to Montenegro.[67] Lichnowsky did make it clear, however, that to him the details of the borders were not worth a European war.[68]

The European monarchies selected their ambassadors to major countries from the ranks of the nobility because, among other considerations, it was assumed that they were better-traveled and, in short, "men of the world." At the London conference kinship, both by blood and by rank, no doubt eased the formality of discussion. But it did not entirely erase petty personality gossip. Mensdorff, the Austrian, said of his cousin, the German Prince Lichnowsky, that he was

> The right man to achieve lasting measures here…whereby his many defects will stand him in good stead. But in a conference he is incredibly amateurish, vague, and impatient. He invariably speaks out on every question without thinking and has made several little *gaffes*. With the best and sincerest intentions, he is the complete bumbler (*konfusionrat*).

Mensdorff liked to belittle his cousins. He found the Russian, Benckendorff, so nervous that it was difficult to talk to him. He reported that London Society said that "poor old Benckie is more absent-minded than ever and getting quite gaga." All this, while German Chancellor Bethmann-Hollweg called the London Conference "a pitiable affair, but it has brought us quite a bit closer to England."[69]

On January 2, 1913, the Conference of Ambassadors resumed after the holidays, by which time the Albanian delegation of three prominent men had arrived.[70] The Albanian Provisional Government had been recognized by the Great Powers. The Albanian delegates called at the Foreign Office and left a memorandum of their desires as to boundaries, etc. They were assisted by Edith Durham and Aubrey Herbert, the Conservative member of the British House of Commons who took a special interest in their cause. His mother was the Dowager Countess of Carnarvon, who ran a charity for Kosovo refugees.[71]

Serbia and Montenegro sent to London the cream of their diplomatic corps (Stojan Novakovic, Andra Nicolic, and Milenk Vesnic for Serbia, and Lazar Mijuskovic for Montenegro.) They thought it was better to have a small, "reasonable" state on their border rather than a great power, but their main concern was the boundary lines and an unqualified outlet to the sea. The latter being denied them, they concentrated on the boundaries. On the other hand, the most nationalistic Albanians were from areas bordering Serbia and so also concentrated on border questions because of their animus toward the Slavs. The Albanians did not get a single border town that they asked for, however, except Scutari, which was occupied by an international force.[72]

Confusion was injected when, on January 13, 1913, Greece formally claimed those areas, including what is now southern Albania, which her army had recently occupied in the war with Turkey. The Greeks claimed that, as most of the people in the area were able to speak Greek, they must *be* Greek. The Albanian delegation pointed out that the Turks had forbidden the teaching of the Albanian language in school, or its use in any public way. Italy challenged the Greeks, and the Conference decided that the Greek troops should withdraw. San Giuliano pretentiously told the Greek *chargé* in Rome that, "I recognize that Argyrocastro and Koritsa are Greek, but the rights of a small nation such as Greece cannot prevail over the interests of a Great Power like Italy."[73]

At a conference called by the Kaiser with his military leaders on December 8, 1912, he said that in a war with Russia, he assumed that Bulgaria, Romania, and Albania would stand with the Triple Alliance.[74] If there is any logic to his assumption regarding Albania, it must have been based on her relationship with Austria.

On December 17, 1912, the Kaiser noted that "the Albanian she-goats [*zeigen-weiden*] were not worth a war."[75] German Chancellor Bethmann-Hollweg hopefully wrote Berchtold in December 1912 that the pacific attitude of Britain in the Balkan crisis "is only one of several symptoms" that British policy might be more favorable to Germany in the future. He concluded:

> But to precipitate a violent solution—even if some interests of the Austro-Hungarian monarchy were to demand one—at the very moment we seem to have the chance, if only a remote one, to have the conflict under conditions much more favorable to us, would be...a mistake of incalculable consequences.[76]

5

1913

The year 1913 was to prove crucial for Albania and for Europe. It was the last full year of Great Power peace before the First World War. It started on hopeful notes.

In January, the Kaiser wrote in English to his cousin "Nicky," the Czar of Russia:

> I think that on the whole the outlook is reassuring, and that the discussions in London which are progressing favorably will continue to be held in a conciliatory and friendly spirit, in which direction the foreign policy of your government so ably cooperates with all the other Powers.[1]

But in that same month in a long interview with Serbian Prime Minister Pasich, the Czar talked of the day when Bosnia-Herzegovina would be part of Serbia.[2] The Czar had toyed with the idea of intervening in the Balkan War. He had called together his Prime Minister, Foreign Secretary, and War Minister, and announced flatly that he was planning to mobilize troops on the Austrian frontier. Prime Minister Count Vladimir Kokovtzev was horrified. Russia, he accurately pointed out, was totally unprepared for a world war, which would be inevitable because Germany would thus also be compelled to intervene. The Prime Minister ended with an impassioned appeal to the Czar not to sign the mobilization, and the Czar acquiesced. "Of course," he smiled, "the mobilization orders will not be sent."[3] Also in January, the Czar wrote to his mother bemoaning a family scandal, "at a time too, when everyone is expecting war, and when the Tercentenary of the Romanovs is due in a few months!"[4]

On January 6, British Ambassador Sir Rennell Rodd in Rome talked to Gottlieb von Jagow (German ambassador, but soon to be foreign minister) and reported:

> His own feeling as regards Austria is that she is very difficult to manage because there is a total absence of leadership there. He thinks very little of Count Berchtold's qualities as a statesman—that he is, in fact, another of [former Austrian Foreign Minister] Aerenthal's mistakes—though it should be said in defense of him that he did not at all seek his present office. ...The real preoccupation which he feels is for the Austrian Empire itself. There seems to be present there and rapidly maturing all the elements of dissolution...

Still, the Austrians were "the only friends we have in Europe," said Jagow. Jagow felt that, at heart, the Kaiser was more English than the English, and that his dream had always been to march hand in hand with the British. Belligerent outbursts by Wilhelm were really due to "*dépit amoreux!*" (lover's spite). A favorite phrase of the Kaiser's when some incident in which Britain was concerned ruffled him, was to blurt out, "and this they say of me, of me, the grandson of Queen Victoria!" His German listeners would have been more gratified if he had referred to himself as "the German Emperor." Jagow said he found no difficulty, when an opportunity was afforded of seeing the Kaiser alone, of being able to state his views. The Kaiser would then be a sympathetic and receptive listener, and accept the difference of opinion in very good part. But it was not easy when others were present. The Kaiser "had a quickness and brilliancy of *repartée* which put his interlocutor at a disadvantage, as the latter had to take into account the obligation not to put the Kaiser at a disadvantage before witnesses." The Kaiser had known Jagow since Jagow's boyhood.[5]

The pugnacious Raymond Poincaré had become premier (*président du conseil,* "president of the council," or prime minister) of France in January, 1912. A year later, on January 16, 1913, he was elected President of the Republic.[6] On March 16, in Paris, a Madame Caillaux murdered Gaston Chalmette, editor of *Le Figaro*, a leading conservative newspaper.[7] She was the wife of a prominent French Minister, angry over scandalous articles in the paper. Incredibly, the shooting was apparently so sensational to the Gallic mind that it distracted not only French public, but also government attention from foreign affairs.

At Scutari, still under siege by the Montenegrins, Hussein (a.k.a. Hassan) Reza Bey, the skillful Turkish commander who had been holding out successfully thus far, dined on January 30, 1913 with Essad Pasha Toptani, his second in command. As he left Essad's house, two assassins, probably hired by Essad, shot him to death. Essad thus succeeded to command and began secretly negotiating, through the Russian consul, with the Montenegrins.[8] Essad commanded, but his officers ran the defense. Essad lived in the citadel dungeons and was never seen in the town. Such orders as he gave to the townspeople were conveyed by his close associate, the Austrian consul, and Suleiman Bey, a well-known cutthroat.[9]

In early February, after Conrad produced new intelligence of Serb infiltrations into Albanian territory, Franz Josef authorized calling up reservists to strengthen garrisons along the Russian and Serbian borders. However, at a dinner in Vienna for his brother-in-law, Duke Albrecht of Würtemberg, Germany, Franz Ferdinand raised his glass and said, "To peace! What would we get out of war with Serbia? We'd lose the lives of young men and we'd spend money better used elsewhere. And what would be gained, for heaven's sake! Some plum trees and goat pastures full of droppings, and a bunch of rebellious killers. Long live restraint!"[10]

On February 6, with Serbian reinforcements, the Montenegrins attacked the Turks at Scutari.[11] The Kaiser wrote to Franz Ferdinand about "the intolerable tension which has been bearing so heavily on Europe for the past six months...to lift it

68

would be a truly epoch-making act of peace, worthy of an *energetic* man who has *moral* courage to speak the redeeming word…" Franz Ferdinand agreed[12] and sent his aide to Conrad to emphasize his position, predicting war with Russia and even loss of the Austrian and Russian thrones if there was a war with Serbia. Conrad ignored him. Frustrated, Franz Ferdinand asserted to the Kaiser that Serbs were beneath their attention, and Wilhelm replied:

> Dear Franzi, Bravo! It can't be easy, that sort of thing. It takes stubbornness and stamina. But success will earn you the enormous credit to have freed Europe from such pressures. Millions of grateful hearts will remember you in their prayers…

Franz Ferdinand showed this to Conrad and to Franz Josef and the reinforcements were withdrawn. Franz Josef had recently said that war with Russia would be the end of his monarchy, and the Kaiser's attitude must have motivated him toward caution.[13]

On February 10, both German Chief of Staff Helmuth von Moltke and Chancellor Bethmann-Hollweg warned their respective Austrian counterparts in separate letters of the danger of making war with Serbia at the moment over the Albanian question. Moltke said that "a European war is bound to come sooner or later, in which the issue will be one of a struggle between Germandom and Slavdom." He proclaimed: "To prepare themselves for that contingency is the duty of all states which are the champions of Germanic ideas and culture [*geistes kultur*]." But he warned Conrad that the Great War "necessitates the readiness of the people to make sacrifices, and popular enthusiasm." Therefore, he was against provoking war with Serbia, especially after Serbia had backed down on her Albanian demands. Now, he wrote, it would be difficult for Germany to "find an effective slogan" for a great war. At the same time, he told the Austrian military *attaché* in Berlin, "When starting a world war, one has to think carefully."[14]

The Kaiser wrote the Czar on February 13:

> I fervently hope with you that the Balkan troubles may soon be finally arranged without further complications and am most anxious to cooperate with you for that purpose. Of course, Austria as a near neighbor to those parts has interests to look after. But I am under the impression that in doing so, she does not reclaim anything for herself but only wishes to make sure that no readjustments of the map occur which might turn out a danger to her in the future.[15]

The Balkan War with the Turks continued. During a siege of four months, the fortress of Janina, in what is now northern Greece, was commanded by Vehid Bey Toptani, brother of Essad Pasha. A final assault by the Greek army, under Crown Prince Constantine, led to Vehid's surrender of the city on March 6, 1913. Argyrocastro (today part of southern Albania) surrendered eleven days later, and the Greeks set about trying to force the Albanians to hold themselves out to be Greek.[16]

On March 11 Grey forcefully told the Serbian *Chargé d'Affaires* (i.e., diplomat temporarily in charge) in London that the Powers, and not Serbia would decide the disposition of the northern Albanian city of Scutari. Therefore, it was useless and "criminal" for their ally, Montenegro, to continue to attack the city. The Serbian contention was that, to discontinue these operations would release Turkish troops to fight elsewhere. Grey replied that this was not applicable to Scutari and repeated his complaint to the Montenegrin "delegate." His advice seemed to be ignored, but there was a lot of coming and going of the Balkan delegates to Grey's office.[17]

As spring approached, the Kaiser wrote to his foreign secretary: "I see absolutely no danger for Austria's existence, or prestige, in a Serbian harbor on the Adriatic. ...I think it inadvisable needlessly to oppose the Serbian wish."[18] By March 18 the Kaiser still had not left for his usual cruise to the Mediterranean. "The damned Balkan muddle," he wrote the Czar, "has deprived me of the possibility of having my heavenly paradise of Corfu!"[19]

This frustration of Wilhem's was understandable. For some years, the German Imperial Yacht, *Hohenzollern,* had been following a regular annual program. After the winter overhaul, the yacht would proceed in mid-February to the Mediterranean, where it would pick up the German imperial family at Venice and transport them to the Greek island of Corfu. There it would lie at anchor while the Kaiser and his family and Court attendants lived ashore in Achilleon "Castle," as it was sometimes called. Toward the end of April the imperial family would board the ship again for the trip through the Strait of Messina to Genoa, whence the party would return to Germany by train.[20]

The Achilleon in Corfu was an understandable pleasure destination for the Kaiser. In 1861, on her return voyage from Madeira to Trieste, Austrian Empress Elisabeth visited Corfu. She purchased the ruined Villa Braila near Gasturi, situated on a wooded hill, a spot from which there is a magnificent view of the blue ocean, the undulating green slopes of the island, and the distant shores of Albania. Here she built a white marble palace and enclosed it with gardens, terraces, and a beautiful park. The villa was planned by Raffaele Carito, a celebrated architect of Naples, who tried to follow descriptions of ancient Greek architecture. The Empress added priceless marble statuary, including the dying Achilles, which gives it his name. The peristyle was decorated with frescoes representing scenes from the Iliad and Odyssey, and opened on a garden ornamented with statues of the Muses to which it is dedicated, between cypress, olive, orange, and myrtle trees of great age. She caused a temple to be built to her favorite poet, Heinrich Heine. The suite of rooms on the fourth floor, on account of the palace being built on the hillside, allowed her to step out of her sitting room into the gardens. There she later erected a monument to her son, Crown Prince Rudolph, who killed himself in 1889. Before the broken column on the pedestal was placed a marble angel stretching forth his right hand as if in protection of the medallion on which was chiseled a portrait of the ill-fated prince.[21]

The greatest remaining problem for the Great Power ambassadors in London in 1913 was the delineation of the boundaries of the new nation of Albania. Serbia and Austria were naturally in direct conflict over this, as Serbia wanted to keep the Albanian territory which she had won, and was winning, in the continuing war. Italy was concerned about Greek claims on southern Albania, which was directly opposite the heel of the Italian peninsula. However, by March 22, 1913, the ambassadors had arbitrarily defined the northern and northeastern boundaries of the country. Scutari, although coveted by Montenegro, which was even then besieging it, was placed well within the new Albanian state. It was considered essential to the viability of the country. On the other hand, numerous Albanians and their market towns were placed within the borders of Serbia and Montenegro. Most of Kosovo province, overwhelmingly populated by Albanians, was given as compensation to Serbia, creating a permanent source of friction which exists to this day. The ultimate boundary decision was called the Protocol of London. On March 28, 1913, the ambassadors advised Serbia and Montenegro of their decision, and requested them to withdraw from their non-sanctioned Albanian conquests, and to stop besieging Scutari. The two nations replied to the Protocol by bombarding Scutari and capturing a mountain above the city. Montenegro formally replied on April 2, refusing to obey the Powers.[22]

Meanwhile, the telegram which Ismail Kemal had sent to the Sultan's Grand Vizier, requesting recognition of Albanian independence, brought the unwelcome reply that Turkey demanded that Albania accept an Ottoman prince as its sovereign.

In April the renewed attack by King Nikola on Scutari, in direct defiance of the request of the Great Powers, lead them to agree upon a "naval demonstration" along the Montenegrin coast at the suggestion of Germany's Prince Lichnowsky.[23] This sort of thing was a common method used in those days by great powers to project their power overseas and to show that they "meant business." Warships were considered the ultimate weapons of war in the days before airplanes and submarines had reached their potential. In London British Permanent Undersecretary for Foreign Affairs Sir Arthur Nicolson pointedly advised Montenegrin *Chargé d'Affairs* Jovo Popovich "to accept without delay the decision of the Powers."

At that time Austria-Hungary was still a naval power, as the Monarchy stretched down the Adriatic coast, with Trieste as its major seaport. On April 1, 1913, Berchtold ordered a division of Austrian warships to the waters off Bar (Antivari), Montenegro, where they would await the ships of the other Powers. Germany hesitated at first, but then sent the cruiser *Breslau* to join the Austrians. The Italians were annoyed by Berchtold's haste and uncharacteristic decisiveness, but soon followed suit with their own ships. San Giuliano had been tempted to join the naval demonstration with Austria alone, but Prime Minister Giolitti pointed out, patiently, that a naval demonstration against a mountainous country like Montenegro would be absurd unless it also contemplated landing troops. And that might provoke Russia to intervene to help her fellow Slavs. He therefore instructed that Italy would only act with consent of all the other Great Powers, as none of this was worth a European war.[24] Russia approved the naval demonstration on April 2, 1913, but declined to send any ships. At first, the naval commanders acted independently, and the senior officer, British Admiral Sir Cecil Burney, on April 5 took the bit between his teeth and sent King Nikola a note in which he threatened a strict blockade of the Montenegrin coast if the King did not cease his attack on Scutari. When Grey got wind of this, it apparently startled him, for he wired Burney to take no further actions, singly or with the others, without further orders. It was decided by the Great Powers to limit the "demonstration" to the area from Bar to a point near Scutari. The naval blockade formally began on April 10, 1913. The Powers called it a "pacific" blockade, since no shots were to be fired unless the ships were fired upon, and no landing of men was to take place without orders from the governments.[25]   The British blockading ships, *H.M.S. King Edward VII, H.M.S. Dartmouth,* and *H.M.S. Defence* (under Rear Admiral Ernest Troubridge) arrived off Bar. Burney was their Vice-Admiral. On April 10, the blockade extended from Bar to the mouth of the Drin River, and, on April 23, down to Durazzo, halfway down the Albanian coast.   On April 20, the Montenegrins actually informed Burney that they had *lost* his note and asked for another copy! Italy and Austria privately agreed to divide Albania into spheres of influence if they had to intervene on land.[26]   When King Nikola refused to evacuate the Siege of Scutari, Austria had threatened to act alone. King George of Britain then spoke strongly to Austria's Count Mensdorff, urging him to warn his government that if they took independent action it might lead to an explosion of Pan-Slav feeling in Russia and create danger of war. When it was then suggested that the Powers send troops to Scutari to push Nikola out, George remarked that he was not going to allow the lives of British soldiers to be risked for so trivial a venture. The Kaiser wrote a comment to this news, *"Seine Majestät is* [sic] *kein Militär."* (His Majesty is no military man.)[27]

In the middle of April, Grey turned the chairmanship of the Albanian conference over to Sir Arthur Nicolson and went fishing. He wrote from the country:

> There is some prospect of rain and if so the sport will be very good. It seems almost too much to expect that everything including the Balkan crises and salmon should go well simultaneously, but things seem to prosper so well in my absence that it would not be in the public interest for me to curtail it. I am in rude health with an appetite for everything except office work.

Upon Grey's return, Prince Lichnowsky imagined that Grey had something to hide and wrote, ironically:

74

I have just had an interview with Sir Edward Grey in which we discussed the situation fully. He regards it with his usual imperturbability and ice calm. He even found time to tell me about the fish he caught on his holiday.[28]

Typical of the problems besetting the ambassadors in early April was the argument between Austria and Serbia over pieces of what had been regarded traditionally as Albania. There were villages where experts might disagree about the ethnic makeup of the population. The ambassadors did not worry too much about such things. On one occasion there was a deadlock over a village called Djakova (Gjakove) claimed by Austria for Albania and equally claimed by Serbia. The ambassadors turned to their governments for instruction. Grey tried his best at private persuasion. One morning a messenger delivered a note at the house on Eccleston Street, not far from Victoria Station, where Grey rented rooms from the Churchills. The note said that Austrian ambassador Mensdorff wished to see him. He agreed, and, in a few minutes, Mensdorff arrived and was invited into Grey's small sitting room, where the servants had placed flowers from his country house on a small table in several glasses of water. Mensdorff was excited and a bit breathless from his haste. He could hardly wait to burst out, happily, "We give up Djakova!" As he was saying this and hustling quickly into the sitting room, his full-skirted frock coat brushed some of the daffodils and tipped over their containers, spilling water onto his coat. Grey fetched a towel and tried to dry him off, as they happily discussed the breakthrough.[29] Grey then at once urged Russia to persuade Serbia to accept Austria's *quid pro quo*, that Serbia cease hostilities and peacefully leave the areas assigned to Albania by the Powers, and this was done.[30]

By the beginning of April, 1913, the Conference had worked out a draft government plan, or statute, providing for:

(1) A neutral Albania. (2) a gendarmerie under officers from one of the smaller European states, (3) a judicial system worked out by an international commission, and (4) a Prince to be nominated by Albania and the Powers.[31]

On April 7, 1913, Grey told the House of Commons that Scutari would go to the new Albania, while Serbia and Montenegro would receive plenty "as the fruits of victory" in the Balkan war, and defended this transfer of Albanian-inhabited areas as "essential for the peace of Europe," and "only just in time to preserve the peace between the Great Powers."[32]

On April 10, 1913 the Russian Foreign Office, putting the best face on developments, formally announced the London settlement of Serbian and Montenegrin claims after "long and persistent negotiations." The "natural tendency" of Slavs toward expansion was "rewarded," the announcement said, but it was added that the interests of the Albanians were being "protected by Austria and Italy, [who] considered the *status quo* in the Adriatic of substantial importance [so] as to admit of no argument on the subject." Scutari was conceded to Albania "in order to preserve peace," because it would have been "absurd" to fight over it, especially as the Russian Vice Consul there confirmed that it was purely Albanian, had a Catholic archbishop, and Montenegro was too small to absorb all those Albanians in any case.[33]

The Montenegrins had made many paper boats and floated them out to sea from the Albanian shores to show their contempt for the "pacific" blockade. The Russian military *attaché* had told Edith Durham, "Faced with a *fait accompli*, the Powers can do nothing!" She replied, "Pardon, sir, they can accomplish another *'fait'*."[34] And they did. On April, 11, Serbia reluctantly agreed to cease fire and pull back from Scutari.[35]

On April 8, the Montenegrin delegate to the St. James's Conference had told Sir Arthur Nicolson that the siege would end if Montenegro could find the money to bribe Essad. The proper Nicolson was somewhat incredulous, and Popovich said that Essad had not come right out and asked for a bribe. Instead, Essad had slyly reported that he had left behind a valise with

£80,000 (about $7,200,000 today) in it when he entered Scutari, and it would be to the advantage of everyone if it was found and returned to him![36]

Despite the apparent diplomatic victory of the ambassadors, on April 21, 1913, Essad sent word to Montenegrins that he would surrender Scutari on condition that he be allowed to leave with his forty- thousand armed troops and he asked to be recognized as Prince of Central Albania, under the Sultan's protection.[37]

On April 22 or 23, di Martino, Director General of the Italian Foreign Office, explained to Sir Rennell Rodd that Italy feared the Straits of Corfu and Valona might serve as an assembly base for a fleet hostile to Italy. Therefore, she did not want Greece to hold that coast line.[38]

On April 23, 1913, King Nikola sent his agreement with Essad's terms via the Italian Consul in Scutari. Essad surrendered in return for only £10,000 (roughly $900,000 in today's money)[39] Scutari was now in Montenegrin hands. Vienna and Berchtold were infuriated. The ambassadors advanced their meeting date and agreed to stand by their demands.[40]

On the morning of April 25, Montenegrin Crown Prince Danilo's guard took their places at the gates of the citadel of Scutari atop a hill, where Essad greeted Danilo. The guards were uniformed gloriously in operetta-style plumed black caps, red waistcoats, blue breeches and shining top boots. A few yards higher stood Red Cross and Red Crescent (the Muslim equivalent of the Red Cross) workers, with a mixture of staff officers of both armies standing at the edge of a small plateau beneath the castle keep. There was a tree in the middle of the plateau and a table under the tree, at which Danilo and Essad sat. The formal surrender did not take long. Essad handed over the keys to the citadel and some papers were signed. Essad and Danilo then shook hands and Danilo went up to the top of the bastion to see the Montenegrin flag raised. A crowd of soldiers stood about, the cannon fired a salvo, and the formal surrender was over.[41] After the ceremony, the citizens celebrated by getting drunk, firing guns into the air and shouting, "Down with Austria." A donkey, dressed in an old dress coat, was festooned with an anti-Austrian placard around its neck, and paraded through the streets.[42]

The London Conference was not amused, and on April 28, 1913, unanimously notified King Nikola that he must give up Scutari. Berchtold wanted to bombard the city and land troops if he did not comply.[43] Nikola stalled and Grey returned from another brief vacation. Grey agreed that the other Powers could take military action, but without British participation. Ambassador Cambon said that "if Nicholas [Nikola] submits to the Powers, Sir Edward Grey hopes to make him certain concessions; if not, he'll abandon him to Austria." Lichnowsky agreed with Grey.[44] The Powers were acting somewhat like today's United Nations Security Council—making demands without acting. Austria had demanded that the Montenegrins and Serbs should be made to leave "by international action," or they would act alone. After "tedious" discussion of how to coerce Montenegro, both troops and bribery were discussed. Britain refused to send troops, but was not averse to a naval demonstration or "the offer of money," which "settled the matter to the satisfaction of Austria, perhaps also to the satisfaction of the King of Montenegro", as Grey later wrote.[45]

On April 27, 1913, Essad proclaimed himself King of the Albanians at Alessio, near the Adriatic coast, midway between Scutari and Durazzo, where he was received with military honors by the Serbian garrison. He then marched south to Tirana with most of the Scutari garrison of Albanian Ottoman troops and their light artillery.

King Nikola had taken a long time to get Scutari because he had no heavy artillery. When Serbia agreed to remove its troops from Albania "once peace is signed and related questions settled," Serbian Prime Minister Pasich told King Nikola to do the same: "The sacrifice is difficult, but it must be borne when the whole of Europe demands it." After the peace of May 30, 1913 with Turkey, the withdrawal of the Serbian troops, mostly by sea through now-Greek Salonika, began with the Greeks and

Serbs agreeing on their respective spheres of influence in Albania (the River Shkombra, or Shkombi, being the dividing line.) But Serbia retained strategic positions in the new border belt and dug in, resulting in a massive Albanian guerilla attack in September 1913 on Dibra and Struga, now on the Serbian side of the new border. The Serb army then counterattacked and crossed the River Drin and invaded the Mati and Malesia areas, causing the Powers to protest.[46]

After the first Serb occupation of Durazzo, Russian Foreign Minister Sazanov had told the Serb envoy, "Watch out. Don't insist on Drac [Durazzo] because you might lose Belgrade. Vienna has lost its head." Unsatisfied, Pasich asked what they should do, Sazanov replied:

> We are ready to defend the political and economic emancipation of Serbia and its exit to the sea across Albanian territory [meaning free transit]...and to work for the drawing of Serbo-Albanian borders as much to the west as possible. But we do not believe that Serbia will be given a sovereign right at any point on the Adriatic coast...Imperial Russia must be sure that Serbia will accept the decision arrived at by the Great Powers. Otherwise, Serbia cannot count on our support, and in that case neither England nor France will help Serbia. Neither Russia nor her allied powers can allow the question of European war to be decided by Serbia.[47]

Pasich's government replied,

> "...with great sacrifice, Serbia has liberated Serbs from the Turks, and reached the littoral which once belonged to her...However, in view of the desires of Austria, which has declared that it cannot agree with the Serbian retention of the littoral taken by arms...The Serbian

government...entrusts to the Great Powers the solution of the Serbian outlet to the Adriatic Sea."[48]

6

WAR CLOUDS OVER SCUTARI

In today's world it is difficult to understand some of the "vital interests" for which countries were once willing to go to war. Austria and Hungary are today happily thriving small countries without empires. Italy, while having a problem with impoverished immigrants from Albania, no longer worries about any threat from Serbia. Russia, much reduced by the fall of the Soviet Union, still worries about its prestige in Eastern Europe, but seems unlikely to wage major war over the attachment of its former satellites to the West. Japan prospers with no empire at all, although it fought several wars to expand and safeguard one. In 1914, however, the concepts of essential national honor and prestige and "vital national interests" were uppermost in the minds of statesmen of all nations which had any pretense to importance. They regarded, with some justification, failure to uphold their honor and "interests" as inviting aggression. They had only to look to the Ottomans as an example.

On May 1, 1913, Berchtold and Conrad presented their respective plans to Franz Josef: either a limited action against Scutari or all-out war against Montenegro, and if necessary, Serbia and Russia. Meanwhile, Grey told the London conference that he had received, *sub rosa*, from Montenegrin *Chargé* Popovich a hint that Nikola might leave Scutari in return for compensation in the form of money and territory.[1]

On May 2, 1913, Berchtold presided over a joint ministerial council of the Austro-Hungarian government to decide their course over Scutari. The council agreed with Berchtold to prepare for action and seek Italian participation. He advised the Austrian Consul General in Albania to prepare for evacuation of Austrian subjects and to prepare for a siege. The other Balkan powers said that they needed peace and could not help Serbia.[2]

On the night of May 3, 1913, in Nikola's palace, the King argued with family, generals, ministers, politicians and citizens that he had to surrender. Prime Minister Martinovich resigned in protest.[3] On May 4, 1913 Nikola wired his representative in London that he left Scutari's fate to the Powers. He even complied with Austria's demand for a formal note expressing this.[4]

On May 5, at the Ambassadors' Conference, Grey read out King Nikola's telegram which formally agreed to evacuate Scutari. Berchtold announced that Austria would give Montenegro time to evacuate, with no time limit. The Powers expressed their satisfaction with Nikola's decision, and the admirals were instructed to prepare to coordinate with Montenegro the occupation of Scutari. The same day, Serbia decided to withdraw the last of her troops from Durazzo. Russian Foreign Minister Sazanov was happy that he would not have to decide what to do if Austria invaded Montenegro. Also that day, the Duke of Avarna, the Italian ambassador to Vienna, visited Berchtold and showed him Italy's outline of a "battle plan" for joint military action in Albania if Scutari was not surrendered. He did not know yet of Nikola's submission. The Italian plan had included recognition of Italian authority in southern Albania. Berchtold took pleasure in telling Averna that the plan was moot. To save face, San Giuliano then said it had only been drawn up to show Austria the difficulties of such a move.[5]

In May 1913, the elections in France returned an imposing majority of Radicals and Socialists, who united in a *bloc des gauches* committed to reduce conscription from three to two years despite Poincaré's opposition. Clemenceau of the Radical Party had said on February 10, 1912 that France wanted peace "because we need to remake our country. We are Pacificists..."[6] Poincaré was not.

Inspired by Austria's success, no doubt, on May 8, 1913 Italy informed Greece that occupation of both banks of the Straits of Corfu could not be permitted and Greece must evacuate Santi

Quaranta on the southern coast or Italy would actually declare war. Italy prepared to land troops at Valona.[7]

Meanwhile, the formative Albanian governmental plan, or statute, was submitted to the Conference, but was not discussed. It was referred to the respective governments.[8]

On May 9, 1913, the new Montenegrin Foreign Minister, Petar Plamenc, met with Admiral Sir Cecil Burney and signed a formal protocol of surrender of Scutari to the Great Powers, dividing the city into sectors for each occupying Great Power. The commanders would collectively rule Scutari until further orders from their governments. Austrian and Italian relief units with food and medicine were allowed into the city on May 7, while the foreign troops did not enter until May 14, allowing the newly-raised Albanian flags to fly freely. Burney became chief city administrator, and the blockade ended.[9]

On May 13, 1913, the day before evacuating Scutari, Montenegrins looted the bazaar and set fire to it. Montenegrin General Becir then handed over the city to Admiral Burney on May 14, less than a month after its fall, and a contingent of marines and sailors from the international ships occupied the city.[10] A perimeter of authority of ten kilometers for the occupying force was set up. Foreign troops would occupy the town until July, 1914. Wary of Essad, Austria and Italy each sent a warship to Durazzo, which was under his control. Essad had some nine thousand demobilized troops under his command, but he professed loyalty to the Provisional Government.[11]

On the same date, the British naval *attaché* in Berlin, Captain Hugh Watson, reported on a conversation with the Kaiser at the Neues Palais in Potsdam. After lunch, there had been animated conversation:

> His Majesty alluded to the outrages of the suffragettes, and said that in his opinion the only way to deal with them was to flog them. There was three quarters of an hour of conversation… it had given him great pleasure that Germany and England had been working together in the Balkan affairs.

"But," the Kaiser said,

I don't agree with a number of things Sir Edward Grey has done; I have however consented to them when put before me because I wanted to work with Grey. As for the Ambassadors' Conference, I consider it a most "clumsy impossible machine" and some of the decisions are quite unworkable. Albania, for instance. There must be international administration. The lot of a Prince of Albania would be impossible. Notices would have to be put up all round the country, like in American bars, "Don't shoot the pianist, he's doing his best." The condition of the country makes it impossible for a prince, there's nowhere for him to make his headquarters, there are no revenues, no roads, no railways, absolutely nothing. It will become a second Macedonia. I have been asked to nominate a prince for Albania and have declined. Four times during the last winter have the diplomats been to me to suggest candidates. The first one they suggested was a Mohammedan. I said, "All right." The next was a Roman Catholic, I agreed to that. When the fourth suggestion came it was a Protestant to which I agreed; but said to this diplomat who brought the suggestion that "I thought you would suggest a Jew, because they would cut his head off, and his money would serve to enrich the country." I was talking to that splendid fellow Mahmoud Mouhktar Pasha [possibly Gazi Ahmed Muhtar Pasha (1839-1918), hero of the Russo-Turkish War of 1877-1878 and governor of the *vilayet* composing of most of Albania][12] about Albania, and he said it was an impossible country to rule. Personally, I don't know the country, but as I see it from my house at Corfu, it appears a black country.

The Kaiser spoke with amusement of the "very clever" sketches in *Punch* over the Balkan business:

> I was very glad of the Balkan source of cooperation with England. Things seemed to be hopeless between the two nations, and I felt that I had exhausted all my efforts to bring about better feelings between the nations. My people were getting angry at the position of affairs. The attitude of the countries to each other reminded me of a scene in "The Corsican Brothers." The two nations were shaking hands with each other, but always looking away from each other when doing so.[13]

The northern Albanian port of San Giovanni di Medua had been occupied by Montenegrins, (although it was kind to call it a port). Santi Quaranta, on the extreme south coast, was occupied by the Greeks. In Scutari the flags of the Powers flew from the citadel. In every quarter of that Turkish-like town, one ran across sailors of various nations. Each Power had its allotted quarter and named the streets with curious results. The Italian *Via Garibaldi* ran into the Austrian *Platz Radetzsky*. On the Catholic Cathedral was a sign informing one that he was in the *Rue Ernest Renan*. The military bands of the Powers played, side by side, in the public garden. In the dining room of the hotel, Austrian, German, British, and French officers ate together at long tables. The officers stood at attention beside their half-filled glasses for the respective national anthems. Admiral Burney had his headquarters in the palatial home of a British nobleman who loved the Albanians and had lived in Scutari for years. Burney was intelligently apprehensive of the possible outcome of the situation, but determined to save the peace of Europe by welding together the Albanians as a nation.[14]

On May 20, 1913 the London Conference on Albania reconvened and French Ambassador Paul Cambon criticized the plan for that country severely because (1) no government existed yet, (2) no prince had been selected, and (3) there would be government by commission.[15] Cambon said that he "...opposed imposing a government and prince from outside...he was doomed to fail and may die *un fin violente* [a violent end]."[16]

On May 23, 1913, two thousand of Essad's Turkish soldiers were camped two kilometers from San Giovanni di Medua, awaiting repatriation to Turkey.[17] The correspondent of the French periodical *L'Illustration* arrived at the nearby Montenegrin port of Antivari (Bar). The proprietor of the Hotel de la Marine there, a Swiss, complained that the international blockade had prevented beer sales for the last three days, and violated his rights as a neutral.

On May 25, 1913 at Durazzo, Italian and Austrian cruisers were on the roadstead outside the harbor, although the blockade had been lifted. No passport or customs were required. The Venetian fortifications were still there, the sea was turquoise, and the little houses sported Albanian flags. Some of the flags also carried a white star, symbolizing the heaven above all religions. The city was in perfect order. Essad had established a council of three Muslims and three Orthodox, presided over by his cousin, Hamid Bey Toptani. The Albanian Ottoman troops were given leave, but the ethnic Turkish troops were "living in distress," not cared for, and uncertain of repatriation.

Essad's headquarters was now a fortress in a building which the Serbs had wrecked, guarded by "Turkish" soldiers. He was now about fifty, "vigorous and with a military bearing." He seemed to know only a few words of French, so his chief of staff interpreted for him in that tongue. Essad acted tough. To the French correspondent, he "combines eastern manners with the harshness of a Prussian." He emphatically denied making a deal with Nikola to surrender Scutari, and claimed that it had been forced by famine. He said that he had been unable to resist a moment longer. In regard to the Provisional Government at Valona, he said,

> The Austrian and Italian consuls have informed me that such a government exists. I know nothing of it. So don't look at me! Now there is a question of my relations with the Turkish Government. Nothing more simple. I await the orders of the Turkish Minister of War… I am ready to lead my men wherever it is desired, provided it is not too far. For example, I will not be at Baghdad or at the end of Asia Minor. That needs no explanation. When I named Hamid Bey [to be] mutessarif of Durazzo, he asked me, 'To whom should I look for orders?' To God, I responded, and next, to whomever you wish, except me… You forget that Austria and Italy consider that there is a government in Valona.

Essad wanted European financial and technical assistance, but without strings and without Austrian or Italian guardianship.

> As for my aspirations to the throne of Albania, thank you, not for me! Let us be left in peace; and with my friends and all the chiefs of the country, perhaps we will do a good job.

He said that he would consider a king who did not belong to one of the country's religions to be "a Godsend."

> Why not a Jew?… What is important and… only important is our independence, and by independence I mean not a crowned title, but a reality, assured and indisputable.

In Constantinople, the Military Governor, Colonel Djemel Bey, said a few days later,

Essad Pasha is the son of a bandit enriched by [Sultan] Abdul Hamid, [and] himself a bandit, having caused Hassan Riza Bey, commandant at Scutari, one of our better officers, to be assassinated, and having allowed the city to give up after having an understanding with the King of Montenegro. There does not exist a man more wicked and more basely ambitious...[18]

By May 30, 1913, Grey was becoming impatient. He said that it would become "misleading and undignified" to continue the ambassadors' sittings "unless we could deal with the question of the Albanian frontier," and agree upon it. "It is almost ridiculous," he urged, "for us to be attempting to make peace between Turkey and the allies if the question of the Albanian frontier is to remain in suspense, causing increasing anxiety and difficulty between the Great Powers." The St. James's ambassadors were still working on the details of the peace between Turkey and the Balkan League.[19] As Ismail Kemal learned, on February 27, the Greek naval blockade had been extended to Durazzo.[20]

The delegates of Serbia, Bulgaria, Greece, Montenegro, and Turkey, somewhat sheepish in their frock coats, were called one by one upon the carpet by Sir Edward Grey. He pointed toward them with an outstretched finger, and, using his Winchester School French, is supposed to have shouted: *"Ou signer, ou partir"* (either sign or leave). They signed. The Treaty of London was signed between Turkey and the Balkan states on May 30[21] by virtue of which Turkey virtually withdrew from the continent of Europe for the first time since the Sixteenth Century. The Balkan nations left the matter of Albania to the Great Powers, reserving to themselves only the right to discuss the proposed borders.[22]

Suddenly, on June 30, 1913, a second Balkan war broke out between Bulgaria and Serbia, and Turkey happily joined in,[23] while Essad decided to cast his lot with his fellow Albanians. On

Broadway production of "The Prisoner of Zenda", 1895

EuropeanTurkey (shaded area) in 1913 before the Balkan Wars

The Royal Palace, Belgrade

King Alexander and Queen Draga of Serbia

Colonel Dimitrijevich, assassin-master

Castle Peles, Romania

King Carol I and Queen Elisabeth ("Carmen Sylva") of Romania

King Nikola of Montenegro

Prince Danilo of Montenegro

Sir Edward Grey

The British Foreign Office, London

Sir Edward Grey's office

Kaiser Wilhelm and Kaiserin Augusta

General Conrad von Hötzendorf

Franz Josef, Emperor of Austria-Hungary

Archduke Franz Ferdinand

July 2, 1913, Ismail Kemal Bey, President of the Provisional Government of Albania, appointed him to be Minister of the Interior.[24] However, on August 1, Essad returned to Durazzo after a dispute with Ismail, and gathered pro-Serb elements around himself.[25]

On July 3, Count Berchtold told von Tschirschky, the German ambassador, that if Serbia had decisive victories, Austria's South Slav provinces could not be held and Austria "might be compelled to intervene." Chancellor Bethmann was absent from Berlin, but through German Under-Secretary Zimmermann he warned Berchtold that:

> Austria-Hungary has stated from the beginning that in the present Balkan crisis, she is seeking no territorial conquests. She has defined it as her interest in the outcome of the Balkan War that Serbia should not reach the Adriatic and that an Albania capable of living should be continued. Her first demand has been achieved without difficulty. In regard to the boundary of Albania she has won a victory in the Scutari question and also, in common with Italy, in the question of Albania's southern boundary on the seacoast. The question still open—the southern boundary on the mainland, the constitution and the choice of a ruling prince, etc., will, it is hoped be satisfactorily settled. The new outbreak between the Balkan powers, does not affect this—let them fight it out. Don't try to diplomatically force Serbia out of any territory she wins. But should [Austria] attempt to accomplish this result by force of arms, such action would mean a European War. Thereby Germany's vital interests would be more seriously affected and I must therefore assume before Count Berchtold takes any such decision he informs us... Against the idea of wishing to gobble up Serbia, since it

would only lead to the enfeeblement of Austria, I
can simply urgently warn.

Zimmerman.[26]

On July 4 Sir Edward Grey met with the Austrian and
Italian ambassadors and made some suggestions for amending
their proposals as to the language of the final decision regarding
Albania. Among other things, Grey suggested that the Powers
guarantee that Albania be "autonomous" rather than
"independent," thus retaining the fiction of subjection to a higher
legal authority. The Austrians, in particular, were anxious about
establishing a regime without a prince, as it might become
permanent. Grey suggested that this could be avoided by
deciding that a prince should be chosen within some time limit,
such as six months, and that an International Control
Commission for Albania should be appointed at once, awaiting
the prince. However, cautious to a fault, he said that the Austrian
and Italian ambassadors must put this forward as their own
proposal as it was only a suggestion by him.

The two ambassadors said that they favored Swedes as
officers to train and run the gendarmerie, but would not object to
Swiss, Belgian, or Dutch officers.[27] On July 30, the Swedish
ambassador told Grey that Sweden could not provide the officers
as they were already heavily committed to a similar undertaking
in Persia (Iran).[28]

On July 29 a slightly modified governmental plan was
adopted, so that civil and financial officers were to be
"supervised" by an International Control Commission.[29] Finally,
on that date, at their fifty-fourth meeting, the Great Powers
proclaimed Albania to be an autonomous principality, with no
bonds to Turkey whatsoever. Its princes were to rule by the
principle of primogeniture (succession by the eldest male) and
independence guaranteed by the six Great Powers. The first
prince was to be appointed within six months and be chosen by
Austria and Italy. Albania was to be neutral, like Switzerland.
The civil administration and finances were to be under an
international commission, composed of a representative of each

of the six Great Powers, and one from Albania, for a period of ten years. The Commission was to decide upon and report the details of a system of government within six months. This "International Commission of Control" was also to be in charge until a prince could be installed. Security and public order would be guaranteed by an international gendarmerie, entrusted to officers chosen (according to the original text) from the Swedish Army.[30] The actual powers of the Prince were thus rendered doubtful from the beginning.

On August 1, the Ambassadors in London met and discussed who would furnish officers for the gendarmerie. Holland, Belgium, Denmark, and Switzerland were discussed. There seemed to be some impression that Holland, having the most colonial experience, might most easily have suitable officers available. Grey said he would send a telegram to the Powers, proposing an application to the Dutch, Danish, or Swiss, in that order.[31] The Ambassadors had considered these nationalities in April, along with Norway and Spain.[32] Nothing was mentioned about the family relationship of Dutch Queen Wilhelmina and Prince Wilhelm of Wied, as he was not the only candidate being considered. The Dutch *Chargé* in London, van der Goes, was not officially notified of the officer request until August 7, 1913. An answer was delayed by a Dutch cabinet crisis.[33]

By now, the Albanian Provisional Government in Valona was collecting taxes and telegraphic contact with Europe was established through Valona. However, there was no central authority of any kind in the mountains.[34]

On August 10, 1913, Bulgaria, thoroughly defeated after a only month of war, signed the Treaty of Bucharest which, among other things, recognized the annexation by Serbia of Kosovo and northern Macedonia. Thus, almost half of all Albanians were now legally under Serb, Greek, or Montenegrin rule. Serbs shot Albanians who came to trade in their old market towns, and Greeks massacred Albanians in the south. Grey protested.[35]

In addition to an International Commission of Control to prepare the Albanian government, the Ambassadors, after much wrangling, on August 11 decided on a means of settling the southern border of Albania. When Albanian questions had been difficult, they worked on the Balkan wars' problems, which they found "more subdued and less harsh."[36] Now they had to turn to Albania again. In the area of southern Albania which Greek troops had occupied during the Balkan wars, it was decided that the border would be delineated within four months by an international frontier commission of six experts, with one selected by each of the Great Powers. They would travel to the area and decide the border based on the sentiments of the inhabitants and their language spoken at home, since Greek had often been the language of official business for Albanians. The Commission was expressly told not to consider any attempts at a plebiscite or political manifestations. On August 11, 1913, the Powers agreed on a southern border which would leave Koritsa to Greece. Greece protested that this placed 140,000 Greeks and all strategic points inside Albania. However, Greece bowed to the will of the Powers, formally, at least.[37]

As Austria took the lead on the largely settled northern Albanian boundary, it wanted Italy to take the lead in the south, and Berchtold asked San Giuliano to make suggestions. The Italian Army Chief of Staff was much alarmed over the possibility of a great Greek naval base if Greece obtained complete control of the Channel of Corfu.[38]

On August 12, 1913, Sir Edward Grey told the House of Commons in broad outline the terms of the settlement by "the Concert of Europe," which had possibly prevented a major war in October 1912 and May of 1913. He concluded by candidly saying:

> I am quite aware that, when the whole comes to be stated, it will be open on many points to a great deal of criticism from anyone with local knowledge who looks at it purely on the merits of the locality itself. It is to be borne in mind that in

making that agreement the primary essential was
to preserve agreement between the Great Powers
themselves, and if the agreement about Albania
has secured that, it has done the work which is
most essential in the interests of the peace of
Europe.[39]

After August, the Ambassadors' Conference did not meet
again as such. They had not settled all the details of Albania's
boundaries, but they had cooled the heated international
atmosphere and given the Great Powers a place to settle their
differences.[40] There was no formal finish, no speeches, no votes
of thanks, and no group photograph. They simply returned to
their regular duties.[41]

Meanwhile, in Albania on August 12, Isa Boletin
captured Dibra (Diber, Debar) just over the new border in Serbia,
provoking the Serbs and presaging future troubles.[42]

Around August 15, the Ambassadors recessed for a late
summer holiday.[43] They would not meet again as a conference
of ambassadors. Thus, the great "Concert of Europe" ended not
with a bang, but with a whimper. They had never exploited the
press for their countries' respective gain. "An atmosphere of
reticence, even to the point of dullness is favorable" said Grey.[44]

On August 18, King George wrote to Grey:

Now that the Conference of Ambassadors
is over... You have by your patience, tact, and
statesmanship secured peace, and gained the
confidence of all the European Powers while
inspiring a similar confidence in the Parliamentary
opposition in this country. I heartily share those
feelings of absolute reliance in your management
of our foreign policy, and join in the sentiments of
gratitude so generally expressed toward you by
your fellow countrymen.[45]

93

Whether deserved or not, Grey was given credit for saving the peace which settled again on Europe.

7

THE SEARCH FOR A KING

The Great Powers having reached a consensus that an autonomous Albania was to be created, they now faced the problem of choosing a prince. How to get a prince? An advertisement in the newspapers was out of the question and, as it turned out, unnecessary. While events continued to unfold in the Balkans and in the diplomatic chambers of Europe, the names of candidates for the throne sprang up like mushrooms even before the country was formally established.

As early as December 1912, Austrian circles, and especially Archduke Franz Ferdinand, had favored the German Prince Karl von Urach of Württemberg.[1] The request by the Albanian Provisional Government to the Sultan for recognition had resulted in the counter- proposal that the Ottoman princes, Burkan Eddine, Abdul Medjid, or Ahmed Fuad Pasha be accepted. However, Albanian President Ismail Kemal Pasha wanted a European prince because he wanted Albania to be European.[2] As the British were considered by the Albanians to be impartial, Prince Arthur of Connaught, uncle of King George V, British Field Marshall Lord Kitchener, and (apparently seriously) English cricket player C. B. Fry, were suggested[3] Other names mentioned were those of German princes Moritz von Schaumburg-Lippe and Karl von Hohenzollern-Sigmaringen, the Italian Count of Turin, Prince William of Sweden, and Marquess Gjon Aladro Castriota of the Albanian colony in Italy. Castriota claimed descent from the famous George Castriota, also known as Skanderbeg (i.e., "Lord Alexander"), who presided over Albania's brief Fifteenth Century independence.[4] Also mentioned was a Romanian of Albanian blood, Prince Albert Ghica, who spelled his name differently from the more aristocratic "Gycas."[5] Ismet [a.k.a. Izzet] Pasha, former Turkish Minister of War, said in January

1914, after Wilhelm zu Wied was already chosen, that he might accept the throne under certain circumstances.[6]

Italy at one time had supported Prince Napoleon Bonaparte[7] and Prince Ahmed Fuad, who thus at one time had the nominal support of both Italy and Turkey. A Muslim Albanian prince in Egypt, Fuad descended from Mehmid Ali Pasha, who ruled Egypt for forty years in the Nineteenth Century.

On January 31, 1913, the portly, mustachioed Prince Ahmed Fuad wrote to Grey in French from Paris. He was the twelfth and youngest son of the Khedive (ruler) of Egypt, and desperate to become king of some place. The letter was received by the Foreign Office on February 3, flattering Grey for his handling of the conference and "England's" reputation for ideals of justice and humanity. Fuad wrote that, "moved by the wishes of the people to whom I belong by blood and tradition," he translated the thoughts and the wishes of "the Albanian elite" in their search, through Grey, for a solution to their situation. To accomplish this, he said, Albania needed "to compose its true life and independence around a national chief," which he felt duty bound to offer in his own person as the desired chief for its rebirth. He "hoped that Your Excellency would wish to accord... the distinguished favor of his approval." The Foreign Office thought it better to leave his letter unanswered.[8]

On February 4, R. G. Vansittart, a junior Foreign Office clerk noted:

> The memo is the usual kind of partisan effusion on this particular subject. If Sir F. Bertie [ambassador to France] wants to go through the polite formality of acknowledgment, he might be told that Fuad Pasha's headquarters are the Hotel Continental, Paris. But I don't think he need acknowledge as we have done so.

R. P. Maxwell, the Senior Foreign Office Clerk, wrote, "leave it alone."[9]

Undeterred by British silence, on February 13 Prince Ahmed Fuad Pasha called in person at the Foreign Office to discuss his letter and the situation in Albania. He was received by Sir Arthur Nicolson, the Permanent Under-Secretary, who told him that the Powers could not consider what form of government to give to the future Albania before the borders were even drawn, a project which was then "engaging their attention." Fuad then said that he hoped the Albanians would not be left under Slav rule, as this would cause "endless trouble." He went on to say that Scutari [then under siege by Montenegro] could be entered and left easily, that its commanding officer was Albanian, as were 35,000 of the 40,000 troops garrisoning the city. He had sent a message to the commanding officer (Essad?) to hoist the Albanian flag. He said that the Greeks had taken Salonika by bribery. He denied that he was a Young Turk, and expressed horror at the recent murder in Constantinople of Turkish Grand Vizier Nazim Pasha.[10] On February 21, 1913, Albanian delegates to a congress in Trieste, Austria-Hungary, wired Fuad an invitation to attend on March 1 at the Hotel Vanoli there. He was strangely evasive, saying that he was "very busy," and wished them luck and unity, but his reply was not read to the congress.[11] Unsuccessful in his quest for the Albanian throne, after World War I Fuad became the first "King" of Egypt.

In response to suggestions that the British Chief of the Imperial General Staff, Horatio, Lord Kitchener, be a candidate for Albanian prince, he wrote to Sir Gerald Lowther, British ambassador in Constantinople, that it was a joke. Lowther and some others in the Foreign Office were not so sure.[12]

A number of the suggested names were quickly ruled out. The Italian Foreign Minister quickly eliminated the Duke of Urach because he was Catholic (as was Karl von Hohenzollern-Sigmaringen) and Italy was still estranged from the Vatican. Some of the candidates were declared ineligible due to their insignificance, stupidity, or limited wealth.[13]

The French-Spanish Duc de Montpensier was a vigorous applicant for the not-yet-created throne. One evening in mid-March of 1913, Ismail Kemal, the Provisional President of

Albania, learned that a yacht flying the British flag had entered the port of Valona and announced that the Greek blockade had been suspended. The next morning, Ismail learned that it was the yacht of Ferdinand, Duc (Duke) de Montpensier, the only brother of the Duc d'Orleans, Pretender to the (by then extinct) throne of France. Ferdinand and his older brother were descendants of King Louis Philippe, the last king of France, who reigned from 1830 to 1848. They were cousins of the Bourbons, who ruled France until the French Revolution, and again from 1815 to 1830. His grandfather, the Duc de Montpensier, was the youngest son of King Louis Philippe, who was ousted by the Revolution of 1848, famously protesting that "it takes a little time, even to abdicate" (*il faut un peu de temps, même pour abdiquer.*) The elder Montpensier became a resident of Spain, even becoming a general in the Spanish army. He was a liberal anti-cleric, and denied any ambition to become Spanish king, only wanting Spain to be "habitable." He had supported the placement of Alfonso XII on the throne of Spain in 1876, however. He married a Spanish princess of fourteen who could not speak a word of French, while he could not speak Spanish. As a consequence, their wedding night was somewhat bizarre. The Duke found a lady-in-waiting behind a curtain in their bedroom, placed there to give some sort of moral support to the bride. Montpensier threw her out.

King Alfonso XII married Montpensier's daughter,[14] so the young Duke who visited Albania in 1913 was well-connected with royalty.

The current Duc de Montpensier was twenty-eight years old, a somewhat stocky bachelor with the usual handlebar moustaches, and fond of adventure and sport, but was thought to have little interest in politics.[15] Perhaps he did not, but his possible candidacy as ruler of Albania was the subject of favorable discussion in royalist circles in France, and it was stated in Parisian society that the Russian Government would be ready to support his bid. However, the same circles believed that Austria, and especially Italy, would oppose it.[16]

Montpensier was, even at his young age, something of a world traveler, author and adventurer, and a crack shot, having hunted in French Indo-China and elsewhere. The Prince was said by the French Vicomte de Cazes to have "the soul of a soldier and the spirit of a scholar," and had "shown on the Moroccan coast a scorn of danger, [and]a swagger in the face of fire." He was said to have "colossal stature, …skill at all sports, …an accomplished cavalier, and a shooter worthy to emulate Buffalo Bill." His numerous voyages around the world were pointed to. Such a French King of Albania, it was suggested, would be "allied to all the reigning families of Europe."[17] Earlier in the year he had begun a Mediterranean cruise in his yacht, *Mékong,* stopping at Naples to visit his sister, the Duchess of Aosta, and her husband, the Duke, a cousin of the King of Italy. From there he had ultimately made his way to Valona, Albania. Upon arrival, he sent a messenger with a letter to Ismail Kemal, the Provisional President, informing him of his desire to become a candidate for the throne. The conservative Paris newspaper *Le Figaro* ran an article on March 21, 1913, by the Vicomte de Cazes (probably secretly paid for by adherents of the Duke), purporting to report a groundswell of demand by the Albanians "from the bosom of the Albanian nation itself," for Montpensier to be their king, despite the opposition of Austria and Italy. The article stated that a French king of Albania, "allied to all the reigning families of Europe… would be the welding point of still distant elements…" A tenuous connection was made by referring to an ancient tomb of an Anjou prince in Alessio, Albania.[18]

The Duke invited Ismail to lunch on his yacht, where, after the meal, they had a long conversation in which the Duke confided that he would like to be chosen king. Ismail, who favored a European Christian king over a Muslim, assured the Duke that he was happy and flattered for Albania to be pursued by such a distinguished personage, but pleaded ignorance of the deliberations of the Powers in London, so that he could make no decision on the matter. The next day, the Duke came ashore and, according to his own account, was received by the Provisional

Government and its Senate with military honors from the little garrison of gendarmes or soldiers. He alleged that they acclaimed him as their desired "*chef*," (leader), despite his "having asked for nothing." He claimed in a French newspaper later that for three months he had been "the object of numerous and pressing approaches coming from the representatives of the Albanian nation..."[19] This article was sent to the Foreign Office in London by the British Embassy in Paris, and thence to King George's attention. Senior Foreign Office Clerk R. P. Maxwell, noted that the "article gives a very exaggeratedly eulogistic version of the Duke's personality."[20] Montpensier rather immodestly commented to Ismail on the excellent impression which he felt that he had made on his visit. On April 1, 1913, Ismail lent some credence to Montpensier's pretensions by accepting the Duke's offer to convey Ismail, along with Louis Gurakuchi and Isa Boletin, to the nearest Italian port, Brindisi, from which they could reach London via Rome, Vienna, and Paris.[21] According to one source, Montpensier's candidacy was already doomed by its presumption. The Albanian congress at Trieste from February 26 to March 6, 1913 included the Albanian Bishop Fan Noli, arrived from America. The Viennese members of the Austrian parliament held a banquet for the visiting Albanians at the Palace Hotel. As Hungarian Baron Franz Nopcsa (1877- ?), a "paleo-physiologist" tells it, he interrupted a pause in the dinner table conversation to say loudly,

> I hear that Montpensier wants to become King of Albania, and that the proclamations have already been printed! Does any one of the gentlemen here have one in his pocket? I am a great collector of material on Albania.

Fan Noli then drew a proclamation by Montpensier from his pocket and gave it to Nopcsa. Nopcsa writes that he mailed it that evening to Count Berchtold, and presumed that it nipped Montpensier's aspirations in the bud. Nopcsa then tells us that he told General Conrad von Hötzendorf that he himself would be willing to be a candidate for the throne if Austria-Hungary would support him. To what would seem a highly unpromising proposition, he added that he needed money to bribe the Albanians into accepting. Once crowned, he suggested, he could marry some rich American woman "aspiring to royalty" to raise funds with which to carry on.[22]

As a further amusing footnote, it is said that Romanian Prince Albert Ghica [a.k.a. Ghika] attended the Trieste congress and there actually sold his claim to the Albanian throne to representatives of the Duke of Montpensier.[23] According to Queen Marie of Romania, there were a number of Ghicas, or Ghycas, in Romania, but "when spelled with a 'Y' instead of an 'I', it spells blue blood."[24] Ghica lived up to this distinction apparently, by selling his "rights" repeatedly, and calling himself King of Albania for years.[25]

It was later said that the Germans, Prince Moritz of Schaumberg-Lippe, and the Duke of Urach, and the Italian Count of Turin, were "canvassed in vain" as candidates for the throne, but seemed uneager for the job.[26]

On April 25, 1913, the Duc de Montpensier, while in London, delivered to M. de Johantho, his Head of Household, a notice to be published in the Paris newspaper, *Le Figaro*. The notice "very noble and very French," requested de Johantho to notify the Albanian Provisional Government and those "committees [and] groups of patriots who have addressed to me their solicitations," that "I am resolved to decline all candidacy to the throne of Albania." He noted that despite all the "pressing" requests he had received, he had always reserved a response. He had, he wrote, "observed, …meditated, waited," and traveled to Europe to seek sympathy for the Albanian cause. Somewhat cryptically, he wrote that he could not foresee the future and his destiny, but that no crown could make him give up his treasured titles of French citizen and prince.[27] The article was duly noted by the British Embassy in Paris and conveyed to the Foreign Office.[28] R. P. Maxwell noted caustically for the files, in reply to Montpensier's refusal of the throne, "As far as we know 'nobody asked you' Sir." Johantho's letter reads rather like a big advertisement for French consumption.[29] Montpensier no doubt had in mind that he was next in line, after his childless brother, to the position of Pretender to the position of King of France.[30] In any event, on April 27, at Alessio, near the Adriatic coast midway between Scutari and Durazzo, Essad proclaimed himself King of the Albanians, and he was received with military honors by the Serbian garrison there.[31] He then marched to his home ground in Tirana.

It has been said that the name of Prince (*Fürst*) Wilhelm zu Wied was first brought into play in January of 1913 by a conversation between the Romanian ambassador in Vienna and Count Berchtold, no doubt at the behest of the Romanian King and Queen.[32]

On May 20, Prince Wilhelm zu Wied wrote to his brother Victor that he was made fun of from all sides about the Albanian throne candidacy. He said that he thought it amusing because he knew nothing about it.[33] Wilhelm asked his uncle, King Carol, for advice. "There's not much of a chance, but you might give it a try," Carol is said to have replied. In view of the king's later statements, this quote may be apocryphal.[34]

At the end of June 1913, the Italian and Austrian ambassadors to Bucharest inquired of King Carol whether he would ask Wied to consider the job, and for Carol to mediate any negotiations. The King agreed. On July 7, Wied advised the Austrian embassy that he would not necessarily decline, although he wisely had doubts about the viability of a state with no finally fixed borders, unclear financial status, and an ominous indigenous figure like Essad Pasha. He wanted time to consider.[35]

In the summer of 1913, President Ismail Kemal Bey, after appealing to the western capitals for a decision, returned to Valona and sent an optimistic appeal to the Powers as "the unanimous wish of the people and the Government for the designation and enthronement of the sovereign, whose mere presence will suffice to unite all classes of the population..."[36]

Shortly thereafter, vague rumors about Wilhelm zu Wied were spread. There had previously been one in Vienna's liberal

102

Die Zeit newspaper on behalf of Ahmed Fuad of Egypt. Now, in the *Österreichische Rundshau* of Vienna, under the byline of "Carmen Sylva" (well known to be Queen Elisabeth of Romania), an article appeared claiming that Albania was vainly clamoring for a sovereign, and evoked the German *Niebelungen* legend of treasure buried in the Rhine. She used Wagner's *recitative* style to suggest consideration of the ancient Wied family of the Rhineland and then gave the genealogy of Prince Wilhelm zu Wied. The article was entitled, "Fairyland Wants its Prince." Soon propaganda began to be openly purchased in his favor in Albania itself. Money, presents, and his pictures were "distributed with equal effrontery." Ismail inquired of the Powers, but was told that Wied was not "officially" under consideration. He therefore took steps to quell the propaganda.[37] The young Roman Catholic Albanian diplomat, Philip Nogga, was allegedly paid thirty-thousand French francs (about $103,500 today) by the Romanian government to promote Wied's cause. He was in Valona around September of 1913, distributing small picture postcards and other mementos of the Prince.[38] After obtaining King Carol's approval, Queen Elisabeth asked Take Ionescu, then the eloquent leading diplomat and cabinet minister of Romania, to informally suggest Wied to the Central Powers (Austria, Italy, and Germany).[39] This was done, and Austria sent its ambassador to Potsdam to sound out the young German officer-prince.

In October, the Acting German Foreign Minister said that even though the Kaiser was against Wied's acceptance, "it would have to be explained to him [the Kaiser] that, in view of the wishes of Austria and Italy, it might cause unpleasantness if Germany raised difficulties."[40]

As early as July 10, 1913, German Foreign Minister von Jagow had written German Ambassador Tschirschky in Vienna:

> For Your Excellency's private and strictly personal information:
>
> Prince William of Wied came to see me today to talk about the candidature to the Albanian throne. Count Larish, the Austrian ambassador,

had been to see him at Potsdam to sound him about acceptance of his eventual election. Prince Wied said that he first asked the Count whether the frontiers of the new state were yet settled; before that was done there was no good thinking of appointing a prince. He would have to consider the matter and consult his relations, and he could not declare his decision until after six weeks,--- Prince Wied is on the eve of starting for Norway.

Prince Wied is hesitating, and my impression is that the position offered to him does not personally attract him, but he cannot reject off-hand the task which is put before him. Besides the general objections, which he feels owing to the strangeness of the country, its economic resources, the utter uncertainty of conditions, he has personal money objections.

I told the Prince that we did not wish to be involved in the question of choice of a prince, and that I could neither advise for or against. Every man must make for himself a decision of this sort, which depended on individual inclination and views of life.

I cannot refrain from saying again---and my conversation with the Prince strengthened my opinion---that the ideas prevailing in Vienna about the choice of a prince do not seem to me very practical. Before the frontiers of the country have even been settled, before there is any sort of certainty about the constitution, government organization, and financial stability of Albania, they can scarcely propose to undertake to select a candidate who will take the matter seriously…

I leave it an open question whether a provisional government composed of commissioners of all the Powers, is the right one. Sir Edward Grey's suggestion of five years' duration [of the International Control Commission's rule], seems to me rather too long. Whether the present Albanian government, which includes so doubtful an element as Essad Pacha [sic] will be a reliable and useful instrument for a new and foreign prince seems to be doubtful, to say the least.[41]

Wied's reticence can be understood. He and his young wife Sophie led a comfortable life in their villa in leafy Potsdam, the Berlin suburb whose statue-topped *Neues Palais* (New Palace) was especially favored by the German Imperial Family. Potsdam was also eminently an elegant army town, for it was here that the elite Imperial Guard regiments had their barracks and held their colorful ceremonies. Germany gave infantry regiments precedence over cavalry, but a Guard Cavalry regiment (of which Wied was an officer) had immense social status. Like all Guard regiments, they had nicknames. Wied's Third *Garde-Uhlan* regiment were called the *Staubigen* or "dusty boys," possibly because of the yellowish collars and cuffs on their blue dress tunics.[42] As a graduate of the Great General Staff College, Wied's military prospects were bright, and Sophie's musicales in their home made them a popular couple.[43]

Events were to prove Jagow's and Wied's reservations entirely justified, but not sufficiently forceful to change the course which Carmen Sylva and Princess Sophie, Wied's young wife, had set.

On August 24, 1913 Wied wrote that the Kaiser had told him, "Don't be taken in by the Albania nonsense" (*Dass Du mir ja nicht auf Unsinn mit Albanien hereinfällst.*) On November 10, Wied wrote that the German Chancellor had told other diplomats that Bethmann-Hollweg made no secret that he had advised him against accepting. (*Der Reichskanzler hatte den diplomaten der anderen Länder gegenüber kein Hehl daraus gemacht, dass er mir abgeraten habe.*)[44] This German reluctance was overcome, in part at least, by the Austrian ambassador who pressed the argument that refusal of Wied's candidacy would only help the Entente Powers, and by San Giuliano, who came to Berlin and secured a promise that Germany would be neutral on the question. Germany still feared however, that choosing a German prince would potentially lead to divisions in the Triple Alliance.[45]

Also on August 24 the diplomat Ferdinand von Stumm, a friend of Prince Victor zu Wied, Wilhelm's brother, wrote cynically that "Albania's throne is strictly for a strikingly rich bachelor who has hunted many dangerous animals." Also, the relatives of Princess Sophie were against the move to Albania. However, Sophie seemed to strengthen and even encourage Wied to take the challenge. At one point Jagow had the impression that family pressure would dissuade Wied from accepting the nomination, while King Carol was comfortable with the candidacy.[46]

In September 1913, Wied and Sophie visited the colorful Romanian royal castle of Sinaia and Take Ionescu brought them the consent of Vienna, Rome, and Paris to the choice of Wied for the throne.[47] Sophie was full of "excited anticipation" but it seemed to Romanian Crown Princess (later Queen) Marie that "quiet William was a little less enthusiastic, not being so deeply moved by the romantic possibilities of this new career."[48]

On October 9, 1913, the first formal approach to the Entente powers (Britain, France and Russia) in Wied's favor was made in Bucharest by conservative Romanian Prime Minister and Foreign Minister Titu Maiorescu. Maiorescu, a highly educated former university professor, was variously described as "steady, full of deliberation" and "oily and polite," but also close to King Carol, which no doubt lent force to his nomination of Wied.[49] Sir George Barclay, British minister to Romania, was approached by Maiorescu and asked what Britain would think of Wied as a candidate.[50] Obviously no opposition was voiced.

By September 1913, both Italy and Austria accepted Wied as a suitable candidate.[51] Germany did not like the possible entanglement of itself in Albania which a German prince would imply, but went along with its allies.[52]

On October 3, in probably the first *public* mention of Wied, The Cologne *Gazette* reported from Vienna that Wied "who is a possible candidate for the throne of Albania" was going to visit Vienna and Rome to discuss it.[53] However, Ismail Kemal Bey emphatically denied his nomination and took steps to expel his propagandists.[54]

It was apparently at this time that Wied made an informal side trip to Vienna where he met Count Berchtold for the first time. Berchtold painted a rather rosy picture of present and future conditions in Albania. He tried to reassure Wied about the financial situation, which Wied frankly (and presciently) declared to be essential. In mid-October, Berchtold and San Giulano agreed to give Wied an annual support of 500,000 kronen (about $1,800,000 today) if he was chosen, designating it as a general aid to the State of Albania in order to get the approval of their parliaments, and to prevent the appearance of Wied being their hireling. Berchtold further lead the Prince to understand that different companies had applied to build railroads and roads in Albania, financed through an Austro-Hungarian and Italian bank. Thus reassured, Wied traveled on to Romania where, his will reinforced by King Carol, be made known in Bucharest on October 23 his agreement to undertake the candidacy.[55]

One of the possible considerations motivating him, apart from his Romanian relatives, was the thought that it would soothe Romanian concerns over the fate of Romanian ethnic *Kutzo-Vlachs* in Albania.[56]

On October 4, 1913, *The Times* of London reported for the first time rumors that Wied had been nominated.[57] Wied had been unknown to London, but on October 20, Grey told German *Chargé* Kühlmann that the nomination of a prince should be made as soon as possible and London would agree to anyone agreeable to Austria, Italy, and Russia. Russia advised that it was agreeable if Britain and France agreed.[58]

On October 29, the Acting Romanian Foreign Minister told British Ambassador Barclay and the Russian ambassador that Wied, who was staying at Sinaia, would be willing to accept

107

on certain conditions: (1) all Great Powers approved, (2) "certain" Great Powers would assist Albania financially, (3) a satisfactory "organic statute," or basic law (i.e., one with no parliament) would be instituted, and (4) the Great Powers would guarantee the frontiers. The British Foreign Office did not care, as long as all deals were revealed and the Prince decided soon. The International Commission of Control (hereinafter ICC) would be asked to watch him.[59] San Giuliano said that Austria had proposed a Roman Catholic, but Italy objected and Austria gave in. Grey said he thought Wied demanded a civil list (personal government salary grant) from Albanian sources and "guarantees in case of his withdrawal, voluntary or otherwise," after his election. Italy thought Wied was probably acceptable.

On October 30, Foreign Minister Sazanov in St. Petersburg said it was "impossible to take [Albania] seriously or to imagine that it would be feasible to make a regularly constituted state out of a collection of uncivilized tribesmen."[60]

On November 14, the Italian and Austrian representatives delivered their countries' acknowledgement of the merits of his conditions to Wied in Romania.[61] On November 23, the Albanian Provisional Government was "officially notified" that Wied had been tentatively selected and Ismail Kemal immediately accepted this, although without enthusiasm.[62]

In November, Grey suggested to Jagow that Germany should act as spokesman for the other Powers and approach Prince Wied with a formal request that he accept the throne. The Germans agreed, on the understanding that they were only acting as the communicator and not the originator of the project, so that the German public would not think that the government was interesting itself directly in Albania. This made life easier for Grey. He was thereby not involved in negotiating with Wied and possibly scaring him off. He told British ambassador Goschen in Berlin to express no opinions to Wied unless he was pressed for them[63]

On November 24, Sir Arthur Nicolson in London said "This question is being unnecessarily dragged out. The proper course would be for Austria and Italy to propose the Prince of

Wied formally."[64] Grey noted that he did not want to embark on an endless discussion with [Wied] which might cause him to withdraw," and so preferred to deal directly with "the Powers who act on his behalf."[65] But Grey notified Goschen that he did not agree that Romania or Italy could speak for Wied. If Wied had conditions, he should communicate them himself. Grey believed that Italy and Austria conditioned their loan on the promised concession of a banking monopoly by an Austro-Italian group for the State Bank which Ismail Kemal had already signed.[66] Grey rightly felt that Britain's only interest was an independent, well-governed Albania, while Austria and Italy put their own interests first. Britain would wash its hands of it if not for the need to consult its friends, France and Russia, as Entente partners.[67]

On December 2, 1913, Wied wrote that his older brother Friedrich still shook his head and "Fritz's" wife, Pauline, was completely opposed to his choice. However, Wied sighed, "now that the decision is made, I am completely satisfied; only the eternal goodbye is difficult for me."

Wied sought advice from his younger brother, Victor, who was active at the German legation in Christiana, Norway, as Secretary, and then as Advisor. Victor formulated ten points, as conditions for Wied's agreement to the Powers to accept the throne.[68] No doubt they were included in Wied's negotiations.

On December 2, representatives of the five Great Powers (other than Germany) formally proposed Wied to the German Foreign Minister von Jagow, who planned to see Wied on December 4.[69] On December 3, von Jagow wrote to Wied the final agreement of all the Powers to his designation.[70]

On December 15, Wied visited Ambassador Sir Edward Goschen in Berlin to thank Britain for supporting him, but said he was unable yet to make a formal acceptance as he was awaiting Austria's and Italy's answer to his loan conditions. If all went well, he expected to go to Albania "some time next month" *via* Trieste to Durazzo, where he would "at first reside." He had arranged for an Albanian delegation to come to Germany to offer him the throne as soon as he had given a formal answer to the Powers, so that it would not appear that he was imposed by them. He hoped that Britain would send a "man-of-war" as an escort from Trieste to Durazzo, as Austria was doing. He had been told he should put his conditions of acceptance to all the Powers.[71]

On December 20, apparently impatient, Wied told ambassador Goschen that he had sent his conditions to all Powers six weeks previously through the Romanian government. He was only waiting to hear from Italy because it had agreed to ask the other Powers to guarantee a loan and let him know. Austria and Italy had promised to do it alone, if others refused, but Wied wanted the guarantee of all the Great Powers so that he would not be considered bound to any one of them.[72] Wied had asked for an eighty million franc (about $276,480,000 today)[73] loan from all the Powers, or by "a few of them." This latter alternative would enable Austria and Italy to act separately and increase their influence, but demanded recognition of their banking monopoly by the other Powers. Grey said Britain could not recognize any concession not international.[74]

Wied had apparently recently informed Austria that he wanted a total loan of £3,000,000 (about $15,000,000 in 1913 U. S. dollars, or roughly $270,000,000 currently) with £800,000 (c. $72,000,000 today) in advance, to be guaranteed by the Powers. Sazanov said that Russia could probably get a loan for her share from Paris, but that Wied should make the request of all Powers and the loan should come through the International Commission of Control.[75]

On December 22, Grey instructed Goschen to try to persuade Wied not to reside in Durazzo, as it was a base of Essad's influence. The Germans had also tried to convince him, without success.[76]

On December 30, the Great Powers were officially informed that Wied would be a candidate. The Austrians and Italians were resigned to guaranteeing the loan by themselves, if necessary[77]

Before leaving Germany to visit his sponsors, Wied sat for a life-sized portrait by German painter Professor Alfred

Schwarz, showing Wied in German uniform, with the order *Pour Le Mérite*, the highest Prussian, and therefore the highest German, decoration at his collar. He presumably received the medal due to his exalted status, since he was not known to have either fought in, or observed, an actual war.[78]

And so, by the end of 1913, it appeared that Albania had a king, or at least a prince. Skepticism was widespread throughout Europe and America. The English journalist and commentator, Lucien Wolf, writing in the London *Graphic*, referred to the Albanians as "the Afghans of Europe" in the social and political sense, because of their wildness and independence. Wied, he correctly surmised, was selected because he was the only "person of princely rank" in Europe who was both willing and inoffensive to all of the Great Powers. While the example of Carol of Romania and Ferdinand of Bulgaria was promising, war pointed ominously to the failures of Otto in Greece and Alexander in Bulgaria.[79]

8

THE POT BOILS

On August 26, 1913, the Dutch ministry asked Queen Wilhelmina of the Netherlands for her approval of the London request to send Dutch officers to train and lead the Albanian gendarmerie.[1] In return, she asked the opinion of her new ministry. They approved on September 13.

On September 1, 1913 the International (Southern) Boundary Commission, agreed upon by the Ambassadors' Conference, met for the first time in Brindisi, Italy to decide the order of its proceedings. They were to go to Cape Styles and Argyrocastro, and Elbasan was then expected to be the capital of Albania. Signor N. Labia, the Italian Consul at Monastir, and Italian Captain Fortunato Castoldi, were to be the Commission's technical experts.[2] Shortly afterward, the Commission was escorted to Scutari by one hundred British and one hundred Italian troops and two doctors.[3]

The Boundary Commission was charged with determining the southern boundary of Albania, primarily that with Greece. It elected as its president or chairman a former British Army officer, Lt. Colonel Charles Hotham Montagu Doughty-Wylie. Born in 1868, his family name was Doughty but he added Wylie at his wife's demand, as it was her family name. He had been a major in the Royal Welsh Fusiliers, with extensive service in China, India, and Africa. He had been badly wounded in both the Boer War and the Boxer Rebellion, and had been British Military Consul in Konya, Turkey, where he organized military protection for Armenians at the time of the Young Turk revolution. He had been the British Consul in Addis Ababa, Ethiopia, and in the spring of 1912 became Director-in-Chief of the British Red Cross. He had once had a chaste romance with Gertrude Bell, the famous Middle East traveler. In the summer of 1913 he accepted the position on the International Boundary Commission for Albania as chairman and British representative, but was back in London by Christmas, leaving for an appointment in Ethiopia in February of 1914. [4]

Doughty-Wylie (hereinafter referred to simply as Doughty), wrote to Gertrude Bell on September 22, 1913, "I am to be president of the crew and a perfectly beastly time I am going to have."[5] He was not optimistic or naïve about his task. While still relaxing at the Naval and Military Club on Piccadilly in London in late summer of 1913, he got reports from friends in the region which was to be delineated, and concluded, "...there'll be a fight [out there] in five years if there is none in ten days..."[6]

Three of the boundary commissioners had arrived in Brindisi by September 3. Doughty found Colonel Boudine Levkovitch, the military *attaché* for Russia at Athens, and the German Major Thierry, a battalion commander from Königsberg, to be "pleasant fellows–especially the German." Doughty brought his wife along "as a reasonable excuse for a separate camp and table." The Russian Commissioner confided to Doughty helpfully that the Austrian delegate Bilinski, who was also the Austrian Consul at Janina (in what became part of Greece), was "some form of bastard." Doughty chafed at Brindisi, which he found "a foul spot," especially since no Italian commissioner had even shown up.[7]

The Southern Boundary Commission arrived at Salonika, now part of northern Greece, on September 22[8] and met first at Monastir, in Serbian occupied territory on October. 4. The delegates then formally elected Doughty as President. The delegates were:

Commandant (Major) C. Thierry (Germany)
M. C. Bilinski (Austria-Hungary)
M. A. Lallemand (France)
S. N. Labia , also Janina Consul, (Italy)
Colonel J. B. Levkovitch (Russia)

Greece protested not being represented on the Commission.[9] On September 6, 1913, the new King Constantine of Greece visited Berlin and the Kaiser pointed out to him how much Greece had won in the Balkan Wars and cautioned him not to be greedy in southern Albania, or "Epirus," as the Greeks called it. However, the Kaiser wisely noted, if Austria and Italy were unreasonable toward Greece,

> We are not to blame! We do not have to join in every folly which they perpetuate. We have already taken overabundantly much at our expense for love of our allies. If the latter just go on making their situation worse in relation to the Triple Entente, we can warn them, but we cannot prevent them. But we do not need to join them.[10]

On September 13, the Dutch Prime Minister advised Queen Wilhelmina that the ministry approved sending Dutch officers to Albania, and she gave her formal approval on September 19, although it was decided that no officers could be sent before the International Commission of Control had started to function.[11]

The International Commission of Control (not to be confused with the International Boundary Commission) created by the Great Powers was constituted as follows (some first names unknown):

Austria: Petrovich (former Consul at Valona and Janina) and Auguste von Kral

France: Léon Alphonse Krajewski (former Acting Consul at Scutari)

Germany: Herr Winckel (former Consul General at Trieste) and Dr. Rudolf Nadolny

Britain: Harry Lamb (former Consul General at Salonika)

Italy: Commandatore Alessandro Leoni (Consul General at Corsica) and Signor Galli

Russia: Aleksandr Petrayev (Consul General at Monastir)

Albania: Mehdi Bey Frasheri (followed by Mufid Bey Libohova when Mehdi entered Wied's Cabinet)[12]

The International Control Commission arrived at the temporary Albanian capital of Valona in September 1913, and met for the first time on October 16, well before a Prince had been selected.

On September 15, 1913 the Albanian Provisional Government granted the request of the Wiener Bank Verein of Vienna and the Banca Commerciale d'Italia of Rome to establish a National Albanian Bank, with the right to deal in real estate also. This was to lead to much jealousy and opposition by the other Great Powers, not to mention other Albanians[13].

On September 18, upon refusal of his demand to make Durazzo the capital or to change ministers, Essad Pasha, then at Tirana, formed a separate government. Faik Bey Konica [sic], of the returned American Albanians, quarreled with Ismail Kemal Bey and joined Essad.[14] One of Essad's additional complaints was that the Provisional Government was extravagant, created unnecessary posts, appointed unfit persons, didn't publish accounts and had given the Austrians and Italians the bank concession.[15]

On September 21, the Carnegie Endowment for International Peace Commission of Inquiry,[16] made up of experts from five of the Great Powers (without Italy) and the United States, issued a report on Serbian ethnic cleansing, massacres, etc. The province of Kosovo had risen in revolt as a result of those atrocities.[17] Edith Durham also wrote an eyewitness account of Montenegrin looting in Albania.[18]

The same day as the Carnegie report, Serbian King Petar signed a "Regulation for the Public Security" (*Réglement sûr la Securité Publique*) to harshly control newly-annexed Albanians. This resulted in an insurrection which was crushed by Montenegro and Serbia. A Serbian soldier wrote: "We collect them in bodies of forty to fifty, and then we pierce them with our bayonets to the last man. Pillage is going on everywhere. The officers told the soldiers to go to Prizren [Serbia] and sell the things they had stolen." This Serbian reaction would lead to the Austrian-Italian demand of October 15, 1913, that Serbia withdraw from Albania, and to an Austrian ultimatum of October 18.[19]

On September 24, 1913, when the Albanians attacked and routed a Serb detachment and Serbia mobilized part of her army, the defunct Ambassadors' Conference issued no joint warning. Grey had become fed up and said "he wanted to hear the name 'Albania' as seldom as possible," and one would not be surprised, said German *Chargé* in London Richard von Kühlmann, if "...yielding to his feeling of irritation he laid the Albanian flute down on the table and recalled Admiral Burney and the English contingent."[20]

On September 23 it was reported from Vienna that Greek authorities in Koritsa had that day seized the American mission schools there, where instruction was being given to nearly a hundred Albanian girls. This information came from a telegram received from Valona. It also said that the Greeks had arrested and persecuted a large number of Albanians who had recently returned to Koritsa from America and other foreign countries, releasing them only when the Albanians promised to aid the agitation for the inclusion of the district in Greece. The British Consul at Monastir, Serbia, sent a vigorous protest to the Greek government on behalf of the Americans. The previous week, Greek officials at Koritsa had tried to take forcible possession of the American mission school building but the courageous housekeeper in charge had refused to hand over the keys, whereupon the Greek soldiers beat her mercilessly and carried her off to prison. The mission was in the charge of Princeton graduate Phineas B. Kennedy, a native of New Jersey, and the school was under the supervision of. the Congregational Church.

Under a convention, made when Turkey was in charge, Americans, in addition to their rights under Treaties of Commerce and Travel, had extraterritorial rights in Turkish lands that protected educational institutions. The U.S. State Department was prepared to protest as soon as it received official notification of the incident.[21]

116

On September 23, Isa Boletin had invaded Albanian areas now part of Serbia with six thousand men, but was forced to retreat on September 25.[22] On that day, as a result of the Kosovo and Macedonia uprising causing heavy losses to their troops, Serbia gave notice that they considered the trouble to be caused by provocations from Albania and Austria, constituting "an act of war." Both Ismail and Essad denied this, but Serbia again sent troops deep into the new Albania, crossing the mountains to the middle of the country, at Elbasan and Orosh. They killed and burned eight thousand people, destroying one hundred villages.[23]

By September 22, Colonel Doughty was in Salonika, Greece, with his Russian, German, Austrian, and Italian colleagues on the Boundary Commission, and the French delegate, Lt. Colonel of Artillery, M. A. Lallemand, was *en route* via Paris.[24] Doughty noted that

> the Greeks are all drunk with victory and Hellenism and general folly [and] …have already organized a monster demonstration at Koritza [sic] to meet us "slaves of Europe" and impress on us the sacred heart of a Christian race for the light and nobility of Hellenism, etc., etc…. the whole thing could be much better settled with German [sic] and me…

Journalists followed the Commission in autos furnished by the Greeks.[25]

By September 25, the Albanian-Greek hostilities moved Doughty to predict war between the Slavs and the Austrians and Italians.

> Albania is most unlikely to last—also and moreover it is a great mistake in German eyes for it is a very real danger to the Triple Alliance. Meanwhile the Greek working as an orderly for the Russian delegate was caught passing notes to Greek police.[26]

117

Even before the Boundary Commission began serious work, Doughty gave his opinion that only rule by a European Power or Powers could give the Albanians a decent life. "These Serbs couldn't rule a dog kennel..." It was clear to him that "... no arbitrary frontier in these countries can be just to all—villages of every kind are interlaced in a hopeless jumble..." The German delegate confided that he felt inclined to back Austria and Italy, while the Russian had instructions to follow the French lead. The whole Commission were nervous about what would happen when they told the locals that "the ambassadors have already decided their fate."[27] Doughty found the existing maps useless for deciding nationality and the Austrians and Italians demanded to actually see the area they were to rule upon. Surprisingly, map makers had not been furnished to the commission, but they were soon requested.[28]

On October 1, the Kaiser wrote Franz Ferdinand that

The situation in the Balkans is confused again. Albania, driven by the Turks (Ismet Pasha and his consorts in Adrianople, Albanians) attacks Serbia to gain these cities without which it cannot exist; and to tie Serbia down for the Turks at the same time, so that the latter cannot assist Greece when the Turks together with the Bulgarian *Komite* will attack Greece to take Casalla from them... [P. S.] I am very happy that Conrad remains. I have seen him a lot during the maneuvers and have learned to appreciate him. He is a remarkable character; this is very rare nowadays.[29]

Between October 1 and 3, 1913 Albanian incursions into Serbian-occupied territory led Serbian Prime Minister Pasich to cut short his vacation in France and hurry to see Count Berchtold in Vienna. Essad and Ismail denied responsibility for the problem.[30] Edith Durham reported that Albanian action was a "revolt" against Serb murders of non-Orthodox Christians and against cattle theft.[31]

After a visit with Berchtold, Pasich issued a communiqué stating that although they could not agree on the issue of Austrian interference in the southern Balkans, he did promise that Serbia would not invade Albania, and he hoped that his pledge would bring friendlier relations.[32]

By October 9, the Southern Boundary Commission had met three times at Monastir, Serbia, and the Italians were becoming more incensed at Greek methods of intimidation of the locals to pretend pro-Greek sentiments. Doughty wrote that a "fat beady-eyed bristling [Serb] general referred to the Albanians as *ces barbares* [these barbarians] who must be taught a lesson". It was an interesting reaction, considering that many nations had similar opinion of the Serbs. Doughty heard that a few days earlier a Serbian band had killed a woman and placed her live baby beside her, laughing at its efforts to nurse. But to the French and the Russians, the Greeks were "patriots fighting for a people rightly struggling to be free—from a cruel Moslem tyranny." As for Wied, Doughty (who presumably had no firsthand knowledge of him), wrote, "He is not the man for the job. He'll never do a thing."[33]

The Austrian and Italian Southern Boundary Commissioners demanded that only the evidence of the older inhabitants of the disputed areas should be accepted, the remaining members of the family being disregarded. The other commissioners opposed this, preventing further examination of persons on the spot. Thus, during their fifty-eight days in "Northern Epirus," only fourteen persons were examined, the majority being old women.[34]

The Southern Boundary Commission had begun its work in October. What the Greeks called Northern Epirus had two important towns: Koritsa and Argyrocastro. After World War I, Manifestations of Greek sentiment in Koritsa were considered by some to be impressive.[35] Argyrocastro, located in the most south-central portion of Albania, was dominated by a fortress. It was in the center of a region inhabited by the tolerant Muslim Bektashi.[36]

The Commissioners set forth from Koritsa into the rough, roadless, mountainous countryside in automobiles, but because of breakdowns and the absence of roads, the cars had to be abandoned for horses and walking. Greek troops had been given until the end of the year 1913 to withdraw from the areas they had occupied in the war. Although there were genuine aspirants for Greek rule, local Greek officials herded Albanian peasants in Greek costumes out to meet the boundary commissioners and shout, *Enosis e thanatos!* [union or death!]. More reticent Albanians were kept indoors.[37] An official protest by Austria and Italy to this Greek obstruction was made to Athens on October 30,[38] and Albanian ICC delegate Mufid Bey Libohova led a delegation to Berchtold to bring him up to date and successfully seek Argyrocastro for Albania.[39]

In the north, boundary commissioners were often stopped and arrested by Serbian troops when they reached areas near Serbian-claimed territory. The French and Russian commissioners tended to favor their friends the Greeks, Serbs, and Montenegrins, while the Austrians and Italians sought as much territory for Albania as possible. Petty disputes were mediated by the British and German commissioners, the latter being torn between Germany's alliance with Austria and Italy, and its desire to win favor with Greece, whose Queen was the Kaiser's sister.[40] Difficulties were magnified by the fact that only two members of the Southern Boundary Commission spoke Greek or Albanian, and one of them, the Austrian Bilinski, was dying and too ill to leave his house. The Italian Assistant Commissioner, Captain Fortunato Castoldi, who had formerly been in the Turkish gendarmerie, made so many mistranslations that his interpretations were mistrusted.[41] Greek guerillas (*hierolochoi*= "sacred batallions") followed the Commission and rushed into towns ahead of them. The same village faces often reappeared and Greek hangers-on menaced the commissioners or their witnesses.[42]

It may be of interest to report the Commission's experience in Koritsa around the twelfth of October, as reported by Doughty:

We arrived here in the rain after a cold ride of 25 miles or so—wet through. So they all came--a deputation from Janina (after the visit to the governor)-- We are not going to receive deputations—therefore I had to explain to them how & why they were refused with each man's long thought out fiery speech hanging on his tongue, & a row of journalists behind. When this was done--the Koritza sacred legion--after them the women of Koritza. They all talked at once, which delighted them to such an extent that after an abortive attempt to go on their knees, they were induced to depart in about seven minutes, quite pleased at having said something—Then came visits—the Archbishop, etc., etc.--& a vast and interesting display of the foreign legion--these *alsteretes* marched through the town--armed & mostly in uniform--old men and children--& the parade of some 2,500 finished up with a party of elderly females armed to the teeth--bells rang, large flags were carried. The streets hung with blue & white streamers *Enosis e thanatos*--bands-- legions, etc., etc. Naturally I refused to be anything more than a very mere spectator on a corner--but it was very interesting & passed off quietly.

Today the Archbishop turned up to return my visit accompanied by the corporation of fiery patriots & assisted by the whole town in procession! However it passed off quietly. Though I had to refuse not quite so suavely to go up to the balcony, to be photographed, etc. Then came the mufti with a tale of Greek benefits in Koritza town—

But riding in I had counted the three nearest villages destroyed—the old mufti could only tell me that across the frontier "the Serbs" were killing—My colleagues who should have been here yesterday had a break down with their motors, (we came on humble economical horses) & have never arrived--they will be here tomorrow I hope--& then on to Colonia, to begin work.

Despite his cynicism, Doughty was able to form an opinion.

The general impression left on me is that the town is really Greek in sentiment, although the language is majority Albanian--or is I am told. No doubt that is the impression intended to be left. It is to be remembered that to a Koritzote there are as alternatives the govt by Hellas [Greece] & priests & eloquence & I think we are bound to say freedom for Greeks--and the unknown Albanian govt which consists as far as they know of Ismail Kemal & his crew--by local Beys with wrongs to even--[If there were] an international occupation, then they would wear a different aspect--let Albania be governed by FOREIGNERS as the only neutrals for a few years (no princeling is going to make any odds) backed by a gendarmerie & a civil service and it is a reasonable proposition to hand them these countries—but not yet—[43]

Back in London, on October 14, Grey noted that although German Foreign Minister von Jagow spoke of agreement with Britain, he made no protest to the threatening actions of Austria. The Germans had recalled their senior naval officer from Scutari after pressure from the Austrians. Sir Eyre Crowe voiced his suspicion in a note to the latest report:

I am not altogether convinced that the Germans are playing quite straight in this Albanian question. They constantly assure us that they do not approve what Austria does but in fact they have at every stage supported her vigorously.[44]

An Austrian ultimatum to Serbia on October 18 and the demand by Austria and Italy jointly to the Greeks twelve days later seemed to confirm this view, as Berlin did not publicly object to Austria's unilateral action.[45]

At its meeting on October 16, 1913 at Valona, the International Commission of Control began supervising the organization of a gendarmerie and a government.[46] The Berlin Foreign Office sent its moral support to Berchtold, but urged Grey to use his influence with Serbia and the Conference to see that the decisions of the Powers were upheld while restraining Austria from acting "independently." Grey was again out of town for the weekend.[47]

Meanwhile, the Serbians had burned several Albanian villages and massacred Albanians in the neighborhood of Dibra, so that the population was in flight toward the coast. Between Dibra and Prizren, nearly all the villages were wholly or partially burned by the Serbs, who pushed their outposts some ten kilometers beyond the provisional boundary of the new country.[48]

In early October, 1913, Berchtold called a ministerial council to deal with the Serbian invasion. As usual, General Conrad urged immediate, all-out war with Serbia, its conquest and the incorporation of most of it into a sort of Triple Monarchy, giving the rest to other Balkan nations. Count Istvan (Steven) Tisza, Premier of Hungary since June, wanted to rely on diplomacy, and was appalled at the idea of incorporating Serbia. He favored an ultimatum. Berchtold vacillated. At one point, he suggested a sharp, swift chastisement of Serbia by seizing some Serbian town without mobilizing. For once logical, if not calm, Conrad explained repeatedly the technical impossibility of such a move. "What are you thinking of? If we mobilize [Austrian Southern Commander] Potiorek will have 80,000 infantry, but now he has only 25,000, and they are scattered all over Bosnia." Berchtold dreaded the complications which could ensue from the sixteen days needed to mobilize, but he still wanted military action without mobilization.[49] He feared that Germany and Italy would not back him against Russia, and finally proposed and sent on October 15 an "amicable request" to Serbia to withdraw, but in her own good time.

On October 16, Germany gave Austria its "moral" support.[50] The Kaiser said, "It's Now or Never! One must finally have order and quiet down there!"[51] With seemingly no hesitation, he had suddenly changed his tune and declined to act as a brake on Austria's potentially warlike actions.

9

ULTIMATUM

War, My Lord,
Is of eternal use to human kind,
For, ever and anon, when you have passed
A few dull years in peace and propagation,
The world is overstocked with fools and wants
A pestilence at least, if not a hero.
             –G. Jeffreys

Serbia showed her contemptuous disregard of Austria's "amicable request" of October 15 by further incursions across the boundary of the new little Albanian state. In the middle of the night of October 17, Berchtold uncharacteristically and suddenly summoned the power of decision, and dispatched an ultimatum to Serbia without consulting anyone.[1] Serbia was to withdraw her troops from Albania within eight days it said, or "Austria would be forced... to have recourse to the proper measure to secure the realization of her demands." In diplomatic language, this was a threat of war. On October 19, Italy sent a similar demand.[2] No doubt the fact that Austria's action defended the Albanian-Serbian border decision of the Great Power Ambassadors emboldened Berchtold.[3] Russian Foreign Minister Sazanov and French Foreign Minister Stephen Pichon, meeting in Paris, advised the Serbs to comply, assuring them that, once Russia was militarily prepared, they could do as they pleased.[4] All of the Powers, even Romania, had warned Serbia.[5] Finding itself without any support, Serbia quickly complied on October 20, but not before further atrocities by its troops.[6]

Sazanov was angered that Russia had not been first consulted by the usually cautious Berchtold, and Pasich said, "I [withdraw] not under pressure from Austria, but out of regard for the friendly advice of Russia."[7]

Grey was at his country retreat, Fallodon, when the Austrian ultimatum to Serbia threatened to turn the Albanian question into a major conflict. As Austria and Italy were using the International Commission to further their own aims, Crowe urged that the British should withdraw before their own reputation for moral behavior was compromised. "My own inclination is in accord with Sir. Ed. Crowe's minute," Grey wrote, "and I would come to that decision and act upon it at once if Russia and France had not to be considered."[8] Grey was apparently already feeling dependent upon the countries with whom Britain had an "understanding."

Even after Montenegrins crossed the Albanian border and pillaged in Albania, Franz Ferdinand wrote Franz Josef: "Our country doesn't want war, as our countless difficulties with conscripts show... We can rid Albania of those Serbs by diplomatic means."[9]

On October 21, 1913, after Serbia backed down, Franz Ferdinand wrote Berchtold while on his way to Konopisht: "I am happy that war has been avoided...I've told you that if one approaches Kaiser Wilhelm with some deftness, avoiding Great Power talk and other chicaneries...then he'll stand fully by us...and we won't need to resort to a single weapon or any Conradian Big Stick to make these [Serb] pigs hoof it back to their own borders."[10]

Years later, Churchill wrote:

The peace of Europe during 1913 rested solely upon the Kaiser's "No." One hand only held the key that could unloose the deluge. From the moment that Austria had quarreled with Russia, William II had the Dual Monarchy in his power. While his veto stood the world was safe.[11]

Unlike his position in late 1912, Kaiser offered no veto in October 1913. Quite the contrary. However, he was now convinced that Russia (and thus France) "could not fight for six years," and he believed that neither country would condone Serbia's behavior.[12] He therefore relaxed his grip on the diplomatic brake.

The other Great Powers were somewhat irritated by Berchtold's sudden unilateral act in October, but Austria's legal position was clearly in line with the Serbian border which had been agreed upon by all.[13] War had again been averted.

10

SETTING THE BOUNDARIES

A German delegate on the Balkan Boundary Commission, von Laffert, called Essad the greatest *gauner* [rascal] in Albania and said that he had a hand in the Albanian 'uprising." Strandtmann, the Russian *Chargé* at Belgrade, reported the Serbian plan to be:

The impecunious Essad will be sent money, and the [Serb] military plans to call for the complete annihilation and dispersion of Ismail Kemal, Isa Boletin, and their friends. Whereupon, Essad Pasha will be set up as governor-general at Valona. The latter, with whom the Serbian Government has been in touch for some time, is prepared to recognize the suzerainty of the Sultan, as is shown by Essad's flag with the eagle and the half-moon. He is also willing to undertake a boundary rectification in accordance with Serbia's wishes up to the Black Drin [river]. At the request of Essad this surrendered territory will be occupied, supposedly temporarily, by Serbian troops in order to maintain order. After establishing his power, Essad will have himself proclaimed Prince of Albania.

In late October, Russian Foreign Minister Sazanov told British *Chargé* O'Beirne in confidence:

Serbia had been more to blame than was generally supposed, in the events which had led up to the recent ultimatum from Austria. Mr. Spalaiković [the Serb representative], had held the most impudent language with regard to Serbia's coming to an understanding with Essad Pasha and combining with him to crush the Albanian Government provisionally established at Valona. The question of Serbian access to the Adriatic would thus, Mr. Spalaiković had said, be satisfactorily settled.[1]

On October 27, despite King Carol's aversion to his heir traveling abroad, Crown Prince Ferdinand of Romania and Crown Princess Marie went to Vienna where they were visited in their hotel by Franz Josef and returned the visit to the Hofburg Palace for lunch, taking young Prince Carol and Princess Elisabeth along. Franz Ferdinand and other Austrian royalty joined them and the Romanians left for home that evening.[2] It seems likely that Wied and Albania were discussed, if only briefly.

In late 1913, the Southern Boundary Commission continued its somewhat fruitless search for a proper border. The following incident, reported by a British observer, was typical:

> The Commission comes by night to a village; They are greeted by a man speaking Greek and they hear the ringing of an apparently Orthodox bell. One of the *Kavasses* [local guards] of the party comes from the village and he assures the Commission that not only are there no Greeks in the village, but that there is not even a church there. It is discovered that the Greeks have rigged up an impromptu belfry in a treetop and are ringing a bell, to hoodwink the representatives of the Commission. A deputation of women and children come to see the Commission and urge them to believe in their Greek nationality. Mr. Bilinski, the Austrian delegate, threw a handful of coppers among the children, and as expected, in the scramble the children excitedly spoke in Albanian despite the protest of their mothers.

In early October, Doughty suggested that an Anglo-German team map the frontier area, as all existing maps seemed inadequate. The Germans were happy to agree.[3] However, by October 31 the Southern Boundary Commission was in deadlock. Doughty took steps to solve the unsolvable:

> I have proposed an arrangement to their Excellencies in London with which all have so far fallen in—except the French & Russian—but they too come in, *les cas échéant*—All it really does is to about halve the country when the thing will be formed—& perhaps to avoid the international trouble and a few other little things.) Anything is better than blood even ink to spill. As for seeing the country that we can do afterwards—The Austrians & Italians will not move from here without some arrangement—As for "determining nationality by examination of the language spoken in families" that we cannot do…So now we wait—if they approve then we go in procession round the country to examine it for nothing in particular, except that people shall not fight because they have not been considered to [sic] their thinking in the settlement—& then we declare a frontier—& then the next adventure—[4]

Shortly after this proposal, however, in November of 1913 a correspondent of the London *Daily Telegraph* saw large numbers of supposedly pro-Greeks lined up beside the road for twenty miles in the Argyrocastro Valley, for twenty-four hours, to demonstrate their desire to be part of Greece.[5]

The Southern Boundary Commission soldiered on throughout October and November. The Austrian delegate, Bilinski, died in Janina on November 18 of "nefritis" after a long illness.[6] Doughty disliked him, but admired his courage and ability and his "gift of talking." Bilinski's wife would not bury him in Albano-Greek soil, for fear of what she understood to be the Greeks' "hideous habit of defiling the graves of their enemies."[7]

In early November, Doughty telegraphed the Foreign Office for authority to visit the whole disputed area, and to rely not merely on nationality, but the "economic, geographic, and strategic features." Britain and the Ambassadors agreed to abandon the language test.[8] After a worrisome silence, by November 23 Doughty was advised that his suggested frontier line had been accepted by Sir Edward Grey and proposed by him to the other Powers as a basis of settlement. But Sir Eyre Crowe sent Doughty a long telegram saying that he could not understand what Doughty wanted—or only with such difficulty that he still had a headache.[9]

On October 31, due to constant interference with the Boundary Commission's work by Greek authorities, Austria and Italy sent notes, independent of the other Powers, protesting the Greek influence in Epirus, and threatening the ingenious solution of regarding automatically as Albanian any villages where Greek interference was encountered. The Commission had already been instructed to make no investigation south of an arbitrary line drawn by the Conference of Ambassadors. To avoid a deadlock, Sir Edward Grey obtained agreement of the Powers to stop the investigation and fix the southern border by using maps furnished by the Geographical Institute of Florence, Italy, where the Commission ultimately proceeded to complete their work.[10] Doughty had maintained so strict an impartiality that the French complained of his lack of enthusiasm for the Entente. Grey defended him, as he demanded that the British representative be impartial.

On November 16, Doughty proposed a line roughly midway between those sketched by the French and Italian delegates. The response was favorable and by December 13, the Commission felt sufficiently confident of success to move to Florence, where an agreement on the southern frontier of Albania was announced on December 20.[11]

The French and Russian delegates to the Boundary Commission had for a time been very angry, not at where the boundary line should go, but whether there should be one at all. They wanted to please the Greeks and the Christians. From their viewpoint, questions were always seen as a conflict between the Triple Alliance and the Triple Entente, and they resented any independent British action. Nevertheless, on December 19, 1913, Doughty sent off from Florence the final documents, along with a signed map of Southern Albania, with the frontier marked on it, and the announcement was made the next day.[12]

When Doughty reported in at the Foreign Office in London on December 23, he learned of the final acceptance of the frontier and even Crowe complimented him.[13]

On November 6, 1913, the rotund, goateed, self-styled "Czar" Ferdinand of Bulgaria, went to Vienna to try to make up with the Austrians. He told them that they had missed a chance to "finish off the Serbs." He met with Berchtold at the Coburg Palace, and later with Franz Josef at Schönbrunn, and finally scuttled back to the Ballplatz to Berchtold again. Ferdinand warned that the Serbs were out to get Bosnia-Herzegovina and were determined to extirpate the Albanian race and destroy Albania.[14] Whether this analysis by a known schemer reinforced Austria's attitude is unclear. Reflecting a common view, Theodore Roosevelt, after meeting Ferdinand in 1910, called him "a twittering wagtail."[15]

The stage was now set for erecting the new Albanian state.

11

PREPARATIONS

[Anonymous Notice in the "personal," or "agony" columns of *The Times* newspaper of London, July 17, 1914]:

> Absolute Rotter, dumb in six languages. Served Rifle Brigade and N.I.D. Admiralty. Can be trusted with money, silly ass. Loves his country, perfect fool, completely brainless but harmless with children, young as possible. Has means. WANTS A JOB. Box H988, *The Times*.

On November 10, 1913, before a Prince had been finally chosen for Albania, Colonel Willem J. H. de Veer, 56, of the Third Regiment of the Netherlands Field Artillery, who was to command the fifteen Dutch officers sent to Albania, arrived at Valona with several enlisted men.[1] All the Dutch officers seem to have been automatically advanced one rank when entering Albanian service. Thus, de Veer became a general of the Albanian gendarmerie.

Since Albania was to be neutral and without an army, its only armed force would be the gendarmerie. That organization was a cross between a national police force and a militia, similar, perhaps, to the *Caribinieri* of Italy. They would wear uniforms (although the Dutch officers continued to usually wear their Dutch Army uniforms) and be lightly armed at first, mostly with rifles and machine guns.[2]

The twelve Dutch officers ultimately sent under General de Veer (and their initial assignments) were as follows:

From the cavalry, Captain Lucas Roelfsema (Durazzo); from the artillery, Captains Wouter de Waal (Argyrocastro) and Hugo J. Verhulst (Elbasan), and First Lieutenants Carel de Jongh, Jetze Doorman (Koritsa) and Jan Fabius (Scutari);

From the infantry: Captains Henri J. L. Kroon (Scutari) and Joan E. Snellen van Vollenhoven (Koritsa); First Lieutenants

Julius H. Sonne (Argyrocastro); Hendrik G. A. Reimers (Elbasan) and Jan H. Sar (Durazzo).

From the general staff: Captain Johan M. Sluys (Durazzo).

From the medical corps: Dr. Tiddo Reddingius.[3]

Many of the Dutchmen seem to have carried their attitudes as colonial masters to Albania with them. Some spoke of the Mirdites, saying, "considered as animals,… [they are] splendid fellows and show as servants doglike devotion." Captain Sluys greeted the Albanian ministers with "Good morning, cads!" Young Lieutenant Fabius considered Turkhan Pasha and Mufid Bey cunning traitors, although they were respectable men. Lieutenant Fabius was only twenty-five, but later became an artillery captain very popular with the volunteers. He sincerely wanted to give Albania a chance to exist, and an observer considered him the most reckless and daring of the Dutch officers.

The Dutch felt that the first task was to eradicate the Albanian vendetta tradition.[4] Roelfsema quietly went about his duties. Major von Trotha, sometimes described as the King's controller and lord chamberlain, was a German, and could not stand the Dutchmen because of what he conceived to be their lack of respect and lack of ceremony. They were not invited to dine at the palace for months.[5]

In St. Petersburg, Sazanov told the British *chargé* in late October that "…it was impossible to take this newly-created state seriously, or to imagine that it would be feasible to make a regularly constituted state out of uncivilized tribesmen." To keep it from completely being a puppet of Italy and Austria, Russia still tried to ensure that the Sultan's ultimate authority would be preserved. A Russian note to Britain stated that:

> The future Prince, to make firm his position, must necessarily ensure himself of a support other than in Albania, a support that the Cabinet of Vienna will be quite disposed to accord him. Inspired by all these considerations the

[Russian] Imperial Government believes its duty to pronounce in favor of a neutral Albania, freely autonomous, confided to the administration of a Turkish *Vali* [governor] and placed under European International control.

Izvolsky, the Russian ambassador in Paris, told the British ambassador there that he was in favor of Austria trying to make Albania a state, although it was impossible, because the people were too wild. However, he thought it would lead to friction between Italy and Austria-Hungary, and that was a result for which Russia would feel no regrets.[6]

Conditions in Albania following the Balkan wars elicited much sympathy in Britain and, on December 2, the British Government sent the following to the German Government:

Aide Mémoire.

According to authentic reports which have reached His Majesty's Government there is lamentable distress among the thousands of refugees in Albania and it is clear that, without immediate assistance, very many will be unable to survive through the winter. His Majesty's Government would be prepared to participate in guaranteeing a loan of £60,000 [$300,000 in 1913, perhaps $5,400,000 today] in all, that is to say £10,000 [$900,000] for each Power, and they earnestly trust that the German Government will be prepared to guarantee an equal share. It would, in Sir Edward Grey's opinion, be perhaps best to instruct the Commission of Control to authorize the Consuls at Scutari in consultation with the Commander of the International Contingents to distribute the funds.

Again on December 12, the British sent another Aide Mémoire:

>   Sir Edward Goschen had the honour to submit to His Excellency Herr von Jagow on the 2nd instant a proposal that the six Powers should guarantee a loan of £60,000 for the purpose of affording assistance to the refugees in Albania who are reported to be in great distress.
>   Sir Edward Goschen has now been informed by Sir Edward Grey that, as His Majesty's Government consider the matter to be pressing, they have decided to make an immediate provisional advance of £5,000 and will be prepared to advance another £5,000 on hearing that the other Powers will do the same and will agree to the suggested joint loan to Albania of a total of £60,000 for this express purpose.

Some relief was granted, but not enough. More international interest in high places centered on the proposed Albanian National Bank. Apparently Germany tried to help its Austrian ally's policy of financial hegemony in Albania. On December 15, Grey warned the German *Chargé d'Affaires*, von Kühlmann, respecting the project of the National Bank of Albania:

>   … the so called Provisional Government at Valona was not competent to grant definitive concessions engaging the economic future of the entire country, of which it controls only a small part. That body as its selfchosen title indicates, is, in any case, not the definitive Government of Albania, a country whose separate existence is due to the six Great Powers, and which was, at the time when the concession in question was granted, subject to the control of an International Commission already designated and on its way to

136

take up its duties. The Provisional Government of Valona must have been well aware, moreover, that, in allotting unauthorized concessions, it was acting against the wishes of a large majority of the population. Much opposition to the Provisional Government has, in fact, been created by this very action.

Grey saw no cause to modify this view after perusal of the terms of the draft concession, which in its then form appeared to him a decidedly one-sided and onerous proposal for the Albanians. After due consideration of this document, he informed Control Commissioner Harry Lamb that the British Government remained of the opinion that no concession granted by the Provisional Government could be considered valid unless and until it had been examined and approved by the Commission of Control. If, in the light of this principle, Lamb considered that the proposed Bank should be internationalized, he was authorised to support a proposal to that effect. Rebuffing a German suggestion of support for Austria, Grey formally replied:

> In regard to Herr von Kühlmann's allusion to the open door, Sir E. Grey is not prepared to accept the statement that the National Bank is the only existing financial institution in Albania, firstly because that institution is not yet in legal existence, and secondly because he understands that the branch of the Imperial Ottoman Bank at Scutari is still open.
> The assumption of the German Expert Bankers, to whom Herr von Kühlmann refers, that no other banks will be inclined to enter the field may be said to depend for its validity largely upon the question whether the present draft concession is or is not confirmed, since Article II of that concession established in favour of the concessionaire group a practical monopoly in

regard to all financial and industrial enterprises in Albania.[7]

Apparently somewhat embarrassed, on December 31 Italy reported that the Austro-Italian State Bank was already in operation, but that Italy would try to persuade Austria to loosen their monopoly.[8] Sir Eyre Crowe of the Foreign Office emphasized Albania's financial insufficiency and doubted that Britain ought to get involved, unless to prevent friction between Austria and Italy. Grey repeated that Albania could be ignored were it not for consideration for France and Russia.[9]

The Imperial German Legation in Bucharest on the 17th of December reported that, according to Minister Maiorescu, it was desired there that not only Austria and Italy, (who were willing), but that several other Powers (e.g., France and England), guarantee the Albanian loan when the Prince arrived in Albania. In that way it would not appear that only the two Powers of the Triple Alliance supported him.[10]

In late November or early December 1913, the Albanian, Philip Nogga, an "intimate" of Wied who had been agitating for some time in Albania for the prince's candidacy, wrote in Italian to a Kristo Mexi. Mexi was an Albanian who had retired from banking in Romania with a good social position there, but a somewhat shaky reputation in some quarters. Apparently Mexi had contacts in Albania, for Nogga asked Mexi to quickly compose a mission of about fifteen notable Albanians to assemble in Durazzo by the 23rd of December and leave immediately for Berlin to offer Wied the crown in conformity with the Great Power decision. Nogga specified that five of the delegates must represent upper Albania, five the middle, and the rest "lower Albania." In turn, on December 12, Mexi sent the Catholic Archbishop of Scutari letters delegating him to choose five representatives from the city and region of Durazzo, and they were to include Abdi Bey Toptani, Hassan Bey Prishtina, the Orthodox Church Metropolitan (unidentified), a "*hoxha*" (a.k.a. "hodja," a Muslim religious leader) of Dibra, and a fifth person, unnamed. All the expense of the trip was to be the responsibility of Mexi.

One Nicoló Martinaj, apparently one of the Wied sympathizers in Durazzo, warned Mexi that he would make a great error if he did not inform "the Prince of Mirdizia" (i.e., Prenk Bib Doda) of this proposed mission. Mexi was happy to get Martinaj's advice, and "urgently" wrote to him to request Bib Doda to also send a delegate with credentials to Durazzo by the 23rd. Martinaj did not know whether Nogga would send an "official" invitation to Mexi to form the mission, but felt duty bound to keep Bib Doda advised of what was going on and, on December 12, hand-delivered a letter in Italian to him (addressing him as "Highness"). In the letter he offered to meet with Doda's representative to keep him up to date and to help with any contact with Essad. He requested Doda to tell him how to reply to Mexi's letter.[11]

This plan was, of course, in conformity with Wied's insistence that he be offered the throne by Albanians as well as by the Great Powers. If not set on foot by Wied himself, this must have been the work of official Romanian circles, either royal or governmental.

On December 24, Berchtold told Sir Maurice de Bunsen, British Ambassador in Vienna, that twelve *(sic)* Dutch officers for the gendarmerie had been "recently engaged" and were on their way, and Holland would send more if needed. He said that the gendarmes were being recruited and organized, and that German ambassador to Vienna, Count von Tschirschky, estimated that it would cost £635,000 (c. $57,150,000 today) a year to govern Albania, of which Albania could only raise one-third. Berchtold thought £416,000 enough, to avoid "extravagance."[12]

Just as the International Control Commission was about to take control in Albania In November of 1913, Control Commissioner Winckel of Germany was bitten by a rabid dog and retired temporarily, to be replaced by career diplomat Dr. Rudolf Nadolny, his deputy.[13] Nadolny was later to act as a spy-and-sabotage-master for Germany in the World War.[14]

From Valona on November 23, 1913, Nadolny expertly summed up the Albanian situation for his Foreign Office in Berlin:

> The political conditions in Albania keep up with great difficulty. There are four provisional governments in the country that pursue the task to maintain order to some extent, to the beginning of a uniform state authority.
>
> In the south, with his headquarters in Valona, Ismail Kemal Bey exercises his power, which he theoretically understands as and also calls the provisional government for the whole of Albania. His influence allegedly extends over the whole area south of the Skumbi [River]. It actually seems to exist in the towns of Valona, Berat, and Tepeleni, though lately it also decreases here more and more. Outside the towns, though, it is probably quite illusory and in the eastern and southern border areas it does not come into play at all.
>
> The middle part of Albania, the land between Skumbi and Mati is ruled by Essad Toptani Bey (usually called Essad Pascha) from Durazzo, namely as "Chief of the Executive of the Senate for Middle Albania." He seems to have quite firm a grip on this area, in fact up to the Serbian border. There are a good deal of complaints about him from his committee, though. The complaints of his neighboring rulers also show that he would like very much to extend his sphere of influence across the two rivers he himself has called the borders of his sphere.
>
> In Alessio together with St. Giovanni di Medua and the vicinity of the Malissor Ded Zoku rules with his notables. He recently wanted to extend his sphere up to the Bojana, but he was

turned back to his original area by the International Control Commission.

Regarding Scutari the question of the formation of a civil authority has not been decided yet, for the time being Colonel [George F.]Phillips, [of the British West Yorkshire Regiment] the head of the international troop detachment maintains the rule in the town and the plain surrounding it. The land east of this, the North Albanian highland and the areas of the Mirdites are without a governmental power.

According to their written assurances the Albanian rulers governing this way understand their role as purely provisional and only lasting until the new ruler's accession to the throne. Apparently they comply with the requisitions and orders of the Control Commission and have also been recognized by the latter for the indicated districts. When they are guilty of infringements and there is friction among them, the Commission reminds them that they had to maintain the status quo and were responsible for it.

If it is possible to talk about a certain order of things in Albania, this easily indicates, though, that this temporary arrangement will not last long. As explained the areas in the north- and southeast are moreover without any government. The four regional governments, though, have too much of the provisional. Uniform points of view in the administration are lacking and—what probably involves the greatest danger—as for the three Albanians the legitimacy of their position of power. Probably a financial administration serving the interests of the country does not exist either. Even though the three gentlemen have taken up residence in the three seaports of the country for good reason and control the customs revenue and thus the most important resources, it seems doubtful anyhow, whether these are spent efficiently and for the best of the community. The International Control Commission certainly takes great pains to be in charge and is willing to try to enable a fairly general use of the revenue. But due to its character and for lack of executive power it can on the whole only restrict itself to redress differences and unreasonableness as far as possible and counteract possibly intended changes of the political development.

In the interest of the country it is to be wished that the question of the accession to the throne will be settled as soon as possible, and that the ruler will not postpone his arrival too long, as the danger is not to be dismissed otherwise that the different administrative powers will adopt their own course and thus the political unity, still supported by all now will break up. Recently a special question has also been noticeable, which also makes the lack of a uniform governmental power felt.

A large number of Albanian refugees have come over from the territories fallen to Serbia and Greece. Especially in Dibra and Elbassan there are thousands of them, who urgently need care. Different states have already given support. So the Austro-Hungarian and the Italian government have contributed (about 26,000 francs each). On top of that 1,000 francs have been donated privately from Austria and 200 pounds sterling for Skutari paid by English charitable societies and 50 pounds sterling promised for Elbassan. Means are also to be expected from the French side. An involvement of German circles in this aid is to be warmly recommended from the humanitarian point of view. It would surely also be recognized—as far as I can judge the considerations from my brief stay here—and possibly have a certain favorable effect on our economic relations to Albania. If means cannot be easily mobilized for this, however, or are more urgently needed elsewhere, it would for the time being be possible for us to leave the aid to those states, which have put themselves into the first row here. At any rate all these donations will not redress the need. According to the Control Commission it would be most advisable to allocate larger sums to be able to employ the needy at various public tasks, urgently necessary for the country, or to settle them in the Tschifliks [sic], partially deserted or depopulated as a result of the war. It will also try its utmost in that respect by influencing the local governments. But effective measures could only be taken by a general authoritative central administration.

Signed: Nadolny.[15]

On November 28, 1913 in Valona, Ismail Kemal, the provisional Albanian president, celebrated the first anniversary of Albania's independence with a reception at his rather square residence on the seashore. He received his cabinet, the International Control Commission, the commanders of the Italian and Austrian warships in the harbor, as well as local notables. People demonstrated in front of the house, cheering and singing national songs. Ismail appeared on the balcony with the Cabinet, spoke to acclaim, and people paraded with the national flag.[16]

The Cologne *Gazette* reported from Berlin that Wied would be officially informed of his selection by the Germans, since he lived in Potsdam[17] and was to spend Christmas and New Year's there.[18]

At this point, the somewhat Bertie Wooster-ish character of Duncan Heaton-Armstrong (hereinafter Heaton) comes upon the scene. A handsome young man of twenty-seven with what was once called a guardsman moustache, he was technically British, although of a cosmopolitan background. His father was of the Protestant Irish aristocracy and a former Member of Parliament, while his mother was the daughter of an Austrian baron. He had been born in Austria, but attended Eton and Cambridge without distinguishing himself in any positive way. He did manage to become fluent in French, German, and Italian. He had also joined a British Territorial, or reserve, regiment, but apparently paid little attention to it, despite allowing himself to be called "Captain Heaton-Armstrong" by the press and others. He liked the gentlemanly sports of riding to hounds and shooting, and he was applying himself to the latter with a cousin in Germany when he learned of Wied's selection. He was considered by several women who met him to be both "youthful, very free and easy, and rather blunt," and "a feeble stick with no ideas...more in place in a Vienna café..." The latter evaluation by the forceful Edith Durham seems a trifle overdone in view of Heaton's very readable memoirs and his perceptive reports on Wied's later predicament. No doubt Durham's opinion was colored by Heaton's flippancy when he told her that he had no interest in exploring Albania because he hated "roughing it" and hadn't the least wish to go anywhere which entailed discomfort. He said that he was only interested in pay and in his comfort.

Heaton did admit in his memoirs, however, that he "was on the lookout for a more stable career [than a professional militiaman]...a trade which had no future." When his eye fell upon the article in the *Daily Telegraph* of London, announcing Wied's election, Heaton got in touch with Baron Esebeck, Kaiser Wilhelm's Master of the Horse, who knew Wied and arranged a meeting with the Prince at a dinner party. During their conversation, Heaton rather presumptuously suggested to Wied that he should raise a reliable bodyguard of troops, but the Prince explained that this could not be done, "as the Concert [of Great Powers] did not allow him to take on foreign soldiers." Just before the party broke up, Wied came up to Heaton and asked whether he would by any chance be interested in being his private secretary, should Wied's negotiations with someone else break down. Disregarding this somewhat demeaning approach, Heaton told him that he could not type or write shorthand, but— "yes." Wied said that he would let the young man know. There were, after all, five hundred applicants.[19]

Nevertheless, at the end of December 1913, Heaton got a wire telling him that he was hired as "Private Secretary and Comptroller of the Privy Purse," and to report to Potsdam within forty-eight hours. Wied could not very well hire a German or Italian, and so found in Heaton a "neutral" who spoke fluent German, plus French and Italian. (Most correspondence was to be in French and Italian.)[20] Apparently Heaton's references were not even investigated.[21] Wied could now spend the year-end holidays contemplating what promised to be a challenging new year.

12

OMENS

The year 1914 did not have an auspicious beginning for Albania. Wied had actually spent Christmas and New Year's week at the family home at Neuwied, and returned to Potsdam on January 6. On the same date, down in Albania, more trouble was brewing. A Turkish major of Albanian ethnicity named Bekir Aga Grebenaly had recruited other such Turks in Scutari and then met with, among others, Essad in Durazzo and Ismail Kemal in Valona. He offered the latter a Turkish alliance against Greece and Serbia, with Kosovo as a reward. Bekir and 50-200 men (depending on the source of the report), and 3,000 gold napoleon coins (about $210,000 today), booked passage on an Austrian steamer for Valona, where they intended to organize a Muslim insurrection against both the Provisional Government and the Greek authorities in Macedonia. Troops were then supposed to come from Constantinople under an individual named Ismet (or Izzat) Pasha. Ismet was a former Turkish Minister of War, Inspector General of the Turkish Army, and a Turkish Senator. Pursuant to this scheme, on January 6, 1914, Ismet announced that he would accept the throne from the Muslims if Albania was only a principality under Austrian and Italian domination for ten years *(sic)*. The plot was betrayed to Mufid Bey Libohova, Albanian delegate to the International Control Commission, and that body thereupon declared martial law so that the Dutch officers could act. Bekir was arrested when he arrived from Brindisi, Italy, and he and his men were court-martialed. De Veer presided over the court-martial at which Bekir and his men were convicted. Sources differ as to whether Bekir was executed or transferred to Scutari to await Wied's pleasure when he took power. The embarrassed Ismail Kemal offered to resign if Essad would do the same. By January 17, 1914, small warships of Italy and Austria lay moored at Valona beneath Ismail Kemal's windows. Essad seemed to agree to resign, and Ismail temporarily "retired" after January to Nice, on the French Riviera.[1]

German Control Commissioner Nadolny had reported the previous November that, at Alessio, near San Giovanni di Medua, Ded Zoku, a Chief of the Kelmeni (Clementi) Tribe, had established a practically independent sovereignty. He was president of a council of Malissors who came in thousands from the mountains to pass each winter in this maritime region with their flocks and herds. Prenk Bib Doda was then ensconced at Orosh, southeast of Scutari.[2]

From Valona, on January 16, 1914, Nadolny sent another of his perceptive reports to Chancellor Bethmann-Hollweg, which is worth quoting at length:

> During the last weeks the political conditions in Albania have strongly approached the state of disarray, which will lead to an intervention by some side.
>
> In the northwest, in the area of Alessio and Medua, the decisive intervention has already taken place. Ded Zoku [a Malissor in the Alessio region] has not been able to hold out. From one side, from Mirdita, Bib Doda reached out for Alessio. Even his own tribesmen, the Malissors, did not really respect him any more, though he willingly took great trouble to organize and administrate the area. They finally turned to Colonel Phillips in Skutari and asked him to appoint an authority, because they did not want to obey a man whom they had to consider being merely their equal. You might perhaps regard this notion as symptomatic and draw a positive conclusion from it for the recognition of the Prince Europe designated for the country. After consultation with the Control Commission, Colonel Phillips has sent the English Captain Francis to Alessio, together with an Austrian and

an Italian officer. And they have taken charge of the administration of the area of Alessio and Medua, appointing local councils for the individual communities. Ded Zoku has voluntarily given up his leadership. Wat Marasch has also offered his services to the head of the detachment. ...it seems no rebellion ensued from this organization. The temporary arrangement has thus taken a shape there, which will not cause any problems to the assumption of power by the new Prince.

Unfortunately a clarification in this direction has not taken place yet in Middle- and Southern Albania. Essad Pascha and Ismail Kemal Bey are still feuding heavily. They scheme against each other in every way, have everyone coming over from one territory to the other arrested and deported and try if possible to outdo the other. In doing so, they go to any length not to let the other get up. And in everything arranged in the other's territory they look for an affront to themselves. So I am convinced that Ismail Kemal has joined the Young Turk plot mainly because the Prince of Wied intends to move to Durazzo and apparently supports Essad Pascha. On the other hand Essad Pascha has e.g. telegraphed the Control Commission, when a detachment sent by the Dutch officers recently marched toward Elbassan, to move to Koritza in order to protect the South. He considered this a threatening measure Ismail Kemal Bey was taking against them and felt compelled to take steps against it. But the participation of the two in the attack by the Young Turks shows that both of them are not trustworthy, regarding the cause of the prince Europe has chosen.

Essad Pascha is the by far more important and dangerous of the two. His and the influence of his relatives and followers in Middle Albania is apparently great and still spreads more and more. So he has sent his policemen north beyond the Mati and tries to gain control of one village there after the other. The Malissors throng in droves from Alessio and Skutari to Durazzo and return home richly rewarded. As he has pointed out himself, when asked about it, so far more than 2,000 have come to him, allegedly to have a look at the building of the castle for the new prince. In the south he has sent his emissaries against Elbassan, in order to snatch this town from the government of Valona. Admittedly the gangs organized by them have so far not succeeded in capturing the town, as the detachment of police mentioned is stationed there for the time being— until the beginning of the evacuation of the south—and would defend the town. That is why they make do for the time being with a pointless shooting at long range. At the time the sly usurper is outwardly loyal and complaisant toward the Commission. As meaningless and evasive as his answers are, he always offers his services and points out, how ready he is to serve Europe and the new prince. But during his participation in the Young Turk plot he has surely not only double-crossed, like Ismail Kemal Bey, but triple-crossed: outwardly he made preparations for the Prince of Wied, secretly for Izzed Pascha, and inmost—for himself, since it can hardly be assumed that he, the Turkish general, would recognize another Turkish general as ruler. His whole personal propaganda also indicates that he had designated himself for this position, if a Muslim should come

149

to power at all. Possibly he actually takes the view the Albanian throne is meant for him

Ismail Kemal Bey has just about reached the end of his rule. Even though he still stands at the head of the provisional government of the whole of Albania in the wider sense and Southern Albania in the narrower sense in name, his influence has dropped to a minimum. His lack of an executive power has contributed very much to this, because the police force, formed and commanded by the Dutch officers, using the beginnings he had established and the funds from the public purse, cannot be used just as he likes. On the one hand it is first of all supposed to serve a certain purpose, the pacification of the South, on the other hand the Dutch officers naturally follow the Control Commission more closely than him. His powerlessness in this respect has especially shown in the fight for Elbassan, where he wanted to use the police detachment for the campaign against Essad Pascha's gangs, while the commanders, in agreement with the Commission, merely consented to a participation in the protection of the town against a possible attack. In the end his participation in the Young Turk plot, which leaked out has also seriously reduced the esteem for him in Valona itself.

Thus both rulers are ready for elimination, one because he can become oversized otherwise, the other because he has come to the end of the road. Ismail Kemal has accepted the necessity of this consequence and declared to the Commission, he would gladly hand in his resignation if his staying in power would turn out to be an obstacle to the development of Albania, but only if the Commission would take command of the whole of Albania. That is to say the other one has to give up as well. During the last days, though, he seems to have regretted his decision again. But he will probably not cause problems in making way. If you really intend to move the country toward the organization desired by Europe, you have to grab the opportunity now. But reason demands that Ismail Kemal Bey is the first of the two to go. This way the other will be robbed of an essential pretext for his further staying on; and probably it will not be easy anyhow, to make him take the same step. But he will be clever enough to visualize the consequences of a refusal and in the end give up. Instead of the two rulers local authorities shall be installed, which—according to the London decisions—will be under the control of the Commission until the arrival of the prince.

If the resignation of the two rulers could be achieved, there would this way be no power in Middle and Southern Albania either that could oppose the prince's coming into power... If the Prince attaches importance to a delegation of the Albanian population offering him the crown, the Control Commission could perhaps be instructed—right after the achievement of his arrangement with the Powers—to see to the selection and dispatch of the delegation.

The present occupation of the North by the international troops and that of the South by the Greeks can possibly be regarded as disturbing for the arrival of the Prince. Regarding the occupation of the North, though, I would hardly assume this, as you might call the Prince the elected representative of the powers which have their troops there... Apart from the fact that the Prince will be in a much better position than the Commission and the command post of the police to give specific instructions for the effective

151

occupation and organization of the area to be evacuated [in the south], the population of that area will also go ahead with greater confidence and calmness with the entry into a finished state, standing under the authority of a sovereign offering all guarantees, rather than a halfway anarchical one, widely open to all kinds of disturbing influence.

(signed) Nadolny[3]

A retired German army officer, Colonel William Shaefer, who knew Albania well, met Wied and Sophie at this time (January 1914) and stated, "I was taken aback by their absolute ignorance about everything Albanian or Eastern...Both the Prince and Princess looked very miserable at having to go to Albania...The Princess seemed to be gifted with a finer perception, but looked a nervous person." The Wieds reported to Aubrey Herbert, the British Member of Parliament who knew Albania and Albanian better than any other Englishman of his day, that they were finding learning the language "pretty stiff work...we felt almost like children learning geography and all sorts of things one has not learnt for centuries. We see heaps of anxieties and dangers for the future, but we try to see the beautiful and interesting side, as well..."[4] These glimpses of reality were no doubt pressed home when Essad sent a teacher of the Albanian language and customs to Potsdam to help the royal couple.[5]

Colonel Schaefer had been both in the Police and the Coast Guard in Egypt, where he was well known to the British overlords Cromer and Kitchener. In December of 1913, he had been asked by some Romanian friends in the diplomatic service to go to Bucharest on his way back to Germany. He did so, visiting Take Ionescu and Take Maiorescu and then was asked to see King Carol. He had a long audience (Kings give audiences, not conversations) with Carol, who allegedly told him that he would very much like to see him go to Albania to give Wied the benefit of his "long experience of men and things in the East."

Schaefer tried to follow this advice, although neither Wied nor Carol employed him. He was reduced to importuning friends in the British Foreign Office to recommend him, which they politely declined to do.[6]

In 1917, Wied denied that in 1914 he had underestimated "the enormous difficulties" which the job would require because Albania was "still largely on the medieval level of civilization," and because there was no regular system of taxation or even regular customs revenue. He said that he had realized that the granting of the loan by the Powers was of fundamental importance. He had initially resisted appointment, he said, but at the repeated request and urging of the two most interested countries, Austria and Italy, he had agreed, upon certain conditions:

- Recognition by the Great Powers;
- Endorsement by "a delegation of the Albanian people," and
- A guarantee by the Great Powers of a loan of seventy-five million francs (about $14,500,000 in 1914, roughly $270,000,000 today).

The loan would be necessary to pay essential administration officials, including tax and revenue agents, as well as the newly organized police, and "the beginnings of a small army." Also, it would pay for urgent construction of streets and ways to permit industry, trade, and agriculture. He was offered the Crown by what he claimed to be "a delegation elected by the Albanian people, headed by Essad Pasha."

Because of alarming reports of all the unrest, not only on the southern and eastern borders, but in the interior, pressure was placed on Wied to make a decision and hurry to Albania, as the absence of a ruler was considered a cause of much of the problem. In order to speed up his accession, the two most interested Powers, Austria and Italy, decided to guarantee, on their own, advance payment of ten million Francs (about $34,560,000 today) on the loan that was supposed to be jointly guaranteed by all Powers. Other ambassadors told him these things in Berlin, sealing his decision to accept the crown on

February 6, 1914, in a letter to the Ambassadors of all of the Powers.[7]

Wied could still speak no Albanian. Vienna recruited an Albanian escort brigade for him, dressed in newly-designed uniforms. Wied's uniform was grey and black, with medals, including some new ones. Vienna prepared new postage stamps, including one with the black Albanian double-headed eagle with the dates 1467 and 1914 (the first being the victory of Skanderbeg over the Turks), and several stamps with Wied's pictures drawn on them. It is doubtful that any were ever actually used, as letter writing was not a usual activity in 1914 Albania.[8]

As Wied prepared for his great adventure, a meeting was arranged with Kaiser Wilhelm, who was still his emperor and king. As Chancellor Bethmann-Hollweg was present, it likely took place in the gloomy Berlin "*Schloss*" or palace. It was a big, ugly square pile of grey buildings standing straight in the street on all sides but the one where it touched the narrow River Spree. Inside was a rather gloomy, sunless courtyard, paved with cobblestones, in the center of which was a statue of St. George and the Dragon. While the Court was in residence, the palace guard spent its time in perpetual rushes and drummings when a princely personage arrived or departed. A long line of soldiers presented arms to the throb of drums, sounding intermittently from early morning until late at night. There was a constant rapid beat of feet on the cobblestones as the soldiers snatched their arms and fell into line; then came silence, the commands, and then the rumble.

A deep archway lead from the large courtyard into a smaller, more secluded one, which was the entrance to the staircase which the Emperor used. On each side of the large "Hof" (House, or Palace) were big, heavy iron gates kept by soldiers, who all day long closed and opened them to the passing carriages and other traffic.

We would be justified in imagining Kaiser Wilhelm, dressed in his favorite uniform, dismounting from one of his saddle-like stools (which he kept in the offices of all his palaces—even in postwar exile) to greet his distant cousin, Wied. Wied, as he was still an officer in the Imperial Guard, doubtless maintained the appropriate respectful demeanor and probably dressed in the colorful uniform of the Third *Uhlan Garde* Regiment.[9] It was the Kaiser's habit to stand close to his interlocutor, looking him in the eye and speaking earnestly and with emphasis.[10] Until the outbreak of war in 1914, when it became too noisy, the Kaiser's office overlooked the busy city.[11]

The Kaiser, in his 1921 memoirs, ruminated (not entirely accurately) about his attitude in 1913-1914:

> At that time…a number of candidates lusting for a crown had already presented themselves before the tribunal of Powers…A number were declined by the Albanians. I looked upon the matter in itself with indifference, and was of the opinion that—as in the case of every "creation of a nation"—the greatest possible attention should be paid to historical development, also to geographical peculiarities and the customs of the inhabitants.[12]

> With this knowledge of the state of affairs [in Albania] as a foundation, I sought to bring my influence to bear toward having a Mohammedan prince chosen, if possible, perhaps an Egyptian prince—not forgetting that he should have a well-lined purse, which is an absolute necessity in Albania. My advice was not heeded by the "Aeropagus[13] of the Powers," whose members were not bothering themselves with the interests of the Albanians but seeking first of all, for pretexts and opportunities for fishing in the troubled Albanian waters in such a way as to benefit their own countries. Therefore, I was not at all pleased when the choice fell upon Prince William of Wied. I esteemed him as a distinguished, knightly man of lofty sentiments,

155

but considered him unfit for the post. The Prince knew altogether too little about Balkan affairs to be able to undertake this thorny task with hope of success. It was particularly unpleasant to me that a German prince should make a fool of himself there, since it was apparent from the start that the Entente would place all sorts of obstacles in his path. I told my cousin all my doubts, laying stress upon the difficulties awaiting him, and advised him urgently to decline. I could not command him, since the Prince of Wied [i.e., Wilhelm zu Wied's father], as head of the family, had the final word in the matter.

After the Prince's acceptance of the candidacy offered him by the Powers, I received him in the presence of the Chancellor. A certain irresolution in the bearing of the Prince, who contemplated his new task with anything but enthusiasm, strengthened the resolve in me and the Chancellor to try hard once more to dissuade the young candidate from ascending the recently invented Albanian "throne." But in vain. The ambitious, mystically-excited wife of the Prince saw in Albania the fulfillment of her wishes. And *ce que femme veut, Dieu le veut.* [What woman wishes, God wishes.]

Carmen Sylva [the Queen of Romania] also worked toward having him accept; she went so far, in fact, as to publish an article in the newspapers beginning, "Fairyland Wants Its Prince."

So even the best meant warnings were useless. I had also strongly advised the Prince not to go to Albania before the settlement of the financial question, since the reasons which had lead me to suggest the selection of a rich ruler now came to the fore. The Prince was not very

156

wealthy and the Powers had to supply him with a "donation," covering the amount of which, and the method of paying it by installments, an unpleasant quarrel arose. At last a part payment was made.

Danger lurked for the Prince and his eventual government in the person of Essad Pasha, an unreliable, intriguing, greedy soldier of fortune, who himself had designs on the Albanian throne and held sway over a certain number of armed adherents. From the start he was an opponent of the new Prince, and he plotted secretly with Italy, which was not favorably inclined toward the Prince of Wied. Now, it would have been quite natural and a matter of course if the new ruler had taken with him in his suite men from Germany whom he knew and were faithful to him. But he did not. An Englishman and an Italian were attached to his person as "secretaries" and they had nothing better to do than to work against his interests, to give him bad advice and to intrigue against him.

As Wied prepared to go to Albania, a pamphlet by an Austrian General Staff officer who had traveled in Albania "appeared." It described the hardships and backwardness of the country and warned against a future ruler living on the coast, rather than showing himself to the people and traveling about the country, which could only be done on horseback, with money to give out. Since there was no army, he must get the loyalty of some of the clans. This nomadic life could have been supported by volunteers from his German Third Guard Uhlan Regiment.

I advised my cousin urgently to study this pamphlet and to follow its recommendations, especially as to his residence, which should be fixed at some point as far as possible from the warships of the Powers, in order that he might not be forced to act under their pressure and arouse suspicion among the Albanians that their ruler needed these ships for protection against his subjects...Things turned out as I had foreseen. According to reports describing the arrival of the sovereign couple, the Princess, although she was a German, addressed the assembled Albanians from her balcony in French, since they understood no German! They lived on the coast, didn't travel inland, spread gold, or "push" Essad out of the way. In this matter, also, I gave honest advice when questioned, based on sound knowledge of mankind.[14]

On January 7, 1914, Wied's mostly British secretary, Heaton, began his duties. He was not used to deferring to others, especially "out of office hours." At first his duties were light. In the morning he reported to Wied's Potsdam villa to receive instructions. There were only a few important letters to write (but hundreds of refusals to appointment-seekers). He had to stave off a number of men "holding high positions" in their own countries and "ne'er do wells" of many countries. "Adventurers, professional snobs, and swindlers" were given short shrift. One man, wearing medals and "distinctly Semitic," as Heaton described him, came repeatedly wanting to see Wied. Heaton was warned about him by his hotel porter. Wied refused interviews with journalists by either himself or Heaton. This was contrary to Heaton's advice and angered the German press, which later was to turn on Wied.[15]

In a comment on the suggestion that the Powers send warships to force Essad to submit to the International Control Commission, Grey said that he would agree to

...send a ship if all the other powers do so, but if it is a case of sending a land force to take active operations we cannot undertake to participate, but we cannot object to other Powers doing what is necessary to maintain the European decision about Albania.[16]

By January 1914, by force and bribery, the two primary methods of achieving results in Albania at the time, Essad Pasha had managed to establish himself firmly between the Mati and Skumbi rivers, commanding most of central Albania, including the towns of Tirana, Kruja, Kavaya, Shiak, and Durazzo.[17]

By January 12, 1914, Wied made it known that he persisted in his intent to land at and make Durazzo his capital.[18] Despite the pressure to hurry to Albania, on January 13 Wied informed Russia and England that he wanted to get a response to his communication on finances before leaving, and the delay was not his fault.[19]

The European press had scolded Wied for not yet accepting the throne unconditionally and going straight to Albania—"a bold course which it is supposed would have impressed the tribes and prevented the recent raiding attempt at Valona." Ambassador De Bunsen sympathized with Wied's caution, however.[20]

By January 16, Germany also had made clear its disapproval of the Austrian-Italian Bank monopoly.[21] Austria-Hungary and Italy had hoped, in return for sixty-percent of the capital, for predominance in the bank and to place their personnel in a majority of the positions, but Russia joined in demanding complete equality for all.[22] Another asset of the country, its forests, had been devastated. Already an Austrian exploring party was in the field under the direction of a somewhat mysterious syndicate organized and financed in Vienna. This syndicate was ostensibly made up of a number of Austrian aristocrats with Count Carl Trautmansdorff at their head, but it was openly said in the Austrian capital that this distinguished gentleman and his associates represented far more "august" personages interested in the matter. ("August" usually meant royalty). The expedition set out as ostensibly a "scientific" one, but was accompanied by mining experts and road building engineers.

Their plan, so far as is known, included first of all a survey for a railroad between Valona and Scutari, and for highways to connect Albania's harbors and Durazzo with the interior, to facilitate the export of agricultural products. It was seemingly a plan for exploitation rather than for development and for the acquisition by outright purchase of whatever promised to pay rich returns.[23]

On January 16, Wied's medical advisor, Dr. Berghausen, arrived at Trieste from Durazzo, where he had been inspecting the building chosen for the future residence of Wied. It was said that the repairs and "adaptation" would be completed the next week, and the doctor even carried a letter to Wied from Essad promising his "fidelity and support."[24]

On January 17, British Consul and International Control Commissioner Lamb in Valona reported that Essad had expelled Serbian Consul (and Serbian Army Colonel) Bozhin Simich from Durazzo, but secretly sent word to the Serbs that he wanted to be friends with Serbia. Simich had been one of the secret agents who contacted Isa Boletin in the spring of 1912 to incite him to rebellion against Turkey. Lamb opined that Ismail Kemal was weak, and Essad too strong to yield to any but force, but felt both had to be "set aside." He suggested sending 500 to 600 British troops from Scutari, where they had been kept within "the ten kilometer zone" along with marines of other nations, to Durazzo. This would preempt any attempt by Essad to declare himself King. Lamb reported that Nogga Bey (presumably Phillip Nogga), Kristo Mexi Bey, Sureya Bey Vlora, his son Ekrem Bey Vlora, and Mufid Bey Libohova were all in the pay of Austria and Djemil Bey. Djemil and his wife went to Potsdam and Princess Wied was rumored to intend to make Madam Djemil a *dame d'honneur* at court, along with "some other mussulman lady," which would be an insult to devout Muslims.[25] However, the rumor proved unfounded and German ladies were selected instead.

In early 1914, Heaton occasionally lunched or dined at Wied's villa in Potsdam and met 32 year-old Ekrem Bey Libohova (later Wied's *aide de camp*) and portly 34 year-old Anglophile Ekrem Bey Vlora (nephew of Ismail Kemal Vlora).[26] They were Muslims, highly cultured and well-educated. They advised (accurately, as it proved) that Wied could not possibly govern without bringing an army. Wied could not be convinced. He said the Powers would not allow mercenaries. A Herr von Trotha, "a typical Prussian officer of the best type, honorable and straightforward," was named Comptroller of the Household. Two German ladies-in-waiting to the Princess were appointed: Fraulein von Oidtmann and Fraulein von Pfuel, sister-in-law of Chancellor Bethmann-Hollweg. There were to be two Political Secretaries, members of a sort of Privy Council attached to the Court: Captain Fortunato Castoldi (formerly Italian Boundary Commissioner and governor of Tripoli), and Vice Consul Buchberger. They would unofficially represent, respectively, Italy and Austria at Court. Castoldi had been strongly recommended by Italy and was to be influential at first.[27]

At Potsdam, Wied worked hard, reading and writing all day, and trying to learn about his new kingdom. Nothing much happened, but a new coat of arms, flag, and uniforms were invented by German and Austrian advisors. Too much time was spent on this sort of thing to suit Heaton. Wied proved to have an amiable disposition but could not make up his mind on even simple matters. He was very popular with brother German officers but they were not optimistic of his qualifications as a ruler. Von Trotha and most of the European staff went to Durazzo to fix up the old *Konak*, or Turkish government building, uninhabited for years, as the palace.[28] Sophie was persuaded to be cautious and leave her best household goods, including many valuable pieces and "historical souvenirs," in Potsdam until things were settled.[29]

On January 20, Grey reported to Ambassador Bertie in Paris that the British Cabinet had agreed in Parliament to guarantee the loan of three million pounds (about $270,000,000 today) if all the Powers did the same, but the loan was not to be issued through the Austro-Italian Bank. As for military assistance, French Ambassador Cambon reported to Grey that Gaston Doumergue, (for the moment both Prime Minister and Foreign Minister of France) agreed that France would send a warship to Albania if the other Powers, except for Russia, did, but would not ever land troops. Grey said Britain took the same position. Let Austria and Italy land forces, if any. But in that case, fretted Cambon, all would have to.[30]

On January 21, Ismet (Izzat) Pasha in Constantinople said he had nothing to do with "the deplorable events" of the recent attempted coup in Durazzo and Valona. Although his family had owned land in Albania for five centuries, given by the Sultan, he said that he would only agree to govern if accepted by all Albanians and all Powers. On the other hand, he said that he thought Wied's arrival "might incur great risk, in view of the excitement of the Musulman [sic] element of the country."[31]

That morning, Greek Prime Minister Eleutherios Venizelos visited Grey in London and suggested an alteration in the southern Albanian border, establishment of Greek schools, and freedom of religion in "Epirus." As usual, Grey was agreeable if Austria and Italy were.[32]

The next day, the International Control Commission at Valona sent Mufid Bey to Durazzo to inform Essad and Ismail Kemal finally that they must go, and they more or less agreed to resign their powers to the International Control Commission, which then appointed Feizi Bey Alizot as "Director General of Internal Affairs." Meanwhile, Turkey (hoping for a comeback) and Italy maintained secret ties with Essad, as every regional power save Austria seems to have done.[33] Also on January 22, Colonel George F. Phillips of the West Yorkshire Regiment replaced the naval brigade in Scutari with an international force. The British contingent consisted of 8 officers and 383 other ranks.

As Nadolny had reported, an able Klementi tribesman, Ded Soko, had set up an efficient administration in the Alessio-Medua area. Prenk Bib Doda, his rival, had contrived the murder of Ded's brother. Prenk considered Ded a usurper, as Prenk's family had ruled the area for generations and he hoped to keep his Serb subsidy by reclaiming it. Ded asked Colonel Phillips to appoint an authority over the two, and after consulting the Commission, Phillips sent British Captain S.G. Francis, one Austrian officer and one Italian officer, along with a British detachment, to Alessio. Ded then retired. Albania was thus finally united except for the area occupied by Greece.[34] The way was clearing for Wied.

On January 24, Ismail Kemal Bey resigned his office as Provisional President into the hands of the International Control Commission and the Provisional Government was dissolved. Essad had been asked to resign as "Governor of Central Albania," and said he would, but on certain conditions.[35]

The International Control Commission began to organize the central government that replaced the provisional government. It was reduced to twelve officials. Each minister was to get 3,500 Turkish piasters a month (perhaps $2,700 today) and "Director General" Feizi Bey got 6,000 (perhaps $4,750 today). The German and British members of the International Control Commission left for Durazzo on January 25 to confer with Essad, the last holdout.[36]

The loan guarantee soon began to hit snags. On January 23, The German Foreign Office noted that it would be impossible for Germany to join with Austria and Italy in guaranteeing the Albanian loan. The Reichstag would not vote the funds as Germany, like Britain, had no real stake in Albania.[37] The Reich Treasury office confirmed this in a telegram to the German Embassy in Rome.[38]

On January 27, King Carol told French Minister Blondel, "the task [tâche] of my nephew will not be easy. I have not pushed him to accept it; I have left him entirely free in his decision, and, when he shall be installed in Albania, I am ready to profit him by the experience that I have acquired of public affairs. I don't want to mix into the actual negotiations."[39] However, the elderly Carol is supposed to have once said to Wied, "as long as I'm on the throne of Romania, you won't leave Albania.[40]

163

From St. Petersburg on January 27 the German Embassy reported that "the Austrian and Italian *chargés* have both been given a letter by Sazanov with which the Russian Government gives its agreement to grant a loan to the Albanian Principality. Sazanov thereupon explained that he has been in principle agreeable with the loan..."[41]

By January 28, Britain had agreed with the French and Russians that Greece would not be responsible for peace in southern Albania after it withdrew its troops. The Powers naively decided that they could always pressure Prince Wied on that score. Britain, France, and Russia decided neither to recognize the contemplated Albanian State Bank nor to guarantee the proposed Albanian loan independently of the question of control over Albanian policy. Britain contemplated the presence of an international naval squadron to observe and enforce decisions of the Powers.[42]

On January 29, Ambassador Flotow reported from Rome to the Foreign Office in Berlin that "from today's telegram from Vienna, Count Berchtold accepts the participation of Austria and Italy together making up sixty percent and the other Powers together, forty percent" of the Albanian Bank. San Giuliano told Flotow he believed that Austria and Italy—if Prince Wied sped up his departure—would be ready to advance the prince ten million francs.[43]

On January 30, Essad made his position clear. He demanded of the British and German Control Commissioners that he be appointed Minister of War in any cabinet as a condition of his resignation from the position that he purported to hold.[44] In response, he was authorized by the International Control Commission, at his request, to meet Wied in Germany as the Albanian people's representative and to return with him.[45] Finally agreeing to resign, he was officially so appointed on February 6.[46]

Austria and Italy now became more realistic about the Albanian Bank. By February 3, German Ambassador von Tschirschky reported to Berlin that the responsible Section Chief in the Austrian Foreign Ministry had told him that, upon the urging of the Roman Cabinet, the Austro-Hungarian government would give up their opposition to the participation by other Powers in the Albanian Bank. Count Berchtold was told by the Duke of Avarna in a lengthy conversation that only in this way would France and Russia participate in the guarantee of the Albanian loan. One could then give the Albanian Bank administration an international character, but still hope as before that the local management of the bank as a practical matter would remain in the hands of Austria and Italy. As a result, Berchtold confidently hoped for effective support of Germany in the bank question. Section Chief Ippen told Berchtold that the representative of the Vienna Bank Association was present in Berlin to speak with German Treasury Counselor Helmreich as agent of the Prince of Wied to discuss the different questions concerning the Albanian Bank. However, the representative of the Banca Commerciale was not able to take part in those discussions.[47] In London Austrian Ambassador Mensdorff proposed to Grey that Britain recognize the special interests of Austria and Italy in the Albanian Bank, but Grey resisted.[48]

On February 6, Heaton had been sent to Vienna to buy horses for the Prince's use in Albania, and bought of team of bays at a low price.[49]

The same day, in a fateful letter addressed by Wied to each of the ambassadors of Britain, France, and Russia in Berlin, he wrote (in French):

Potsdam, February 6, 1914

Mr. Ambassador,

The Ambassadors of Austria-Hungary and Italy in Berlin have just informed me in the name of their governments that an Austro-Hungarian bank institute and an Italian Bank institute— acting under the guarantee of their respective governments—are ready to place immediately at my disposal, for the government of Albania, a sum of 10 million francs,[50] as an advance on the total amount of the 75 million loan [$15,000,000 in 1914], to the guarantee of which the other Great Powers have in principle shown themselves likewise disposed.

In bringing the preceding to Your Excellency's attention, I have the honor to declare to you that I have decided to accept the throne of Albania and to proceed to Albania soon.

Would you please, Mr. Ambassador, accept the expression of my highest admiration.

Wilhelm[51]

However, before he left Germany for his courtesy calls to his sponsoring Powers, Wied received a letter at his villa at No. 12 Albrechtstrasse in Potsdam (addressing him correctly as "*Durchlaucht*," and not "*Hoheit*"). Dated February 7, it reported on the financial discussions which had taken place between the German Treasury representative and others in regard to the proposed Albanian State Bank and stressed that the Austrians were only giving up their joint monopoly in the bank with Italy in return for a majority interest in the bank. The treaty which the French and other Powers had made in 1904, setting up the Moroccan State Bank, was given as an example to be followed.[52]

It was learned that, in Albania, Wied was to officially be addressed as "*Madheri*" which was the equivalent of "Majesty," and have the title of "*Mbret*," which is, roughly, "King." But the diplomats, not the grammarians, decided that the English meaning of *Mbret* is "Prince." A diplomatist "who had a great hand in the creation of the Albanian State," explained that they wanted to first be sure Wied was firmly and permanently planted on the throne, as it would be embarrassing to have another ex-king running about in Europe. The London Agreement called merely for a "*principauté*" or principality.[53] Wied was quoted as telling a Potsdam friend on the eve of his departure for Albania, "I prefer to be 'Prince.' It will be easy to go back to the title of Prince of Wied after having been Prince of Albania, but a dethroned 'King of Albania' would be a ridiculous figure to the end of his days."[54] Sadly prophetic words.

13

THE TRAVELING PRINCE

On February 7, Greek Prime Minister Venizelos was in Berlin and had a cordial conversation with Wied regarding the promised Epirus evacuation of Greek troops and settlement of the frontier.[1] Unfortunately, events did not conform to this beginning.

Wied planned to pass through Rome, see the King of Italy, travel to Neuwied to receive the Albanian deputation which would offer him the throne, and then arrive in Albania on February 20.[2] Such a slight to Russia was unwise, however, and von Jagow convinced Wied that he must visit Russia as well, before going to Albania.[3]

In early February diplomatic luncheons and other hospitalities were held in Berlin for Wied by the Austrians, Hungarians, Italians, and Romanians living there. Wied's furniture and some of his officials had already left for Albania. It was "semi–officially" announced that all six Powers had now agreed to guarantee the Albanian loan of £3,000,000 (about $270,000,000 today) and Austria and Italy agreed to advance up to £500,000 ($45,000,000 today) "for immediate requirements."[4]

On February 9, Wied departed for Rome "incognito"[5] and arrived that evening, staying at the Hotel Excelsior, which flew an Albanian flag in his honor.[6]

The French ambassador reported to his government that Wied did not meet the Pope on this visit because Italy opposed it. The Italian government's estrangement from the Vatican dated at least from the unification of Italy in 1870, when the Italians seized Rome from the popes. The French ambassador added that, "I have heard pronounced in other terms by other diplomats and by Italian political men, that the Prince of Wied generally produced a good impression, but I have encountered none who had discerned in him the faculties necessary to surmount the difficulties of all sorts which oppose the consolidation of his ephemeral royalty."[7]

On February 10 Wied spent the morning in "prolonged" visits to San Giuliano and Prime Minister Giolitti. In the afternoon he paid the customary visit to the Pantheon and then to the Quirinal Palace for a long talk with King Vittorio Emmanuele. That night he was given a state banquet and the King awarded him the Grand Cordon of the Order of Saint Maurice and Saint Lazarus.[8] German Ambassador Flotow was the only foreign ambassador invited to the banquet. Presumably this invitation was not only because of Wied's nationality, but in hopes of influencing Germany's cooperation on the bank question. Echoing the Kaiser's advice, King Vittorio Emmanuele warned Flotow that it was essential that Wied form a devoted life guard of some one hundred Albanians from "loyal houses" to ensure his security.

The Prince had made a hit in Rome with both the press and Italian leaders. They were struck by the fact that he visited Rome first, before Vienna, and by his "elegant looks" and obliging appearance. San Giuliano told Flotow that, after he overcame Wied's "peculiar reserve," he found him to have a clever and full understanding of all conditions. The Italian was also pleased that Wied was well-advised by a devoted and "clever advisor," Capitano Castoldi, who just happened to be Italian.[9]

The same morning, Wied's doctor, Dr. Berghausen, his German major-domo von Trotha, and a male and female servant arrived in Durazzo. They told enquirers that they knew little of Wied's movements except that he was to leave Trieste for Durazzo on February 25.[10]

Wied called on Sir J. Rennell Rodd, British Ambassador in Rome, and, to Rodd's eye, "seemed to have little conception of the elemental social conditions prevailing in the primitive land, to which the Princess was to follow him with state coaches, liveries, and all the equipment of a little court."[11]

On February 11, Wied lunched at the German Embassy in Rome and then visited the dowager Queen Margherita.[12] He met with Herr von Gwinner of the (German) Deutsche Bank in Rome with regard to the difficult question of participation of German capital in the economic development of Albania. There is no record of Wied making any specific commitments, especially in view of his very tentative situation.[13]

Later in the day Ambassador von Flotow arranged a meal at the German Embassy to honor the Prince, and the Marquess di San Giuliano and other prominent political personalities participated. Two points proved delicate upon this visit. First of all, the question of a visit to the Vatican. The Prince told Flotow that the Austro-Hungarian ambassador, whom he had also sought out, had fairly urgently recommended the visit to the Pope. Franz Josef of Austria-Hungary was a Catholic monarch. Wied was of opinion, however, that the "incognito" nature of his presence made a visit to the Vatican unnecessary. In addition, he felt that, to the majority of the educated Albanian population, the visit would make the worst impression, especially upon the Muslims. He correctly believed that, both Palace and Government in Rome would not be happy to see such a visit. Flotow cautiously asked Marquess San Giuliano his opinion, and the minister replied with great decisiveness that a visit to the Vatican would doubtless ruin the favorable impression of the Prince's visit.

The second difficulty concerned the method of arrival of the Prince in Albania. He told Flotow upon parting that he had been reminded in Rome that a voyage to Albania from an Austrian port in an Austrian ship would be felt by the Italian public as a one-sided tilt toward Austria and as a preponderance by the Danube Monarchy in the future Albanian state. He had already feared this and had fought those impressions by the priority he had given to his visit in Rome. It seemed to him, however, that this was not felt to be enough, although San Giuliano had not yet spoken of the matter to the German ambassador.[14]

With typical journalistic unreliability, certain Italian newspapers, especially the *Corriere della Sera*, reported that Prince Wied had, during his visit in Rome, sought an audience with the Pope. The paper pretended that it was informed of the exact details of the audience and that it had actually observed the ceremony. The news was widely circulated, although Wied made no visit to the Pope. The Cardinal State-Secretary, with whom the Prussian minister dined along with Sophie's brother, Prince Gunther Schönburg-Waldenburg (part of Wied's suite), "betrayed a certain upset over this omission." The suspicion was left with diplomatic observers that the report of the audience was a trial balloon (*ballon d'essai*) from the Vatican. Prince Schönburg reported further that the Austro-Hungarian ambassador to the Quirinal, Count Kajetan Mérey von Kapos-Mére, again sought out Wied and asked the Prince if he would be presented to the Pope. Wied emphatically declined and declared his regret.[15] He left for Vienna the night of the 11th.

Meanwhile, in Albania, in early February 1914, Essad spent eleven thousand Turkish pounds (about $871,200 today) for a ceremony in Durazzo wherein "Mountaineers of Skutari" come to "do homage" to him. He refused to allow an Austrian school to open in Tirana (no doubt to please Italy and Serbia) and hoped Wied would confirm him as Minister of War, a move which Lamb predicted would be "fatal to the prince's chance of success, though inevitable."[16] Essad was said to intend, with Austria's blessing, to address Wied as "Your Majesty" (the proper salutation for a king) in his greeting speech, so that Wied would have equal rank with the King of Montenegro.[17]

In Berlin, a Professor Dopler designed a new coat of arms for Albania to replace "a somewhat emaciated-looking eagle," which, since Ismail Kemal's arrival in 1912, had been their symbol. Now, a traditional double-headed black eagle on a red shield held in its claws a thunderbolt, and on his breast bore a peacock with outspread tail, which was from the arms of Wied's house. From between the eagles' heads shone a white star.[18]

On February 12, Wied's train was met at the Austrian frontier by Baron Buchberger, former Austrian Vice-Consul in Albania, who was now to be part of Wied's suite. That day Essad gave a speech in Albania, expatiating upon the historical importance of the day, and saying, "with the arrival of the prince will begin a new era of freedom and progress."[19] He apparently had been assured of his position in Wied's cabinet. Essad and twelve deputies then left Durazzo on an Italian steamer, and (to taunt the Austrians) sailed to Bari, Italy, rather than Austrian Trieste, and thence headed by train to Rome and Neuwied. He also finally formally resigned his Provisional Government Commission. The delegation which he headed was to tender the throne to Wied.[20]

Early on February 13, Wied's train pulled into Vienna. He was met at the station by an Austrian officer who was to be attached to him for his visit at the command of the Emperor Franz Josef. He was then greeted by a representative of the Ballplatz, a large crowd, and by a number of Albanian boys being educated in Vienna, who cried, *"Rroft Mbreti!"* ("Long live the King!"). He and his suite were then taken to the palatial marble and gold Hotel Imperial, where he was the Emperor's guest. The hotel flew the yellow and black flag of the Habsburgs instead of the new Albanian banner. Imperial carriages were put at Wied's disposal and he visited briefly with members of the Austrian imperial family in Vienna and various ambassadors, including the Papal Nuncio. Berchtold gave a breakfast in his honor, attended by the German Ambassador von Tschirschky, Italian ambassador the Duke of Avarna, Prince Schönburg, Austrian Prime Minister Count Stürgkh, the Catholic Bishop of Durazzo, and a Foreign Ministry official. In the afternoon he went to the German Embassy. In the evening, he was received by the Imperial Master of Ceremonies at suburban Schönbrunn Palace and immediately taken for a private audience with the Emperor in his private room. All the Palace officials and Wied's suite, including the German Ambassador, von Tschirschky, were in full dress uniform. Heaton was introduced to Franz Josef, who spoke kindly to him in German. The Emperor twice expressed to Wied his regret and chagrin that Wied did not visit the Pope in Rome. Wied stood his ground and replied that he would have to deal in Albania with three different religions, and could not appear to favor any one. He said that the Papal Nuncio in Vienna had made the same complaint, to which he had given the same reply.

The old Habsburg empire, in its twilight, could still produce elegant hospitality. In the evening, a dinner was given by the Emperor in Wied's honor at Schönbrunn at which the Prince was decorated with the Grand Cross of the Order of Leopold. Both Franz Josef and Count Berchtold reported to the German ambassador that, despite Wied's reserved manner, their impression of him was favorable. The Austrians had reported the complicated situation in Albania to Wied and he seemed to take a thorough interest in what they said. Despite all that, he told them that he looked forward to dealing with his task, but with caution. He was very pleased by his warm Viennese welcome. The next day, he was taken to the *Hof Reitschule* (Spanish Riding School) at the Hofburg Palace in Vienna to see the famous white stallions go through their paces. Before leaving Vienna, Wied paid a long visit to the Bank Verein, the principal bank in the Austro-Hungarian group interested in the Albanian State Bank. No doubt exhausted by his busy schedule, after another lunch at the German Embassy and a further talk with Berchtold, Wied and his retinue boarded a loaned Imperial train carriage to leave for Berlin. At the German border they were returned to reality when an officious German railroad officer made them buy twelve tickets before they could proceed over the German rails.

On the same day Wied had arrived in Vienna, Essad and the Albanian delegation, charged with offering him the crown, had arrived in Rome. To demonstrate Italy's interest in them, they were met at the railroad station by Italian Foreign Ministry officials and a group of Albanian residents in Rome. Essad met with San Giuliano that afternoon at the *Consulta*, and was treated with "cordiality" according to reports. In many respects, Essad was to become Italy's man in Albania—insofar as he was for anyone other than himself.[21]

While Wied was busy in Vienna, on February 13 British Ambassador Elliott handed Greek Foreign Minister Streit a note from the Great Powers, jointly ordering Greece to hand over Northern Epirus to Albania and warning of dire consequences should there be a Greek-supported uprising in that province. The Epirus Greeks and the Greek government feared a massacre of ethnic Greeks by the Muslim Albanians when the Greek army withdrew, but the Greek government yielded to the Powers.[22]

Wied arrived back in Berlin the morning of February 15.[23] After two days of rest, on the morning of February 17 he left Germany for Flushing, Holland, the jumping off point to London. He had decided by now to also visit Paris and St. Petersburg to avoid the appearance that he was under the sole patronage of the Triple Alliance.[24]

Essad's character (or lack thereof) did not escape the notice of the German Embassy in Rome. One of its informants, a reporter for the German newspaper *Die Lokal Anzeiger*, named Nebel (a *nom de plume*, perhaps?), who knew Albanians and their language well, spoke to Essad and Sureya bey Vlora in Rome. Nebel felt that Sureya, from one of the great Albanian families, had much influence upon Essad. Sureya told Nebel that housing conditions in Durazzo were so bad that Wied could not stay there, and would be forced to stay in Essad's *konak* in Tirana, where Essad could control him. Nebel further reported that Essad seemed to have entrée to high government circles in Rome, even attending Palace balls, and boasted of what he was doing for Wied. The German Embassy concluded, with some inadvertent understatement, that "It seems not out of the question that the Italian Government will later make use of him."[25]

On the morning of February 18, Wied arrived in England at Folkestone by the Flushing Boat Express, and traveled from there to Victoria Station in London in a reserved train compartment. He was met at the station by King George's Master of Ceremonies, the Honourable Sir Arthur Walsh, along with members of the German Embassy staff. German Ambassador Prince Lichnowsky supplied a carriage to convey him and Walsh to his suite at the Ritz Hotel. After breakfast, he made the obligatory courtesy visits to the German, Austro-Hungarian, French, and Italian embassies. At 1:30 p.m. he was taken to Buckingham Palace, where he and his retinue were received at the entrance by Lord John Hamilton (who was soon known as "Jack" by Heaton) and Wied was escorted to meet King George and Queen Mary for lunch. Probably the talk was confined to generalities, as Grey and Asquith controlled political matters. Heaton lunched with the household staff, and Hamilton joked that Heaton disappointed them as they had expected him to look a bloodthirsty bandit, which would have been a change from their dull routine. The King awarded the Grand Cross of the Victorian Order to Wied in a red morocco case, and the Prince was soon on his way to the Foreign Office to meet Foreign Secretary Sir Edward Grey, after dropping off calling cards for Prime Minister Asquith and Under-Secretary Sir Arthur Nicolson.

Grey told Wied that he was sure all Powers wished him well. Though there would be many difficulties, he said all reports from "unofficial Englishmen" (and Englishwomen, perhaps, like Durham?) who had traveled to Albania, were in favor of the people of the country, especially since the heavy hand of Turkish rule was now lifted. He pointed out, however, that he had told Austria and Italy that the advance they were making to Wied from the loan to be guaranteed by all the Powers should be spent "by arrangement with the International Commission of Control." In other words, Wied would not be able to spend the money as he pleased. There were points still being discussed by the Powers. First, the necessity of all Powers having an equal share in the National Bank of Albania, or else Parliament might not agree to guarantee the loan Wied required. If shares were unequal, Grey could only urge upon Parliament that Britain, as one of the founders of Albania, had a moral obligation to it, even if she were not to have an equal voice in the Bank. Second, it was important that the expenditure of advances from the loan should be controlled by the International Control Commission. He then said diplomatically that, "in order that these troublesome financial questions should be as little disagreeable as possible" to Wied, the governments would do the discussing of the matter between themselves. Wied's reply is not recorded, but he either did not grasp the ominous import of Grey's words, or he changed the subject. He expressed his pleasure at his reception by the King but said that he was leaving for Paris at once, and regretted that the distance to St. Petersburg made it impossible to go there before receiving the Albanian delegation which was to formally offer him the throne.

Prince Lichnowsky reported to Berlin that Wied had, as he had done in Rome and Vienna, made an excellent impression during his short visit, on both Grey and the King. Grey had told Lichnowsky that the British Government wished Wied well, and would gladly support the loan guarantee of one-sixth if Britain participated equally in the National Bank, and if the loan was controlled by the International Control Commission. Lichnowsky replied that, although he had no exact instructions, he assumed that Germany would agree with Grey. The International Control Commission financial guardianship would be hard on Wied at the beginning, but he was expected to do well.[26]

Meanwhile, back in what had become southern Albania, a meeting of Representative Epirotes had taken place at Argyrocastro at which outrage was expressed at Greece agreeing unconditionally to withdraw from Albania. The Epirote leaders told a reporter that they considered their position desperate, and preferred to send their families to Greece and die fighting "rather than be exterminated by Albanian brigands." The Greek government had tried to persuade them to accept the situation, as resistance was hopeless and only caused trouble for Greece. The Epirote Commission said that they would, on February 19, appeal to the representatives of the Powers in Albania for "adequate safeguards," or else "the fight will begin in earnest."

Essad and the Albanian delegation arrived at Cologne on February 20.[27]

The *Taurus*, formerly a yacht, which up to that time had acted as the token Austrian Naval presence at Constantinople, would now be loaned to Wied and soon play a more prominent role in Albania.[28]

In St. Petersburg on February 18, German Ambassador Count Pourtalès reported to Bethmann-Hollweg that Russian Foreign Minister Sazanov had told the Italian ambassador and

175

the Austro-Hungarian Commercial representative that Russia would agree to the loan advance to Wied as Wied conceded that it be made through the International Control Commission. Sazanov said that Russia had yielded to the request of King Carol of Romania that no difficulties should be put in Wied's path, and observed, "one cannot refuse the King of Romania anything good." Although secretly allied to the Triple Alliance, Romania was being busily courted by Russia.

Wied's visit to Paris met with little enthusiasm. When his train pulled into the Paris station early on February 19 after the overnight trip from London, he was met by only a secretary from the German Embassy. As Wied alighted from the train, a bright flash and loud report of a photographer's magnesium powder flashgun aroused momentary fear of an assassination attempt. The French government did not provide a carriage, a festive reception, or an escort of colorful Republican Guards on horseback, as was usually provided to the heads of state and other important visitors. The French were given an excuse by German Ambassador Baron von Schoen's earlier remark to them that the visit was unofficial and by the low-key reception in London. Wied had reserved rooms in the Hotel du Rhin, where he had stayed before, but the French were not paying for them. President Poincaré did invite him to breakfast at the Elyseé Palace, however, and they were joined by the Prime Minister and Foreign Minister of the moment, Gaston Doumergue, by M. de Margerie, a French Foreign Office (*Quai d'Orsay*) official, and by some members of the "institute." Wied then met with Doumergue for further talks. The talks went pleasantly enough, and de Margerie commented somewhat undiplomatically to Baron von Schoen later that Wied "had none of the disagreeable characteristics commonly associated with the idea of a Prussian officer." He said further that Wied should "lean" on the International Control Commission until he got his footing and let it approve expenditures of the loan advance so that no one could question them later. France opposed Austria and Italy's claims to thirty percent, each, of the Albanian Bank, which those Powers had based on France's similar predominance in the

Moroccan State Bank when it was set up a few years earlier. The advances to Wied by Austria and Italy would be at their own risk, the French asserted.

Before leaving Paris, Wied met privately with Baron von Schoen and reported that the French had told him "in a friendly way," that it would be in the interest of Albania to remember that it was created by *all* the Powers, and was an independent state.

Wied had made courtesy calls in Paris on Russian Ambassador Isvolsky and the ambassadors of the other Great Powers, and Isvolsky told him not to forget to visit St. Petersburg before he ascended the throne. This put Wied in something of a bind, as he was to meet the Albanian delegation in a few days, and was being pressured, especially by the Albanians, to take charge there as soon as possible. Wied asked von Schoen's opinion, and he told the Prince that failure to take Isvolsky's "hint" could lead to "uncomfortable consequences." Wied said that he would consider the trip if Chancellor Bethmann-Hollweg would send him a statement that it would be a good idea. This would give him an excuse for further postponing his removal to Albania.

As they prepared to leave Paris, Heaton went to settle the account at the hotel and found that the proprietor, one of Wied's countrymen, had padded the bill![29]

In 1922, a wealthy American divorcée with a somewhat chequered past, Roberta Menges Hill Tearle, made the claim that she had renewed an acquaintance with Wied at the Hotel Continental during this visit to Paris, and loaned him some $125,000 (about $2,250,000 in today's money). Wied supposedly then promised to make her "unofficial ambassador of Albania to Paris."[30] Although she dropped some fairly specific names of people and places, and Wied was in need of money in 1914, her story is rendered highly unlikely by the brevity of Wied's Paris visit, the failure of his Secretary Heaton-Armstrong to mention her in his memoirs of Wied, by Wied's exalted status at the time, and by his apparent assurance of funding by the Great Powers. Of course, as Mrs. Tearle said, "You can't ask a King for an I.O.U., you know that."[31]

Wied and entourage left Paris the same evening of their arrival and reached Neuwied by late the next morning. They stayed at *Mon Repos*, the modern country home owned by Wied's two spinster sisters overlooking the town of Neuwied,.[32]

As Wied arrived in Paris, Ambassadors Cambon and Benckendorff came, together, to see Grey. Cambon wanted to be sure that all agreed to (1) equal participation in the bank, (2) disbursement of advances to be controlled by the International Control Commission, and (3) after Wied's arrival, all powers except that of the executive, would be retained by the Commission. Grey agreed, saying that he thought "…the proper course would be for [Wied] to consult with the…Commission as to the formation of an *"Autorité Indigène"* [native authority] which would be the executive, the Commission of Control retaining the powers that had been assigned to it at the reunions [sic] in London…" One might well ask what powers this left to Wied. Grey suggested that Wied discuss with Premier Doumergue what would happen if Austria and Italy made the entire loan. Cambon felt that Italy wanted support against Austria.[33]

On March 4, 1914 Cambon and Benckendorff again came to Grey's office. Doumergue had refused to give Austria and Italy sixty-percent of the bank. The ambassadors proposed an English president of the bank, but Grey would not be drawn into that formula unless all requested it.[34]

14

THE CEREMONY

On February 21, 1914, Prince Wilhelm zu Wied and Princess Sophie borrowed his elder brother's palace, *Schloss Neuwied*, in which to receive the Albanian delegation who bore the formal offer of the crown. The *Schloss* is a barn-like, canary yellow Seventeenth Century structure of two main stories and a Mansard roof. At the appointed time, Wied, wearing his Prussian Army major's uniform with fringed epaulets, and Sophie, in impressive flowing royal robes and diadem, joined the other members of his family to await the delegation. To the irritation of Secretary Heaton-Armstrong, all male non-military participants were expected to wear white tie and tails or frock coats, after the continental fashion, even though it was daytime.

The little town of Neuwied was gaily decorated for the occasion. Near the train station was a triumphal arch draped with the colors of Germany, Albania, and the Wied family, and the black double eagle of Albania rested beneath a golden crown. Every window was filled with sightseers. The day before, the Bishop of Durazzo had told a Berlin reporter that Essad was "a brigand in the best and worst sense of the term, and a fox who would require an iron hand to keep him under control." This idea spread quickly among the journalists at Neuwied, and they were keen to set eyes on Essad. A curious crowd assembled outside the little train station.

Due to a lack of coordination, Wied's brother and his retainers went to greet the delegation at the same time Heaton and the others were dispatched, each unaware of the other's mission. The result was that each group "tried to elbow each other out of the field." When the train from Cologne bearing the delegates arrived at noon, Wied's Lord Chamberlain and the town *bürgermeister* (mayor) met them at the station. The mustachioed, barrel-chested Captain Castoldi alighted as ostensible head of the Albanian group, most of whom appeared

179

rather uncomfortable in their new top hats and frock coats. Essad, however, gave no such sign, and appeared very much the capable patriarch, which delighted the onlooking children.

The delegation of eighteen Albanians from different districts then proceeded to the *Schloss* by autos and carriages, where a German military band played a selection of music. Heaton and the reporters arrived last.

Sophie stood beside Wied (contrary to Muslim custom) to graciously receive the guests, and the delegate Miltiades Salvari tendered a small casket containing sand, earth and water from Albania. There was a small ceremony at which Essad made a speech in Albanian, not a word of which the royal couple understood until Ekrem Bey Vlora translated it, saying that the deputation represented all of Albania and that they were happy to welcome their new sovereign and would be true to him. Essad had at first addressed Wied as "Serene Highness," (presumably in Italian or French), but ended by calling him *Mbret*, or "king," as there was no Albanian word for Prince, and *Mbret* (a corruption of *Imperator*, Latin for emperor) meant "holder of supreme power." Wied replied in German, which few if any of the delegates understood, and accepted the throne of the tiny kingdom. He spoke with surprising candor, saying that he had made his mind up only after very much consideration, and at first the difficulties and the responsibilities had frightened him. Now that he had accepted the crown, however, he would give all his heart and strength to Albania, which he hoped had a glorious future. The Albanians cheered, and he the shook hands with the delegates as each was presented and each kissed his hand. A solemn group photograph was taken on the front steps of the *Schloss*, and everyone retired to a banquet with table music, including compositions by Wagner and Tchaikovsky, among others, and parade marches by Torgauer and Hohenfriedberger. The banquet was uneventful save for the customary belches of appreciation by the Albanians. Next the party removed to sprawling *Mon Repos* villa for tea and one of the new-fangled silent movies (subject unrecorded) which bored everyone. The boredom was somewhat relieved when several reporters who had slipped in were unceremoniously ejected.

A telegram was dispatched by Wied to Valona, formally announcing his acceptance. Upon hearing this, crowds there paraded the streets and cheered for Wied. In the afternoon a mass meeting of Valonans was held with patriotic speeches and telegrams were sent to Wied expressing gratitude and loyalty.

The evening after the ceremony, the royal couple prepared to leave Neuwied for Sophie's home in Waldenburg, thirty miles south of Leipzig, where another ceremony was to be held, this time for her. Wied then reviewed local veterans and five brigades of soldiers before leaving. Unfortunately, upon arrival at Waldenburg, it was discovered that Sophie's lady-in-waiting, Fraulein von Pfuel, had come down with measles. Undaunted, Prince Schönberg, the proprietor, gave hospitality to all. The "coronation" ceremony was repeated by the Albanians for Sophie's benefit. Due to the language barriers, Essad and his hosts often resorted to good natured back slapping.

Some of the Great Powers took a special interest in Wied's title. Austria was happy that Essad called him "king," while Britain and France were not. The Germans thought it important to be consistent, as even some of Wied's retinue called him "Highness," as did the Austrian minister when he later presented his credentials in Durazzo. The Powers looked to the 1878 example in which it had been decided initially to call the new ruler of Romania "Royal Highness."[1]

15

BEWARE OF GREEKS

On the evening of February 21, British Ambassador Sir Francis Elliot spoke in Athens to Prime Minister Venizelos at a party. Responding to Epirote concerns, Venizelos said that Greek troops would withdraw slowly to protect Epirote Greeks, and would only hand over to "regularly constituted Albanian forces," not "irregular bands." He predicted that Essad would become Prime Minister and hoped Wied would take a pro-Greek person, such as Essad's secretary Dr. Tortoulis, into his cabinet, as was ultimately done. Venizelos denied that Essad was friendly to the Greeks because they allegedly subsidized him. "No," he said, "we have had enough of that with Ismail Kemal."[1]

By February 23, contributions of relief from abroad received at Scutari in the north were not enough to relieve the Albanian suffering, especially among the refugees. The small international military force had restored order to the Alessio district and Ded Zoku had been pacified. Friendly relations had been established by the government with northern chieftain Prenk Bib Doda. Opinion in Albania was that international troops were needed until the gendarmerie was organized, and that residence by Wied in Durazzo would cause jealousy, as it was in Essad's bailiwick.[2]

In Berlin, Ambassador Sir Edward Goschen wrote to Foreign Secretary von Jagow on February 24 his understanding of Austria's position on the loan to Wied. He said that Austria's consent to International Control Commission control of the loan to Wied depended upon (1) whether the other Powers would agree to repay most of the advance of ten million francs to Wied (which Austria and Italy would make) from the total loan to be guaranteed by all, and (2), upon "the adjustment of the question of participation in "the Bank." Austria was playing the only card in its weak hand, as Von Jagow had suggested that the International Control Commission control the money. Goschen added that he thought it was good that Wied was taking von Jagow's advice that he go to St. Petersburg. "It puts him right with all the Powers," he said.[3]

On the morning of February 25, Wied arrived in Berlin from Waldenburg and received the Russian and Italian ambassadors at his hotel, and then visited von Jagow at the *Auswärtiges Amt* (Foreign Office) on the Wilhelmstrasse.[4] About this time, Wied received the following letter from Count Szögyény, the Austrian Ambassador in Berlin:

> To His Highness (*Durchlaucht*)
> The Prince Wilhelm zu Wied
> Potsdam

> Your Highness

> I have the honor, upon the instructions of my government to bring the information that an Austrian and Italian Bank Institute, under the guarantee of their governments to Your Highness, for the Albanian government, are ready to guarantee an advance of 10 million francs from the loan of 75 million francs of which the entire Great Powers are *in principle* ready to participate.

> Your Highness is authorised to make declaration of the project to the remaining Great Powers.

> Your Highness will receive the assurance of my special respect.

> The I.[mperial] and R.[oyal] Ambassador:
> C [ount] Szögyény[5]

Note carefully the use of the word, "principle", which was not highlighted in the original, but should have been.

Wied left the same day by train for Wirballen, the tiny frontier station at the Russian border. At midday, he and his suite were met by a Russian Colonel who showed them into the Imperial Waiting Room in the station for lunch, while the Colonel attended to the luggage and passports. They were then installed in an Imperial saloon car. It was comfortable, but they could not speak Russian to the attendant, who consequently gave them so much food and drink they became tipsy and had trouble getting back to their sleeping compartments.[6]

Meanwhile, Essad and the Albanian delegation were now in Vienna as the guests of Emperor Franz Josef in a hotel which flew an odd new Albanian flag. It did not bear the Albanian eagle and consisted of longitudinal stripes of red and black, and red and white, with a five pointed star in the middle. Perhaps this banner was a concoction of Essad's. Upon his arrival on the morning of February 25, Essad had been officially welcomed and had an interview with Berchtold. The delegation then went to the historical museum to see Skanderbeg's sword and helmet, which are still there. The whole delegation was given the signal honor of a dinner at Schönbrunn Palace and a Dr. von Löwenthal, hitherto counselor of the Austrian Embassy in Constantinople, was appointed Minister to Albania.[7] The little country did not yet rate an "ambassador."

George Christaki Zographos was born in Argyrocastro Epirus (now southern Albania), and was the son of a father famous throughout Greece. George Zographos had himself been both Greek Foreign Minister and Governor General of Epirus during the Greek Army occupation of 1913-1914.[8] On February 26 Zographos left Athens and arrived in Argyrocastro the next day.[9] The rebellion by Greek "Sacred Battalions" in Epirus was spreading. M. Varatassis, the Greek Prefect of Corfu, was ordered to Durazzo to cooperate with the International Control Commission over evacuation of Epirus by the Greek Army, and to arrange all details thereof.[10] However, the Greek troops had orders to stay in Koritsa, "North Epirus," until the Albanians took over. Three hundred Albanian gendarmes under Mustapha Bey had reached Moglitza on the Devol River near the frontier of the area occupied by the Greek army. All roads south from Elbasan in Albania's dead center were reported to be safe for travelers except at Starovo.[11]

According to a British journalist, despite efforts by the Greek Army, some thirty Greek officers, along with about 100 Greek army men, deserted to the Epirotes with some machine guns and joined them in the mountains, as did some 300 Cretans arriving in small boats.[12]

On February 26, German Control Commissioner Winckel reported to the German Foreign Office from Valona that the Commission had decided that day to write to the Six Powers, asking them to quickly approve payment of 20,000 francs (about $69,000 today) for the Dutch gendarmerie officers.[13]

When the train bearing Wied and his party pulled into the station at St. Petersburg for the promised visit to Russia on February 27, they were greeted by Count Totleben, one of Czar Nicholai's aides-de-camp, who took them to the Winter Palace, although the Czar was then at the suburban palace of Tsarskoe Selo. Heaton was indignant at being left to deal with "gesticulating porters," who gibbered at him in Russian, one of the few European languages which he did not speak. He was consoled somewhat, however, when a butler at the palace who spoke German took him to breakfast with the Prince. Unlike its French ally, the Russian government gave their guests handsome suites of rooms and furnished them with carriages. Wied availed himself of the latter to pay an early, brief visit to the German ambassador, Count Pourtalès, and then leave for Tsarskoe Selo, where he shared an intimate family breakfast with the Czar and Czarina. When Wied mentioned that large areas populated by only Albanians had fallen to Serbia, the Czar expressed astonishment, which, if genuine, shows him to have been an even bigger ignoramus than history has suggested. Nicholai told Wied of his special interest in a proposed "Danube-Adria" railroad for a Serbian port on the Adriatic Sea, presumably in keeping with the London promise that Serbia would have access to that sea.

In the afternoon Wied visited some grand dukes and grand duchesses, Foreign Minister Sazanov and the prime minister, as well as the usual remaining Great Power ambassadors. Sazanov advised Wied to keep his relations upon a "very broad basis" with the Great Powers and with the different ethnic and religious groups in Albania. He said that Wied must be able to prevent Orthodox Christians from being suppressed by the Muslims. If he did those things, Sazanov assured him, the goodwill and support of Russia would be secure. The Foreign Minister also advised the Prince to take his uncle, King Carol, as his general model and highest advisor on important matters. That evening Wied dined at the German Embassy and took part in a relatively small party attended by Pourtalès, Sazanov, the other ambassadors and diplomats, and some palace officials.

Pourtalès reported to Berlin that Wied made an unusually favorable impression upon the Russians and the Prince was very happy over his reception by both the Czar and Sazanov. Usually such "favorable impressions" referred to the impressions of the important government figures in a given locale. However, even the Russian press, not usually fond of Germans, had a slightly friendly tone and the *Rjetsch* newspaper wrote a friendly greeting article.

The next day, before leaving, Wied was received by the Czar's mother, the Dowager Czarina, and he afterward lunched with the Grand Duchess Marie Pavlovna. After the ambassadors lined up and said their farewells at the train station, a number of local Albanians, "unknown and unpleasant looking," forced their way into the Imperial waiting room to see their new ruler, but Heaton had them promptly ejected.[14]

In Albania on February 28, British Consul-General and ICC commissioner Lamb reported that painted placards had been discovered in Valona announcing the autonomy of Epirus. That morning, Zographos sent a telegram from Corfu to the President of the International Control Commission, announcing that he had been appointed President of the "Provisional Government of Epirus" and demanding that Albanian gendarmes respect their "borders."[15] The Greek army began its withdrawal the same day.[16] Another ominous threat with which Wied would have to contend had materialized.

On the evening of March 11, Wied returned to Berlin from St. Petersburg. The next day he received representatives of the Austrian and Italian Embassies and paid another visit to the Deutsche Bank.[17] The same day regular Greek troops evacuated Koritsa, to be replaced by fifty Albanian gendarmes under a Dutch officer.[18]

Wied wrote in 1917 that,

> Even though I was aware of the difficulty of the tasks awaiting me in Albania, I had not been able, just like the great powers, to form an impression of them corresponding sufficiently to reality. Like the European diplomacy, I was not yet familiar in detail with conditions in Albania in those days. In the rest of Europe, Albania was indeed almost more unknown than central Africa at that time, as has been rightly said. Today, with the experience gained in the country, I am endowed with the valuable treasure, of that sure knowledge of all conditions..."

He admitted rather pitifully that, "filled with the high cultural Central European conceptions of law, justice, and truthfulness, I am not equipped with the antidote against the lies, malice, and schemes of the Serbs and Italians."[19]

In early 1914, with British Colonel Phillips in control of Scutari, the whole situation in northern Albania seemed to Wied "such that the takeover of power by the new ruler would not meet with any difficulties." But the situation in middle and southern Albania was different. Essad's behaviour even aroused the suspicion of the International Control Commission. Also, many refugees came from the areas which had been newly assigned to Serbia and Greece by the treaties. In Dibra and Elbasan there were thousands who lacked everything and needed support, although some aid came from the Austrian and Italian governments as well as English private sources.

187

The Dutch Officers were being hindered by Essad in organizing a gendarmerie, as he claimed that he had already formed an Albanian police force of his own, while the International Control Commission did not have any real executive power.[20]

On March 2 the Austrian ambassador in Berlin, Count Szögyény, wrote to the Prince that not only the Greek Prime Minister and the Greek Secretary of State considered a quick accession to the throne urgently necessary due to the conditions in southern Albania, but also Count Berchtold called it "extremely desirable and important to avoid any delay and take over the Albanian government as soon as possible." Therefore, Wied urgently speeded up his preparations for departure.[21]

He could not, of course, govern without ministers. The pool of educated talent was shallow. He was seeking distinguished expatriates and someone advised him to appoint a south Albanian from Valona to be his prime minister. This man, Ferid Pasha, had actually been "*Grand Vizier*," (prime minister) of Turkey from 1903 to 1908, and was a cousin of Ismail Kemal. Ferid declined the offer, and Wied turned to the distinguished old diplomat for the Ottomans, Turkhan Pasha, who had just been having a long interview with Count Berchtold in Vienna. Upon receiving the offer from Wied, he wired his acceptance and left for Durazzo in early March.[22] Essad, of course, had successfully demanded to be Minister of War.[23]

Prenk Bib Doda had succeeded his father as chief, or prince, of some 30,000 Roman Catholic Albanians in the northernmost mountains of Albania. They were called Mirdites because their region was named Mirdita.[24] Under Prenk the Mirdites made a show of supporting Prince Wilhelm zu Wied against the Greeks and rebels, although Prenk and his family were very half-hearted about it.[25] In March 1914, even as Wied prepared to come to Albania, Bib Doda was in Rome, and asked the French Ambassador to use his good offices with Belgrade for the Mirdites so that they could get arms and money from them to keep their autonomy.[26]

On March 2, the Greek Minister in London said that Venizelos was in a difficult spot and would be glad if Greeks in Albania were guaranteed their churches, their own schools, and places in the gendarmerie. Italy had said that this was not consistent with an independent Albania. Always cautious of becoming entangled in the Balkans, Grey hesitated to take the lead on this and said that he would let the Powers reply.[27] The same day, the last Greek Army troops were leaving "Epirus," and the "Epirotes" then raised a blue and white Greek flag with the Byzantine double-eagle superimposed on the white cross in the field.[28]

The next day, the Epirotes named Greek Army Colonel Demetrius Doulis, stationed in Argyrocastro, and born near Santi Quaranta, as Minister of War and Commander-in-Chief of their forces, which included Greek Army deserters and men from Crete. The Greek general staff was furious at this and General Anastasios Papoulas telephoned Doulis on March 3 to verify the report:

> Papoulas: "Is it true that your countrymen have declared you Chief of the autonomous State's Army?"
>
> Doulis: "My countrymen have given me a hearty, universal, and armed reception upon my arrival here yesterday."
>
> Papoulas: "I'm asking you if you've accepted the command."
>
> Doulis: "Not yet. However, should matters call for it, I shall accept."
>
> Papoulas: "Then you will inform me?"

In a call later that day, Doulis repeated his report. Papoulas blew up and demanded that Doulis hand over his regiment. Papoulas said that the Greek Army had given its oath to obey their King and his government and did not want to hear from a "Minister," but from Doulis. He should "advise the officers to remove themselves," he was told. Doulis said that they wanted to be under the rule of King Constantine and reminded Papoulas that Constantine had told them after the Bulgarian War to always be prepared to defend their territory. Papoulas insisted that the Greek Army had to obey orders, and quoted the cipher telegram he had received that day from the King.[29] King Constantine's personal telegram read as follows:

> Inform as final in my name Colonel Doulis, that the first obligation of a soldier is obedience to the orders of his King and preservation of his oath. Unless he carries out his duty he will be considered a deserter. I do not consider his act justifiable under conditions of which he is unable to be the judge.
> Constantine, Rex

Doulis replied that, "I now find myself unavoidably obliged to deviate from my idolized King's commands." He was then stricken from the Army rolls.[30]

The British cruiser, *H.M.S. Gloucester* arrived at Trieste the morning of March 3 to escort Wied to Albania. The French cruiser *Bruix* had already been there for a few days. The German newspaper *National Zeitung* reported that Wied had obtained leave for German officers to be sent to Albania to be military instructors.[31]

In early March of 1914, the Greek Army in Epirus under a zealous Colonel Contoulis had, upon hearing that Argyrocastro had proclaimed its autonomy, along with General Papoulas, ordered martial law and threatened to shoot the first person raising the Northern Epirote flag. He arrested the Metropolitan (an Orthodox archbishop) when he came to Ersek to proclaim the autonomy there. The Greek Army confined the Greek population of Koritsa to their homes and turned the city over to the Albanian forces, which consisted of an administrator and 150 Albanian deserters from the Turkish army. These Albanians had, with one mortar, invested the city. Their commander was Lt. Leon Ghilardi, a Croatian formerly in the Austrian army.[32] Venizelos believed that Epirotes could defeat the Albanians, but he impounded their funds and spoke harshly to Zographos, as he saw the danger of international complications in the Epirote position.[33] Greece even joined in the blockade of Santi Quaranta with its warships, *Alpheius* and *Eurotos*, despite the bitter opposition of a large segment of the Greek Parliament.[34] Venizelos had assured the Powers by "formal engagement to oppose any resistance (and) not to support nor encourage, directly or indirectly, any resistance" to the state of things established by the six powers in Southern Albania.[35]

16

TRIESTE

On March 4, 1914, the Wieds, Heaton, two ladies-in-waiting, servants, and a few dogs left Waldenburg by train for the Austrian Adriatic seaport of Trieste. Before pulling out, one of the dogs escaped at the station and, when caught later, had to be brought to the next station by automobile. Though all had read as many books as they could find about Albania, they had learned very little about the new kingdom. Meeting in the train corridor the next morning, both Wied and Heaton were wearing the newly invented grey Albanian uniform for the first time. "Good morning, Your Majesty," said the secretary. "We'd better go a bit steady with the 'majesty' at present," cautioned Wied.

They arrived at Trieste at nine o'clock in the morning to twenty-one gun salutes from naval and land batteries, and were received at the station by *Statthalter* (Governor), Prince Hohenlohe, a number of other government officials, local dignitaries, officers commanding the international naval escort, and a crowd of Albanian residents. Wied descended from the train and a military band struck up "a weird and rather cheerful tune." (Allegedly the Albanian anthem, possibly *Himni Mbretnor*.) They marched solemnly to the tune along the platform to inspect a smart guard of honor, the Austrian 97th Infantry. The streets were decorated, the crowd excited, and the princely couple were cheered on their drive to the quay. A motor launch conveyed them to the *Taurus*, the 1,200 ton motor yacht put at their disposal by the Austrian Admiralty. They received several deputations on board, and then landed again to pay a complimentary call on the *Statthalter*. The Wieds were addressed by all as "Highnesses."[1]

The party walked to the *Statthalter's* "Palais" just opposite the quay, a way being cleared through the crowd, but closing behind them. Heaton caught a spur in an old lady's skirt and had to remove the spur, but it was returned by an "Italian

192

rough" as he entered Government House. After lunch, the Prussian "*Junker*" (country aristocrat), Major von Trotha, who was to be Wied's lord chamberlain and controller, and Dr. Berghausen (called a "charlatan" by Harry Lamb[2]), arrived from Durazzo and came on board. Berghausen had not been expected but insisted on coming. For lack of room on the yacht, he was sent to the French cruiser *Bruix*. He was "of a very sensitive and nervous disposition" and ever after felt slighted by royal controller von Trotha.

In the early afternoon they visited the Austrian flagship, *Tegethoff* and the other foreign cruisers, the Wieds being much impressed by the smartness and cleanliness of the Austrian and British crews and ships, such as *H.M.S. Gloucester*. British Royal Navy Captain Eustace LaTrove Leatham commanded the escorting international squadron. In the evening, to the sound of bands and guns, the *Taurus* weighed anchor, surrounded by the escort, and steamed into "a still Adriatic night."[3]

As late as March 5, 1914, inhabitants of Scutari had passed a resolution that it should be the capitol, since it was the "home of the historic warrior Albanians," and because it considered that it was the strongest, largest, finest, and healthiest town, and the only one with the necessary buildings for the government and foreign consuls. A telegram conveying all this, signed *inter alia*, by the Archbishop of Scutari, the Abbot of Mirdita, the Mayor, and "a number of Mohammedan notables," was sent to Wied, ending with "long live the King of Albania," etc.[4] That same morning the International Control Commission arrived in Durazzo from Valona, and separate steamers delivered both the Greek envoy Varatassis and General de Veer to the town.[5]

17

ARRIVAL

On the morning of March 7, 1914, the royal passengers sighted the mouth of the Boyna River at Scutari, with its towering castle atop the dominating mountain. *H.M.S. Gloucester* sent a signal of congratulation to Wied. Genial Austrian officers pointed out places of interest along the shore, but were unable to answer Wied's inquiries about local hunting prospects. The *Taurus* and her escorts passed San Giovanni di Medua ("the third port of Albania"), a mere village of whitewashed cottages. The coast of Albania, with its occasional Venetian castles, was impressive and the sea was dotted with fishing smacks manned by baggy-trousered Albanians who had come to see their new king. The men on the *Taurus*, smoking peacefully and watching the scenery, spent most of the morning on deck. Princess Sophie was "enthusiastic about every rock," and there were plenty of them. The sea became a bit rough, so the ladies and some advisers went below. Calm weather and seas returned by midday as they rounded a cape and headed into the bay of Durazzo, a city of about 7,000 people, including not a few gypsies. The climate at this time was like the Riviera—superb.

Their first glimpse of Durazzo, shortly after 2:00 p.m., was of the white houses nestling close under a great hill against a grey-green background. Trees were scarce, but Durazzo boasted a beautiful bay with deep blue water, and in the distant south, across the water, was the mountain of Tomor with its snow-capped peak. In front of Durazzo, Pompey had made his last successful stand against Julius Caesar in 48 B.C., and in 1501, the Turks captured the city. Durazzo is located midway down the coast of Albania. In 1914 it was made up largely of squat stone or mud brick houses, threaded with alleys and cobblestone streets in places. A crowded restaurant could be found there, furnished with rickety wooden tables and benches, and the floor

194

littered with sawdust and spittoons. The walls were decorated with prints of their new king and queen, probably taken from a magazine, a large Albanian flag, and a bearskin. The city had decayed for centuries.

There were sea breezes, but they merely shifted the city's dust around and rain turned it to mud. The fierce sun would then dry it again. From June to November, the almost tropical sun beat down on the hot, dry earth. Nearer the seashore it was cooler and there were fewer mosquitoes than inland. A beach about ten miles long and in many places more than fifty yards wide was very near the city.

Durazzo stood on a slight promontory at the southern end of a range of low hills five miles in length, which rose steeply from the sea. Behind the range was a big marsh, divided in its northern and southern ends from the sea by strips of sand. Where an ancient Roman channel or canal used to be, there were ruins of fortifications and harbor works known as the Porta Romana. The dilapidated canal passed through the marsh and was crossed by a bridge. No doubt Wied soon was told of good duck and snipe shooting which the marsh provided in winter, but in summer it also provided malarial mosquitoes.

In 1914 there were no buoys to mark the harbor and it needed dredging. Passengers had to come ashore by barge or launch, a problem in rough weather. There was no main automobile road to the harbor, only a rough, winding lane. A Venetian wall ran fairly close to the coast, down the northern hill, and ended in a fortified tower. From the harbor one could see a number of warehouse-like buildings clustered near the waterfront. The city boasted a fine mosque at the highest point of the town, alongside the main square. From there, the road crossed the old marshes, leaving a lagoon on the north side and the very long, sandy beach to the south. The road itself then divided south to all the main southern towns, and straight ahead to the town of Tirana. On the road to Tirana one soon reached low hills which lined the road on both sides. Then there was a zigzag climb over a hill. The journey to Tirana from Durazzo was approximately twenty-five miles and, just beyond that town, the road branched off northward to the northern city of Scutari. To go south from Tirana, one had to return to Durazzo and take the southern road from there. The ancient Via Ignatia led southeastward from Durazzo through Elbasan to Salonika, Greece.

As the *Taurus* entered the Durazzo harbor, cannon in the old Venetian fort fired a twenty-one gun salute, as did the foreign warships in the harbor. A little government motorboat, hired at an exorbitant price by Essad, brought local bigwigs to the yacht. Not only Essad, but Feizi Bey, Aziz Pasha, and the chief officials of Durazzo and Valona, including the Mayor, climbed aboard. Essad boarded first, wearing white tie and tails, and his companions *salaam*ed in frock coats and American shoes, their heads topped by newly-created reddish grey fezzes. After perfunctory courtesies, Essad was appointed a general. He then retired below deck to remove his civilian clothes and put on the general's uniform which Wied had caused to be made for him in Potsdam. Like Wied's and Heaton's uniforms, it was a blue-grey cavalry uniform with black piping suggestive of that on some native Albanian jackets and a white astrakhan cap, topped by a tall white aigrette plume. Wied, Heaton, and Essad were to wear this outfit on almost all public appearances.

The Prince and his party then boarded motor launches to take them to the long rickety wooden pier which jutted southwards into the open sea from a little kink in the coast which formed Durazzo harbor. Sophie, dressed in white flowing robes reaching to the ground, walked beside Wied, non-Muslim style, and their entourage followed behind on the narrow wooden walkway. They then stepped onto a red-carpeted landing, with Essad walking only slightly behind the royal pair so as to emphasize his importance. Behind him came von Trotha, the two ladies-in-waiting, then Heaton, Castoldi, and Buchberger. They passed between somewhat scruffy, fez-wearing soldiers with rifles held clumsily at "present arms." Both banners and saluting Albanian and foreign officials bracketed the landing stage. The royal pair were greeted by Dutch General de Veer, commander of the gendarmerie, in full dress uniform of the

Dutch Army (with feathered cocked hat), the foreign consular corps, and the heads of the various religious communities. All the while, an Italian band played the new Albanian national anthem, *Himni Mbretnor* (Royal Hymn), composed by the Italian musician Nardella. In his greeting, Essad said that Wied would be the new Skanderbeg. British International Control Commission delegate Harry Lamb thought that Wied's speech of reply bothered some hearers as an unnecessary emphasis on withdrawing as much control from the International Control Commission as possible, in line with the wishes of his "more intimate advisors." The members of the International Commission of Control waited at the entrance of the "President's Avenue." Signor Leoni, the Italian Commission delegate, greeted Wied formally and handed over the Commissions' executive powers to him. They then proceeded, with Wied saluting and Sophie waving her handkerchief. Lamb thought the population's demeanor was "throughout sympathetic, but not enthusiastic."

Along the avenues and gardens were ranged in local dress the representatives of as many Albanian towns as could be obtained on the relatively short notice. In the crowd were a few white fezzes and *fustanellas* from the south, and low red fezzes with long blue tassels from the Elbasan district. Also the pupils of the Italian schools presented bouquets to the Princess amid general enthusiasm. Although the open space between the landing jetty and the Palace was scarcely half filled due to Wied's delay in saying when he would arrive, the market square was crowded to overflowing and the people there cheered and applauded. The town was festively decorated. There were mountaineers from the north, with long, narrow heads, and there were fair, shorter, round-headed Tosks from the south, as well as Gypsies. Flowers were strewn in the royal pathway and two white pigeons were thrown into Sophie's path. She was cheered when she picked them up. One hundred yards more brought them to the pretty royal gardens (formerly a public park) where blossoming almond trees running down to the shore perfumed the air. They then mounted the steps of their humble palace with green shutters.

Once inside the Palace, deputations and officials had to be received. These included not only those who had greeted them at the dock, but deputations from nearby towns and Albanian colonies in Italy and the United States, who filed before the royal couple watching from the balcony above. Many were ushered into the Palace by von Trotha and Heaton, but not before they were searched for guns. The Albanian reputation for firearms was apparently well known to the newcomers. A few of the visitors made little speeches in French or Italian, but a local dignitary usually had to translate. Many of the Albanians had not bathed and ate garlic, but bowed gracefully and displayed good manners. Many wore gold decorations or silver chains and Turkish medals.[1]

The old Turkish government *Konak*, or administrative building, had become the Royal Palace. It was a long, low, barn-like building of three stories and forty rooms, with a large gabled upper floor or attic. It had undergone extensive repairs, with freshly whitewashed walls. Presumably modern plumbing, including toilets, had been installed, as opposed to the hole-in-the-floor facilities which even the best Albanian hotels boasted.[2] Edith Durham thought the Palace very large "and got up very swagger," but it proved to be somewhat crowded for all the people it had to hold. The royal gardens were directly in front of the palace and there was a cool, stone-paved courtyard in the middle of the building.

The living quarters were on the second (British first) floor, as was the Throne Room, which had a balcony overlooking the gardens. The Prince's study was next to Heaton's one room, where Heaton both worked and slept. The Throne Room had a fairly low vaulted ceiling, damask wallpaper, a large mirror, a rather plain carpet, and Louis XV furniture with porcelain figurines on a side table. On the wall hung a large portrait of a woman—no doubt a royal relative. Next to the Throne Room was a drawing room through which one reached Sophie's little boudoir. Then there was a large, comfortable dining room with a good view onto one of the old Venetian towers and the sea. The other half of the second floor was divided off as servants' quarters. Wied's study had large bookcases and gun cupboards around it and a solid old work table with a large settee opposite it. He put up few pictures as he expected to hunt and hang trophy heads in their place. There was a broad passage all around the inner side of the palace, the King's half divided up with curtains, practically converting it into three additional living rooms. The one on the end was furnished, oriental-style, with sofas, cushions, and the like, and used as a sitting room by the "entourage," who took black coffee after meals. The Palace was clean and fitted with electric lights, but they were not adequate for a palace. In looks, at least, it was not even comparable to the palaces of other Balkan monarchies, such as Serbia, Bulgaria, or Romania. Wied had an English butler of the "old school" and German footmen who had worked hard to get the Palace ready, helped by numerous maids and multi-national "dailies." In fact, there were plenty of servants. There were Germans, Austrians, Albanians, British, Italians, and an Egyptian Arab, all of whom usually got on well together. French and German were the usual languages spoken at court, unless necessity compelled otherwise. The cuisine and wine cellar were excellent, as was the supply of cigars and cigarettes. The packing crates had only recently been opened, but not until the somewhat forlorn appearance of the Palace, with the children's rocking horse in plain view, had been photographed by an Italian journalist for public consumption. When Wied landed on March 7, he brought with him, among other things, not only his police dogs and a piano, but ten million francs in gold coin (now about $34,560,000) which Austria and Italy had advanced from the full seventy-five million francs ($270,000,000) the other Powers had not yet all agreed to pay.

As the first evening wore on, the royal couple were called upon to show themselves on their balcony several times. Chinese lanterns lit the square below and an Italian brass band from Bari played popular tunes, ignored by the crowd. Everyone in the Palace was in good spirits at dinner and Wied inquired about the best places to hunt, what was the best game, and what

European princes should be invited to hunt. He also set about creating the Order of the Eagle of Albania, and brought with him "Accession Medals," which showed his profile on one side and a star-topped crown above a large "W" and "VII-III-1914"on the reverse.[3] One of the guests later said, "I saw the beginning of a tragic operetta."[4]

In Albania, Wied was now officially addressed as *Madheri*, which was the equivalent of "Majesty," and *Mbret*, which is the equivalent of "King." The word for "Queen" is *Mbretersha*. Henceforth we will accord them the Albanian accolades of King and Queen,

After dinner at the Palace, Heaton explored the little town and found Dutch officers at the Hotel Clementi with other foreigners, celebrating. The Clementi was by no means luxurious, but was expensive nevertheless. Food was served on a long communal table, which was lit by an oil lamp and covered with a dirty tablecloth, with guests sitting on kitchen chairs and empty packing cases. A couple of gaudy postcards decorated the walls. The foreign officers welcomed Heaton and they toasted the occasion with champagne.[5] The reign had begun.

18

THE SHORT HONEYMOON

Wied's day started at 9 a.m. After settling in, Wied often retired to his study for hours on end with Captain Castoldi until dinner.[1] The Palace staff took breakfast in the dining room, while the King and Queen ate in their own rooms upstairs. From 10 o'clock until lunch, Heaton busied himself at his secretarial duties, which consisted mostly of seeing people. He then worked the hours from 2:30 until "tea," which Heaton and the King's staff took with the Wieds in the passage drawing-room. One or both Wieds then usually went for a walk with an aide, Sami Bey Vrioni, or a lady-in-waiting went with Sophie. They would be escorted by a squad of gendarmes in front and one behind, with the Queen's dog yapping at everyone. Dinner was at 8 o'clock, followed by chess or cards, and occasionally music. The Queen played several stringed instruments well and sang old songs. Trotha played guitar and sang German songs rousingly. Two to three times every week the Wieds rode horseback. They were escorted by Heaton and Ekrem Bey and clumsy mounted gendarmes, galloping along the sands, with the royal police dogs nipping the horses' legs. Like most aristocrats of the era, the Wieds rode well, with Sophie mounted on a chestnut mare which only she could manage.[2]

Soon it was time for Romanian minister Burghele to present his credentials to the new King. As he was the emissary of Wied's uncle, this was an important relationship. Heaton and a detachment of mounted Albanian gendarmes were dispatched, along with Essad's carriage, borrowed for the occasion, to pick up Burghele at his hotel. Burghele and his legation staff, consisting of Prince Michel Sturdza and M. Ranette were introduced to the King and Burghele read out his credentials in French. They all then retired to lunch in the "Yellow Room," after which coffee was served in the Oriental Room. The Romanian minister was the first foreign diplomat to present his credentials, in order to avoid showing a preference for either Austria or Italy. An Englishman reported at the time that there were only three duly accredited diplomatic representatives to the *Mbret*, those from Austria, Italy, and Romania. The first two diplomatically agreed to remain in hiding until the Romanian had presented his credentials, so that neither would struggle to be first. They carefully watched each other's building through shuttered windows until M. Burghele had presented his letters. The Austrian "legation" had several secretaries, but the Italian mission had only a loaned secretary, the Marchese Durazzo.[3] Those countries, however, had the best consulates and soon presented not only their ministers, but a whole bevy of *attachés* and functionaries.[4]

On the evening of March 9, members of the International Control Commission had a long interview with Wied in Durazzo on diverse questions, but he was most concerned with the "very precarious" treasury. There would have been more money if not for considerable sums dispensed for "a campaign for personal influence by a person whom the Prince recognized," but did not name—obviously Essad. Finances were considered "desperate." Colonel Phillips of the international military forces said that he could not assume the payment of functionaries and the gendarmerie. Commissioner Krajewski told Wied the precise figures that were required and directed attention to the need to provide for these. His Albanian colleague on the Commission advised the impressed King to draw upon the "two million francs" (*sic*) advanced to him by the Austro-Italian banks. In his turn, Wied reserved the right to control movements of the gendarmerie and nomination of the functionaries, despite Corfu negotiations over the "Epirus" question. He asked for information on the proposed organic law, or constitution, and for copies of the parts finished. The Italian Commission delegate prompted Captain Castoldi, who got the Prince to ask the Commission to observe the situation in Scutari, which Italy thought Austria was stirring up. The Frenchman Krajewski's impression: Wied would act "under his own inspiration and ignore as much as possible the ICC."[5]

In early March, Wied attended ceremonies in honor of the royal couple at the different religious houses of worship in Durazzo, but Sophie did not go to the Mosque. Because Austria was traditionally a "protector" of Catholics, its diplomatic minister, von Löwenthal, was seated opposite the Court at the Catholic ceremony, while all others were seated near the royal ministers. The Italian representative, Baron Aliotti, protested, but things were smoothed over and Aliotti and Löwenthal walked arm-in-arm down the street.[6]

A few days before Wied's arrival, protocol problems had arisen in the north at Scutari. On Monday, the second of March, Colonel Phillips had invited the military detachment commanders to see him and asked whether they would agree to his greeting the Prince of Albania in the name of all the international troops. The German naval Commander Schneider asked him what form this would take. He said that he would go to Durazzo, although this was not yet definite, and take with him Captain Crossman, his adjutant, as well as the Austrian and Italian captains on his staff. Commander Schneider demanded thereupon that a German captain must also go with him. Later, the French Consul demanded the inclusion of a French captain. On Thursday, March 5, Colonel Phillips informed Commander Schneider of his definite decision to go to Durazzo, and that the German and French captains should go with him. Only on that day did they learn of the definite arrival date of the Prince. The German Commander received a telegraphed order from Germany to go to Durazzo. However, it arrived so late that it was impossible for him to be on time for the festive occasion, as the only means of transportation available to him was an un-seaworthy Austrian vessel! The proposal of the German Foreign Ministry met the approval of the Austrian and Italian representatives, however, and they at once telegraphed their cabinets to inquire whether a later joint trip would be desired. Because of the critical local situation, both representatives thought it necessary to keep the detachment commanders in Scutari. After all of this, on the morning of the seventh of the month, the German Commander merely sent a welcoming telegram to the Prince in the name of the German detachments.

The day of the "Prince" of Albania's arrival passed in Scutari in a brilliant celebration, entirely without the Muslims, however. On the morning of the seventh of March, there was some friction between the Christians and the Muslims because the Muslims would not close their shops for the occasion. Around six in the evening, some tried again to open their shops, which greatly agitated the Christians, who were milling about the streets in thousands. The crowd rushed toward those businesses known to be open, but were held in check in front of the foreign barracks by five foreign soldiers, probably German. The Albanian gendarmerie was powerless against the mob. If the international troops had not been there, the hatred between the religions would have been expressed violently that day. Toward evening, a crowd of around a thousand demonstrated sympathy for Germany, in contrast to the other Powers, as they surrounded the German flag. In explanation, the Archbishop of Scutari assured the German commander that the people were tired of Austrian and Italian politics.

On March 8 the Archbishop celebrated a High Mass in the Scutari Cathedral. Invitations went to all representatives of the Powers and detachments in Scutari. Only the Italian General Consul was absent,--due to illness, it was reported. The German naval commander, Schneider, visited the Consul at noon, but found him at his desk. The Consul said that he supported the heartiest relations with the Germans and went out of his way to be kind to them. Schneider reported that this was also true of the Italian officer corps at Scutari, the young men of which had almost all received German training. He did not give as good a report of the Austrians. He said that the presumptuous and incautious remarks of the Austrian officers, urging the Germans to shun the Italians, had thrown a shadow over local conditions. He felt that the Muslims, once they knew that Wied was really in Albania, and Essad was exposed as a fraud, would telegraph their loyalty to the Prince.

On the afternoon of March 8, a crowd of one thousand loitered at the Scutari Citadel as music was played, wanting to raise the Albanian flag. The acting governor cautiously refused permission, however. At nine o'clock, a Muslim who had been forced to close his business at seven, shot and killed a Christian.

The next day, the Archbishop visited the German commander and expressed his joy over Wied's arrival and declared his hope that northern Albania would develop further under the protection of the international garrison. He later asked Schneider to review and advise upon reception plans for Wied. The only remaining dispute seemed to be whether Scutari would become the capital.

Schneider proudly reported that the German detachment protected the Muslims and the Christians equally, and was popular with the people as a result, as evidenced by the demonstration before their flag on the seventh. He hoped that Wied would recruit from Albanians for both military and civil service. Schneider remained suspicious of Essad, however, despite the latter's generous praises of Germany and his asserted intention to send his nephews to enter the German Army, and to encourage other Albanians to do so.

Schneider's view of the Great Powers locally was equally skeptical. He felt that Britain merely pursued her own interests through currying favor with the Muslims. He gave as an example the high salary paid to the local Imam upon the instruction of Colonel Phillips. He accused Phillips of attaching former convicts to the civil service, with higher salaries than locally appropriate, thus threatening the local treasury. When the chiefs of the Hoti, Gruda, and Kastrati tribes complained to Schneider of their desperation in resisting Montenegrin attacks, he advised them to contact Colonel Phillips. They replied that they would have nothing to do with him, as he had not protected their interests, and they only wanted to deal with the "Germanen." Phillips had told Schneider that a Mr. Kraja had been producing strong propaganda for Germany. Schneider curtly replied that he was happy to hear this, and that it was no crime. He felt that the French supported Montenegrin and

Serbian interests, while the interests of Austria and Italy clashed strongly. On the other hand, he thought that Italy was cozying up to the British and was hoping for a protectorate over the Muslims.[7]

Matters were not yet alarming to Wied. In March of 1914, Greek gangs had invaded southern Albanian border villages but were driven back across the border by Albanian policemen together with armed inhabitants. Wied had been informed of this upon his arrival in Trieste on the way to Albania. At that time, it was not considered extremely serious. The International Control Commission had instigated Ismail Kemal Bey's exit from Albania before Wied arrived, but they lacked the power to force Essad to go. He had only given up his governmental power on the condition that he go to Germany as head of the delegation offering Wied the Crown. He had repeatedly assured Wied of his loyalty and devotion, and Wied, knowing his powerful position in middle Albania, tried to co-opt him for his government by giving him special distinction and inclusion in the government as Secretary of the Interior and of War.

The first weeks of Wied's reign were given over to the appointment of the officials of his government, the formation of governmental departments, the setting up of the subordinate authorities, the organization of the police, the centralization of finances, and his visit to the areas around Durazzo.[8]

On March 8, 1914, the countries of the Triple Alliance notified Greece that the International Control Commission, meeting in Valona, had decided at Austria's request, (1) upon religious and language freedom for Epirus, (2) upon adoption of the Greek frontier previously agreed with Venizelos, (3) that Greece must evacuate Koritsa, and (4) that the Commission would recommend to Wied that Epirote Greeks be included in the gendarmerie. This met most of Greece's requests. A copy of the note was given to British Ambassador Elliot in Athens as a courtesy by the German Minister. This infuriated Sir George R. Clark, Senior Clerk of the British Foreign Office, and Sir Eyre Crowe, assistant Under-Secretary of State for Foreign Affairs.

They suggested that it was the third time the Triple Alliance had presented a *fait accompli* (the previous one being in October and November 1913) to Britain. They suggested that Britain wash its hands of Albania.[9]

The International Control Commission were in Valona to keep an eye on the Greek army evacuation from Epirus. It was thought that King Carol had told Greece that Romanian help with Bulgaria in future depended on fulfilling Greece's obligations to Albania.

Wied appointed Dutch Major Ludovic Thomson as his "Representative Extraordinary and Plenipotentiary," and "Commissioner General for the South" in the districts of Koritsa and Argyrocastro to maintain peace and organize the administration. Several Dutch officers went with him. He was to play a prominent part in Wied's brief reign. General de Veer, with whom he had disputes, had engineered his appointment to get him out of his way. Thomson was a logical choice, however, as he was known to the Greeks from his recent service as a military observer of their battles.[10]

On March 11, Colonel Thomson arrived on the island of Corfu with plenipotentiary powers to discuss the Epirote situation with its "Foreign Minister," Alexius Carapanos. Thomson's offer of limited local self government was rejected in favor of full autonomy. Thomson rashly exceeded his instructions and promised Epirus autonomy as an opening gambit. He told reporters, "It will be quite agreeable to name Mr. Zographos as Administrator-General of Argyrocastro..." The Greek governor of Corfu, Varatassi, later to be Greek *Chargé d'Affaires* in Wied's Durazzo, tried to pretend that he had nothing to do with the Zographos "government" in Epirus. However, Varatassi agreed to take the proposals to Athens for Greek Government consideration.[11]

Wied did not have long to bask in the glow of his arrival reception. Soon the telegraph office in Durazzo, one of the few facilities with at least Nineteenth-Century technology, was clicking with telegrams for "His Majesty the King." He was so addressed in French by Feizi Bey Alizot, his "Director General of Internal Affairs" who, on March 11 and 12 telegraphed from Valona that in some villages of the Premeti region, as soon as the Greek regular army pulled out, they were re-occupied by Greek Christian bands and soldiers in disguise who claimed that they would only submit to Greece. It was reported that they then persecuted "the peaceful population." The royal governor of Berat reported that in the *kaza* of Permeti, a Greek captain of artillery with 300 soldiers disguised themselves as civilians and took part in an insurrection "in the Kosnia villages." Persecutions against the Albanians had taken place in the Termishta area, and one of the leaders of the "bands," named Varda, had sent a menacing letter demanding Albanian evacuation of Frasheri, newly surrendered by the Greek army. The *komitadjis* commanded by a chief called "Agrenaga" in the vicinity of Colonia continued their persecutions. Loyal detachments and auxiliaries were being sent against them. General de Veer telegraphed from Valona on March 15 to the "Princely Chancellery" of troubles in the Koritsa area occupied "by certain Albanians." He had attempted to telegraph the local Dutch Commander Snellen for information, and to give him orders, but the telegraph bureau reported to de Veer that Athens reported telegraphic communication with Koritsa was "interrupted," and that de Veer's telegram, sent via Salonika (Greece) was still sitting there. He asked the International Control Commission to request Greece to re-establish this important channel of communication.[12]

Around Koritsa, "grave disorders," were reported in which some Albanians allegedly attacked Christians, ransacked their homes, and "outraged" their women. Essad's partisans in the village of Bograditch refused to recognize the Albanian authorities at Koritsa and occupied the villages between Starevo and the River Deboli. They retired after a fight with Ismail Kemal's followers at Malik, but invited the Albanian gendarmerie to occupy it. One hundred gendarmes under Dutch officers went out, but the officers were imprisoned and fighting went on. The Christians were said to be in great danger in the district.[13]

At a dinner party which he gave around this time Wied said, somewhat cryptically, "If Albania is to be ruled peacefully, three persons ought to be hanged: Ismail Kemal, Essad Pasha, and myself. If all three of us were dead, Albania would fare much better."[14]

The International Control Commission only sanctioned a minimum expenditure from the loan funds for the gendarmerie, and the Dutch government threatened to withdraw the mission if the Powers did not support it. The mission had no non-commissioned officers and was inadequate. Albania, required to be neutral, could not raise an army except for some mountain artillery units.[15]

The Italian government shared the view of the German government that it was necessary to pay ten million francs for the support of the Albanian gendarmerie from the Italian and Austro-Hungarian guaranteed loan. The Italian government was even of opinion that the Albanian government's most urgent need was to spend a part of the one million francs (*sic*) which the King had been advanced, in order to raise the level of the gendarmerie. (The reported amount of the funds advanced to Wied varies widely, depending upon the source of the report).

On March 14, 1914, elderly, snow-bearded Turkhan Pasha Premeti arrived in Durazzo to help his new sovereign organize a government. Born in Albania, he had been for many years Turkish ambassador to Russia. In fact, he had served the Ottoman Empire in one capacity or another for forty years. Perhaps because of his experience and that rare quality, honesty, he had reportedly been recommended for the job by "official Romanian circles." Even Essad approved of him, apparently considering him no threat to his own power.

After several days of delay during which Wied, (upon whose advice is not recorded), rejected two ministries submitted by Turkhan, a cabinet was finally announced on March 17. The International Commission of Control, in an attempt at thrift, had only provided for four main ministries in their proposed organizational "organic statute." However, Wied sought to avoid offense to supporters and appointed eight ministers, hoping to obtain later ratification of the move by the London ambassadors. He accomplished this in part by raising the departments of Mines and Forests and Posts and Telegraphs to cabinet level. The appointments were as follows:

Turkhan Pasha Premeti was named Prime Minister and Foreign Minister. Essad Pasha Toptani was named Minister of the Interior. This gave him nominal control of the only legal armed force at the government's disposal, the gendarmerie. There was not a War Ministry because Wied considered that Albania was not permitted to have an army, although he hoped that London would later reconsider this. The terminology did not bother Essad, who was satisfied for the time being that he held the most powerful post.

Dr. Themistocles Adamidis Bey Frasheri, an Orthodox Christian from Koritsa originally, was named Finance Minister. He had been a physician and landowner in Egypt for twenty years before returning to take up the post. Mufid Bey Libohova, appointed to be Justice and Religion Minister, was an attorney. He had studied law in Constantinople but spent much of his time as a deputy in the Turkish Parliament and in the Turkish Foreign Service. He had most recently been Albania's delegate to the International Control Commission. He was to be replaced on that body by Mehdi Bey, the former governor of Durazzo.

Another physician who was an Orthodox Christian from Koritsa was Michael Tortoulis Bey, who was appointed Minister of Public Instruction and Health. He was extremely wealthy and considered to be very cultured. Hassan Bey Prishtina, a northern Albanian, was one of the organizers of the rebellion of 1912 against the Turks and was at first in the Provisional Government of Ismail Kemal before joining forces with Essad. He was now appointed Minister of Posts and Telegraphs. Aziz Pasha Vrioni, a large landowner, was appointed Minister of Agriculture and Commerce.

Prenk Bib Doda, the Catholic chief of the northern Mirdite tribe of Orosh, was named to be Minister of Public Works. These "works", being few or non-existent, and Prenk being a cautious man, returned to his own mountain bailiwick to await events, but proved very loyal to Wied.

Major Ekrem Bey Libohova was made Wied's *aide de camp* or personal attendant. He was well qualified for the job, having been educated in Belgian military schools and served with the Turkish army in the recent Balkan Wars. He spoke French, Turkish, passable German and Italian and was a perfect diplomat, preferring to pass bad news to Wied through Heaton or von Trotha. Selim Bey Wassa, a young Catholic from the north, was made orderly officer. The nominees were received at the Palace, swearing "...before God and upon mine honour that I will well and truly serve the Mbret, the Mbretersha, and the realm."

The Cabinet soon began their work, meeting each day late in the afternoon at Essad's house near the Palace. They would talk, drink strong Turkish coffee, and smoke. Meetings would last until after midnight. At first they busied themselves with patronage, giving plum appointments to their friends and to Essad's men. They even set up an elaborate judicial system which never functioned. It was intended to send "ministers" to Vienna, Rome, Paris, and London. Albania was not yet an important enough state to be so presumptuous as to send "ambassadors."[16]

In the north on March 19, the Albanian flag was hoisted over "the castle of Scutari" in the presence of the consular body, the international army of occupation, the local authorities, and some 30,000 other spectators.[17]

Meanwhile, a new deal had come to Albania. On April 7, it was reported that the government had decided to install foreign specialists as advisors in some ministries in order to instill European model management. There was to be an advisor for Posts and Telegraphs, one for the Ministry of Public Works, one for Agriculture, and one for Forestry. The Austrian and Italian governments had been skillful in naming appropriate servants for the jobs.

On March 19, the French representative on the International Control Commission was disturbed to learn that the

Austrian and Italian bankers from the Wiener Bank-Verein and the Banca Commerciale were in Durazzo. What were they up to? The French wanted the International Control Commission to ask the Albanian government to hold up on any negotiations with the bankers. The request was voted down on Triple Alliance vs. Triple Entente lines, but the German delegate, Winckel, soothingly proposed that the Austrian and Italian delegates find out what was going on and report back to the Commission, and matters cooled down.[18] Nothing of consequence was reported.

On March 31, Prime Minister Turkhan Pasha wrote to Mehdi Bey, the Albanian delegate on the International Control Commission in Valona. He wrote in French, as was common between educated Albanians in this polyglot country. He asked Mehdi to officially inform the International Control Commission that the new government would formally notify them each year of the Budget of the State, and reported that two million francs ($6,912,000 today) had been, "in accordance with the preliminary discussions between … the Great Powers," put at the personal disposition of "the King" [du Roi] to get his reign started. Turkhan was confident that the International Control Commission could oversee all expenditures as the Powers had agreed, including the first draw of five hundred thousand francs (sic; $1,728,000 today), but hoped that they would not expect to have to approve every penny of expenditure and would be satisfied by the government keeping the Commission advised of draws and not strictly bound by the contract with the bank syndicates.[19]

On March 21, Essad offered to raise twenty-five thousand men to clear the Greeks from Epirus. If Wied agreed, Essad would be all powerful. If he refused, Wied would appear weak.[20] Here was one of the many equally bad choices Wied was to face.

An Epirote force had gathered in the south at Vigilista under Epaminondas Charisiades, waiting for the Greek army to leave Koritsa. On March 22, they cut the telegraph wires between Koritsa, Pogradets and Colonia and took up positions near the city, whereupon the local Greeks donned uniforms and assaulted the Albanian gendarmerie in Koritsa. The royal administrator panicked and left the city to be defended by the Dutch Major Snellen and the local Albanian police under an ethnic Greek named Themosticles Germeni. A furious street battle followed, with both Sneller and the Epirote commander being wounded, and the Epirote flag was raised over Koritsa. The Epirotes fired mortars on the Albanians for five days, until their ammunition ran out. The town was retaken by the Albanians on March 29 and held until July 8. Essadists treacherously freed a number of Epirote notables who had been taken prisoner by the Albanians.[21]

On March 22, a dispute arose in the International Control Commission over whether Albania could have a militia, as opposed to a gendarmerie, since only the latter was expressly authorized. The distinction, if of any practical meaning, was that a gendarmerie performed police and semi-military duties in a military manner, while a militia was a reserve military force only. Lamb, Kral (of Austria), Winckel (of Germany), and Leoni (of Italy) agreed to allow a militia, but Petraiyeff (of Russia) made it a condition that they have Dutch officers, like the gendarmerie. This was impractical as there were not enough Dutch, so Albania asked Austria and Italy for ten instruction officers each to make up the foreign complement. Essad already had thirty-five Turkish officers and ordered fifty more. The next day, Wied told Löwenthal that he wanted no Turkish officers— better to have Italo-Albanians, and Romanians[22] he thought, and Baron Aliotti sponsored his legation *attaché*, Colonel Muricchio, to be one. A militia was still in the planning stage when World War I made it moot.[23]

In early April, the gendarmerie and Albanian irregulars appeared to have held their own against an Epirote attack at Koritsa. Official reports to Durazzo, however, said that Epirotes, using machine guns manned by Greeks, made the situation precarious at Koritsa and elsewhere. Telegrams from Valona said that recruiting for the Epirote "sacred battalions" or "sacred legions" (*Hierolochoi)* was proceeding generally and that arms and ammunition for them was being landed at Santi Quaranta.[24]

These guerilla bands already had the arms which Greece had given them in the war against the Turks.[25]

On the night of April 6, 1914, local Greeks in Koritsa joined supposedly wounded Greek soldiers who left the hospital, ran into the streets, and joined Epirote rebels with machine guns to stage a *coup*. They captured the public buildings and strategic points and laid waste to the Christian quarter of town, according to Romanian Prince Sturdza, serving with the gendarmerie. The Albanian townsfolk however, rallied in support of the gendarmerie under the Dutchmen Commandant Snellen and Captain Doorman. After four days of street fighting, they expelled the invaders, restored order, and rebel Orthodox Bishop Ghermanos was carried off to Elbasan. Guerrilla warfare also broke out at Tepeleni, where a detachment of the gendarmerie was massacred.[26]

By March 23, complaints began to be heard around Durazzo that nothing had changed, that Wied surrounded himself with foreigners, including a German *aide de camp*, two to three Austrian court functionaries, an Italian soldier, and an English secretary. They noted especially that he had "scarcely" left the Palace and "nobody ever sees him." Men went in and out of Essad's house as before, but the Palace was "unapproachable." In Essad's anteroom lounged armed retainers. "Those who came with boons to ask seldom went away unsatisfied; they might receive a gold 'Napoleon' coin [perhaps $70 today],[27] a lamb, some wine, etc.", it was reported.[28]

At the end of March, 1914, the nine horses Heaton had purchased in Vienna arrived and were landed on the rickety "landing-stage" with difficulty, a mare falling into the sea. The Royal infants, a girl aged four, a boy aged one, and Fräulein von Pfuel, arrived on the Italian yacht *Misurata* and were received "in state." Crowds cheered little Crown Prince Carol Victor. From then on, the children and their English nanny were rarely to leave the little garden in front of the Palace.[29] Around this time the government had obtained an advance of nine million francs (c. $31,104,000 today) from Italy and Austria-Hungary, making a total of ten million francs ($34,560,000), if it is accurate that

Wied had brought one million with him. Strangely, in view of Wied's desire for autonomy, Finance Minister Adamidis insisted that the expenditure be controlled by the International Control Commission, which considered it to be an advance on the total loan. The government also purchased a number of machine guns and mountain artillery pieces from Austria and, to avoid favoritism, rifles from Italy.[30]

On March 27 the Kaiser visited Archduke Franz Ferdinand at "Miramare", the latter's beautiful seaside castle near Trieste. At lunch in the marble dining hall, Franz Ferdinand said he was unhappy about Wied in Albania. His own choice for the Albanian throne had been Duke Wilhelm von Urach, but he had been turned down by Vienna, the archduke said. Franz Ferdinand warned that, if Wied fell, Serbs would try to grab more Albanian territory. The Kaiser then left on the yacht *Hohenzollern* for Corfu. Emperor Franz Josef caught a cough about this time, which was soon public knowledge and became quite serious.[31]

On March 24, Colonel Thomson returned to Durazzo from Epirus and Corfu where he had been negotiating with the Epirote leader, Zographos, at Wied's behest. He had offered the Epirotes virtual autonomy and complete religious freedom. However, because his proposal had not insisted on the Albanian language being taught in the schools, and, because the proposal did not mention that Wied retained nominal sovereignty as "*Statthalter de l'Epire*," (*sic*), the Albanian cabinet angrily rejected it. Essad and Mufid Bey chastised him, and he flew into a rage. Turkhan Pasha, the new prime minister, was kind, but even he was upset.[32] They felt that Thomson had conceded too much.

Specifically the Epirote demands were:

(1) A Greek Orthodox governor of the province and Greek sub-governors, approved by Greece.

(2) Greek to be the official language, but Albanian to be optional in schools.

(3) Gendarmes to be recruited locally and only serve locally, with Greeks to be exempt from regular military service.

(4) Freedom of religion for Christians and Muslims.

(5) The special privileges of the coastal cities of Himira (Khimira) and Santi Quaranta to continue, the latter to be a free port for transport of goods from Greece.[33]

Upon receiving the Cabinet's criticisms Thomson, always temperamental, became furious and threatened to resign his commission and return to Holland. Turkhan Pasha had to intervene to soothe his rage. Thomson was, however, soon relieved of his position as commissioner to Epirus because of illness, and replaced by Mufid Bey. In May, Wied turned the negotiations over to the International Control Commission and General de Veer was urgently recalled to Durazzo. The Epirote matter was far from settled.

Apparently the seriousness of the insurgency in the south was not appreciated by the Wied government until late March or early April of 1914. Greek "bands" continued to kill gendarmes and the almost helpless Albanian government formally called the "regrettable situation" in the south to the attention of the Powers, begging them to put a stop to it. Every report confirmed that it was the Greek Army which had organized and armed the *Komitadjis*. Koritsa and its vicinity had been captured and pillaged. Wied, who was, after all, a highly trained professional soldier, wanted to raise and personally lead an army to the south. The whole police force of gendarmes was to be mobilized, strengthened by Albanians on official duty. On April 6, a notice was posted in Durazzo, proclaiming a *levée en masse* of all Christian and Muslim men of certain ages "for the occupation of Koritsa and Argyrocastro." Letters to the same effect were addressed to the chiefs of the different religious communities by the Mutessarif of Durazzo. An appeal was made to Albanian officers in the Turkish Army to come home and help. The proclamation stated at its close that Wied would lead the fifteen thousand men, including three regiments of former Turkish Army reservists expected to be raised. Essad pretended to agree, but secretly ordered his followers not to enlist, and few rushed "to the colors." A Greek who aroused suspicion, Dr. Viola, had contacted Essad and frequently took money to him.

Leopold, Count von Berchtold

Count Albert Mensdorff, Austrian ambassador

Prince Lichnowsky, German ambassador

Count Benckendorff, Russian Ambassador

Paul Cambon, French ambassador

Marquis di San Giuliano, Italian foreign minister

MONTENEGRO

Kosovo

SERBIA

Prishtina

Cetinje

Gusinje

Albanian Alps

North

Prizren

Scutari L.

Scutari

Drin R.

Kukus

Tetovo

Jordar R.

Kushneni

Orosh

Gostivar

S. Giovanni
di Medua

Alessio

Pishkopeja

SERBIA

C. Rodoni

Kruja

Dibra

Kičeva

Durazzo

Arzen R.

Tirana

Kavaya

Elbasan

Okhrida

Shkumbi R.

Prens

Monastir

Ljushna

Okhrida L.

Prespa L.

Pta Samana

Semeni R.

Devol R.

Fieri

Berat

Tomoritsa

Koritsa

Grikal

Osum R.

C. Glossa

Valona

Kanina

Viosa

Klisura

Ersek

Ljeskovik

Premeti

Khimara

Argyrokastro

Drino

Konitsa

of Otranto

Santi-Quaranta

GREECE

Corfu

Jannina

ADRIATIC SEA

Strait

ALBANIA
English Miles
0 10 20 30
Kilometres
0 10 20 30

(A) Long. East of Greenwich (B)

21°

Austro-Hungarian marines

Gottlieb von Jagow, German foreign minister

Durazzo street scene, 1914

Ferdinand, Duc de Montpensier

THE THRONE PERILOUS.

AUSTRIA AND ITALY (*to the new Ruler of Albania*). "BE SEATED, SIR."

Princess Sophie and Prince Wilhelm zu Wied

Wied is painted by Prof. Alfred Schwarz

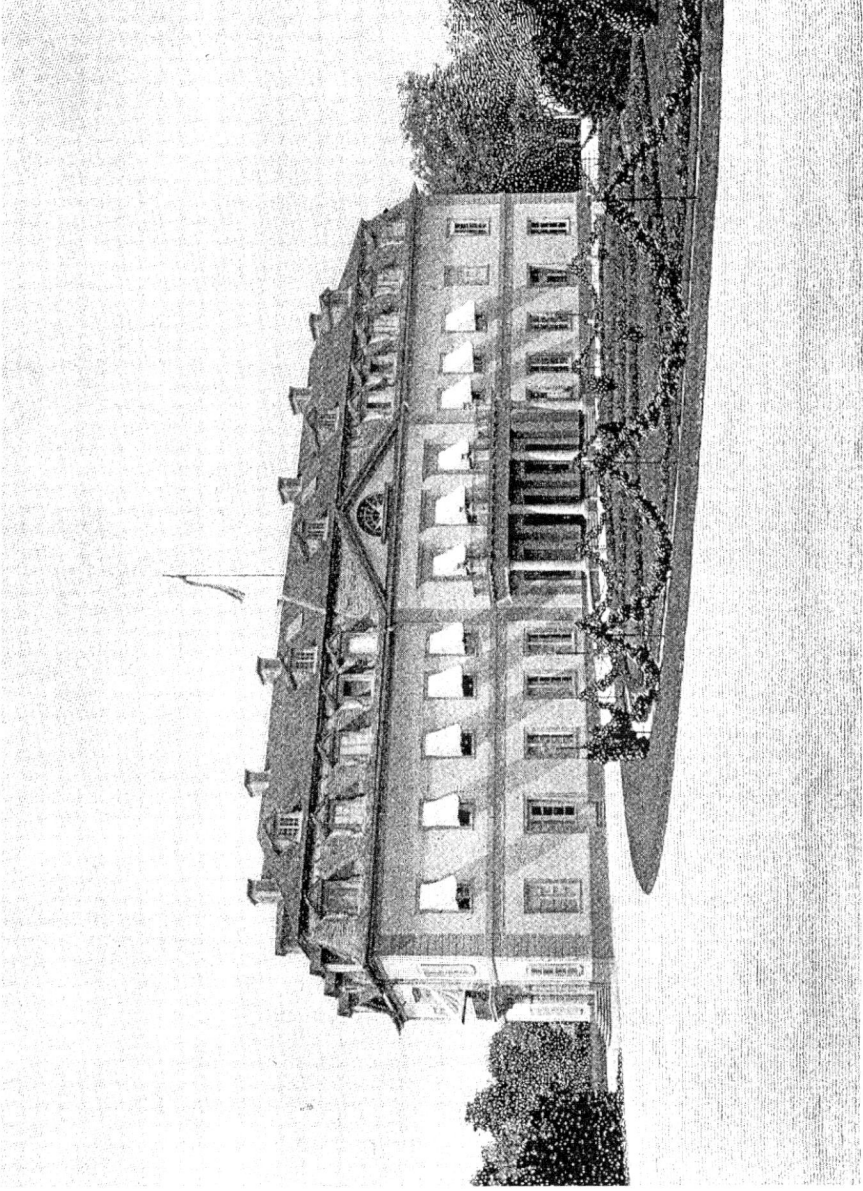

Schloss Neu Wied

Schloss Mon Repos

From all sides, cold water was thrown on the mobilization idea. The International Control Commission came to Durazzo for two days to offer their advice. The French Commissioner, Krajewski, told his former Commission colleague Mufid Bey Libohova (now Minister of Justice) that the move was dangerous. Mufid replied that Italian minister Aliotti had advised, "March against Argyrocastro. If you succeed, it is well, if not, Italy will not abandon you." But Krajewski, no doubt reflecting France's pro-Greek policy, urged concessions to the Epirotes to avoid bloodshed and possible setbacks. Revealing the labyrinthian world in which these men were functioning, Krajewski believed Essad was Aliotti's creature and for that reason Essad had publicly favored the attack.[34]

British Commissioner Harry Lamb also opposed mobilizing the Albanian and Turkish reservists, many of whom were presumably veterans of Essad's Turkish command. He emphasized to the Albanian government the "unsatisfactory state of the finances," the scant hope of success with an untrained, unequipped army without artillery, and the dangers of complications with Greece and Montenegro "over the frontier question," and on general principles.[35] De Veer joined in this advice, also fearing the power which such an army would give War Minister Essad.

Wied gave in to the pressure and was considering naming a Dutch officer as field commander of the available forces, which now numbered 1,500 gendarmes trained by the Dutch and 2,000 raw recruits. Then Essad again offered to raise either 20,000, 25,000, or 30,000 men (depending on whose account is believed) in central Albania for service in the south. Although the recently-purchased Italian rifles were distributed to Essad's recruits, the Dutch officers wisely prevented his removal of the mountain guns from Durazzo to his stronghold in the Tirana area. Essad's grandiose plan to raise an army had the same practical objections as Wied's had, so that it was not realized either.

More suspicions of Essad were not long in coming. He was constantly in friction with the Dutch officers, who, whatever their shortcomings, were trying to do their jobs without ulterior political motives. At one point, Essad offered to resign.[36]

On April 6, four Italian destroyers arrived at Valona to "carry out soundings" of the bay, presumably to facilitate any future military landing.[37]

In April, Emperor Franz Josef's cough became serious, with inflammation of the lung. His life hung in the balance. All night long, a special train stood fully coaled in the railway station at Konopischt, to bring Franz Ferdinand with all speed to Vienna if the worst happened. However, to the surprise of many, the old emperor recovered and, until June 27, resisted his doctors' advice to go to Ischl to relax.[38]

On March 30, 1914, Sir Rennell Rodd reported from Rome that he was assured (through "well-informed sources") that it was only the paramount necessity of first securing a settlement of the Albanian question which caused a submissive attitude by Italy regarding the treatment of Italians in the Austrian Empire. Once Albania had been fairly started on her path, "there would be a considerable change in this respect," he predicted[39]

Crown Prince Ferdinand of Romania in late March told French Ambassador Jules Cambon privately in Berlin that Wied had to accept Essad while things were disorganized, but "it would be necessary at some given moment to discard him so that he could do no more harm." However, for the present, he thought "Essad is better experienced than anyone about [local] sentiments…"[40]

On April 4, British Ambassador Maurice de Bunsen in Vienna reported that Berchtold had received a telegram from the Austrian Minister in Durazzo, saying that the gendarmerie was unable to handle the Epirote bands, and the Metropolitan of Koritsa reported that town on fire, a Dutch gendarmerie officer wounded, and Greek regulars helping the Epirotes. Berchtold expressed regret that talks between the Dutch Colonel of gendarmes, Thomson, and the Epirotes had been broken off.[41]

In April, Kaiser Wilhelm, in his usual clumsy way, proposed to Vienna the confiscation of the Montenegrin seacoast and that it be given as a present to Albania. This, he said, would force the Serbians to turn to Austria. The Austrians considered the project, but Italy would not permit a common frontier between Albania and the Austro-Hungarian Empire. The Italians said that they would at least have to be given the southern Austrian Province of Trent, which was largely inhabited by Italians, in compensation-- a politically impossible solution[42]

On March 30, 1914, Wied, seriously concerned about the Epirote problem, wrote the Kaiser, asking him to mediate, especially with King Constantine, who was to visit Kaiser Wilhelm at Corfu in a few days. Wied said that for the sake of national unity he could not afford the precedent of concession. He predicted warfare if the Greeks continued their present course. Wied entrusted this letter to the German *chargé* in Durazzo, Nadolny, and asked him to give the Kaiser some personal information, but Nadolny was not able to speak to the Kaiser.

King Constantine denied Greece's responsibility for the problem and blamed it all on the Bulgarians![43] A Romanian newspaper reported that Wied was also asking King Carol to intercede with Greece.[44] On April 6, the Kaiser did telegraph from the Achilleon on Corfu to his Foreign Office regarding his concern over events in Epirus and urged a quick decision on sending a German diplomatic representative to Albania, especially as he had gotten the impression that the International Control Commission was overstepping its authority.[45]

The German Foreign Office replied on April 9 that the matter was under study, but that "a longtime civil servant of the Foreign Office, Legation Counselor Nadolny," had already been sent to Albania to study matters, although he had only been able to visit coastal areas due to the bad climate and unsettled conditions of the interior. As Nadolny was also a member of the International Control Commission, he could watch over German political and commercial interests while the matter was under study. When a diplomat was appointed, the Foreign Office predicted, there would be a general consulate at the capital. They noted, somewhat disdainfully that as an undeveloped country of only about 900,000 souls, there was no need for separate diplomatic and economic representatives. It was true that Austria-Hungary had an embassy or legation with an attached consulate in Durazzo, a general consulate in Scutari, and a consulate in Valona, while Italy had the same. Of course, those were the two Great Powers with the greatest interest in Albania. However, France had an legation, with a consulate authorized, in Durazzo, and a consulate in Scutari, while Russia had a general consulate in Durazzo and vice consulates in Scutari and Valona. Romania and Greece had legations in Durazzo, but Britain as yet had no official diplomatic representative other than Harry Lamb, who was on the International Control Commission.[46]

Nadolny reported on April 10 that Albania intended to send diplomats abroad, especially to Vienna and Rome. Sureya Bey Vlora was elated to be the first minister to Vienna, but was expected to move on to Rome in a short time, because Finance Minister Adamidis hoped to be relieved of the burden of his ministry. In fact, a lot of the local beys hoped for some government position.[47]

Despite his question about an envoy to Durazzo, during his annual visit to Corfu the Kaiser's attention was so focused on the ancient ruins being excavated that his entourage was concerned about the lack of interest he paid to European affairs. On the way back from Greece, he visited Franz Ferdinand again at Konopischt.[48]

Around April 7 or 8, Koritsa repelled another Epirote attack, with one Greek officer and one Greek non-commissioned officer killed and numerous others wounded on both sides. The people of Koritsa formed a volunteer corps including the one thousand gendarmes trained and led by Dutch officers. It had been decided to expel the "Greek Committee" (club) from Koritsa for its pro-Greek propaganda which caused friction, including the killing of Father Kritzovech, a leading anti-Greek activist. On the other hand, Greeks complained that the gendarmerie, aided by Muslim Albanians, were disarming "the Christians of Koritsa" and that on April 8, there was much bloodshed. The remaining Greek insurgents in Koritsa laid down their arms.

A longtime American missionary in the Skrapari district named Phineas Kennedy reported from Valona that ten villages in the district had been burned by the Greeks and the population was in "a pitiable condition." A Dr. Shaw, an English "Honorable Secretary" of the British Epirus Relief Fund in England, said that it had spent its last two thousand pounds and had 230 sacks of flour at Santi Quaranta in a warehouse, but could not get them out without payment of two hundred pounds. He asked British subjects to help.[49]

Wied addressed a plea for peace to his southern subjects, In reply, on April 8, he received a telegram from "Ahmet", the Mayor of Koritsa, co-signed by "Thesistakli Germeses [an Orthodox Christian respected by the Muslims], Pandeli Tsale, Llanite, Kristag Xafer Bey, Malig, Rossi, Islam, Mehmet Ali, and Mohammed Belil." It was addressed, in French, to "His Majesty the King of the Albanians," and professed lifelong loyalty. It then proceeded to assert that all the troubles in the District of Koritsa were brought on by "bands organized in Greek territory, amidst which are a great number of regular soldiers disguised, and officers of the Hellenic Army." It reported that two villages in the vicinity of Bilishta had been burned and the village was being "menaced on two sides."[50]

In early April, British Member of Parliament Aubrey Herbert in London stated that a "reliable source" had told him that Midhat Bey, Provisional Governor of Colonia (Ersek), reported that the "*andartis*" (an Epirote "sacred battalion") together with the regular Greek Army, had burned all the houses in the village of Kosee and fourteen houses in the village of Delvine. They also reportedly burned all the Muslim houses in Ogran, and the home of the Albanian priest in the village Mellan, where many women and children were burned alive. Edith Durham wrote that her informant had confirmed this.[51]

By April 13, 1914, a "severe encounter" between Albanians and Epirotes had taken place near Premeti, where the Epirote insurgents were trying to reoccupy the villages which they had evacuated. There were "several" casualties on both sides and some Greek soldiers had been captured. The

221

southernmost point reached by the Albanian gendarmerie was the bank of the Voinea River, where the opposing forces faced each other. The Albanians felt that they were better at guerilla warfare, and could beat the Epirotes if the Greek army left.

To try to deal with the situation, the newly-appointed royal Governor of Koritsa was to leave Durazzo on May 12, with an additional force of five hundred gendarmes. Koritsa was then a four or five-day journey from Durazzo, depending upon the state of the roads.[52]

Between April 11-13, 1914, the Albanian forces under Dutch Major Snellen captured Greek soldiers. They took statements, written in English because the interpreter did not speak any Dutch. Three of the men giving statements were regular soldiers in the Greek army, and one was a Greek mercenary who was offered one franc a day (now about $ 3.45) to serve with the Greek troops. Three hundred and fifty of them under a Lieutenant Sterios and a Colonel Mavraza of the regular Greek army came to Koritsa where they had been involved in a stiff fight on April 2 at the local girls' school, following which they were taken prisoner.[53]

In April Colonel G. F. Phillips, of the West Yorkshire Regiment, along with a British detachment of eight officers and 383 enlisted men of the regiment, was stationed in Scutari. Phillips had also commanded the international military force at Scutari since the previous October, when it replaced the naval brigade, and was now temporary civil governor of Scutari. His authority was originally limited to a 6.25 mile radius[54] from the city, but his personal influence reached farther. Every week, "chieftains in gorgeously picturesque and variegated costume" came to him from the surrounding tribes for his advice and help in settling disputes. They kissed his hand. The chiefs of the Hoti and Gruda had been there in the first three days (of April) to voice their refusal to be incorporated into Montenegro. Phillips had persuaded them that to attack Montenegro before the International Frontier Commission for Northern Albania had definitely drawn the frontier (although it had in reality already been decided) would be wrong. The tribes of northeast Albania understandably complained that they were cut off from their market towns of Ipek, Djakova, and other places which had been assigned by the Powers to Serbia. When Phillips said that they could still go to the markets, they answered "but we may not take our rifles." They had heretofore been pacified by funds from Phillips, but these were now exhausted. As a consequence, they might be moved to raid Serbs.

Captain S. G. Francis had been administering the northern cities of Alessio and San Giovanni di Medua with detachments of the West Yorkshire Regiment and Austrian and Italian troops. He had been obliged to try to collect the old Ottoman taxes to meet fiscal debt, and met with great difficulty in doing so. Albanians did not understand his actions. The fish tax had always been earmarked for this purpose, and the fish market had to be surrounded by gendarmes before the tax could be collected, although Francis kept their respect. It was now proposed to send in an Albanian civil governor.

General de Veer, commanding the gendarmerie, had arrived at Durazzo from Valona along with Major Henri J. L. Kroon, who was raising gendarmes at Scutari. The registration of reservists was going on in the country and all was temporarily quiet in Koritsa by April 11.[55]

However, by April 17, 1914, two Dutch officers had left Durazzo for northern areas still occupied by the Montenegrins where fighting had broken out. It was the country of the Hoti and Gruda tribes, which for centuries had had defensive truces, or *besas,* with other northern Malissor tribes such as the Clementi, Skreli and Kastrati.[56] The International Northern Boundary Delimitation Commission had been waiting for winter to end, leaving off their work the previous winter at Prizren. In future they were to be accompanied by Austrian and Italian troops to prevent further dispute at the Malissor country and Lake Scutari.[57]

On May 5, Grey somewhat belatedly urged the French and Russians that Albania should have access to traditional markets in the areas given to Serbia. This message was also sent to Colonel Granet of the Northern Frontier Commission.[58]

However, as usual, Grey was not prepared to do more than suggest and protest.

On Easter Sunday, April 12, 1914, Berchtold was at the Freudenau race track in Vienna, nattily dressed in black top hat and grey topcoat. He ate coffee ice cream in his box near that of Prime Minister Count Karl Stürgkh. Rumors had reached Vienna of clashes between the Austrian and Italian advisers of Wied's inner council. When asked about affairs, Berchtold evaded the question, asked who would win the Handicap that afternoon, crossed his legs and nonchalantly leaned back in his box seat. He bet on the winner and ate a chocolate truffle.[59] This was Vienna, after all.

Prenk Bib Doda, who had assumed the title of Prince, arrived in Albania April 12 from Rome and left on the 13th for Scutari, finally refusing to become a member of the current Albanian cabinet. He claimed the Ministry of Public Works was beneath him, and laid claim to the Ministry of Interior, which Essad naturally refused to give up. After his return from Italy, Prenk Bib Doda spent two days in Durazzo, strolling down the only street followed by a half-dozen faithful retainers, gravely returning salutations. When he still could not get the office of Interior Minister, he retired to Scutari.[60] Prenk's influence in the north made the possibility of an actual defection serious. It was also reported that M. Adamidis, Minister of Finance, would soon resign and become Albanian Minister in Rome.

Someone referred to as "a Protestant Albanian missionary" telegraphed to Aubrey Herbert on April 11 from Koritsa that he and his men had captured or killed a "band of eight men" of whom two were Cretans, and six came from Constantinople, Athens, and other parts of Greece. Greeks had burned many houses, it was reported, killed the Vlach (ethnic Romanian) priest and his brother and cousin, and mutilated them as well as other men. A number of Albanian villages had been burned and sacked, some being "utterly destroyed." The Greek Ambassador in London "officially" denied this in a letter to *The Times*, blaming only a few deserters, and "understandable hostility" from a civil war in Epirus, where there had been "terrible suffering endured by Christians for many generations at the hand of Albanian Mussulmans."

San Giuliano left April 13 for Austrian Abbazia to meet with Berchtold and Mérey (Austrian Ambassador in Rome) and the Duke of Avarna (Italian Ambassador to Vienna) on the heels of meetings between the Kaiser, Franz Josef, and Vittorio Emmanuel.[61]

Dressed in Panama hat and spats, Berchtold boarded his salon car in Vienna for Abbazia, a "palm-dotted" Habsburg resort on the Adriatic, not far from Franz Ferdinand's "Miramare". His meeting with Marquess San Giuliano was to discuss complaints by Italians in Austria, and also Italy's desire to invest in Albania. They lunched in a zeppelin, 1500 feet in the air, on poached salmon and cold champagne, as they viewed the coast. Other pleasant activities followed.[62]

A ship chartered by the Austro-Albanian Friendship Committee arrived in Durazzo on April 15 with a large deputation headed by Prince Fritz Liechtenstein and a Count Harrach. They were received by Wied that day, and the next night they gave a big banquet on board their ship. Sophie's two Ladies-in-Waiting, along with Heaton and Ekrem Bey Vlora, were sent, accompanied by most cabinet ministers, to represent the Court. Lots of windy speeches were given about good relations, etc.

Some days later, one of the Court's "regular informants" reported a conspiracy to kill Wied, and the Black Hand (a Serbian terrorist group) was reported to be operating in Durazzo with plans to kill Essad, although they were loyal to the Throne. This was not taken seriously, and Heaton and Selim Bey told Sami Bey Vrioni as a grim joke that his name was on the hit list. They sent him an impression of Selim's hand in ink in an envelope by a servant, who was told to say that a strange Scutari man had left it. Sami soon figured out the trick and sent it back to Heaton with "some threatening remarks added to it!"[63]

Prince Michel Sturdza of the Romanian Legation was sent to Northern Epirus to study the situation, and in due course sent an official report. Von Trotha and Heaton continually urged

Wied to send home the ladies and lead his nation in person against the insurgents. However, Wied seemed to them to pretend that Epirus was not that important. The people of Durazzo no longer cheered the King as he rode down the main street, and people, mostly "nationalist," daily came to Heaton with tales of woe. The general complaint in Durazzo was that only Muslims or "Turks" could get government jobs. Heaton was one of the few who would report bad news like this to Wied.[64]

Everyone in Durazzo was not as concerned as they might have been. A young Englishman, visiting Durazzo on business, suggested a horse race meeting, which actually took place on the sandy shore, was attended by Wied and much of the town, and was a great success. There were races for officers, European civilians, town dwellers, and peasants from the surrounding villages. With Wied's approval, Heaton set up a committee to encourage sports in the schools and started a sporting club for adults, for golf, tennis, shooting, and horse races, but it was stillborn due to the unrest.[65]

On April 16, "mountaineers" arriving in Durazzo reported that, at the instigation of the Serbs and Catholic priests, an "autonomous state" had been formed in the extreme northwest of Albania between the White Drin River and the Montenegrin frontier. The capitol was Reshan and the President was Arif Bey, a Huchnite tribesman. A force of two-hundred gendarmes had been formed and were paid three Turkish pounds (about $230 today) a month by Serbia. "No postage stamps have been issued … the citizens of the new republic not being in the habit of writing letters," *The Times* of London joked.

Greek regulars and "holy battalions" prevented Albanian forces from coming south. From the stretch of land from Voina, near Premeti, to Mount Grammos, local bands occasionally sallied forth to intimidate inhabitants to rise up.

In Wied's Cabinet, the only Epirote and one of the three Christian ministers, Dr. Themosticles Adamidis (later to serve in the Greek government) offered to resign. He had favored all national expenditures being submitted to the International

226

Control Commission. Prenk Bib Doda had still refused to appear in Durazzo, favoring Scutari as the Capitol. Thus, the only remaining Christian in the Cabinet was the aged Dr. Tourtulis, who, until only a few weeks before, was practicing medicine in Egypt.

At this point, the British Army Council gave notice that, until further orders, officers might not visit Albania without War Office approval.

The Kaiser was still in Corfu with Chancellor Bethmann-Hollweg on April 20. Venizelos and the Greek Foreign Minister, Dr. Streit, had a "satisfactory" visit with the Kaiser there, in which Venizelos received an autographed photo of the Kaiser, and Streit got the Order of the Red Eagle.[66]

In Russia on the morning of April 3, Sir George Buchanan was received by the Czar. Nicholai said the only European question which caused any anxiety was that of Albania. He did not know whether it would be possible in the long run to keep Austria and Italy in line with the other powers or whether they would leave the concert of powers and adopt a policy of partition. In the latter case they were all certain to quarrel, and, as this would mean a weakening of the Triple Alliance, he confessed that it would have some countervailing advantages for Russia. He was very sorry for the Greeks as they were being "rather hardly treated", both with regard to the present situation in Epirus and the question of islands in dispute since the Balkan wars. He did not know what could be done. It was the old story, he felt: Europe was divided into two camps and it was impossible to get the Concert to work together.[67]

Down in Abbazia On April 17, Berchtold and San Giuliano spent most of the day on a "motor car excursion" and were believed to be discussing Albania and Montenegrin troop incursions.[68] Their conference concluded amicably on the 19th, and they telegraphed their agreements to Bethmann-Hollweg.[69] San Giuliano reported that they had concentrated on Albania, where "the position of the Prince did not seem well assured." They agreed that, of the three border problems, the Montenegrin one should be settled first. Colonel G. F. Phillips, the British

Commanding Officer at Scutari, had suggested that a portion of the International Control Commission should be moved there. Berchtold opposed weakening the ten-kilometer radius around Scutari which would result from sending troops north to the border, as had been suggested. Both foreign ministers favored concession to the Epirotes. As to the remaining Greeks, the two debated how to forcefully but politely ask them to be withdrawn, as the Greek Government needed the cover of such a message. Austria would say the withdrawal was "expected" (*erwarten*) and the Italians would say "requested" (*demandare*). They thought Venizelos was the only one strong enough to cause the evacuation. They agreed "so far as practical measures were concerned," only to advise the Albanian Government to continue with more energy the measures which had apparently already been initiated in organizing a militia, with perhaps some further addition of foreign officers.[70]

In response to Wied's call in early April for an army, provincial beys had responded immediately, promising around thirteen thousand men. But then, nothing happened. Meanwhile, Essad daily visited the Palace and was at all functions. Diplomatic and court receptions were still held, and all seemed well on the outside and the honeymoon mood continued.[71]

Two hundred of the five hundred gendarmes being sent south with the new Governor of Koritsa were Essad's men, and they deserted as soon as they got a few miles out of Durazzo, saying they did not know they would have to leave Central Albania ("Essad's country.")[72]

Wied and his advisors decided that the King should not stay cooped up in Durazzo, but should get out into his country. They decided to visit Tirana, east of Durazzo, which was the heart of Essad's and his family's landholdings and sphere of influence.

At 4 a.m. on the morning of April 23, von Trotha and Heaton donned their dress uniforms with tight tunics and Astrakhan caps. They set out with Wied's mounted escort commander, Dutch Major Lucas Roelfsema, the coachmen, and the horses the Wieds were to ride through Tirana, where Heaton and party intended to arrive first at 11 a.m. and wait. The rest of the royal entourage were to follow in automobiles. Heaton et al, crossed the swamps outside Durazzo and passed the heights of Raspul before the sun rose. They arrived at Shiak, "a picturesque village" some seven kilometers (five miles) from Durazzo. There they crossed over the river by a high wooden bridge and rode through the narrow streets already crowded with spectators. Some miles beyond the town they stopped in beautiful surroundings and enjoyed breakfast from their saddlebags, as it already was becoming warm.[73] The landscape on the route to Tirana was fertile, with orchards, prairies, forests, wild roses, clematis, jasmine, and a breeze from the sea. Tirana itself is protected on the north by high mountains and was then hidden from view upon approaching by the leaves of its plane trees, mulberry bushes, cypresses, and innumerable gardens with orange and lemon trees. Water from springs cascaded everywhere.

About 10 a.m., the advance party spotted Tirana and rode on through the valley until they met gendarmes, who, surrounded by children and the curious, awaited the Prince outside of town. Dervish Hima, a well-known Albanian politician and popular agitator, was rehearsing the populace on the road. He told them how to cheer and how to behave when Wied came. He waved his arms and shouted "*Rroft*" [long life!] repeatedly, making the crowd repeat it, and then joined Heaton and company resting under a tree and sucking oranges brought from a nearby fruit stall. Essad was originally to have shared the third automobile with Turkhan Pasha, the Prime Minister, but, after the royal cars left, his was brought and something supposedly went wrong with it at the gate. While the chauffeur was tinkering with it, Essad slipped away and jumped into a waiting two-horse carriage, which rushed to catch the King's car halfway to Tirana. Around 12:20 a hooting of auto horns was heard and two cars came slowly up, discharging the King's suite and a smiling Essad. Poor Prime Minister Turkhan only arrived after lunch.

Tirana was in the center of the large land holdings of Essad's Toptani clan. The town itself was decrepit, muddy and gray, but there were almond blossoms and dark cypress trees and minarets against the background of the snow-clad mountains on the east. Often a cloud of blue smoke hung over the dull red roofs of the houses, saturating the air with the smell of burnt wood.[74]

Essad rode horseback behind Wied's carriage through the town, which was packed with thousands of people from the district. Tirana was bigger than Durazzo, lying in a fertile valley. On all sides, Essad's "militia," or henchmen, pretended to keep order. The procession rode slowly through the streets, stopped every few yards by deputations who made speeches of welcome. The crowds seemed sincere. An old cannon was fired in salute every ten minutes, as it took that long to reload. As it was a Muslim area, the women were completely veiled in black robes from head to foot, with wooden sandals.

The party went up a private road to Essad's villa on a hill overlooking the town for lunch. Heaton found the meal horrible, served in quick succession by attendants "who didn't look too clean." It consisted of "soup, meat, and pudding; all tasted of mutton fat and all other imaginable nastiness," he thought. Sophie diplomatically ate some and praised it, but the rest of the Europeans stuck to bread and mineral water. As a gesture to their guests, the Albanians did not smack their lips or belch, as was customary. Good coffee followed.[75]

On this occasion, Wied unwittingly committed a *faux pas*. He had helped his wife from their carriage and allowed her to walk before him, an action which the people interpreted as a sign of feebleness![76]

After lunch the group headed to the town schoolhouse. On the way, a little girl fell from a second floor window of a house with a piercing scream, and landed on the heads of spectators. She was uninjured and her mother led her away. Undaunted, the Wieds then received deputations for two hours in the school. They adjourned for tea to the house of respected Abdi Bey Toptani (later Agriculture Minister), which was "run on more European lines." Although Essad's cousin, Abdi was

230

estranged from him. As customary, as the host he personally served food and did not sit at the table until the meal was over.

The trip seemed a great success and Heaton, von Trotha, and Roelfsema left at five o'clock in the afternoon, reaching Durazzo over the "white, dusty road" at eleven-thirty that night. The Palace ladies were waiting up.[77]

At the end of April an Italian naval squadron, commanded by the Duke of Abruzzi, a cousin of the Italian king, called at Durazzo. A dinner was given for the Duke by Wied at the Palace, and the next day the Palace staff (including the ladies) had lunch on his ship, the *Regina Elena*. The Duke was very popular due to his "open, breezy manner." He showed everyone around the ship, including his stateroom where his pinup pictures were turned to the wall in consideration of the ladies.

Some days later, the Wieds visited the picturesque town of Kavaya, southeastward from Durazzo, and received a good reception from thousands of people who turned out. Their carriages drove over a crude road and two rickety bridges, maintained by Essad. An imam spoke from a second floor window to the crowd, stating that his Muslim and Christian fellow-citizens were united in loyalty to the King. (About a month later, however, he and they became rebels.) Unable to bring themselves to eat much native food this time, the visitors satisfied their hunger with a picnic on the way home.[78]

At the beginning of May 1914, while negotiations proceeded in the south, hostilities had been suspended, but the Albanians attempted to advance. Argyrocastro was threatened by them until Epirote reinforcements drove them off and captured Colonia (Ersek) after a heavy battle, in which an Epirote chief and thirty Albanians were killed and sixty Albanians were wounded. Essad was blamed for the unfair attack and losses.[79] The International Control Commission stated that it would act as intermediary and telegraphed Zographos that the Albanian Government agreed to "concessions," which the Epirotes would receive upon a cease-fire and which would be delivered at Santi Quaranta at that time. Zographos agreed and notified Durazzo that the cease fire would begin a noon on May seventh.

Unconfirmed reports began to be received in Vienna that the Albanian gendarmerie had found in the village of Kodra, near Tepeleni, in a half-burned church, the charred corpses of two-hundred Muslim Albanians, crucified by the Epirotes.[80] Early in May, this was confirmed when Captain Wouter de Waal, leading a volunteer group, crossed the Vrina River near the village of Kodra, where they found inside the Orthodox convent the remains of 218 people, old men, women, and children who had been butchered, some being crucified.[81]

On May 4, Durazzo reported that Colonia had been captured and burned by Epirotes armed with artillery and machine guns, and that they were advancing. However, it was also reported that Albanian forces won back many villages and got as far as Bonati, near Colonia. Some two thousand loyal "*franc-tireurs*" (guerillas) enrolled at Tirana and were supposedly marching on Koritsa. It was expected that more volunteers would come from the north and middle of the country, and all were expected to join at Koritsa.[82]

By May 4, Commissioner Nadolny was able to report from Durazzo that negotiations on the Epirote question were proceeding with Varatassi, erstwhile Greek Governor of Corfu. The Greek Government wanted to name him their ambassador to Albania once diplomatic relations had been established, but he had already had informal discussions with Wied. Officially, Greece maintained that it had carried out its duty to evacuate Epirus, so that there was technically nothing for Varatassi to negotiate. However, he obviously could play a role in any negotiations between Albania and the Epirotes, and the International Control Commission could monitor conditions in the south. Nadolny felt that the British and German delegates to the International Control Commission would be the best persons to deal with the Epirotes. In the meantime, the gendarmerie could keep up pressure on the rebels.

By now, Wied mistrusted not only Varatassi but all the Greeks and Epirotes, and still wanted to use force, as many were advising.[83]   Turkhan Pasha pointed out to Varatassi that it would be more respectful for Greece to name him ambassador or minister, rather than a mere "diplomatic agent." He had told the same thing to the Russian Control Commission member, who was also only Russia's "diplomatic agent," and to the Serbian Consul General.   Nadolny wrote to Chancellor Bethmann-Hollweg, suggesting that, in view of German budget problems, the Consul General be named *chargé d' affaires* as well.[84]   On May 15, Greece, prodded by Romania, had finally ordered Varatassi to apply to the Albanian Government as Greece's Resident Minister.[85]

France did not want to be too heavily committed in Albanian affairs. On May 13 French Minster de Fontenay at Durazzo was instructed by the *Quai d'Orsay* that, "The Legation of the Republic [of France] in Albania is, … from the political point of view essentially an observation post."[86]

At Koritsa, the rebels did not observe the May 7 ceasefire and captured Mount Morava, later claiming they had not received word of the truce. At Santi Quaranta, "President" Zographos suggested to the ICC and Mehdi Bey that the parties meet at "neutral" Corfu, a Greek-ruled island. This being agreed upon, Zographos arrived on the motor launch *Puglia*, and they talked at the Hotel Bella Venezia. Nine days of difficult talks followed, during which Mehdi bey Frasheri was stubborn, and Zographos actually got into a fist fight with the Italian delegate, Leoni. However, they finally agreed on the "Protocol of Corfu," by virtue of which (1) the Koritsa and Argyrocastro districts would be controlled by the International Control Commission under the nominal rule of Wied; (2) the Epirote Sacred Bands (*komitadjis* or "holy hosts") would become gendarmes under Dutch officers; (3) elementary schools would be bilingual, with Greek preponderant in Orthodox schools, and (4) there would be local autonomy under the Epirotes, but under the nominal rule of Wied.[87]

The Albanians ratified the Protocol on June 25, but the Epirote government never did.[88]   They finally refused on July fifth.[89]

At this time, a Scot, Miss Katherine MacQueen, visited the Durazzo Palace on many days and sat with Queen Sophie and her two German ladies-in-waiting, cutting out and sewing clothes for refugees in Epirus. She found Sophie very easy and pleasant, full of ideas for helping the people, especially women's work, visiting hospitals, etc. Sophie apparently had not yet lost her optimism. Miss MacQueen also recognized the Ruritanian imagery of the whole adventure, commenting, "Oh! It is an extraordinary little place, like an Anthony Hope kingdom."[90]

While events simmered in Albania, on May 12, General Conrad met German General Moltke and had tea in the sitting room of a hotel suite in Carlsbad, then in Austrian Bohemia. They discussed the next war. Conrad grumbled that Serbia's provocations in Albania and elsewhere could no longer go unanswered. Belgrade, he told the German Chief of Staff, was presuming too much on the patience of Conrad's imperial masters (an allusion to Franz Ferdinand's pacifism and the ill Franz Josef's caution.)[91]

In Albania auxiliaries to the royal gendarmerie were springing up. Attached to the irregular royal Albanian bands were Captain Leon Ghilardi, a Croatian and former Austrian Army officer, and the American Harold Sherwood Spencer. Both were doing excellent work fighting rebels.

Suddenly, on May 8, with Captain Castoldi translating, Essad tendered his resignation to the King, telling him that he knew all the stories that had been circulated about him, and that there was no truth in them. He said government was impossible with him in the cabinet if he was not trusted. He was loyal to the King, he said, but would go to the United States for a few years to prove his honesty, and if he had a thousand souls they would all be at Wied's disposal. Wied refused to accept his resignation. He coaxed and flattered Essad to stay, to the surprise of some who thought it a great opportunity to be rid of the scoundrel. Soon long caravans of ponies left Durazzo for Shiak, Tirana, and Kavaya at Essad's instance, laden with rifles and ammunition to arm the natives. Word soon came back that the recruits took the arms but refused to march "against their brothers." Essad went to talk to them and returned in a few days, claiming that they had been offended by some minor royal official, but he had talked them back into readiness to march.[92] Two days after his return to Durazzo, news arrived that a rebellion had broken out in Shiak, near Tirana. The next day, Essad attempted to have some machine guns taken to Tirana without the King's knowledge, but this was prevented by the Dutch officers. Essad declared that the recent troop rebellion was of no importance, but Wied now had him watched.[93]

Despite the truce, Albanian forces were defeated on May 12 near the Monastery of Cepo by Epirote bands reinforced by Greek regular infantry and artillery. At the time, Epirotes reduced more than 150 villages in southern Albania to blackened ruins and reportedly caused the deaths of thousands, bringing about a state of terror.[94] On May 13 the International Control Commission and Zographos agreed to set up a neutral zone on the basis of the forces' positions on May 9. In Vienna, Berchtold announced his and Italy's support for the Corfu concessions on religion, language, and gendarmerie.[95]

On May 14, the Italian member of the International Commission for the Delimitation of the Northern Frontier disagreed with the Frenchman, who was felt to be too pro-Montenegro, so the Commission returned to Scutari.[96]

On May 13, Turkhan Pasha went to Rome to find out whether Aliotti's apparent relationship with Essad was approved by Italy, and Aliotti followed him there.[97] Turkhan was not entirely happy with the Dutch officers in Albania either. While talking with the Austrian Ambassador to Rome, Mérey, Turkhan remarked of the officers that they were "expensive, pretentious, insubordinate, and too rude to the people."[98]

Becoming more alarmed about the situation in the south, on May 15, Heaton wrote in his private capacity to British Ambassador Sir Francis Elliott in Athens, asking him to tell the British Government of the "infamous conduct of the Greek Government" and the Greek atrocities in Epirus. Still distancing themselves from the fray, the Foreign Office told Elliott to take no notice of Heaton's "pardonable attempt to find a remedy."[99]

Now it became very clear that, squeezed between the Muslim Essadist areas and the Greek-dominated south, Wied's power was effectively confined to Durazzo and some areas in the mountains of the north.[100]

19

THE PLOT THICKENS

By May 17, a major of the Ottoman Turkish General Staff and several minor officers of the Turkish army had organized an uprising under one Arif Hikmet, an Albanian, against the Wied government. The Turks had spread the rumor that Wied was a Jew, a much despised entity in Albania, and, rather inconsistently, that he intended to suppress Islam and place Christians over Muslims. Also active in this agitation were the Mufti of Tirana, Musa Kasim, along with Mustafa Broka, and Kamil Haxifesa of Elbasan, who, with help from the Serbs, was purported to be their commander-in-chief. The International Control Commission traveled from place to place, hoping to come to some sort of understanding with the insurgents, but in Tirana some of the populace greeted them with shouts of "Long Live the Sultan!," about which Czar Nicholai later commented "delightful country!"

Wied had wisely taken the precaution of ordering eight quick-firing mountain artillery pieces from the Skoda works at Pilsen in the Austrian Empire, and, at Wied's request, that country sent a captain, two lieutenants, and several non-commissioned officers to train the gendarmerie in their use. Their arrival created some surprise, and the officers were later ordered by Vienna to take no part in actual fighting.[1]

The town of Shiak (also known as Bazar Shiak), located about five miles east of Durazzo, between that city and Tirana, was garrisoned by two hundred gendarmes from Essad's town of Kruja. On the morning of May 17, a telegram from Shiak was received by Wied to the effect that armed men were concentrating in the neighborhood and that the gendarmes there were surrounded and desperately needed reinforcements to hold out. After much dithering, Wied sent Heaton out to investigate unofficially, in civilian clothes. Having decided this much, the King and Queen and their mounted escort rode their horses south along the Durazzo beach around 7 a.m., as was their habit by now. After Heaton left on his mission, the royal party neared the *Sasso Bianco*, which was a rocky hill which rises close to the sea. Suddenly, an escort officer spotted the glint of sunlight on rifle barrels on the hill, and a few men were observed there. Wied's *aide de camp*, Ekrem Bey, urged a return to Durazzo, and Wied readily complied.

Upon return to the Palace Wied sent for Essad, who laughed at the matter, saying that there was no cause for worry. He also reportedly made "several palpably false statements," the nature of which was not recorded. Wied and his staff naturally became more suspicious.

Meanwhile, Heaton trotted over to Shiak on his pony. To his surprise, he found that everything appeared normal and safely in government hands, with gendarmes guarding the bridge and the mayor professing loyalty, although Heaton was warned of rebels nearby. As he rode on between Shiak and Tirana, however, he encountered two bands of rough-looking men, armed with modern rifles and supplies. Upon meeting with them and using his limited Albanian, he learned that, while they were loyal to the King, they were rising against the King's ministry, which they rightly considered representative of the landlord class which had long oppressed them. Heaton noted that passing Essadist gendarmes seemed to know the insurgents and were comfortable around them, while they paid his known position little respect. He trotted back to Durazzo with this intelligence, which Wied was in no hurry to hear, and about which he appeared rather blasé. Of course, he was probably already considering what to do about his problems.[2] Suspicion of Essad was now severe. Captain Castoldi paid close attention to Heaton's report and there was a general Palace fear of a night attack or an Essadist coup in Durazzo.

At this point, Essad, as Minister of War (technically, of Interior), ordered the town commandant, Dutch Major Sluys, to turn the mountain guns over to two Italians of Albanian origin, Captain Moltedo (an experienced artilleryman) and Colonel Muricchio. Sluys did not like that at all. He wanted the guns to

238

be served by the Austrian artillery instructors, Klingspor and Tomjenovic. The argument which ensued between Sluys and Essad at Essad's house almost came to blows. Sluys then went to the Palace and protested to the King, who suspended Essad's decision temporarily. Essad then rushed to the Palace himself to protest this interference with his decision and offered to resign unless Sluys apologized. Wied missed another opportunity to be rid of Essad, and urged him not to resign. In his usual state of indecision, and at the instigation of the Italian Minister Baron Aliotti (who always seemed to be hanging about), Wied sent Mufid, who was acting as temporary Premier in Turkhan's absence abroad, to ask Sluys diplomatically if he might not be ready for a furlough. He also asked that he apologize to Essad. When Mufid spoke to Sluys, he made it sound like an order, and Sluys prepared to turn his city command over to Major Roelfsema. Hearing of this, the Romanian *attachés*, Prince Sturdza and M. Ronette, quickly advised Sluys to first talk the matter over with the King.

Back to the Palace went Sluys, who met with both Wied and Queen Sophie. They expressed some surprise and denied that he had been sent an order to leave. One source says that Sluys persuaded them to order Essad's arrest. Others say that Sluys took it upon himself.[3] Wied himself later implied that it was the Dutch officer's decision.[4] It may have been, as has been suggested, that Sluys had at some previous time been given blanket authority to *disarm* Essad when necessary.[5] It is also unclear whether Essad ever resigned.

Apparently a council of ministers was held on the evening of May 17 at Essad's house. The house stood on a high embrasure of the old Venetian wall, which ran from an ancient watch-tower on the summit above Durazzo down to the shore. The house had become known as a kind of barracks for Essad's armed retainers, whose number was daily increasing, all within two hundred yards of the Palace.[6] Unlike most of the other pashas in Durazzo who had reduced their armed retinues to two or three men when Wied arrived, Essad kept about thirty guards in his house and at least one hundred more in the town, with the main body stationed in the old Venetian tower on the hill.[7] Word now came that Essad had concentrated about two hundred men at his house.[8]

Concern about Essad was now great in all royal quarters. The foreign warships in the harbor were signaled to stand by to send landing parties to protect the Palace, if necessary.[9] That night, a group of "Nationalists and foreigners," most of whom were in the service of the Albanian government, plotted Essad's neutralization. During the evening, Dutch officers could be seen posting men on various points of the rising ground behind the town. Armed Albanians were leading sturdy little Bosnian horses, recently bought for the artillery, through the streets. Austrian cavalry instructors brought in a whole contingent of gendarmes from the adjacent plains. At nine o'clock a line of men marched silently into a small building adjoining the mosque. At the Palace, all was tense, and even the Queen and her ladies, guarded by Heaton, stayed up late. The Durazzo garrison only consisted of about one hundred gendarmes, and they had been recruited by Essad. Sluys took the precaution of recruiting about 150 loyal locals, and about one hundred Catholic Malissors from the north had come to help. The Italian destroyer flotilla returned to the harbor and a distress signal was arranged with the senior Italian naval officer, who had come ashore to ask what he could do. Ministers and officials met with the King constantly. Sami Bey, Essad's son-in-law, however, expressed doubt that anything was wrong and left for home about midnight. The King then went to sleep in his study.[10]

Early in the morning of May 18, while the King was supposedly asleep, Sluys asked the Austrian gunner Klingspor to place two of the mountain artillery pieces in the garden behind the Palace, aimed at Essad's house.[11] About 3 a.m., one of the local beys reported the plan to Palace officials, including the Queen and Heaton and presumably, the King.[12] At about 4:30 a.m., at sunrise, Sluys, accompanied by ten gendarmes, sent nobleman Ayet Bey Libohova-Arslanpashali, a first cousin of Essad, to request the sentries in front of Essad's house to disarm. They were willing, but Essad came to an upstairs window and demanded, "Who dares give orders to my men?" Fifteen or twenty of Essad's men had rushed out of an adjoining house. Major Sluys looked up at Essad, saluted, and replied, "I, Your Excellency, in the name of the King and the nation, call upon your men to lay down their arms." (Sluys later reported that he had told Essad that he was acting on his own authority.)[13] Essad then said that he would only surrender to the King or the Italian Minister, and gave an order.[14] Several of his men snatched up their rifles, opened fire on the gendarmes and one of Sluys's men was wounded. Thereupon, the signal was given by someone to the mountain gun to open fire. A British newspaper correspondent reported that seven rounds were fired,[15] but the consensus seems to be that only three shots were necessary. The first shell blew a hole in Essad's roof and the third entered his bedroom (apparently without exploding), at which point Essad's wife appeared at a window waving a white sheet, and Essad surrendered.[16]

At a signal from the Palace balcony, within fifteen minutes of the firing naval detachments from Austrian and Italian ships landed and took up protective positions around the Palace and the foreign legations.[17] Austria had a cruiser in the harbor and Italy alone had a flotilla of eleven destroyers, one sloop, and the cruiser *Vittor Pisani*, which had been recalled from Valona the previous night. The Italians landed 140 men, while the Austrians landed 60.[18]

Sluys at once reported to the King and asked what to do with Essad, as the King purported to have been ignorant of the plan to disarm him. It is difficult to believe that Wied was entirely ignorant of the scheme. Perhaps the pretense was maintained by all to protect the King from foreign as well as domestic opprobrium. He hesitated, and then, apparently accepting advice from the Austrian Minister, Löwenthal, and the German Nadolny, decided to have Essad sent to the Austrian cruiser, *Szigetvar,* to cool things off. The idea initially was that Essad would be returned to Durazzo later. However, after Sluys was sent on this errand, the Queen, and possibly the Romanian Minister Burghele who was at the Palace, persuaded Wied to

241

have Essad imprisoned. Wied sent Heaton to catch up with Sluys, who was not well pleased by this reversal of plan. Amazingly, when Sluys returned to the Palace, Wied had *again* changed his mind and decided to send Heaton to actually arrest Essad and take him to a warship. Essad was to be asked to sign a written oath, on his honor, to cause no more trouble and to leave Albania and not return without the King's permission. Essad let it be known that he wanted Dr. Nadolny, Sturdza, the Austrian *attaché* Hornborstel, and the Italian *attaché*, the Marquess of Durazzo, to witness his surrender. Baron Aliotti had already warned Wied not to try to court-martial Essad.[19] Apparently, suspicion had also fallen on Mufid Bey, and he was put under house arrest for a while.[20]

At 9 a.m. Heaton led a procession of Austrian and Italian sailors, as well as "dragomen" (local employees) from the Austrian and Italian legations to act as interpreters and insure fair play. They returned to Essad's house. There was a great gateway to the house, which Heaton and the dragomen entered. The front door opened to reveal Essad, his wife, their retainers, and Dr. Berghausen, whose reason for being there was a mystery. The good doctor apparently liked to appear important. Heaton told Essad that he was under arrest and that he was to be escorted to the "landing stage," there to be delivered to Captain Schmidt, the commander of the Austrian cruiser. Essad's wife begged to go too, and Heaton agreed. To protect Essad from assassins, the Italian officer and Heaton took Essad between them. Essad was nervous about taking the shorter route through the town and persuaded Heaton to go down a path beside the town wall and through the Palace garden. This turned out to be a wise move, as it surprised three assassins in the town who were waiting at windows to shoot Essad. The procession crossed the square in front of the Palace, which had been cleared by the police, but a crowd assembled behind the gateway leading to the town. They jeered Essad, who bore himself with great dignity, occasionally saluting, as gendarmes and Heaton led the way. His wife, clothed in black from head to foot and heavily veiled, followed him sadly to his left. The King and Queen appeared for a moment at the window of the Palace to watch, and other windows were filled with chattering Palace servants. At the jetty, Essad was handed over to Captain Schmidt, whereupon he turned to Heaton to say that he was loyal and a victim of intrigue. As he said this, two of his sinister-looking luggage bearers tried to melt into the crowd. Then a waiting launch took him to the *Szigetvar*.[21]

As Essad departed, an armed crowd entered the Palace gardens, where Wied and Sophie and their children responded to wild cheering and *"Rroft Mbreti!"* cries. An excited patriot hurried to deliver an impassioned speech and then the King thanked his people with one word in Albanian (not recorded) which apparently was the right one, as it evoked a fresh outburst of enthusiasm. The King and Queen then reentered the Palace.[22] An official communiqué was issued, stating that Essad would remain on the Austrian ship at Wied's "disposal."[23]

The Austrians and Germans in Durazzo seemed well pleased. Everyone but Baron Aliotti congratulated the King. Essad's house was now searched and some trunks of documents seized and taken to the police station. Wied sarcastically said later that he did not expect to find many incriminating writings, as Essad could barely write his name.[24] The foreign sailors guarded the Palace so closely that they were even in the passages and stairways, but the Italian officers thought this amusing and unnecessary. Later the sailors replaced the regular Albanian palace guards. In the afternoon there were lengthy discussions about what to do with Essad. Some wanted to hang him, some to court-martial him, and the Italians wanted him to retire to Italy.[25] Aliotti's request apparently soon turned into a demand, and Edith Durham maintained that the Austrian and Italian warships in the harbor actually cleared for action against each other for twenty-four hours before Wied finally agreed to turn Essad over to an Italian ship, having been advised by the Romanian Minister, Burghele, to concede that point.[26] This concession seems also to have soothed the Tirana rebels after the Italian legation auto had driven out to them with the news.[27] Having won this concession, Aliotti now demanded that Wied send his hundred or so Malissor defenders home, upon the ground that failure to do so would anger the rebels, who were Muslims. The Italian Minister threatened to withdraw his sailors if Wied did not comply, and the King reluctantly agreed. However, Wied then asked the ministers of the other Great Powers to send troops to defend Durazzo.[28]

Whether Essad was plotting against Wied, or merely insuring his own power base, has never been satisfactorily established. Heaton seems to have had his doubts. But it was certain that Essad was without any fixed loyalties to anyone other than himself, and was what the English of the times would have called, "a thorough bounder," and what the German-speakers called a "*gauner.*"

Years later, Essad claimed rather implausibly that it had become evident to him that Wied's purpose was to weaken the Albanian people so that they might, without further resistance, fall into the lap of Austria, and thereby cease blocking "the march of the Germans to the sea." As his relations with Wied became "much less cordial," he said, he had to summon guards to protect his life against the machinations of the King. Perhaps he also resented having had to vacate the Palace to make way for Wied in the first place.[29]

20

AFTERMATH

On May 20 Aliotti and, surprisingly, the weak-willed academic Romanian Burghele, went to the Palace and blamed Austria for the treatment of Essad. Suddenly placed on the defensive, Wied denied that he had caused Essad to be arrested. He said that all he had done was to take the precaution of previously authorizing Sluys to disarm him, if necessary. The Italian and Romanian ministers had then talked Wied into transferring Essad into Italian custody and sending him into exile in Italy, provided he signed the pledge not to cause trouble from abroad and not to return without the King's permission.[1] De Veer and Thomson had returned to Durazzo, and Thomson told the King that he had intercepted cipher telegrams of Essad's in Valona. In his zeal to avoid complications, Wied ordered these and Essad's other papers returned to Essad unopened, and refused the advice of some (including Heaton) to court-martial the fallen minister. Heaton warned that Essad would be more dangerous abroad than in custody or dead. In a conversation with Austro-Hungarian envoy Löwenthal, the King's German lord chamberlain, Major von Trotha, took the blame for ordering the arrest in order to cover up the probable fact that Queen Sophie had talked Wied into authorizing Sluys to disarm Essad.[2]

Having readily signed the required promise, Essad told Heaton again that he had been loyal and that Wied would regret his hasty action and recall him, at which time he would gladly return and work for the good of the country. The two parted in a friendly manner. Essad was then transferred to the Italian steamer *Bengazi*, which sailed at 3 p.m., for Brindisi.[3]

The foreign sailors (sometimes referred to as "marines") continued to guard the Palace and the foreign legations for the time being. De Veer ordered Major Roelfsema to occupy the strategic hill-chain of Raspul, between Durazzo and Shiak. Roelfsema commanded Isa Boletin's Kosovo volunteers and a detachment of gendarmerie, but he was unable to keep the restless Kosovans at their posts when nothing was going on. Wied announced that he would keep his same Cabinet for the present, (less Essad), but Mufid Bey would be acting Prime Minister and Foreign Minister in Turkhan's absence abroad.[4]

The evening of Essad's departure, Durazzo was startled by the arrival of two hundred men from Kruja, in Essad territory. Ekrem Bey Libohova was very concerned and Heaton put von Trotha's secretary, a non-commissioned officer on leave from the German Foot Guards, in charge of arming the male Palace servants. Most of them had served in the German or Austrian armies, and should have been familiar with firearms. However, somewhere in the process, one of them managed to fire a rifle into the wall near the cook's head, and, despite Heaton's admonitions, into the ceiling just below the ladies' boudoir! Von Trotha then appeared and gave them a drill-sergeant's cursing. As a precaution, the men from Kruja were locked up overnight in the schoolhouse, although they protested their loyalty. They were released the next morning and actually made a loyal demonstration outside the Palace, after which they were allowed to leave town.

After these serio-comic events, on the night of May 20 Essad arrived at Brindisi. Before boarding his train for Naples, he was interviewed by a reporter from the *Tribuna*, in which he professed complete loyalty to Wied and protested his innocence, blaming the influence of "certain foreigners" in Wied's entourage for the misunderstanding. Official Italian circles suggested that Wied was too hasty in believing rumors. On May 22, Essad arrived in Naples and there said openly that Austria fomented troubles in order to get him out, and that Albanians did not like foreign officers.[5] Meanwhile in Budapest, where Berchtold had gone to meet with the "Deputations," a joint Austro-Hungarian governmental body, he tried to distance Austria-Hungary from the appearance of meddling in Albanian affairs without justification. He told the Delegations that a *coup de main* by Essad had been thwarted by Austrian and Italian troops and that Essad was arrested at the Wieds' request because he wanted to make himself "sovereign." In answer to an "interpolation" (question) in the Delegations, and in the presence of the German and Italian ambassadors, Berchtold said that the commanders of the Italian and Austrian ships had sent sailors ashore at Durazzo, but they did not have to fight.[6]

With Essad gone, Durazzo was temporarily quiet. In Scutari, a body of Catholic Malissors was being raised to protect Wied. Prenk Bib Doda, head of the Mirdites, was calling up a levy to take the field against the insurgents. Trenches had been dug and guns placed in position commanding the road from Shiak to Durazzo, and arms distributed to volunteers.[7]

Between May 18 and May 22, Heaton made urgent attempts to recruit contingents of Catholic soldiers from the Malissori tribes of northern Albania. Meanwhile, he was becoming famous abroad. His exploits were reported in the London *Daily Sketch* of June 18, 1914, in which he was described as "Captain Armstrong, the British officer who keeps the Albanian King on his throne…" He was given credit for "tap[ping] Essad on the shoulder, and saying 'come with me' and marching him off under fire."

Heaton later wrote to a friend that he found the system of employing chiefs to raise armies ineffective because they claimed pay for double the men actually brought into the field.[8] Encouraged by his exploits, his bemonocled brother Jack, newly arrived and seeking adventure, later led a long march with Bib Doda from the north.[9]

On May 20, the ever-cautious Grey wrote Lamb

> It seems to me that the Prince should not have taken a step of this surprising nature [i.e. exiling Essad] without giving previous or at least simultaneous information as to the reasons for it to the International Commission. I certainly cannot accept any responsibility for the consequences and it may end in our having to withdraw from the International Commission… but I will await further information.

247

A carbon copy was sent to Colonel Phillips "for confidential information."[10]

On May 21, Aliotti asked Wied to authorize return of the sailors to their ships. The next day was the birthday of Queen Sophie, so all the ships would be gaily decorated.[11]

General Conrad later reported a conversation with Berchtold around this time regarding Albania:

> Berchtold: "Let us hope there will be no hitch. But what shall we do if there is?"
> Conrad: "Nothing at all."
> Berchtold: "Even then, we can do nothing. Somebody else must take the throne in his place. Anybody will suit as long as he is not under foreign influence."

It was rumored that Austria had just refused a request by Wied that he might live on a yacht rather than in Durazzo.[12]

On May 22 in Berlin, Jagow sent for British Ambassador Goschen and told him, in answer to his inquiry, that the first intimation he had received of the arrest of Essad Pasha and the landing of Austrian and Italian sailors was from the press, but he added that the matter had been so pressing that there had been no time for consultation with other powers. Of one thing Jagow seemed quite certain, "That it was a thousand pities that Essad had not been shot."

Jagow was amused by a remark in a German paper to the effect that it was by no means certain whether the ouster of Essad arose from a plot of Essad against "the Prince", or a plot of "the Prince" against Essad. He was also rather amused by a report he had received from the German Consul General at Budapest saying that he had just seen Turkhan Pasha. The Albanian premier had told him that he was going to Vienna to attend a dinner, but that his subsequent movements were uncertain, as he was not quite sure whether he was still Prime Minister of Albania or not! Jagow said that he had read in the newspapers that

Turkhan was coming to Berlin. He hoped to goodness it was not true as he had nothing whatever to say to him. In fact, like Grey, he wished to have as little as possible to do with Albanian affairs.

Goschen said that he was very sorry for the poor Prince, to which Jagow replied, "Yes, but why the devil did he go there?" His presence was, in fact, awkward for the German Government as they wished to hold aloof from Albanian political affairs and were in perpetual dread that danger to the King might call for their intervention. Jagow was dead against sending to Durazzo the international forces, especially the German troops."[13]

Jagow wished to know Grey's views on sending five hundred international troops to Durazzo, and said that while personally he was disinclined to send German troops, he would not of course refuse it if all the other governments were agreed as to the necessity for employment of international troops.[14]

Instead of a guarantor of the peace, Wied was becoming a nuisance to the Great Powers.

21

COMPLICATIONS

When sorrows come,
they come not single spies,
but in battalions.
                                    --Hamlet

By May 21, 150 northern Catholic Malissors and Mirdites arrived in Durazzo under the command of Prenk Bib Doda's nephew, Simon Doda, to serve as the King's bodyguard. However, Aliotti persuaded Wied to use them against the rebels, and to place them under the command of Dutch General de Veer for that purpose. Reports from Kavaya, a few miles south of Durazzo (which had welcomed Wied in late April), and from surrounding districts, came in that the gendarmerie had been driven out of the town by the populace, and that the barber (or someone) had pulled down the royal flag and put up the Turkish banner, declaring himself president of still another new republic. The governor of Tirana wired that his position was critical and that he and his small garrison needed reinforcements. Wied had a long debate with de Veer and finally decided to send a relief expedition. He must have been anxious about his decision for, late on the evening of the 22nd, he asked Heaton (who knew nothing about it) whether it had left yet. Though reports vary, the force was apparently composed of one hundred Malissors and fifty gendarmes, aided by the two foreign "sportsmen," Romanian *attaché* Prince Michel Sturdza, and the French Count de Pimodan, who were in charge of a mountain gun and one machine gun.

De Veer placed Dutch Captain Sar in charge of the force and ordered him to pacify Shiak, on the road to Tirana. Sar led his men across the Rastbul hills on May 23rd and approached Shiak. As Major Sluys had previously forbidden the carrying of arms in Tirana Province, when Sar encountered a large body of Bosnian Muslims, armed (as just about every male

Albanian was), he ordered them to disarm. They refused and behaved in a menacing way. He then gave the order to open fire. This upset the Malissors and Mirdites, who felt that Sar's action violated the *besa*, or peace oath, which all had given upon Wied's arrival so that the King would have a fresh start. Furthermore, they said, they had only volunteered to be the King's bodyguard, "and had no wish to leave their bones in central Albania, where they might not even get a Christian burial." Finally, they pointed out that they were wearing their best clothes, which they did not wish to spoil. Neither the pleas of Simon Doda, Prenk's kinsman, nor threats to shoot them, could persuade the northerners. Sar telegraphed de Veer for instructions and, contrary to Sar's advice, was told to proceed without the Malissors. The reduced force was soon surrounded by about fifteen hundred angry Bosnians and forced to surrender, along with their cannon and machine gun.[1]

When word of this disaster reached the Palace, Wied was in his bath. Major Sluys named a young German ex-officer volunteer, Baron von Gumpenberg, to command a relief expedition, yelling to him, "Go acquire the Skanderbeg Order for yourself!" However, the Albanians would not accept the German as their commander and he was forced to turn command over to Melek Bey Frasheri.[2] Soon de Veer rode to the front on horseback to take overall command, whereupon he found that his incompetent artillery was dropping shells on their own men. He returned to the bridge which lead into Durazzo and looked for reinforcements, taking a civilian geographer named Seiner along as interpreter. He was able to rally some of Sar's deserters and got the artillery to stop firing after refusing to do their job for them. He was headed to the Palace to ask for foreign marines when he ran into Baron Aliotti. The two argued for a while and then de Veer returned to the front to lead a new attack, assisted by Major Roelfsema and Baron Gumpenberg. They found Melek wounded, and were soon surrounded. De Veer and Gumpenberg escaped capture, but the other royal prisoners were to have the remarkable experience of being congratulated and having their hands shaken by the rebels for their bravery. The only fatality so far had been a foreign lawyer-volunteer named Berger.

Durazzo was now well and truly in a panic. The Italians erected barricades at random. Colonel Thomson took charge of the artillery.[3] Word now spread among the Albanians that Wied had broken the *besa*.[4]

Around May 21, 1914, Prince Sturdza wrote about the dilemma:

> "The truth is that all work is, at this moment, devoted in advance in Albania to a certain failure. Whatever may be the method chosen, the complicity of neighbors, large and small, guarantees failure. Be soft, [and] innumerable agents will preach violence and insurrection, all the frontiers will permit the infiltration of arms and munitions, foreign money will be at the disposition of agitators. Take arms yourself, [and] no one will support you, all difficulties will be made for you, and you will soon remain short of everything [*resterez à court de tout*]."[5]

On May 23, Heaton went to the Palace garden to gather more information when he ran into Aliotti, who was very agitated and said that eight thousand fanatics were on their way to attack the town. He seemed to think that Heaton was the cause of the problems because of his role in arresting Essad. Aliotti warned Heaton that he should leave, as "something" might happen to him. Frightened, Heaton walked across the square and reached the old Venetian Tower behind the Custom House. From there, he watched through his field glasses the Tirana Road and the heights of Raspul from which the enemy would come. He could hear firing on the far side of the hills and saw insurgent advance guards on the skyline on both sides of the road, driving the troops at the royal outposts inward to the main lines. These lines were near the bridge, stoutly defended against about fifteen hundred rebels by seventy gendarmes commanded by Baron Gumpenberg. The Baron had left his junior post in the German cavalry over some unknown disagreement with his superiors, and served with the Turkish Army in Tripoli and some of the Balkan Wars. Von Trotha had obtained a commission for him in the Albanian militia and he led a gallant charge that day, being slightly wounded. In the afternoon his men ran out of ammunition.

Around 11 a.m., the Austrian field gun which had bombarded Essad was brought into action, fired by untrained volunteers. Ekrem Bey Vlora, a couple of German commercial travelers, and an Austrian waiter. The Austrian officers who knew how to use the gun were confined to their ship, ostensibly to prevent a breach of neutrality, but the Austrian Minister, Löwenthal, told Wied he could use the officers if he would make a written request. Wied declined for fear of complications with Italy.

The tiny defense force now consisted of Gumpenberg's seventy men and about eighty men under Major Roelfsema in the firing line. Another hundred or so were in reserve. There were a number of foreign volunteers who happened to be in Durazzo on business. They were mostly Austrians and Germans, but included the Englishman William Walford, who acted as dispatch rider to General de Veer. Though the town was full of Italians, they were conspicuously absent from the fighting.[6]

On May 22, Harry Lamb feared that the selfish motives of the Austrian and Italian competing consulates might lead to war between their forces and said the Powers should insist on equal participation by all. In London, Crowe noted that Lamb should tell Wied, "if a suitable opportunity offers," to submit any suggestion from any one Power to the International Control Commission. Grey disagreed, for fear Wied would then expect Britain to send troops to enforce any International Control Commission decision.[7]

Count Forgach, as the representative of Count Berchtold, addressed the Budapest Delegations on May 26, and said, somewhat disingenuously, that the Austrian officers who participated in the skirmish to arrest Essad were simply there to test cannon sent by Austria, and only cooperated by "chance," as Austria and Italy had agreed to non-intervention. Also that day, San Giuliano in Rome told his parliamentary Chamber, indirectly, that the Dutch officer Sluys had been "precipitate" in his action against Essad and a grave error had been committed afterward in sending Catholic Malissori against the insurgents, causing a religious feud. He said that he and Berchtold were in agreement to work to keep Wied on the throne. The two were asking the other Powers to send troops from Scutari to preserve order.[8]

22

DISGRACE

Early on the morning of Sunday, May 24, Muslim insurgents, apparently led by Akif Hikmet (a.k.a. Arif Hikmer and Arif Hemet), who had taken Tirana and Shiak, began to march toward Durazzo. The gendarmerie under their Dutch officers, along with volunteers, went out to meet them and give battle. The 124 Catholic Malissors who had come from Scutari fled at the opening of the engagement, and it was left to the gendarmes and the volunteers, along with the badly-aimed artillery, to resist. The defenders put up a stout defense three kilometers from Durazzo for about three hours, despite their own artillery shells occasionally dropping on them. The French International Control Commission delegate, Krajewski, along with the Briton, Harry Lamb, went to the front lines and assisted in arranging order in the retreat of the volunteers. An attempt to send a negotiator from Wied was refused by the rebels.[1]

Around noon, Baron Aliotti came to the King, very excited, and reported that the rebels, who he said numbered eight to ten thousand, were near Durazzo and had either killed or captured fifty gendarmes as well as the four Dutch officers who had led them. Colonel Thomson, the deputy commander of the Dutch officer mission, confirmed that the officers had been surrounded and captured when on reconnaissance with their men. He said that he had been forced to retreat due to the great superiority in numbers of the rebels. Aliotti urgently advised Wied to board the *Misurata* in the harbor, otherwise Aliotti could not guarantee the royal family's safety. When Wied refused, Aliotti threatened to withdraw all the Italian sailors who were guarding the Palace and legations in order, as he said, to protect the *sailors*! Also, he warned that the Italian ships would not fire a single shot to defend the town. Wied again refused, stating that he did not see the necessity of removing to a ship at that point, whereupon Aliotti said that he would refuse any personal protection for the King and his family. Although many Palace personnel now joined in Aliotti's advice, Wied still refused to flee. Sami Bey remained calm and told everyone but the King that flight was both unnecessary and would make a bad impression. Desperately, Wied sent for Löwenthal, the minister of his chief sponsor, Austria-Hungary, for advice. Although Löwenthal had been confident in the morning, even he now urged a hasty retreat to the *Misurata*, as he thought the Italians were trying to pull off some sort of a coup in cooperation with the rebels. At that point Wied reluctantly agreed to send Queen Sophie and the royal children to the ship for their safety. However, Sophie refused to go without him, as did some of his staff and Malissor bodyguards, apparently.

Upon leaving the Palace, Aliotti met Secretary Heaton and warned him ominously that he had better immediately grab the nearest boat and board an Italian warship. Somewhat shaken, Heaton entered the Palace and "found it necessary to visit the butler for a glass of brandy to keep me going." At around 3 o'clock, Aliotti mounted the steps of the Palace, and seeing Heaton, told him that it was too late for *him* to escape, but that he could still save the King. Aliotti then told Wied that the situation had further deteriorated and that he was going to withdraw the sailors guarding the Palace. When Heaton spoke to the King, Wied appeared shaken, and, with tears in his eyes ordered Heaton to prepare a hasty departure, packing trunks and getting servants ready. One can imagine the chagrin of this man, a Prince, an able German officer, a well-meaning ruler, and a public figure on the job less than three months, being forced into an ignominious flight. He looked around his study and expressed his anguish: "It seems such a pity to leave all my old things here. Why must it be?" Heaton replied impertinently, "Well, it was bound to come sooner or later, so we had better make the best of a bad job."

Heaton packed Wied's and his own things along with the seized Essad papers and put them in the Palace passageway for the porters. The lord chamberlain, von Trotha, gave him forty thousand gold francs (around $138,000 today) from the privy purse to pack, and this heavy load he dragged to the foot of the stairs with the other luggage. The Italian Legation sent word to hurry or the pier would be under fire.[2]

The red royal standard was lowered from the Palace to the consternation of the populace of Durazzo and its defenders. The city was effectively left without a government. The sad procession marched silently across the square with foreign sailors lining the route, at the salute. They then boarded launches which took them to the *Misurata*. A comic opera incident then added to the general depression. It was discovered that the King's English butler had been left behind. The Italian captain of the ship refused Heaton permission to leave the ship to retrieve him, and said that he had orders that no one was to go ashore. Italian sailors with fixed bayonets were posted about the deck, ostensibly to "prevent undesirable refugees from trying to get on board." Permission was given, however, for the royal children to be sent to the Austrian warship, *Szigetvar*, and the Austrian Minister, who was also aboard the Italian ship with his wife, begged Wied to transfer to the Austrian ship as well, at least for the night. He believed that the rebel attack would come that night and he expressed worry that the Austrian sailors would suffer casualties defending the Palace, rather than the Austrian legation. The *Misurata* pulled farther from the shore and closer to an Italian warship.[3] Wied later wrote that he had intended to immediately return ashore when his wife and children were safe, but did not demand a dinghy for that purpose as he knew that it would be refused.[4]

Having arrived safely aboard, Wied and his party assembled on the boat deck from which they could see with binoculars that the royal forces were holding their own and that firing was dying down. In fact, Thomson's artillery was doing some damage to the rebels. A truce had been called in Durazzo, and they could see persons apparently conferring, and an auto with a huge Italian flag going to and fro. Krajewski and Lamb, the only International Control Commission delegates in Durazzo at the time, took it upon themselves, along with former Provisional Government Minister (and Kosovan) Mehmet Pasha

Dralla, to negotiate with the rebels. They asked Aliotti and Löwenthal to join with them, and Aliotti agreed, while Löwenthal stalled and refused at first. Later, however, an Austrian Legation First Secretary and the Romanian Burghele accompanied them. On the way to meet the rebels, they encountered Major Sar, a prisoner under escort by the rebels. He had been sent to demand an interview with Wied.

On board the *Misurata*, Wied and company were served tea and then the Italian Admiral Trifari joined them. He and Wied retired to a salon for a private conversation. Trifari told Wied that the insurgents claimed that they had Durazzo in their clutches, but that they would parlay with the King if he would meet them at the Palace. When Wied asked why they couldn't come on board, the admiral told him that they refused. Wied sensed a trap, but the admiral insisted (prompted no doubt by Aliotti) and he agreed. The King emerged from the meeting pale and agitated.[5] French delegate Krajewski and Commissioner Mufid Bey also sent their unsolicited suggestions that Wied should disembark, so Wied landed around 8 p.m.

Aliotti had the nerve to tell de Veer that, "whoever advised [Wied] in this is very unwise, indeed," and asked the general and Minister Nogga to bring Wied back. However, it appears that the Italian secret service was at work while the royal family were afloat. De Veer had gone to the vacated Palace and found only Italians in evidence. He saw Captain Castoldi actually looking through secret state papers.[6]

When the King's party returned to shore and left their motor launch at the dock, they were relieved to be met by loyal subjects, weeping at Wied's safe return. While crossing the square, one warned them that "the Italians were playing some low game." Captain Castoldi met them in the Palace garden and the *kavass* (gate guard), who had been sitting at the gate with his rifle across his knees, welcomed them with joy and led the way inside the Palace. They found that the electric lights had been switched off at the main, so that they had to dramatically make their way up the stairs in the dark, Browning pistols in hand, until servants brought candles stuck in empty beer bottles.

For the next two hours, ministers, the Control Commissioners, and loyal beys came to the Palace to discuss the matter. Captain Sar, now paroled, had to report that not only was he a prisoner, but also another Dutch officer, the Secretary of the Romanian Legation, fifty gendarmes and a machine gun had been captured. He estimated that there were three thousand well-organized rebels menacing the capital. The rebels demanded a letter of amnesty for themselves in return for a promise to spare the prisoners and not attack for the present. Wied consented and had a letter to that effect prepared and signed. He sent Sar in a royal carriage to convey the letter and sent the royal auto to bring in the loyal wounded, although its regular chauffeur was still on board the *Misurata*. As the Italians now assured him that all was safe, he sent Heaton to retrieve Queen Sophie from the ship. Upon seeing him, she feared the worst, but he soon assured her of Wied's safety.[7]

By the time Sophie reached the Palace the electricity had been restored. Apparently de Veer had told Heaton of Castoldi's burglarious activities in Heaton's room at his desk. Heaton had made some "over-truthful" remarks about the Italians in Durazzo that morning and Castoldi now blamed Heaton for Essad's arrest.

A cold supper with champagne was served and then a.d.c. Ekrem Bey was told that the Italians were going to pull out all their sailors from the shore and the Austrians would not send any to replace them. Ekrem managed to get the Italians to reconsider, although the Austrians, indecisive, at first both refused and then landed a machine gun detachment on the lading stage, apparently fearing a clash with the Italians. It is difficult to believe that the respective governments were responsible for these maneuvers. It seems more likely that they were instigated by people on the scene like Aliotti, who was acting semi-autonomously, or hotheads like Conrad, who was always spoiling for a fight.

Meanwhile, the King's physician, Dr. Berghausen, resigned "apparently under some compulsion," for reasons not apparent. It may be that his presence in Essad's house on the fatal night did not sit well with the King and his advisors. It may be that he was some sort of spy or intriguer. He would later pop up in Valona. The doctor blamed his resignation on court chamberlain von Trotha.[8] The doctor's former residence was now rigged up by two Austrian naval doctors as a hospital, and the King set about pinning medals (brought in large quantities from Austria) on both wounded and unwounded loyal soldiers.[9]

Wied had now learned his lesson and no longer trusted Aliotti, although he could not openly show his feelings. Others showed their feelings about Wied's flight, however. His fellow German officers in his homeland were contemptuous of his action, feeling that he should have fought for his rights. His officers club at Potsdam struck him off its rolls.[10]

23

PICKING UP THE PIECES

On May 24, at about 1 a.m., the royal automobile returned with three or four seriously wounded but stoic and brave men, one a Mirdite. It was then found that someone had stolen Heaton's case containing the King's forty thousand gold francs, an act hardly calculated to reinforce the monarch's sense of security.

On May 25, Aliotti, some Albanians and de Veer, along with the rest of the International Control Commission, went to Shiak to negotiate with the rebels. Commissioner Auguste Kral, the Austrian member, spoke fluent Albanian. The Commission was received courteously and it was agreed to send back the prisoners and the guns captured from Sar's force. The rebels seemed to have no specific demands other than return of the Turkish regime, and their real leaders did not seem to be present. Red Turkish flags, with their white Islamic crescent moons, were everywhere.[1]

On May 26 the prisoners were returned, but, as Durazzo had sent no ponies to pull the artillery pieces, those could not be returned. This annoyed the rebels, who did not want the guns, but, fortunately for them, still had them later when they besieged Durazzo.[2]

At 8 a.m. on May 26, the French Diplomat Fontenay arrived in Durazzo and found the situation had been "the most critical imaginable" during the Shiak battle. The King's troops had abandoned a cannon and the two machine guns, and the Austrian Legation had left with all its baggage. After the battle of May 27, there were only about ten gendarmes guarding the Palace.[3] He was told that Wied had said that he never gave the order to arrest Essad, while Essad's people said that Wied assisted from the Palace window in Essad's forcible deportation.[4]

On May 25, Grey wrote to Lamb that, "in light of repeated incidents in the past," he did not believe that the necessary agreement of all Powers to send troops to help Wied could be obtained. He noted for the Foreign Office record that

> In explaining to Mr. Lamb it would be well to point out that Austria apparently does not want real international action. Italy desires it only to be left alone with Austria but will continue under cover of it to play for her own hand. ...it would be difficult in any case to work a real condominium of six Powers but... the action of Austria and Italy and their special interests make it impossible...[5]

In late May, 1914, when the rebellion had picked up steam, Consul-Commissioner Lamb urged Britain to help on humanitarian grounds. Grey and Germany had both refused to join the other Powers even in sending warships to Durazzo. When Grey's position was reported to the Kaiser, he noted, "exactly my point of view. He says precisely the same as I do." Grey still would not ask the British Cabinet or Parliament for troops to be sent when Britain had no direct interest.[6] This was especially so as Britain was on the brink of a civil war in Ireland because of the imminent grant of home rule to that island.

By May 25 the Dutch officers were freed after the King rode out to confer with the insurgents and meet their demands to place their case before him and the International Control Commission. Journalists spent their time second-guessing the situation. Viennese papers called the situation "awkward" and "chaotic," and Austrian papers said "diplomatists" caused Wied's flight "in too great haste." Rome papers reported 120 killed in the previous two days, saying that the insurgents wanted Muslim predominance.[7]

On May 25, after long negotiations at Shiak, the questions in dispute seemed to be settled and some of the rebels returned to their villages.[8] However, there was little optimism elsewhere in Europe. To the Marquess di San Giuliano's written question to his German colleagues, "If the international troops arrive at Durazzo, will the rebels give up?" the Kaiser wrote in the margin: "The situation of the Prince will be settled and impossible."[9]

Pessimism was warranted. On May 27, a letter from the Muslim insurgents to the International Control Commission asked that "the sovereign of Albania may raise the standard of the religious teaching of their faith," and pointed out that Wied had appointed persons who had always persecuted them. As most of his cabinet were Muslims, this reference must have been to the upper class backgrounds of the government. The rebels said that they wanted to return to the Ottoman Empire and asked that the Powers protect them from the Albanian government.[10] They said that Wied was a bloodthirsty tyrant and they would have nothing to do with him. At that point, negotiations in Kavaya were broken off.[11]

As the whole Cabinet had made a *pro forma* resignation after the Essad expulsion, a new cabinet was chosen on the evening of May 28, after long negotiations. It would again contain eight ministers, although Wied had been advised by several sources to follow the proposed organic statute and narrow the number of ministers to four or five, and to take foreign advice on their appointment. The Cabinet was now as follows:

Turkhan Pasha – still Prime Minister
Prenk Bib Doda – Foreign Minister (his acceptance not yet received)
Mufid Bey Libohova – still Justice Minister
Dr. Philippe Nogga – the young Catholic diplomat, Finance Minister
Dr. Michael Tourtoulis Bey – Public Instruction and Health Minister
Midhat Bey Frasheri – Aged 35, a Nationalist and skilled in languages, Public Works, Posts & Telegraphs Minister
Abdi Bey Toptani – Agriculture Minister
Akif Pasha Elbasan – Interior and War Minister[12]

Everyone was on edge. Late in the evening of May 29, a Dutch officer fired two shots out of his window at the Hotel Clementi, near the Palace, at a stray dog. This called the Italian and Austrian sailors to arms, and they quickly and efficiently set up a road block on the main road before the source of the shots was discovered.[13] Afterward, all was quiet.

Earlier that day, Krajewski had returned from Tirana where the Control Commission had again negotiated with the chiefs of the rebel movement. There was now a demand to join a Turk to the Commission and a refusal to recognize Wied. "The 101 villages of the Tirana district are in the movement, which is from all evidence organized by the Young Turks," Krajewski reported.

Fontenay presented his credentials from Poincaré as "Envoy Extraordinary and Minister Plenipotentiary" of France to "William I," the same day. Wied made a nice speech and they then had a lunch with Turkhan Pasha, who had returned. Afterward, they retired to a Palace salon where the King suddenly said that the Powers must send three thousand troops. When Fontenay said that it was hard to get the Powers to agree on anything, Wied backtracked and said that five hundred to six hundred men would suffice, but were needed soon. He asked help in getting Austria ("the Ballplatz") to accept equality in the proposed National Bank, thus demonstrating that he was not their puppet[14] This thorny bank problem had still not been resolved.

On May 28, German Ambassador Flotow in Rome had sent the following astonishing telegraphic report to Berlin from Rome:

> Local government continues effort to convince Powers to send detachment Skutari to Durazzo, but has not yet received the agreement of the English.
>
> Minister of Foreign Affairs [San Giuliano] told me – apparently in order to apologize for the Italian ambassador – that not the latter but all the other foreign ambassadors had advised the Prince

of Albania to board ship.[!] *Misurata* appears to be not really an Italian ship, but a yacht which has been put at the Prince's disposition jointly with Austria and on which the Prince flies the Albanian flag so that he is considered to be on Albanian soil. Prince must now be supported absolutely, above all to avoid differences with Austria over the selection of the successor. Austria would otherwise propose Duke Urach again. Moreover, it is said that Kemal [Ismail?] was here secretly and reported that a son of ex-Sultan Abdul Hamid has apparently applied to succeed to the throne of Albania. Position of Prince Wilhelm is considered weakened, but not impossible. If international troops were to arrive in Durazzo, the insurgents would surrender of their own accord. In spite of Stefani communication, it is said that Essad has not been received by the Minister; however, he thinks to return and that, sooner or later, he cannot be refused a reception.

Very Confidential: Prince of Albania is said to have written to the King of Rumania that he did not know about the measures against Essad Pasha, and that he himself has nothing against him.

Local journalists claim to know that the Prince of Albania already treats privately with Essad.

Flotow[15]

Italy, through Aliotti, having contributed to the chaos, now tried to distance itself from it.

On May 29, Sluys was furloughed to Holland due to fears for his safety. Thomson replaced him and was now "Director of the Armed Force."[16] On May 30, a simmering dispute between General de Veer and Colonel Thomson broke out over control of the police. A Dutch newspaper had said that de Veer allowed

Essad to control the police. De Veer suspected that Thomson was the author of this rumor, but he denied it. Having complained to the International Control Commission, and received their support. De Veer took the matter up with Wied and Turkhan. To his consternation, they said that Thomson had fourteen days earlier made sure Essad had no control over the police and had taken control as city commander. [17] This upset de Veer, but Löwenthal supported Thomson and Thomson was appointed commander of the armed forces after a chat with Wied and Turkhan. To placate de Veer, Wied sent him a note appointing him commander of the Scutari gendarmerie. This was a meaningless gesture as the gendarmerie in Scutari were under the command of the International Forces' British Commander, Phillips.[18] De Veer protested without results, and so asked for a six month furlough. He complained not only to the Dutch War Minister, but, indiscreetly, to Dutch and German news correspondents. The German paper, *Die Zeit,* reported the conflict, taking Thomson's side. De Veer angrily headed for Holland.[19]

On May 29, Wied's master of the household, Commandant von Trotha, called by journalists "a garrulous chamberlain," had arrived in Berlin. Speaking freely to German journalists, he said nothing could be done until Wied got a military power, instead of what he called fifty gendarmes at Durazzo, and fifty at Valona.[20] At the instance of Wied, no doubt, he asked to meet with the German Under-Secretary of State for Foreign Affairs, Zimmermann, who said that he was too busy, but agreed to see him on June 2. French *Chargé* De Manneville told Zimmermann he was sure Zimmerman would give von Trotha good advice. Zimmerman replied, "Oh! Yes, (laughing) I will advise him to return as soon as possible to Potsdam." Wied's "flight" had been badly received in Berlin.[21]

Wied now had a spy system of loyal Albanian nationalists who happened to be pro-Austrian, and therefore somewhat biased. They reported that Italians seemed to be on good terms with the rebels. It is probable that Aliotti had advised Wied to fire von Trotha and Heaton, "as they had intrigued against Italian interests, in his view." The King refused. Heaton received several new Italian warnings to flee. He persuaded Harry Lamb to ask Aliotti their source. Aliotti seemed caught off guard and said he had heard that the nationalists were displeased with Heaton and wanted to remove him, although he did not know the details. In retrospect, Heaton concluded that Aliotti wanted to scare him so that he would not reconnoiter again and discover that there was no such serious threat as Aliotti had described to Wied to convince him to flee to the ship.

About this time Heaton was detailed to take the place of the Muslim *aide de camp* Sami Bey at the funeral of a loyal Muslim soldier who had just died in the Court hospital. Heaton had to send for and pay an Imam to pray over him, as none volunteered. The next afternoon, he had to perform a similar duty for an Austrian reserve officer, walking behind his rough casket, through which blood dripped.

By May 29, Italy had withdrawn its marines from Durazzo but was notified by Austria that it would send a squadron shortly to Durazzo, thus placing Austria in a more influential position.[22] Vienna received a telegram dated May 31 reporting that Finance Minister Philippe Nogga Bey had gone north to discuss the employment of some six thousand Catholics whom he had collected in Alessio and for whom he had asked that a large number of rifles be provided. At a cabinet meeting with Wied it was decided to reinforce the gendarmerie as stated, and also enroll an equal number of Muslims. Seven hundred Albanians loyal to the government were assembled at Lossnia, thirty miles south of Durazzo, under Captain Ibrahim of the gendarmerie, while Colonel Thomson had been appointed commandant of Durazzo. No word had been received from the cautious Prenk Bib Doda.[23] At Kavaya, southeast of Durazzo, where the King had been happily greeted only a month earlier, the Commission of Control found that almost everyone had left for the south to oppose Aziz Pasha Vrioni, the former Agriculture Minister, who was marching north for the King.[24]

The best analysis for the causes of the central Albania revolt against Wied seems to be as follows:

The peasants were profoundly disappointed that Wied had surrounded himself with the landowning beys (including Essad) who leased their land on the most onerous terms to these serf-like tenants who were sharecroppers for one third of their crops. All surrounding Slav and Turkish powers agitated this discontent. The central insurrection appears to have been sparked by Turkish agitators of whom Akif Hikmet seems to have been chief. They spread the rumor that Wied was a Jew. Musa Kuasim, the Mufti (religious leader) of Tirana, and Mustafa Ndroga (a.k.a. Broka) were the principal organizers, and Kamil (or Quamil) Haxifeza of Elbasan the commander-in chief, probably aided by Serbian officers and Essad's veterans.[25]

24

FRICTION

It was the custom of the Mbret almost every night to stroll into Heaton's apartments (which adjoined his at the Palace) after the day's work, and there, over a pipe, discuss the latest doings. The discussions must have been gloomy if Heaton was as frank as he later claimed to have been.[1] Heaton already resented Queen Sophie's "regal" manner toward him. (Of course, she *was* regal!) In May, a Scottish visitor described Heaton as youthful, very free and easy, and rather blunt. He confided to her that the Palace was over-crowded, the staff living three to a room, and that nobody had even taken any notice of his offer of references when he was hired.[2]

Heaton and von Trotha often spoke their minds and pessimism openly, but they were not taken seriously, while Sophie appeared to resent their comments. She disliked Heaton. Heaton was told (probably by the ambassadors) that the Powers were disappointed in Wied and would not help him, as he was unfit. Heaton also was apparently told by members of the International Control Commission that they would not help Wied raise funds, but Wied refused to believe this. Wags in the town, and even one foreigner in the government service now mockingly called Wied "Bürgermeister of Durazzo" and "the Houseowner."

By June 1, Wied had already requested through Colonel Phillips the despatch to Durazzo of a portion of the international military detachments at Scutari and this was repeated to the International Control Commission. The Italian Foreign Minister promised to renew this request to the Powers, but several foreign ministers were away from their capitals and the "Whitsuntide" holiday was given as an excuse to delay an answer. The International Control Commission was due to meet again with the insurgents in the next few days.[3]

Around this time, Nadolny reported to Berlin his opinion that the Austrian-Italian contrast was so great that Germany must push a "wedge, or better call it a buffer" between the opponents where she could. He preferred that the two countries even be somewhat hostile to Germany over the matter, rather than to each other. The "Italian representative" (presumably Aliotti) had already expressed to Nadolny that Wied should unconditionally have some advisor by his side, preferably a German or Romanian.[4]

Apparently, by June 3 Wied had asked for a German Privy Secretary or Cabinet Counselor to replace Castoldi and Buchberger. The so-called "small cabinet Castoldi-Buchberger" was about to expire. It had been opposed from the beginning by the Albanian ministers, who seemed to consider the two to have been a foreign intermediate or "shadow government" between themselves and the King, which they would gladly see removed. The ministers had been seeking, in an official manner, to transfer them. This resistance could perhaps have been overcome if it were not the case that the king's trust, especially concerning Castoldi, who had worked against the Greeks but for Essad Pasha, was wavering. Wied must have had the insight that Castoldi was not working for him or for Albanian policy but for Italy's interest, so he determined to renounce both men. Unfortunately, in carrying out his intention, he made a mistake. Upon being asked by the Italian Ambassador the grounds for the abolition of the arrangement, he declared openly that he had lost confidence in Castoldi. Not surprisingly, Baron Aliotti was upset by that statement, and took it as a vote of no-confidence toward his government, whose favor Castoldi enjoyed. Unfortunately the Italian press, in their usual excitable way, was in an uproar about the matter. The conflict had reached the point that both ambassadors had reported to their governments and awaited replies. Austrian consul Baron Buchberger intended to leave Albania. Of Castoldi, it was said that he would remain there with the Italian Embassy, which certainly would not be very comfortable for anyone.[5]

In Berlin on 15 June, the Under-Secretary of the *Ausrwärtiges Amt* noted his belief that "… the appointment of a Romanian [as Wied's advisor] seems to us unthinkable."[6]

When in 1912, Ismail Kemal Bey had declared the independence of Albania, Austria had sent instructors for the infantry, as did the Italians. An Italian Major was sent to Albania and immediately became a citizen there. Alfred Rappaport, Ritter Von Arbengau, the Departmental Chief of the Austrian Foreign Office for Albania and Deputy Chief of their Oriental Department, used his contacts to make it possible that Austria received the ultimate control of the artillery development, and Albania, as mentioned, had purchased some mountain guns from their Skoda factory. When it was rumored that the King would receive some officers from Romania as instructors for his army, General Conrad and Chief Rappaport agreed that this could not be in the interest of Austria and, together with the *Evidenzbureau* (Austrian Military Intelligence), they managed to secretly transport fifty thousand old Mauser rifles as a present to an "Albanian Tribal Chief," (unidentified; perhaps Bib Doda). In fact, Austria did not have enough rifles, so they had to borrow them from the Germans. To arrange this, Urbanski from the *Evidenzbureau* talked "unofficially" with German Chief of General Staff Von Moltke, who allegedly received the Kaiser's permission, and both sides agreed not to inform their particular Foreign Ministers of their gunrunning.[7] More intrigue was yet to come.

25

INTRIGUE AND STRATEGIES

On the first of June, 1914, a detachment of seven hundred Catholic Mirdites and other Malissors arrived in Durazzo harbor by boat from Alessio. Their commander was Marco Gioni, a cousin of Prenk Bib Doda. The Bishop of Alessio, who was known as a fighting priest, accompanied them. They wore traditional clothing, including baggy white trousers and small caps, and carried various types of rifles, including the more modern Mausers and older British Martinis. They especially liked the louder noise the Martinis made. Heaton's brother, Jack Heaton-Armstrong, who was looking for adventure like so many Englishmen of the time, had arrived on the same boat with the northern Albanians. Probably because of his brother, Jack was allowed to pitch his tent on the Palace grounds.

The International Control Commission had tried to negotiate with the Muslim rebels, but were met with coolness and repeated demands that Wied leave and a Muslim prince take his place.[1] A small place twenty-five miles north and east of Durazzo had been captured when its gendarme defenders deserted. In Romania, Take Ionescu's personal newspaper waxed pessimistic and opined that a small force sent earlier would have been enough to restore the overall situation, while more would now be required.[2] The insurgents were angered to learn of the arrival of the Mirdites and, at a meeting with the International Control Commission at Shiak, tempers flared and the Muslim demands were repeated. The Commission gave up in frustration and returned to Durazzo.[3] The insurgents, still at Shiak, then asked to reopen talks, but, as they were obviously stalling, the Commission refused.[4]

Wied had been making "vigorous remonstrations" to Aliotti about the daily car trips of the Italian legation car to the rebel lines, and the Italian finally agreed to stop them.[5] Spies sympathetic to the King, including the Austrian Comptroller

General of Police, Baron Begeleben, as well as officers of destroyers in the bay (obviously not Italian), reported that they had for three nights seen Morse lamp signals from a house in Durazzo to the rebels on the heights of Rastbul. Begeleben had been a Police Commissioner in Graz, Austria, and presumably knew his business. A lookout was posted on the terrace of the Austrian legation who pinpointed the house which was signaling. This was reported to Captain Jan Fabius, "the most reckless and dashing" of the Dutch officers, and he called in Austrian Minister von Löwenthal. The signals were in code and some sort of "Italo-Albanian dialect" which they could not read. This information was passed to Colonel Thomson, the commandant of Durazzo, and he obtained Wied's permission to make an arrest if he caught the signalers red-handed.[6]

Apparently exceeding his orders, Thomson sent Fabius with several policemen and volunteers to raid the house, and they found there three Italians, a Colonel Muricchio, who was attached to the Italian Legation, a Captain Moltedo, and a Professor Chinigo. Muricchio and Chinigo were said to be of Italo-Albanian stock. They were found with a "roller-blind" kerosene signal lamp. Upon the Fabius group's entry, in the best Ruritanian novel tradition Moltedo threatened them with a revolver, jumped out a window and ran to the Italian Legation.[7] Fabius arrested the remaining pair and sent a test signal to the rebels, who replied. A search of the house revealed incriminating papers, including a list of spies in the Italians' pay and the information that Italian troops were at Bari, ready to cross to Albania at any time.[8] Colonel Thomson and Baron Aliotti were on the scene almost immediately, and Aliotti protested that the invasion was a violation of the Capitulations, which were treaties the Turkish Sultans had made with various European Powers to give those Powers virtual diplomatic immunity or extraterritorial rights over their own citizens. Albania had inherited those agreements. Thomson, not one to give in easily, argued that there was an exception under which this incident fell, as the city was under martial law. An excited argument ensued, with voices raised and the onlookers cheering for their favorites. Thomson finally left the prisoners in Aliotti's custody upon his promise to keep them in Durazzo.

Aliotti then rushed to the Palace, of course, and had an audience with the King, at which he raised his voice and demanded Thomson's immediate dismissal or dispatch to Holland, and a public retraction in the newspapers. Wied felt forced to agree to release the prisoners, but Thomson would not so agree, and would not apologize, saying that it was not compatible with his honor as an officer. Then Justice Minister Mufid Bey pointed out that, technically, the Dutch officers were appointed by the Great Powers, so that only the International Control Commission could fire them. However, he begged Thomson to apologize for the King's sake. The Colonel refused, saying in French, "Willingly, I would give my life for the King, but never my honor."

In Rome, San Giuliano, who constantly suffered from gout, was so angry at this exposé of Italian chicanery that, at a diplomatic banquet the next night, he made a point of sneering at everything Dutch.

To placate the Italians, Wied had promised to invoke a commission of inquiry under Ekrem Bey, and if it found no guilt on the part of the Italians, to fire the Dutch officers involved. Ekrem heard seventy witnesses, and, although he personally had no doubt of the Italians' guilt, he diplomatically or expediently reached no conclusion. Wied was thereby released from his promise to dismiss the Dutchmen. Durazzo Mayor Djurkevitch, of Montenegrin descent, and formerly Essad's secretary, had been arrested due to compromising papers found in his home. No doubt he had been under suspicion, or a "tip" had been received. He was released, however, when the Russians intervened in his behalf.[9]

On June 5, Isa Boletin arrived in Durazzo. By now Wied had approved the Corfu agreement on Epirus, virtually surrendering control of the southern third of his country. Austria was rumored to have advised Wied that he now had three choices: (1) Take the offensive against the remaining rebels, (2) move his capital or, (3) negotiate again. He was to choose the first alternative.[10]

Almost every day volunteers arrived from both the north and south to join the King, and the Durazzo garrison increased to more than a thousand men. More Malissors were expected.[11] Everyone in the Government now thought that the rebellion could only be ended by force, and were optimistic that it could be done. The Mbret was now supported by some well-known Muslims as well as Isa Boletin. Von Trotha had returned from Berlin. Plans were drawn up in the King's study to surround the rebels and thereby force them to surrender and go home. Prenk Bib Doda claimed pay for five hundred to seven hundred Mirdite and Malissor men in the north, while Muslim chieftan Ahmed Zogu Mati (someday to be king, himself) boasted two thousand men, more or less, in the northeast, who were supposed to take Kruja for the King and then head for Tirana. Loyal forces from midcountry Elbasan and the southern forces at Berat and Valona were supposed to surround the rebels somewhere between Tirana and Shiak. There was to be an attack from Alessio by Doda, and from Durazzo and the south by the gendarmerie and volunteers.[12] A mountain gun and many rifles and cartridges were sent to Bib Doda in Alessio to stiffen his spine, and two guns were sent to Valona. The Romanian Prince Sturdza, the French Count de Pimodan and Jack Heaton-Armstrong, plus a few gendarmes and two or three American Albanians (who were to act as interpreters and assistants) went north by tramp steamer to Alessio.[13]

Unfortunately for the plan, however, on June 6 a portion of the eight hundred northern Albanians, under the command of Prenk Bib Doda's cousin, refused to march against the insurgents for the second time. Insurgent outposts were now within a mile of Durazzo. A state of siege was proclaimed. The insurgents had a Skoda quick-firing gun and a couple of machine guns, captured two weeks earlier. Wied was left with only about 150 gendarmes and some foreign residents who had learned to fire artillery somewhat.[14]

The three European gunners, including Heaton's brother, arrived at Alessio and found Doda's forces lounging about.

275

Dutch Major Kroon attempted to train these bands of irregulars, who had made no sanitary or water arrangements for the troops. The ample supplies which the government had bought, including ammunition, had not arrived. Later, when Kroon had to return to Durazzo after Thomson's death, an Albanian officer, Shefket Bey, took his place. Jack Heaton-Armstrong chose twenty-five men and trained them with a mountain gun, a small wheeled piece of artillery, despite his own limited experience.

The royal forces proved unequal to their task. After a late start, Doda's force of about 2,500 finally left Alessio, but many Mirdites had gotten bored and deserted. Doda's force advanced about six miles a day, and some of the Malissors happily pillaged the villages through which they marched. After two or three days they reached Ishmi, which was about twenty miles north of Durazzo, built around an old citadel on a hill. About this time, Romanian *attaché* Prince Sturdza, who had applied for leave, was reprimanded by his government for his undiplomat-like actions, and recalled to Bucharest. De Pimodan was used as a messenger to Durazzo. A German commercial traveler and an Austrian ex-soldier took the men's places, along with Jack Heaton-Armstrong. Unfortunately, the royal force had somehow mistakenly bombarded a friendly village called Malkuts. Rumors of an impending attack by rebels soon reduced Doda's force, by then about 700 men, the others melting away. The army retreated to Slinza, where it re-assembled. There, it retreated again under rebel harassment to Alessio, the Roman Catholic stronghold, from which they had started. Some disgusted Scutari Albanians decided to leave Doda and return to Durazzo. The rest of Doda's army dispersed.[15] So much for that wing of the attack.

Meanwhile, from the mountains of the northeast, the loyal Muslim troops of Zogu from Mati captured Kruja without difficulty and took a strong position overlooking Tirana. However, they then did nothing but negotiate, as his army, although well-armed by Wied, also drifted away.

The eastern army, which included regular gendarmes, was beaten in one or two minor engagements, and lost Elbasan, south of Tirana, when two Dutch officers were captured and some of the royal forces simply changed sides.

The first southern army, made up of fierce but thieving Albanians called Laps, set out from Valona, looting the friendly inhabitants as they went. When attacked by the rebels, they retreated, with the locals understandably helping the rebels in retaliation for their mistreatment. The Laps stopped at Valona, as did the rebels, probably fearing the Italian interest in that town. The second southern army from Berat, in central Albania, led by Aziz Pasha Vrioni, hardly moved at all due to internal squabbling and desertions to the rebels. Berat's defense had been decimated by two weeks of fighting and the principal Nationalist leaders had been killed. Captain Leon Ghilardi with a mixed following of volunteers, including forty Bulgarians, one American named Harold Sherwood Spencer, and several hundred Albanians, succeeded in breaking through the insurgent lines from the south and entering Berat on June 10th. Ghilardi mounted one field gun and four machine guns on the old Venetian citadel above the town. The insurgents, using a mountain gun captured at Elbasan, dropped shrapnel on the citadel from the northwest. The defenders used a dozen old Venetian cannon, dating from 1489, which they loaded with the original stone balls, of which a plentiful supply was available, as they had been mostly used as door-stops. They used rags for wadding, and black powder for propellant. Ghilardi reported that some of the guns were actually those presented by Lord Nelson to Ali Pasha, the Lion of Janina (1740-1822), to encourage him in his hostility to Napoleon.[16]

On June 11, the insurgents occupied a position to the northeast of Berat, hiding among the women and children who had been placed there for safety, thereby paralyzing the fire from the town in that direction. Insurgent rushes on the citadel were checked by the defenders bringing down the old Venetian wall on them. At midnight, the citadel was evacuated by the royal forces, taking the field gun and the four machine guns, and "a vast concourse of refugees" to Valona, which was reached on June 12th. General De Veer did not propose to resist there, "to avoid the possibilities of excesses," but Ghilardi was to remain outside Valona with his guns to protect incoming refugees, thousands of whom were now arriving, as was Edith Durham, who was trying to organize relief.[17]

A stiff defense of Koritsa had been made by the loyal troops, but Epirotes joined the rebels and the city was surrendered. Ghilardi, Spencer, and some others eventually managed to escape to Valona with the guns and machine guns.

While these events proceeded in Albania, in Germany the Kaiser was his usual ebullient self. June 1 was a great day in Germany, the *Schrippenfest*, wherein the Kaiser entertained with great pomp officers and representative enlisted men, as well as diplomats and visitors at his Potsdam Palace. He drank beer with the enlisted men and then went inside a large dining hall with the officers. He usually did not discuss political matters with foreigners without a Foreign Office representative present, since his outlandish remarks to *The Daily Telegraph* of London a few years earlier had produced a diplomatic and governmental crisis.[18] However, later that day, he spoke with American "Colonel" Edward M. House on the palace terrace, out of the earshot of others nearby. House had been sent to Europe by President Woodrow Wilson to evaluate the likelihood of a European war. House reported the conversation as follows:

> "The last thing Germany wants is war.
> We are getting to be a great commercial country.
> In a few years Germany will be a rich country like
> England and the United States. We don't want a
> war to interfere with our progress…Every nation
> in Europe has its bayonets pointed at Germany.
> But we are ready." He smiled and gestured
> towards his officers.[19]

By now, the French, British, German and Russian warships had left Durazzo harbor[20]

On June 4, Grey sent a message to Rodd in Rome that he maintained his position that Britain would send a warship back to help protect Wied if others did, but would not send troops to occupy any place but Scutari. However, he was agreeable for others to send troops to Durazzo. The Italian Ambassador spoke to Grey on June 4, hinted at regret for unilateral actions by Italy and Austria, and said that Italy now truly wanted to internationalize the situation and keep Wied in Albania, but had to pay attention to Austria's wishes and placate her. Grey said that Britain would send only ships (which could easily be withdrawn) and not troops, to protect the King; but he would only send them if all the Powers then having ships in the Mediterranean (i.e., all but Russia) did so. The Italian ambassador expressed fear of "a European war" if Albania was left to Austria and Italy alone, and said that Italy feared Austria and Serbia.[21] That same day, the Germans told Ambassador Goschen that Germany also was ready to send a ship to Durazzo to protect "the Prince" and his family. But nothing was done.[22] Dr. von Flotow reported from Rome to Berlin that San Giuliano complained of losing prestige in his Parliament and the "Authoritative Press" because of his friendship with Austria, which opprobrium he found "most unpleasant." Any further development on the present path (in relation to Albania) really brought the threat of this "estrangement," he felt. Aliotti had skillfully gotten the press, the Chamber, and the "Rome Salons," all on his side, and opposing him might cause San Giuliano to loose his office.[23]

Flotow reported that Wied knew of Aliotti's criticisms of the King, but "retaliated" them. Giuliano said that he was looking for a way to get Aliotti out of Albania without creating a storm in his parliament, and to have a *rapprochement* with Wied He wanted criticism of Italy and Albania soft-pedaled. The Kaiser noted on this report:

> That's the last straw! After all Aliotti's low-down tricks...Italy treats [Wied] as an adversary...In other words, Italy has betrayed the Prince and he has noticed it; he is to act as if he

had noticed nothing and was to say nothing more!"

A further comment of the Kaiser was considered unprintable.[24]

In Germany on June 5, Goschen and all his staff attended a luncheon at the New Palace at Potsdam to celebrate the Kaiser's birthday. The Kaiser agreed with Britain not to send "a single German soldier" to Durazzo, no matter what the others did. He had objected to Wied's candidature, he said, and had tried to dissuade him from going to Albania. He had warned both the Austrian and Italian governments that the Prince, with all his good points, had not the qualifications, still less the experience, necessary for a ruler of a new and turbulent principality. Everyone, including the Prince, he said, had turned a deaf ear to his advice, and he was not now going to risk the lives of German soldiers to get the Prince out of the hole in which he had landed himself. He had been certain all along that the Prince would come to grief sooner or later, and it had been sooner. Thanks to the loyalty and efficiency of the Dutch officers, he said, Essad Pasha had been removed in the nick of time. Had Essad been allowed to remain a few days longer he would, the Kaiser felt quite certain, have "the Prince" assassinated or caused to be assassinated. Of course it was not true that Wied had deserted his post "in a moment of panic," as his personal courage was beyond all question, but he had committed a grave error of judgment and had not had the strength of will to resist what he ought to have known was bad, and probably interested advice. It was a bad business altogether and he had hoped the Prince would take the first opportunity of withdrawing from a position with which he was unable to cope, with as much dignity as possible under the circumstances. He felt that it was a mercy that the Prince had followed the advice given to him not to allow himself to be proclaimed King of Albania, as now he could, if forced to abdicate, return to Germany and live quietly on his estates under his own original title an without the prefix of "ex-King!"[25]

No help would be forthcoming from France, either, even had it been so inclined. On June 5, Colonel House arrived in Paris but found no government stable enough to even talk to, due to the excitement over the scandalous Caillaux Affair involving a former minister.[26] There had been three French ministries in two weeks.[27]

In an early June visit by the Czar to the royal family of Romania at the seaside resort of Constanza, the Czar was informed by King Carol, who as an ostensible ally doubtless made the comment reluctantly, that Romania could not look on with indifference at an Austrian attempt to weaken Serbia. The Austrian minister wrote to Berchtold on June 22 his opinion that the secret Romanian Alliance with Austria was a dead letter. "Romania's swing over to the Triple Entente, which had been expected for a year, took place before the public eye today at Constanza," he reported. Carol, however reluctantly, was forced to put Romania's foreign policy on a footing broader than his loyalty to Wied.[28] In the final analysis, even family ties could offer Wied little assistance.

By early June of 1914, the Great Powers had still not even decided amongst themselves what title of dignity should be accorded poor Wied. Was he still only a prince, or had he somehow graduated to the status of a king, no matter how modest his kingdom? On June 6, the German Ambassador in St. Petersburg, Count Pourtalès, reported to Chancellor Bethmann-Hollweg that Russia believed that the Great Powers should agree on Wied's proper title, but what that was to be, they were not yet prepared to say, "in view of the present unclear situation in Albania."[29] Von Tschirschky in Vienna reported that the Austrians were currently still regarding Wied as a "Highness" ("*Hoheit*"), the accolade given to a prince. They pointed to the fact that the credentials which the envoys of Austria, Italy, and Romania had presented to Wied all addressed him as "Highness." However, they were aware that Wied's own court, including his Prime Minister, Turkhan Pasha, addressed him as "Majesty," as befit a king, and thought that perhaps the time had come to adopt a similar attitude.[30] The French did not seem to much care,

Baron Schoen reported from Paris, although they had merely used the term, "Highness" in their minister's letters of credence to Wied. They were willing to do whatever the other Powers agreed upon.[31]

Italy, through its foreign minister San Giuliano, took an even more indifferent attitude toward things Albanian. The German emissary in Rome on June 11 found it hard to induce the Marquess into a serious discussion of a title for Wied, as he did not even hold the current Albanian situation appropriate for discussion, and he used his "well-known wit" to deflect it. He may still have been smarting over the Essad affair and Austria's obvious current influence over Wied. He professed to be indifferent to what Wied was called, and noted that the Italian King's cousin and naval war hero, the Duke of Abruzzi, had already called him "Majesty" in an after-dinner speech. Also, the Italian minister to Albania, Aliotti, had told Wied that he would be happy to address him thus, but could not do so until given official permission by the Italian government. San Giuliano used the conversation (probably with Ambassador von Flotow) to repeat his low estimate of Wied and his doubts about the demeanor of Queen Sophie. He quoted Essad, who said of her, "she is a woman who has much imagination and has read many novels."[32]

On June 10, while Wied reviewed the Durazzo garrison,[33] the Duke of Avarna, Italian Ambassador to Vienna, suggested formally on behalf of San Giuliano to the Austrians that Wied "might not be able to maintain his position." Berchtold rejected this and said that Wied must be kept in power and strengthened.[34] San Giuliano then dropped the subject, but Italy's attachment to Wied was now tenuous. On June 14, Berchtold sent, via the Duke of Avarna, proposed instructions supporting Wied, to be circulated to all Austrian and Italian diplomatic and consular agents in Albania and their representatives on the International Control Commission. San Giuliano replied evasively.[35]

Austria and Italy eventually agreed that their representatives should be instructed to cooperate to maintain Wied, but "to observe the greatest circumspection" in dealing with the International Control Commission, and that France, Britain, Russia, and Germany, which had withdrawn their warships from the International Squadron, should be asked to send back one warship each to Durazzo to put up a united front. The Powers complied, and Admiral Troubridge in *H.M.S. Defence* came from the Bojana in northern Albania.

At dawn on June 15, the rebels attacked Durazzo with some determination, causing surprise to all but the Italians, whose newspapers even reported that the city had fallen. During the attack, Wied courageously rode along the firing line, encouraging his men, and was greeted with much enthusiasm.[36] He was a soldier, and physical cowardice was not one of his flaws.

On June 11, Djemal Effendi, "*cadi*" (magistrate) of Scutari, in the name of the Muslim community, reported their intention to publicly support the other Muslims and stated confidentially to the French Vice Consul in Scutari, Billecocq, that the Albanian Muslims did not wish "at any price" to recommend Wied as Prince. According to Djemal, Wied had fired at them when they came to present their grievances and used "indignant" means against Essad. They placed all their hopes in France he said, and sought her instant protection.[37]

On the night of June 14, Sheik Hamdi, currently leader of the rebels at Durazzo, received signals causing him to attack the next day.[38] There had been some shrinking in rebel numbers in Shiak and Tirana due to many locals returning to tend their fields temporarily and to some dissention in Tirana. On June 14, Wied held a luncheon for the "Malissori Beys," and that afternoon there was a great demonstration of their loyalty before the Palace.[39]

In the south in mid-June, the Greek Commandant at Gramosta District pledged his word to the Dutch officers that the Epirotes would not cross the frontier of Kayan District. However, six detachments in full Greek Army uniform (minus only badge and cap) overran the whole eastern frontier from Gramosta northwards, burning all the villages. The same happened farther south. From the northwest, Albanian rebels lead by Turks advanced. Other Muslims and Nationalist Christians fled toward Berat, and the gendarmerie dispersed.[40]

Meanwhile, on June 12, the Kaiser and his Naval Minister, Admiral von Tirpitz, were at Konopischt, Franz Ferdinand's antler-bedecked Bohemian castle. The Archduke took them for a ride through the extensive gardens and park.[41] On June 12 through 14 they discussed, among other things, Romania's loyalty to the Triple Alliance. Franz Ferdinand expressed the gravest doubts about Italy but the Kaiser, who had great confidence in the integrity of monarchs, reassured him that King Carol and King Vittorio Emmanuelle were entirely loyal to Franz Josef.[42] The Kaiser left Konopischt on June 13. Berchtold arrived the next day with his wife and they spent the day with the Archduke. One concern they discussed was Albania, which it had been assumed would be Austro-German in orientation, but they were aware that Italy was maneuvering and becoming a rival.[43]

On June 14, 1914, in a telegram to Franz Ferdinand, the Kaiser said:

> The roses in my garden are blooming. Rhododendrons are also blooming despite three weeks of rain. *Waldmannsheil* [forester's greeting]. Many greetings to all.[44]

> The Kaiser was never to see his imperial friend again.

26

THE DEATH OF
THE KING'S CHAMPION

The Durazzo of 1914 was situated in a bulge, or semi-peninsula, which projected into the Adriatic. By Monday, June 15, the royal forces had dug trenches in an inverted "U" across the outskirts of the town. Looking upon the area from the sea, one would see hills behind and to the left of the town, the old Porta Romana Road running generally north from Durazzo, and, to the right, the beach and the road to Shiak and Tirana running eastward through woods and across the heights of Rastbul. Just north of the beach and the Tirana Road, which ran to the east of the town, was a petrol dump and a watchman's hut. Major Roelfsema commanded an artillery position with a machine gun emplacement northwest of the town, where the rebel menace seemed to be concentrated. Behind him, Captain Fabius commanded a battery of the small artillery behind the "barrack hill," which apparently was so-called because it overlooked the barracks. To the northeast of the city were both open meadows and swamp and flat, marshy ground. There was a royal outpost on the Tirana Road at the point where an old Roman canal emptied into the Adriatic.

During the night of June 14-15, Captain Fabius was on duty, alert for an attack, despite the recent lull in combat. He had ordered that no foreigners leave the city. He encountered Edith Durham as she left the Hotel Clementi (also apparently known as the Europa) in the early hours of the 15th. He told her that he was especially suspicious of the Italians, a not unreasonable position in view of recent events. Very early that morning, rebels had taken the outposts near the Porta Romana and shortly before sunrise Fabius had seen people crossing the shallow swamps to avoid the guarded bridge. He quickly called down artillery fire upon them, which served the additional purpose of alerting the other defenders. A general rebel attack had begun, and, aided by the covered character of the ground, the rebels had come as near as 325 yards from the royal lines. Stray bullets plopped on the square outside the Palace, kicking up little clouds of dust. Prime Minister Turkhan Pasha went to awaken Heaton-Armstrong with the news. It was 4 a.m. The King had already been awakened by the firing and his first impulse was to mount his horse and ride to visit the defenses. However, Turkhan and Heaton persuaded him to await a reconnaissance by Heaton and a report by Colonel Thomson.

About two hours earlier, another shipload of 1,200 Mirdites had arrived from Alessio, this time led by two "fighting bishops." The King and Queen now reviewed them as they passed in review on their way to the trenches.

Aliotti and his staff from the Italian Legation stood on the edge of the city, at the castle above Durazzo, watching the whole scene with satisfaction, no doubt. Aliotti claimed that bad dreams had awakened him. Heaton went to the area of the "petroleum magazine," as he called it, which had become the main position of attack. There he found two big defense trenches on both sides of the Tirana Road, manned by Mirdites and Kosovans, who were rapidly firing rifles and a pair of machine guns. There Heaton also found Colonel Thomson, like all the Dutch officers, still in his Dutch Army uniform, standing in the open behind the row of trenches. He told Heaton that the position was perfectly secure for the present, although a number of rebels had been able to get rather close under cover of the tall grass. It was hard for the rebels' shots to be heard due to the firing by the royal troops. Thomson then told Heaton that the Englishman had better leave before he got hit. As it was too swampy to proceed much farther, and as bullets were coming uncomfortably close, Heaton took the opportunity to ride along the firing line, yelling *"Rroft Mbreti!"* ("Long Live the King!") to buck up the troops. The loyal soldiers echoed the sentiment, while the rebels shouted the somewhat redundant, *"Allah il Allah!"* (God is God!"), at which point Heaton made a discreet retreat, still drawing fire.

A number of foreign correspondents were in the area of the petrol dump, including Arthur Moore, the "Special Correspondent" of *The Times* of London,[1] as well as a French correspondent of *Le Matin* and one from a Russian paper. Thomson had told them, "The place where you are now standing is dangerous. You would do well to fall back." When they declined, he said, "Well, if you like to run risks like that, that is your affair." Thomson had other problems besides the newsmen. Although there was much firing going on, it was having little effect and much ammunition was being wasted. Thomson tried to persuade the Malissori to leave the trenches and advance, and went in front himself, causing several to follow him. However, they "promptly returned to their trenches, where they stuck fast." as *The Times* reported. He actually dragged some men by the arm from under cover, but they quickly ran back to safety.

Meanwhile, Wied had decided not to await Heaton's report and had left with Ekrem Bey to visit Fabius's battery on the hill behind the barracks. He had hardly arrived when a flank attack sent a hail of bullets toward the battery. Wied behaved coolly and only left when Ekrem urged him to do so. As the King rode back into town, the townspeople cheered him.

Back at the petrol dump front, Colonel Thomson was speaking to Major Roelfsema and ordering some *baraiktars* (chieftains) and their men into the trench. At that moment, the rebels rose for an attack, but were halted by Captain Fabius's quick-firing artillery piece. Around 5:45 or 6:15 a.m., with his face to the enemy, a bullet struck Thomson in the right chest, close to his neck, exiting higher on his right shoulder. He turned to Roelfsema and said in Dutch, "*Ik ben gowond, laat me wegbrengen*," ("I am wounded, carry me away.") He then took a few steps and collapsed. The Albanians nearby did not move, so Roelfsema and correspondent Arthur Moore ran forward under heavy fire to bring Thomson to cover. They carried him to the nearby watchman's hut where Dr. Reddingius, the Dutch surgeon, pronounced him dead from hemorrhage of the carotid artery. Roelfsema was now senior Dutch officer remaining in

Durazzo. Moore was later given Albanian and Dutch medals for this action.

The Mbret was shocked to learn of Thomson's death and Löwenthal broke into tears. After breakfast, Heaton rode out again, seeing many rebel bodies in the valley below royal lines, and went through the trenches, acting as royal cheerleader, calling out "*Rroft Mbreti!*" He found that the royal forces had six artillery pieces, manned by volunteers, some of whom were reserve officers in the Austrian and German artillery. An Austrian civil engineer and reserve officer, Herr Hassler, commanded two guns. The heaviest part of the fighting apparently took about three to four hours, but by the afternoon, largely as a result of artillery fire, the rebels were returning to their original positions. During the fighting, several Austrian and German ladies had tended wounded in the trenches, despite the danger. As the fighting died down, Heaton returned to the Palace and resumed his character as secretary, spending the afternoon preparing proclamations and letters of thanks to loyal chieftains.

The royal losses from the battle were about forty officers and men, while the rebels lost over twice as many. Thomson's body was transported from the watchman's shack to a tent in the yard in front of the former court doctor's house. After taking tea like a good Briton, Heaton had food and wine sent to the artillerymen. During the day, Rear Admiral Ernest Troubridge arrived off Durazzo with *H.M.S. Defence.*[2]

In Italy, the Albanian situation was causing concern, if not confusion. At 8 a.m., while fighting was still going on, Aliotti is reported to have sent a telegram via his stock broker to the Trieste Stock Exchange to the effect that Durazzo had been occupied by the rebels. If he did so, it would be consistent with his reputation as a scoundrel, out for personal gain. Apparently the Italian government then sent a note to the Albanian government, seeking confirmation of the report.[3] In the Italian Chamber of Deputies, a Signor Galli asked for information and paid tribute to Colonel Thomson who had, he said (not entirely accurately), died in defense of his new homeland and prince. San Giuliano replied that Wied and his government's situation had seemed deplorable even before the recent attack. He noted that Aliotti had, the day before, pressed the matter of the arrest of the two Italians for spying, but Albania had agreed to "give satisfaction" for the Muricchio affair, even though Thomson had approved of the arrests. The Marquess noted that Italian sailors were defending the Palace and the foreign legations, and that British, French, and Italian warships were expected at Durazzo. In fact, the Italian squadron was ready at Ancona, Italy. Of the battle leading to Thomson's death, he said,

> The Government, feeling sure that it is interpreting the wishes of Parliament and the country, will act in such a manner that the great interests of Italy may not be compromised, whatever may happen. Meanwhile the Government and Parliament should follow the events in Albania with the greatest calm, *sang froid*, and firmness.

Hinting that Aliotti was difficult to control, San Giuliano said that the baron had been instructed that the Italian Cabinet were satisfied that the arrested Italians were innocent, and "no regard was to be paid to any further inquiries by the Albanian government or the Dutch officers." He was to bear in mind, when demanding satisfaction, the prestige of Italy, but also "Italy's interest in the consolidation of the young and sorely-tried state." Meanwhile, leading Austrian newspapers attacked Aliotti.[4]

Back in Albania, late in the evening, Major Henrik Kroon, Dutch commander of the northern gendarmerie, arrived at Durazzo by ship with 1,000 Mirdites from Scutari. The ship had been urgently sent for reinforcements that morning. Heaton and von Trotha superintended their disembarkation and the new troops were drawn up on three sides of the square and reviewed by the King around one in the morning.

Earlier that day, Wied had received a telegram from Kaiser Wilhelm, exhorting him to resistance and pointing out that a Prussian officer only retires at the last moment, when all resistance is useless. The Kaiser advised him to put his wife and children on a ship and defend the Palace with the last bullet, "when he, too, should retire to the ship, leaving the settlement of the issue to the decision of the Powers." What use Wied could make of this advice is uncertain.[5]

The next day, Kroon led about 3,000 men in an attack on the rebels. They got a slow start, but Isa Boletin and his men fought "like a lion." Unfortunately, his troops under Marco Gioni on the right flank decided to visit a tavern and disappeared. Kroon was able to save most of his men and cannon, however. During the fight, the freighter *Herzegovina*, leased from Austria to transport troops, was mounted with a gun and placed under the command of a German named von der Lippe. He bombarded the rebels until the vessel grounded itself, and the rebels later demolished it with their fire. A rebel named Hamdi Rebeiki was captured. Apparently as a result, the rebels asked for an armistice, and Wied, without consulting the Dutch officers, agreed.[6]

Durazzo was happy to receive British Admiral Troubridge, now the senior naval officer of the multi-national ships in the harbor. A burly, suntanned figure with snow-white hair, he came ashore with his flag lieutenant and an orderly. On the morning of June 16 he was given an audience by the King, who was happy to see him and in hopes that he would be willing to bombard the rebels with his powerful naval guns. Troubridge was forced to tell Wied that his orders forbade such intervention into Albania's affairs. He did become a familiar figure at the Palace, however, often smoking a cigar with Heaton in the evening to get the latest news, and then returning to his ship.

Later in the day on June 16, Thomson's funeral took place. The whole of Durazzo, as well as local diplomats, foreign naval officers, and even insurgents under safe conduct passes, turned out. The King, no doubt sweating in his usual fancy uniform, followed by his staff and all the notables, walked behind the coffin, passing between foreign sailors with their rifles at "present arms." The temporary burial site was the enclosure of the central sheep pen or *karakul*, which was decorated with wreaths bearing inscriptions such as the Austrian Minister's, which said "Albania's Gallant Defender." The British naval chaplain from *H.M.S. Defence* read the funeral service, and this was followed by speeches. The Dutch Government wanted to bring Thomson home for a hero's burial, and they soon sent the Dutch warship, *Noord Brabant* to Durazzo. De Veer returned from Holland and, for the first time, he and the Dutch officers dined at the Palace. Thomson was reburied on July 18 with full military honors in Groningen, Holland, where Queen Wilhelmina had already unveiled a hastily-crafted bust of the colonel.[7]

Following the Durazzo funeral, the royal forces planned a predawn attack for June 18th, hoping to surprise the enemy by sneaking up to the supposed rebel lines at the base of Raspul heights. Major Kroon was not optimistic. Unknown to Wied's planners because they neglected to send out patrols, the rebels had begun to dig ditches all over the heights of Raspul, turning it into a strongly fortified position with a field of fire over the approaches. The evening of Thomson's funeral, however, the rebels sent two emissaries with a white flag to open negotiations. Their losses had been heavy, and many dead bodies were lying about. One of their leaders, Hamid Bey (Toptani?), had been captured, wounded in five places. He declared that the attack on Durazzo had been made after receiving lamp signals from within the town.[8]

27

FALSE HOPES

Durazzo remained besieged by insurgents. Admiral Troubridge could only offer refuge at any time on *H.M.S. Defence.* Still smarting from the *Misurata* affair, Wied said that neither he nor his family would "under any circumstances" again embark in a foreign ship.[1] On June 16, Wied asked Troubridge to blockade the coast against the import of arms, but he refused and advised the King to consult the International Control Commission.[2] Wied now attributed all his troubles to Italian Intrigues. Troubridge reported to the Admiralty that, "What stands clearly out, is the universal impression that Italy is doing her utmost to compel the King to leave the country."[3]

On Wednesday, June 17, Sir Eyre Crowe, the British Assistant Under-Secretary of State for Foreign Affairs, advised Lamb that Grey had said that, while a small body of troops from Scutari might have been enough to nip the insurgency in the bud, it was now physically impossible to get enough troops to Durazzo to make a difference. Grey added sarcastically, "unless the Prince had shown unusual capacity for rapid and energetic decision, he would probably have missed his very brief opportunity." Britain's "direct interests with Albania are practically non-existent," he said. British public opinion would not support military action, and Austria would make six power cooperation impossible. The Powers had formed Albania to protect it from being gobbled up by other states and to forestall Austrian and Italian rivalry that might have led to "an European conflagration." Britain offered expertise and money, but not internal control of Albania's development. The International Control Commission was there for Wied's advice, Grey said, but the Mbret did not use it. The troops in Scutari were only there to protect the naval officers who took over from the Montenegrins, and they would probably leave when Albania took effective control.[4]

On that same June 17, Wied's troops had suffered a defeat. The Malissors were brave behind their mountain rocks, but were out of their element in unfamiliar territory. Major Kroon wanted to march from the front, parlay with the chiefs, and use all means to get the Malissors to follow. However, the rebels prepared an ambush which left numerous dead and wounded Malissors. It was a rout, and the frightened troops rushed back to the city's lines of defense. At the same time, a handful of rebels flanked the city and a prolonged fusillade rattled in the suburbs, the bullets whistling in the streets. There was a terrible panic. Immediately the usual barricades around the Palace were raised and the situation appeared so critical that the Austrian and Italian Ministers made ready to disembark new contingents of sailors from their ships to protect the Palace and the legations.

Admiral Troubridge, who found himself in the city at the time, ordered eight "embarkations" of sailors, but the cruisers were anchored so far from the city that by the time the British boats neared shore, calm had returned. From the Palace one could follow the phases of the battle at least two kilometers away, and the Malissors, at last rallied by their priests and chaplains, had stopped the impetus of the insurgents. The battle was pursued all day with results soon unfavorable to the besiegers. Meanwhile, the gunfire ceased with the coming of darkness. A certain number of Malissors came back to a strategic point on which the city depended to protect Durazzo against a sudden attack. But the capital remained surrounded by insurgents, cut off from the rest of the country, without communication with the interior, and without telegraph lines to keep the Government informed of what was going on in Albania. Austrian Minister Löwenthal sent a naval cadet at full speed to the outposts, taking it upon himself to give the order to refuse to receive negotiators. He would watch from the height of the observatory of the Imperial and Royal Legation. The cadet arrived too late. As mentioned in the previous chapter, negotiations were already going on in the city, and the chief negotiator had carried to the Government a letter addressed to the

International Control Commission. This letter never reached the Commission. Those who saw it said it contained a request for a three day armistice to remove the dead and wounded. To forward the proposal to the Commission would mean that the Government admitted that the insurgents rose to the dignity of belligerents. To the Government, they were only rebels who had nothing to submit. But Wied's government had been abandoned by the Powers, having to rely on Albanian Catholics, when 500 foreign troops could have restored order, and the awareness of this situation was keen at the Palace.[5]

When the British landing parties sent by Troubridge were near shore, they had been ordered back to the ship due to the return of calm. However, their approach had produced great relief in Durazzo. A Government official had cried to French Minister Fontenay, "Finally we are delivered from the mercy (*bon plaisir*) of our executioners; the Triple Entente pays us some attention [*s'occupe de nous*]". At the Palace, the British admiral was surrounded and given to understand that salvation had come from him. The population had been terrified.[6] The same day, the Government sent hastily to Alessio for troops, and 1,300 "Malissores" arrived in the night by an Austrian Lloyd Line steamer. They were received by the King and Queen and were soon at their posts. A night attack was resisted. The city was calm, "thanks to the energetic attitude of Turkhan Pasha," the French ambassador reported. Berchtold told French Ambassador Dumaine in Vienna that Austria was happy with reports that the rebels were repulsed and that Wied had been seen at the head of his troops. Berchtold said, "Happily he made a good figure. It's none too soon."[7]

The Thursday, June 18, 1914 royal counterattack was six hours late starting due to petty quarrels between the Mirdite and Malissori chiefs and the laziness of their men. They did not like any orders from the Dutch and casually sauntered out along the Tirana Road in groups, smoking and talking. On the other hand, Heaton, awakened at 8 a.m., could see from his window loyal Kosovans advancing along the seashore with a huge Albanian flag, which they planted some hundreds of yards beyond the bridge to indicate their position to their artillery. The Mirdite-Malissors soon came under heavy fire and they ran for cover until they spotted the enemy positions and then they cautiously worked their way forward in open order with artillery support. Seven foreign volunteers, including an Austrian reserve officer who had been shot in the shoulder on the 15th and wore a sling, charged up the hill to within 200-300 yards of the rebels, calling unsuccessfully for the Mirdites to follow. Their reluctance forced a retreat.

At 11 a.m., Marco Gioni, commander of the Mirdites, rode to the ordinance depôt to ask for "Vaseline" for his men's rifles, which he said were beginning to jam from the heat. There being none there, he proceeded to the Palace, where everyone was too busy to help him, so he went for a beer at the nearest café. He then returned to the Palace and, asserting that he had urgent information, got to see Wied. He said that Abdullah Effendi, the gendarme officer in charge of the gun at the bridge was a traitor and was firing on the royal forces. Heaton found this to be untrue.

A Red Star (replacing a Red Cross or Red Crescent to avoid religious friction) station was set up by some Albanian doctors on the outskirts of town, aided by foreigners, including Italians and educated townspeople. Reserves leaving for the front passed wounded troops and many who were simply going home. At the bridge, Isa Boletin rode up, asking for someone to help retrieve the forward gun being held by the Kosovans on the royal left flank, as they were under heavy attack. From the bridge onward, the road leading across the swamps was raised a couple of yards above the general level of surrounding land. On the right of it, looking towards Raspul Heights, there were a number of low mounds of sand, overgrown with long, coarse grass and grey-green weeds. The Kosovans were holding this broken ground and formed a sort of protecting screen for this, the only line of communication for the royal forces. The troops would pop up for a moment to fire and then lie down under cover. Occasionally a man ran back and took cover behind the embankment on which the road was built, firing again over the heads of his comrades in front. Further on, crowds of Mirdites were streaming back from the left and center of the position, some wounded, but mostly running away, although they muttered *"Rroft Mbreti"* when they saw Heaton. The rebels were only 300-400 yards from Major Kroon and the six German and Austrian volunteers who were manning their little artillery piece calmly. Having received Isa Boletin's message to retrieve the threatened gun protecting the Kosovans, Kroon ordered a retreat and the gun was disassembled and packed onto ponies along with the ammunition. They reached the bridge, but had to hold the rebels off with their automatic pistols. The Kosovans fell back to the bridge where Isa Boletin was, but forgot to bring their flag with them and rebels now surrounded it. Heaton directed the batteries at the barracks to fire on the flag area. This stopped the rebel advance. Heaton reported to Wied, who sent Selim Bey Wassa of the northern Catholic Kastrati clan, to try to stop the government rout. He failed, but the troops helpfully told him they would return to fight later in the day, after some rest and refreshment. The loyal trenches were found to be abandoned, and it took the Bishop of Alessio to get them re-manned, just in time to repulse the rebels attacking from the hills beyond. Italian laborers at the "brickfields" close to the sea became hysterical, spreading false rumors of enemy numbers. After noon, the fighting died down. The royal Muslim troops had fought well. Rumors had swept the Mirdites, causing their earlier flight. The Austrians blamed the Italians for the rumors. The Mirdites blamed Marco Gioni for bad leadership and failure to pay the money they had been promised, apparently suggesting that he embezzled it. He was sent home to get him out of the way.

In the afternoon, British and Italian naval doctors set up hospitals, the former in a mosque and the latter in an Italian school. They did such good work that they were able to decline the offers of the French, German, and Russian ships' doctors to help.

The royal forces had suffered at least 150 casualties, including 60-80 dead, who were buried in a heap beyond the bridge, but so poorly that foxes got at them. The rebels' losses were probably less, as they retreated in an orderly manner back to their trenches. One rebel Muslim leader was captured, badly wounded, but later recovered and was pardoned.

It was clearly a decisive defeat for Wied. Durazzo was still cut off. Wied's English butler, hearing a false rumor that the rebels had gotten into the town, said he was sick of all the shooting and panic, but said, "Well, I don't care, let 'em come if they want to, but these scares delay dinner so!"[8]

In the battle of the 18th, Duncan Heaton-Armstrong's brother, Jack, serviced the one Austrian mountain gun and taught Mirdites to use it. Colonel George Fraser Phillips of the West Yorkshire Regiment (commanding the small British detachment at Scutari) told Lamb later that Doda had only about 2,000 men left and the one cannon, serviced by a "Romanian prince [Sturdza?], a French Count [Pimodan?], and a young English barrister [presumably Jack], none of whom have the faintest idea of how to use it."[9] By the end of the 18th, Durazzo was quiet and the Italian and Austrian sailors had been withdrawn.[10]

The French cruiser *Edgar Quinet* arrived at Durazzo harbor the evening of June 19 and took its place beside the Italian, Austrian, and British ships to join a group framed by destroyers and Austrian and Italian torpedo boats. It was announced that the German warship *S.M.S. Breslau* was expected. The ships which had marines guarding the Palace and their legations were Austrian and Italian. The Russian gunboat *Teretz*, being small had been able to approach closer to land, while the British and French cruisers anchored more than three miles out and the Russians two miles from the *Edgar Quinet*. They would be useless in an emergency as the rebels were only one or two kilometers from Durazzo. The rebels realized that the ships would not fire. The local population had been terrified. They could not understand why the Powers internationalized Albania and then left it up to the Austrians and Italians to vie for control of the Palace. They felt that the 500 troops in Scutari which the King asked for should have been sent, and he would then not have had to send for the Catholic Malissors, thus angering the Muslims.[11]

During the day of June 19, Durazzo was quiet. In the afternoon the Muslim inhabitants met and four *"hodjas"* (Muslim religious leaders)[12] went to the insurgent camp at Shiak to urge them to lay down their arms and submit. Later, two *hodjas* returned with the rebel reply that they were ready to recognize the King, but wanted a three-day armistice. The rebels were told that only twenty-four hours could be granted and they must give up hostages to keep the truce.

That night there was heavy firing in Durazzo, "generally causeless." Rifle shots were heard in the town, and the Dutch commander, Major Kroon, was so exasperated that he issued a notice that anyone firing shots in the town would get five years in prison. The British and Austrian warships threw searchlights on the hills at night to reassure the inhabitants, while the Italian ships "[lit] up the town." Also that night, the temporarily Albanian steamer *Herzegovina*, manned by volunteers, again went along the coast, bombarding rebel positions in the direction of the Porta Romana and Kavaya.[13]

On Saturday, June 20, after a few quiet days with some firing at night, a carriage flying a white flag and surrounded by a crowd of people appeared on the Tirana Road by the Heights of Raspul. It signaled that a deputation (identity unknown) from Durazzo had been sent to the rebels to try to arrange an armistice. Akif Pasha, Minister of the Interior, reported this to Wied, who was very annoyed at not having been consulted, but Akif, although loyal to the King, supported it. The next day, the King acquiesced in a 48-hour armistice although Prenk Bib Doda's forces, according to the previous strategic plan, were supposed to be converging on Shiak within two days. Wied had no way to communicate the armistice to him, and the rebels would consider an attack by Prenk as a violation of the truce. Heaton had begged Wied not to agree to the truce, but he ignored the advice. Von Trotha, an honourable but quick-tempered martinet, took no interest, as he had long since lost hope and only wanted an honorable way to exit from Durazzo. He felt that Wied should leave voluntarily before he was thrown out, as he had proved unfit for the job. When the Dutch officers learned of the truce, they were ready to resign *en masse*, but level-headed Major Kroon dissuaded them for the sake of avoiding total disaster.[14]

Two of the three bodies of loyalists supposed to converge in an attack on the rebels had not been heard from. Prenk Bib Doda demanded and got another gun, but his third army was "tardy." Wire entanglements had been erected around Durazzo.

To settle finally the spying debacle, on the evening of June 21, Turkhan Pasha, the Premier, handed Baron Aliotti this groveling letter, composed by Aliotti, no doubt:

> I am glad to note that among the papers seized at the residences of Colonel Muricchio and Professor Chinigo nothing compromising has been found. Consequently the innocence of the Colonel and the Professor has been demonstrated. The Albanian Government deplores this regrettable incident, which led to a violation of the Capitulations. It is superfluous to add that the government will employ all the means in its power that such incidents may not be repeated.[15]

Italy had received its pound of flesh.

On Tuesday, June 23, Edith Durham wrote from Durazzo that the whole situation was a hopeless mess. She said that:

> Wied is a poor creature – evidently absolutely unfitted for the post – with no initiative and swayed by any and all. Does not even play the game – such as it is – but gives orders and makes plans without consulting his Officers – the Dutch. These, who are honest and plucky fellows, are consequently furious. I am surprised they haven't resigned yet.

Both sides had suffered considerable losses. The Dutch officers thought it important to agree on terms as soon as possible. However, when Wied interfered and ordered the 48-

hour truce on Sunday, the Dutch officers were outraged, as this gave time to the insurgents to concentrate again and bring in reinforcements.

On May 22, deputations from Tirana who had, (unknown to Wied) come to petition the King, had been fired upon by the King's troops. Since then, they had demanded his removal. Every day there was a rumor that Prenk Bib Doda was coming with many Malissori. Durham considered the Mirdites the most inferior of the tribes and they had showed no fight on the 17th at all, she said. She said that the Italian newspaper reports that there had been fighting in Durazzo were lies. Berzewsky, a Russian correspondent, gave an account to the reporter Dillon of *The Daily Telegraph*, about the death of Thomson, which was completely false. Dillon accepted it in preference to the account by *The Times'* Arthur Moore, although Moore and one of the Dutch officers, Roelfsema, were the only people actually present besides the Mirdites. Despite Dillon's reports of bullets falling in the town, Durham said that she heard none. She said Italians had run about building barricades and pretending that the enemy was entering Durazzo when it was not in sight. The Italians paid children twenty piasters (about $15.00) a month to come to their school and gave free medical assistance to each schoolchild's relatives. Durham and Consul-Commissioner Lamb believed that the Germans were the only honest persons in Durazzo. Someone named Raymond Duncan was working on "a big American propaganda" to give all of southern Albania to Greece. Lamb confirmed to Durham the reports of Greek atrocities. He said the report of a massacre in the church at Kodra was perfectly true and she was told that photos were taken of the mutilated bodies. Disgusted, she agreed with the Albanians who had invited Lord Kitchener to come and rule Albania.[16]

June 22 being the British Coronation Day, the estimated three British subjects in Durazzo were invited to lunch on board the *H.M.S. Defence* with Admiral Troubridge. Edith Durham, who was in Durazzo from the northern mountains to help with the wounded at the British hospital, was there. It was on this occasion when they were looking at the beautiful mountains that

Durham asked Heaton if he was not longing to explore them, and he said the hated roughing it and hadn't the least wish to go anywhere uncomfortable. She: "What on earth did you come for?" He: "Because I'm paid." He said he could see no fun in camping or riding about. He liked good food and comfort. He said he had been expected to eat roast mutton in Tirana at a bey's house, but refused to eat anything, rather than that. She said, "That's insulting," and he replied that he was just working for the pay and wouldn't put himself out. She concluded that he had never "knocked about." "He is more at home in a Vienna café," she opined.[17] It is difficult not to believe that Heaton was having a bit of fun at Miss Durham's expense. At least he later wrote that he had dreamed of remaining in Albania and making a career of his royal service.[18]

At 2:45 a.m. on June 22, Heaton was awakened by the *Kavass*, who announced the arrival of Catholic educator (and then Under-Secretary for Education), Louis Gurakuchi, and the Count de Pimodan, both just returned from Slinza, a coastal town about 25 miles north of Durazzo where Prenk Bib Doda's northern army was now based. They wanted to discuss strategy with Wied and did so, along with Major Kroon.[19]

Also on June 22, Dumaine, the French Ambassador in Vienna wrote:

> In the place of exceptional gifts, which in spite of his distress, permit him to cut a good figure, William of Wied is considered, as even Count Forgach admits, paralyzed by the most distressing irresolution, and this lack of will and of decision is enlarged by the incoherent energy of his wife by whom the list of projects that are formed are upset.[20]

On June 23, with real or feigned indignation, San Giuliano said that Italy resented Austrian press accusations of Italian meddling and *denied any such thing being authorized* by the government. Ambassador Rodd naïvely believed that it was not in Italy's interest to destabilize Albania, and so accepted San Giuliano's word on the subject. The British Foreign Office was more skeptical, rightly believing that Italy supported Muslims to offset the pro-Austrian Catholics, thereby consciously or unconsciously undermining Wied.[21]

Meanwhile, in London, Lichnowsky visited Grey and passed on Bethmann's pleasure at past cooperation on the Balkans and his desire to keep in close touch "if new developments or emergencies arose…there."[22] Perhaps the two Powers were, after all, growing closer.

Fieri, some 60 miles due south of Durazzo and north of Valona, fell to the rebels because the government tribesmen had gotten all the loot they wanted and headed home. A Dutch officer, Captain Carol de Jong, gallantly saved the breech blocks of the mountain guns, however, making them useless to the rebels. The armistice was extended but the Russian gunboat at Valona reported rebels advancing on that town from Fieri.

On June 23, King Nikola of Montenegro arrived in Berlin incognito, with his Crown Prince Danilo, to consult a specialist regarding the king's ailment.[23] On June 24, King Petar of Serbia left for the baths at Vranya, Serbia, due to "ill health," and delegated his authority to Crown Prince Alexander, since Prince George, his eldest son, had been forced to resign his rights in 1908 following the somewhat awkward killing of his servant.[24]

On June 26, Colonel George Phillips, who had commanded the small British detachment in Scutari since September, 1913, happened to be in Durazzo on a "flying visit" to report on the situation in the north when word was received that the rebels wanted to negotiate with an "English" officer. Phillips drove with his interpreter to Shiak, where the rebels were barely courteous and demanded a Muslim prince as a non-negotiable term, so that nothing was accomplished. Their specific terms were: (1) Wied must abdicate, (2) the International Control Commission must become an interim government, and (3) There must be a Muslim prince elected by delegates from all of Albania. A debate with Phillips followed in which the "rebels revealed a surprising and peculiarly intimate knowledge of the bypaths of European politics." The majority seemed disposed to yield to the persuasive arguments of Phillips, but five anonymous leaders remained unyielding, their answer being frequently prompted, strangely, by an Orthodox priest.[25]

The weather was hot now. The foreign naval officers dressed in their white uniforms visited each others' ships, but the Germans and British seemed to get along best. Heaton was invited to dinner one evening on the soon to be famous German cruiser, *S.M.S. Breslau*, where several British naval officers from *H.M.S. Defence* were already enjoying the hospitality.[26]

But all was not well with Albanians. On Sunday, June 21, 80 government soldiers were killed and 120 wounded. A Russian gunboat landed a member of the International Control Commission in Valona along with 120 cases of cartridges sent from Durazzo. On June 25, rebels finally captured Elbasan in the south.[27] The same day, de Bunsen in Vienna reported that Serbian Ambassador Y.M. Jovanovich had visited him and denied that King Petar's appointment of Prince Alexander as Regent put the war party of Serbia in power or amounted to an abdication. He said that it was because Petar "was completely broken in health," and couldn't face the "anxieties and fatigues" of the upcoming Serbian elections. With some justification, he said that the whole problem in Albania was caused by Austria and Italy intriguing for power and profit. He maintained that Albania had been formed to placate Russia in order that that there would be no war with Austria over ejecting Serbia from Durazzo. He felt that it would have been better to let Serbia and Greece govern Albania, but Austria and Italy had opposed this. If Serbia had the northern ports, he said, they could be neutralized by treaty and only used for commerce, which would keep Serbia busy and relieve Italy's worry of being bottled up. The "Albanian experiment [has now]…hopelessly broken down," he concluded.[28]

Becoming desperate, on June 24 Wied asked Aliotti and Löwenthal to find out how their governments would regard the sending of Romanian troops to aid his government, since theirs were obviously not going to help.[29] The Albanian government having little choice in dealing with the Epirotes, the next day the Austrian International Control Commission delegate Auguste Kral telegraphed to C. Zographos, "President of the Autonomous State of Northern Epirus" as follows:

> His Highness the Prince of Albania and his government have unconditionally accepted the Corfu agreement in its entirety...As regards our other declarations, which are attached to the text...these have already [been given effect]. Under these conditions, the definitive settlement of the question comes within the exclusive competence of the Great Powers, represented by the International Commission of Control. As soon as we receive a definite reply from you, we shall communicate to you officially the decision of the Great Powers, and notify you of the date of my own arrival at Santi Quaranta.[30]

In the north, the armistice was extended over the objections of the industrious Finance Minister Philippe Nogga and others. Nogga had visited Prenk's northern army and considered it strong enough to defeat the rebels there.

On the evening of June 25, Queen Sophie's younger brother, the scholarly Prince Gunther Schönburg-Waldenburg, aged 27, arrived in Durazzo on the Austrian steamer *Baron Bruck*. After the usual family greetings, he sat up with Heaton, who told him frankly of the desperate position, hoping he could thereby talk sense to the Wieds.[31]

Wied's only professional supporters, the Dutch officers, were becoming more and more discouraged. On June 25 and 27, respectively, de Veer and Sluys returned to Albania, while Sar left on June 30 for health reasons. Fabius had gone to Scutari for his luggage. This left the Dutch contingent in Durazzo for the moment consisting of de Veer, Kroon, and Dr. Reddingius. At Valona were Sluys (as city commander), de Groot, de Waal,

Mallinckrodt, Sonne, de Jong, and van Vliet. Verhulst and Reimers were prisoners at Shiak.

On June 27, an office for the open recruitment of volunteers to aid Wied in Albania was opened in Vienna. About 2,000 men applied on the first day. Many felt that they would be fighting for Austria. When the German and Italian ambassadors urged the Austrian government to be cautious, the Austrians told them disingenuously that nothing could be done unless persons liable for Austrian military service were recruited. But by allowing the recruitment of its citizens, Austria would be permitting another area for potential armed conflict with Serbia.[32] The Austrian government apparently realized this, for when, the next day, it was reported that 1,600 more men had enlisted (including several American doctors, 200 college students, a professor, and several nurses) the government refused them permission to go to Albania.[33] With Wied's consent, Heaton had written to William Gurschner, a Viennese sculptor who had designed Wied's uniforms and medals, and who was an Austrian reserve army officer, to accept his standing offer of volunteers. Gurschner opened a recruiting office in his home in Vienna and signed up 100 men before the police, at the request of Aliotti, shut him down. Nevertheless, on July 4, about 100 to 150 of the volunteers arrived in Durazzo and Gurschner followed them. The city was already swarming with Austrian officers unofficially there.[34] On June 28, Emperor Franz Josef left Vienna for Ischl, his favorite resort, little knowing the fateful events that day would bring.

The precipitate withdrawal of the Italian sailors from the Palace on May 23, the signals to the rebels from the Italians, Aliotti's unnecessary encouragement of the King's withdrawal to the *Misurata*, and the hostile Italian press, all made Wied begin to lean heavily on Austria-Hungary. In contrast to the Italians, von Löwenthal was diplomatic in his manner. Retired Austrian soldiers worked the cannon and machine guns night and day during the attack on the city, and an Austrian Steamship Line furnished two steamers to Albania, in one of which (the *Herzegovina*) it had installed cannon to police the coast.

Austrian torpedo boats carried Wied's messages north to Alessio to Prenk Bib Doda and the Malissors. Austrian sailors served in the artillery and the Austrian Legation (whether bluffing or not) let it be known that its battleships would open fire on the next rebel attack. Löwenthal was constantly at the Palace and spoke menacingly to the ministers. He played the role of a Resident General, and some wondered whether he exceeded his instructions, as he no doubt did.[35]

A more helpful attitude now seemed to develop in Rome and Vienna. On June 26, the two countries formally proposed to the other Powers that Colonel Phillips form five battalions of 500 men each, four mountain batteries of 100 men, and five machine gun detachments of 20 men, totaling 3,000 men in all to aid Wied. Each international detachment at Scutari would furnish an officer to instruct one battalion and one machine gun party. Italy and Austria would each instruct two batteries. Officers and Albanian "underofficers" would be chosen by the King without regard to religion. The International Control Commission and the Albanian government would pay expenses. The British and French stalled, saying that they had to consult Phillips and their International Control Commission delegates to see if this proposal was practical. On June 25, Grey asked Lamb and Colonel Phillips their views on this proposal, and on July 16, wired Phillips that the question of financial support alone delayed the formation of such a force, although the Powers had agreed.[36] If events had not rendered this plan moot, it might have given Wied the boost he needed. In one of his numerous marginal notes on diplomatic reports, the Kaiser wrote, "the Prince should fight and conquer, or die at the head of those who remain loyal to him."[37] Might the Kaiser have been thinking of poor Maximilian of Mexico, who followed just such a course?

On July 2, the rebels wrote a note to the authorities in the southwestern town of Berat, north of Valona, demanding surrender and including the following odd warning: "We make common cause with the Greeks, who advance in the south, with the Triple Alliance and with Italy." The Berat town council

306

forwarded the note to the Secretary of the Interior in Durazzo, and all foreign ambassadors were advised about it.[38]

As if Wied did not have enough to contend with, he was confronted with a public relations problem in the person of an American, George Fred Williams, U.S. Minister to Greece. Like most U.S. envoys to European countries, Williams was a political appointee. Born in Massachusetts, he was a Free Silver, anti-imperialist Democrat, appointed by President Wilson at the behest of Secretary of State William Jennings Bryan. He was an ex-congressman and a former attorney and journalist (a dangerous combination). As Albania was in the news, and as The United States had no representative in that country as yet, the State Department gave Williams permission to investigate conditions there. He entered onto this mission with unusual enthusiasm, circulating (without authority) a memorandum to all diplomats in Athens saying that he was going to investigate ways to bring about peace and other desirable conditions in Albania. He apparently landed at Valona, which he found hemmed in on the north by insurgents and on the south by Epirotes. He then proceeded to Argyrocastro, where he claimed to have been greeted warmly by Zographos and the Dutch officers in that city. Williams began negotiating with Zographos, who supposedly promised him that no more massacres would take place. If Williams' story is to be believed, the Albanians must have made no effort to determine by what authority he negotiated, for he had none. A week later, after the Valonans had allegedly agreed to some of Williams' suggestions, the German Consul General and International Control Commission delegate, Herr Winckel, arrived on an Austrian warship and ordered the negotiations to be stopped, and they were.

Williams then traveled to Durazzo, where he said that he found "no one in authority," although he said that he had talked with government ministers and others. He said, "I found a prince calling himself a king, with no powers, no subjects except his wife and children." From his hotel room Williams could see the Palace to his right, guarded by "foreign marines," warships in the bay in the corner of his view, and a "malarial marsh" on his left, from which he heard "musketry."

Returning to Athens, Williams realized that due to his meddling, his career as a U.S. diplomat was over, and prepared his resignation. On June 28, however, before it could reach his superiors in Washington, he gave the local reporters the benefit of his written views "to avert further threatened disasters." He condemned Wied, the International Control Commission and the Great Powers for the state of anarchy which he had found. He placed the primary blame upon Wied because the King had summoned Catholics from the north and Muslims from Valona to fight the rebels, thus pitting Albanians against each other. He also blamed the atrocities in Epirus on the existing administration of Albania, which he considered a blot on civilization. He rather accurately said that the proceedings of the International Control Commission had been reduced to a "comedy," in which the other Powers looked on, while Austria and Italy wrangled and intrigued. He described the members of the International Control Commission as "men of consular station, unfitted by training or character to create a government." Winckel's interference in his negotiations in Valona meant, he said, that "Another district was thus betrayed by fraud at Durazzo." He thought that the result was that the Muslim insurgents and the Epirotes, who might have become allies, were advancing, each against the other. "The insurgents will descend upon Epirus, flushed with victory, and all the horrors of religious war may be expected."

Local diplomats were amazed at Williams' statements. *The Times* of London's column headline chuckled, "American Minister's further indiscretions." Not surprisingly, the U.S. State Department expressed astonishment when it heard of the statements, and said that his actions must have been the result of the emotions aroused by the sad sights he had seen. It publicly disowned and deplored his views and, by July 8, he had resigned.[39]

Whether the cause of Williams' behavior or not, he no doubt saw things which would have stirred the emotions of anyone. Aubrey Herbert, President of the Albanian Committee in London and a Conservative Member of Parliament, in the House of Commons cited the case of the massacre of defenseless Albanians by Greek regular troops at the monastery of Kodra, which the Greek ambassador to London had denied. Sir Edward Grey answered this and other atrocity reports by stating simply that he had no "official information." This was not a surprise, since Harry Lamb was "the only possible informant of the Foreign Office, and he [was] with the International Control Commission in Durazzo." Herbert wrote a protest letter to *The Times* on July 15.[40]

Herbert's report of incidents, including shooting and burning all the local men in a church at Kodra on June 18, was backed up by *The Times'* local correspondent James Bourchier. After Zographos allegedly ordered the whole region from Tepeleni to Koritsa burnt to drive Albanians out, de Veer and Williams pointed out that the Albanians had committed no atrocities. Britain still kept a "hands off" position and Grey stated in the Commons that,

> Though His Majesty's Government are responsible, with the governments of the other Great Powers, for the creation of an autonomous Albania, I cannot admit responsibility for maintaining order there, and I do not wish to assume such responsibility... [He later elaborated that consuls could not be sent to Albania without armed escort, and] We have taken the line that we are not prepared to send British troops into Albania. On the other hand, if you are not prepared to send troops of your own to use force, you must, of course, stand aside when things are very bad and other Powers take a different view...The most I can say is, that while we are not prepared to do things ourselves, we are not going to obstruct the steps other people will take for themselves.

In the House of Lords, the Marquess of Lansdowne, a former Foreign Secretary, said that Britain should do SOMETHING to "arrest the carnage," and Lord Loreburn exclaimed that the Government's position was "what I would call a decadent answer." Grey told Venizelos how bad it made the Greeks look. He said that Britain had contributed £5,000 (perhaps $450,000 today) for relief of the refugees, but that Wied had refused Italy's offer of supplies, presumably on account of Italy's complicity in the discomfiture of Wied.[41]

28

ANOTHER ROYAL MURDER

Around noon on July 28, 1914, Archduke Franz Ferdinand, next in line to become Emperor of Austria-Hungary upon the death of Franz Josef, was paying an official visit to Sarajevo, in Bosnia-Herzegovina. The province, some 250 miles north of Durazzo as a crow might have flown, had been officially annexed in 1908 by Austria-Hungary. The Archduke had brought his wife with him for company, and so that she would receive the honors not accorded her in Vienna. But the great hunter was being hunted. A short time after surviving an assassination attempt by bomb, the couple were murdered in their open car by the pistol shots of a Bosnian Serb, who was part of a band of scruffy conspirators. These murderers had been actively assisted in their plot by some of the same Serbian military officers who had hacked up their own king and queen in 1903.[1] After the initial shock and expressions of sympathy by most of the civilized world, it appeared on the surface that there was no reason to expect the crime to become a cause for war between Austria and Serbia. But the private reaction in the Austrian and German seats of power was not so restrained.

Emperor Franz Josef's relaxation at his modest villa in Ischl was interrupted that afternoon when his *aide de camp*, General Count Paar, handed him a telegram informing him of the death of the heir to his throne. This old man, who had received so many reports of the violent deaths of beloved family members: his brother Maximilian, his son Rudolf, and his wife Elisabeth, could only comment on this, his nephew's death, that the natural order of things (i.e., no commoners in the Imperial family) had been restored.[2]

The news was flashing around the world. When Serbian Premier Pasich heard it, he stroked his long beard and said, "It is bad. It will mean war," and then went to bed without ordering an investigation, which he must have known would incriminate

Serbians.[3] At 3 p.m., during the Kiel Regatta in Germany, a motor boat approached the Kaiser's yacht, the *Hohenzollern*. Coming alongside, the messenger was told that the Kaiser was not to be disturbed, so he put the assassination notice in his cigarette case and tossed it to a sailor on board, where it soon reached the German Emperor.[4] Knowing the Kaiser's pacific position in the previous crisis, two days later German Ambassador Tschirschky in Vienna reported that he was taking every opportunity to "advise quietly but very emphatically and seriously against too hasty steps" against Serbia. Kaiser Wilhelm's anger, now aroused by this attack not only upon royalty, but upon a close friend, noted on the margin of Tschirschky's report, "Who authorized him to act thus? That is very stupid…it is solely Austria's affair what she intends to do in this matter…Tschirschky will please stop this nonsense! The Serbians must be disposed of and that right soon!"[5] From June 29 to July 6, the Kaiser remained in Potsdam.[6]

Back in Vienna, the two Counts, Berchtold and Forgach von Ghymes und Gacs (new Under-Secretary of Foreign Affairs) thought over matters in the "golden and red chancellery of the… Foreign Ministry" as "a scent of limes from the Volksgarten… wafted through the tall open windows…" Not only did they have to decide what to do about the assassinations, but they had to decide what mourning clothes to wear.[7] After reaching a decision on the sartorial question, Berchtold turned to the other problem. He wrote to his ambassador in Rome that exploring all the possibilities in the next few weeks would be like taking a walk through a labyrinth.

> At present, I have the impression that I have been selected by Providence to become one of those ministers… who wished to make a policy of peace and were forced into one of war. I hope I shall have better success than the last man who took this course.[8]

Back in Albania, on the same day as the murders in Sarajevo, Turkhan Pasha had received "strong Nationalist representations" that his departure from the country would be advisable. A majority of government ministers were perceived to be willing to resign power to the International Control Commission, and on June 29, a group of Nationalist leaders actually asked the Commission to place itself at the head of affairs. The commissioners were considering the matter. On July 1, the venerable Turkhan Pasha left Durazzo to visit European capitals in a desperate search for tangible help for the faltering royal government.[9]

Also on the fateful day of June 28, Wied entrusted the Romanian resident of Durazzo, Kristo Mexi (also known as Meksi), with a letter to Wied's uncle, King Carol of Romania, asking for 4,000 soldiers.[10] By this time the Belgrade newspapers were gleefully referring to Wied as "The Mayor of Durazzo."[11]

29

THE POT SIMMERS

On July 1, Berchtold told Hungarian Premier Count Tisza that he meant "to make the horrible deed at Sarajevo the occasion for a reckoning with Serbia." He needed the assent of both the Austrian and the Hungarian prime ministers, as well as that of the Emperor for this dangerous move. Both Tisza and Franz Josef said that more proof of Serbian guilt was needed.[1] Receiving Ambassador Tschirschky, Berchtold asked Germany's position and was now told that she would back any definite plan. Tschirschky told Emperor Franz Josef that Austria would have to decide whether its vital interests were involved. If so, Germany would be solidly behind them. "My emperor would stand behind every firm decision of Austria-Hungary," he said.[2] The next day, Franz Josef approached Tschirschky "with elastic step," upon the former's entrance to his "cabinet," and requested him to take a seat at the old emperor's writing table, whereupon the ambassador conveyed the Kaiser's regrets at being unable to attend the funeral of the Archduke Franz Ferdinand and his wife. Franz Josef said that the times were very serious and he did not know how long it might be granted to him to live, but he feared that he was to be granted no peace during the last days of his life. He spoke of the increasing danger "down there," and said, "I see a very dark future," but that one had to look forward and take all precautions possible at present. He then said that everything was going very badly in Albania. One could do nothing with those people; every Albanian could be bribed, and one could rely on none of them. Wied certainly had the best of intentions, but apparently he was not the man for the task placed before him, although the Emperor would not undertake to say whether someone else could do a better job. It was, he thought, undoubtedly one's duty to uphold "the Prince of Albania" as long as possible, and to guarantee his personal safety. But further he could not go. The Albanians would then have a chance to see how they could settle matters among themselves. Austria, he said, was interested only in the integrity of the Albanian nation. As long as that was preserved, there was no thought in Vienna of any intervention. He thought that Turkhan Pasha also appeared to be a very bad leader, and had now for the second time left his country and his prince in the lurch. As for Aliotti, it was regrettable and evidence of the weakness of the Italian government that a person "of such evil repute" had been sent as Italy's envoy to Durazzo. On the other hand, the Marquess di San Giuliano was in every way worthy, and fortunately things were now going decidedly better in connection with Austrian-Italian relations. The London Conference had not been exactly brilliant, but it had the good result that Germany and even Austria had been brought closer to Britain, and Grey was viewing "our" policy a little more justly than before. He then sighed that, "Everyone is dying around me and it is too sad," but then his mind shifted and he spoke of his plans for the summer at Ischl and the prospects of stag hunts. Tschirschky reported that the old monarch dismissed him "in the most gracious fashion," after the conversation of nearly an hour.[3]

For all the good it did, on July 1 the Great Powers informed the Greek government that they had approved the Corfu agreement in regard to "the constitution of Epirus."[4] Meanwhile Heaton, without authority, wrote to an English friend (for transmission to the British Foreign Office) that only a well organized "little army," sent by the Powers, and composed of foreigners ready to strike in any direction on short notice, could save Wied's government. The Albanians were, he wrote, "savages and will understand nothing but force," as had been repeatedly pointed out to Wied.[5] Heaton's brother Jack told reporters the same thing: "the manner in which the Powers have left him unaided is shameful..."[6]

On July 1, beginning a poignant pilgrimage, Turkhan Pasha met with San Giuliano in Rome to request soldiers and materiel to end the rebellion, or, at least, for the warships to bombard the rebels. In what must have been a highly frustrating reply, San Giuliano said that this request was "illusory," and that

315

the remedy lay in Wied offering to discuss all demands other than leaving. He said that Young Turks and Ottoman officers were behind the Muslims, and that discussions could be had with Constantinople.[7] However unhelpful this advice was, Italy was apparently willing to share responsibility for the use of force to save the Albanian situation, and to maintain some influence over Albanian affairs. San Giuliano suggested to the Russian ambassador, Krupenski, that in view of the chaos, international troops might be dispatched. Krupenski replied that Russian troops would not participate because Russia had only reluctantly agreed to the creation of Albania in the first place, and that it would only turn out to be a new Muslim state under the Turks.[8]

Aliotti arrived in Rome at about the same time as Turkhan and reported to the *Consulta*, no doubt pointing out Austria's increased influence in Durazzo and stiffening San Giuliano's resistance to unilateral aid to Wied. Reports were coming in that the rebels were fighting among themselves and that Ahmed Bey Mati (Zogu), instead of advancing on the rebels at Tirana, was still at Kruja, 20 miles north of there. Bib Doda was reported to be assembling his forces at Alessio.[9] On July 4, Zographos telegraphed the International Control Commission that, "in view of the threatening attitude of the insurgents," the Epirote commander had been forced to take possession of Koritsa to save it from anarchy.[10] The Epirotes had sent an ultimatum to the Dutch officers protecting Koritsa, seeking permission to enter the city to protect the Christians from the "Turkish insurgents." The officers asked them to wait four days while they negotiated with the insurgents, but this had been refused. The Dutchmen had not been paid for two months the eight thousand pounds (perhaps $720,000 today) owed them, and this had naturally made them less than bellicose.[11] At nightfall on July 6, Major van Vollenhoven and Captain Doorman, along with fifteen of their men, one field gun, three machine guns, and a vast number of refugees, withdrew westward to Berat. The Epirotes were just three hours away. That same day, after bombardment by the regular Greek Army (according to the prefect), Berat had fallen and both Epirotes and "insurgents," (reported to be Turkish) advanced. The insurgents hoisted the Turkish flag. Up to that time the Turks, Serbs, and Greeks had been cooperating on the eastern front.[12]

At about this time, U.S. Secretary of State Bryan issued a formal repudiation of former Minister Williams' remarks, which seemed to some "…to have occasioned more amusement than resentment."[13]

In Vienna, General Conrad was champing at the bit. On Sunday, July 5, he had an audience with Franz Josef. The Emperor brought him up to date on the Serbian crisis, which most of the world had assumed to be over.

Franz Josef: "Yesterday evening a note was sent to Germany in which we called for a clear answer [whether or not Germany would support war with Serbia]."

Conrad: "If the answer is to the effect that Germany is on our side, do we then go to war against Serbia?"

Franz Josef: "In that case, yes…The German Emperor is on a journey to Scandinavia. In any case we must wait for the answer."[14]

Privately, Franz Josef had said of the ultimatum, "Russia will not accept this. There will be a big war…I will be happy if we get out of this thing with nothing more than a black eye."[15]

Having read Franz Josef's letter, after lunch at the New Palace in Potsdam on July 5 Kaiser Wilhelm told Austrian ambassador Szögyény that, while he must hear his Chancellor's opinion, he had no doubt that Bethmann-Hollweg would agree to support "action" against Serbia, and as soon as possible, even if Russia was willing to fight Austria. But he thought the latter unlikely.[16] That afternoon, he repeated his belief that Czar Nicholai would never side with a murderer of royalty and that neither Russia nor France was ready for war.[17] Two days later, he blithely left Potsdam early for his annual cruise in Norwegian waters.[18] On July 7, the *Hohenzollern* put to sea.[19]

Meanwhile, the Russians having refused to participate in an international force to help Wied, Austria and Italy supported the suggestion that Romania send three thousand troops to keep order. King Carol and his prime minister considered the matter and reluctantly agreed, upon the ground that it might prevent a European war. But they conditioned the agreement upon receiving a formal request from all the Great Powers who had created Albania, and upon token contingents of 50 to 100 men from each Power to make the force seem international. Otherwise, they felt, Wied's blood relationship to the Romanian royal family would make it look "like a dynastic affair." Grey asked Take Ionescu, who had brought the Romanian proposal to him, whether 50 to 100 men each from Italy and Austria would be enough, since Britain, Germany, and Russia certainly would not send any.[20] Britain was somewhat smug. On July 6, in famous words now dripping with irony, Sir Arthur Nicolson wrote that, "Apart from Albania, we have no very urgent and pressing question to occupy us in the rest of Europe." [21]

On the morning of July 7, Austrian ambassador to Germany, Count Hoyos, back in Vienna from Berlin, gave the fateful report of unconditional German support in case of war with Serbia.[22] By noon, Berchtold had met with the entire Austro-Hungarian cabinet to report this good news. Still cautious, Hungarian Prime Minister Count Tisza urged that any demands sent to Serbia be such that it could accept. Only if it rejected just demands should an ultimatum be sent, and no surprise attacks or annexations should be considered. He understood the consequences of what Berchtold and Conrad were up to. He worried that an attack on Serbia might "provoke the world war," and obtained time to write to Emperor Franz Josef about the matter.[23]

The same day, von Tschirschky's Vienna embassy received a telegram from Berlin, relaying the Kaiser's message that "it would not be understood in Germany if we allowed the opportunity to pass without striking a blow."[24] The next day, Berchtold told the eager General Conrad that the Austro-Hungarian ultimatum would give either 24 or 48 hours for acceptance, and it was to be expected that Serbia would refuse, at which time mobilization would ensue. Berchtold wanted to hold the attack until "after the harvest and after the close of the Sarajevo inquiry." That is to say, to wait 14 days, until July 22, before mobilizing. He urged Conrad and the War Minister to go on leave, "to preserve the appearance that nothing is happening."[25]

30

THE SHADOWS DARKEN

In Albania chaos still reigned. On July 8, four royal gendarmes deserted and crossed the lines to turn and fire upon their former comrades. By some peculiar Albanian logic, they sought to avenge the death of one of their relatives among the insurgents who had been killed in recent fighting. The same day, a deputation of twelve, including several *hodjas*, arrived in Durazzo from Argyrocastro, declared that the population in Epirus was in a state of great destitution, and asked for help. Officials of the French Forest Exploitation Company were now missing, having previously been arrested by the rebels near Ishmi in the north. At about the same time, a band of Catholics from the neighborhood of Derveri were attacked by rebels and about 800 fled into the woods on the banks of the river Mati north of Durazzo, where they suffered terrible privations. On July 7, nearly 100 refugees from Kosovo somehow arrived in Durazzo and more were expected, while on a brighter note, 48 Romanian volunteers with two officers arrived also, and were presented to Wied by the Romanian Minister.[1] The next day, 100 Austrian and German volunteers, including many ex-officers seeking adventure, arrived in Durazzo.[2] By that time Turkhan Pasha was in Vienna and had spoken not only with Count Berchtold, but also with the Italian and Romanian ambassadors and others regarding "the Albanian Bank loan" as well as more effective support of Wied by the Powers.[3] To date, Austria had been Wied's most sympathetic friend, but was now secretly planning to fry bigger fish.

While Turkhan was pleading his case in the European capitals, Wied had become increasingly frustrated by the chaotic situation into which he had allowed himself and his little family to be placed. On July 10, he decided to confront the Powers which had sent him to Albania. Thoughtlessly failing to consult his own acting foreign minister, Mufid Bey Libohova, the King summoned the ministers of Austria-Hungary, France, Germany, and Italy to the Palace. Britain and Russia as yet had no diplomatic representatives accredited to Wied.

Speaking from written notes (presumably in French, the language of diplomacy), he ascribed the present "hopeless" situation in the country in the first place to the failure of the Great Powers to settle the question of Epirus in accordance with their own decisions, urging them to compel the Greek government to get the Greek military bands out of the region. Forgetting that he had pretended to believe that he had been summoned by the will of the Albanian people, he reminded the Powers that they had themselves placed him on the throne. He said that, following the advice of the Powers, his government had made concessions to the Epirotes, submitting the matter to the International Control Commission and accepting the Accord of Corfu, which was advantageous to the Epirotes. He had tried to unite some of the militias to assist him. Despite the armistice with the Epirotes, Zographos had taken advantage of the domestic unrest and seized Koritsa. While the German minister to Albania, Baron von Lucius, had stated that the Greek ambassador in Berlin denied that Greek Army soldiers had joined in the fighting in the south, Wied had received reports from the Dutch officers there to the contrary. They reported that they had been told by a Greek officer that the Albanian forces had been fighting regular Greek troops. Moreover, the Dutch had taken statements and photographs of their Greek Army prisoners as evidence.

The rebellion in the south, Wied asserted, had only encouraged unrest and aggression in other parts of the country, exploited by Montenegro and Serbia. Wied reminded the diplomats that, in the case of other Balkan monarchies, the Great Powers had sent assistance upon their formation, and he was entitled to the same, both financial (in the form of the promised loan), and military, in the form of international or Romanian troops.

He concluded the audience by urging the ministers to telegraph their governments, and handed them each a note

321

written in French, which read as above and included the following:

> ...you know that the Epirotes have taken Korytza [Koritsa] and are advancing on all the line toward the north. ...Thus,...paralyzed from the beginning by the question of Epirus which was supported by Greece, the Government has been unable to do any work in the country and has had to spend its money to defend its frontiers guaranteed by the Powers...I am persuaded that Albania will in some years have attained a great development, but foreign powers have impeded it. To have a period of peace, it is necessary to have money and foreign troops. That is why I beg you to insist from your government [sic] the loan that has been promised me and the dispatch of international troops or Romanians and to press Greece to withdraw her troops from Epirus and compel Zographos to accept the accord of Corfu and send back the Greek bands which have still finally burned several Albanian villages... If the Great Powers decide to accord us this help, we will very soon have order in the country and be able to recommence work...

The same note was to be delivered shortly to the local British and Russian consuls. Wied was evidently as oblivious as most of the rest of the world to the greater crisis between the Great powers which was even then developing in Vienna and Berlin. He had not directly mentioned abdication, but the implication was there. Admiral Troubridge, who may also have been present, reported that after the three ministers left, Wied had asked his erstwhile countryman, Baron von Lucius, to linger a while. Described by a former colleague as, "quick, intelligent, shrewd, and essentially cynical," the Baron was also probably one of the clique of Germans favoring a preventive war against

France and Russia.[4] The King asked him what he ought to do. Von Lucius replied that, speaking only as a German, he did not see what remained for the King to do but to go. Rather pathetically, Wied then said that he would be glad enough to do so if he had anywhere to go. He must have been keenly aware of the ignominy and ridicule which would await him in Germany, especially.

Learning that he had been completely left out of this important diplomatic event, Mufid Bey resigned the same evening. He had made enemies, so Wied appointed him to be the Albanian Diplomatic Agent in Rome, as the previous appointee Dr. Adamidis Bey Frasheri, the physician from Egypt, had disappeared.

There now seemed to be general agreement among the nationalists and the insurgents that the International Control Commission should "take up the reins of government" as a first step toward restoring order. It would only be necessary for the Albanian minister to be present at deliberations of the Commission to act as a link or buffer between them and the country, and to be the nucleus of future Albanian cabinets. On the Control Commission, however, France and Russia never disguised their skepticism concerning the success of the Albanian experiment, despite the continuing arrival of some Romanian volunteers. Wied had also received a delegation from Argyrocastro, assuring the King of their loyalty.[5] About the same time, Edith Durham had the occasion to see Wied up close at the Durazzo English Hospital. The doctor, the chaplain, and the hard working German and Austrian nurses had lined up by the entrance for the King's visit. Durham wrote rather harshly that she "never saw a more pitiable show than Wied giving putty-medals to the wounded…as though he were feeding nuts to monkeys." She thought he looked bored to death, gave no speech, and ignored the staff lined up by the door. He frequently gave a nervous laugh and asked Durham about some of her travels, although he "evidently [had] not the vaguest comprehension of what life up-country means. I believe he imagines he is roughing it."[6]

323

Unfortunately for Wied, however, on the same day as his impassioned plea to the ministers, the Romanian prime and foreign ministers were telling French ambassador Blondel in Bucharest that they had formally rejected the "*démarche*" of Austria and Italy to send troops to Albania. The foreign minister said that Romania would act only as part of a Great Powers intervention. With the facility of one who had not had to confront the problems facing Wied, he said that Wied had never lived up to the hopes that were reposed in one of his capabilities. The German *Chargé d'Affaires*, Count Heinrich von Waldburg zu Wolfegg und Waldersee, chimed in and told Blondel that Germany would have no regrets if Wied left Albania.[7] The same day, von Waldburg was received by King Carol and afterward breakfasted in leisurely fashion with him and Crown Prince Ferdinand at half past noon [sic] at Castle Peles in Sinaia. Carol considered the political situation to be very precarious ("rightly," the Kaiser noted later), particularly with regard to Albania. He showed much dissatisfaction with Italy's attitude in that country and described it as especially incredible that such a minister as Aliotti should have been sent there. "That man had at one time to leave London in haste on account of cheating at gambling," he said, and had once threatened Wied with having the troops withdrawn if he did not go aboard a ship.[8]

On July 9, the peripatetic Turkhan Pasha arrived in St. Petersburg, while back in Greece, Army Major Tsouras, who had led Epirote troops in the attack on Koritsa, faced the wrath of the embarrassed Greek government, and was forced to resign his commission. Two other officers who helped the Epirotes were "struck off the strength," while others were court-martialed and some privates were sentenced to two months confinement.[9] The International Control Commission made representations to Zographos about the advance of Epirotes into the neutral zone laid down in the armistice which had preceded the Agreement of Corfu, but he replied that the advance had been against his wishes and that he had even ordered a withdrawal.[10] Apparently the responsible Greek authorities realized that things were getting out of hand. Fieri in southwest Albania fell to the Epirotes on

July 13, and the Greek government denied any intervention except by 100 deserters from their army, and had "severe measures" taken against them. Zographos threatened to resign as Epirote President if the rebels did not desist and respect the boundaries of the Corfu Agreement.[11] On July 15, Greek King Constantine told French ambassador Deville that he had exerted all his powers to prevent Greek regulars from going into Albania and blamed Aliotti for reports to the contrary. He said that even Greek deserters had left and that the true solution to Albania would be to divide it between Serbia in the north and Greece in the south. He said that Berchtold's policy was idiotic (*idiote*) regarding Serbia, and he hoped that Franz Josef would restrain the partisans of war.[12] Edith Durham reported by telegram from Valona that

> ...the Epirotes are advancing rapidly towards the coast, burning all the remaining Muslim villages on the way, and the town at Tepelen [a.k.a. Tepeleni]. At Batska they massacred all the inhabitants, including the women and children who were strangled and cut to pieces. Destitute refugees are streaming in, having fled for ten days over the mountains. Some who were too exhausted to proceed killed their own children. The Epirotes at Scrapari attacked the wretched peasants as they fled, slaughtering many of them. The Greek Minister at Durazzo admits that all the criminals of Crete are now in Epirus [as guerillas]. The Albanian population begs Europe to save them from these barbarians.[13]

On July 15, *The Times'* "Special Correspondent" [perhaps Durham] was visited by a deputation consisting of the prefect, the judges, the commandant, and other notables of Koritsa. They begged that their appeal for help on behalf of the over 100,000 starving refugees accumulating at Valona be transmitted to the world. The distress far exceeded local capacities, and a shipload of provisions was needed urgently. The principal necessity was food and water, while clothing was secondary. Panic bred by the Epirote atrocities around Koritsa raced throughout the countryside and the dread of the Greeks who were reported to be devastating southern Albania was said to be "only comparable to the fear of pestilence."[14]

In Vienna on July 11, Count Berchtold dispatched Dr. Friedrich von Wiesner, a legal counselor of the Ballplatz, to Sarajevo to investigate the Archduke's assassination on the spot. As the Foreign Minister already knew what he intended to do, this was presumably for the purpose of obtaining as much incriminating evidence as possible, and to make Austria appear reasonable.[15]

On the same day, Turkhan Pasha was in Russia, where he pressed his case with Sazanov. He then went to see French Ambassador Paléologue and insisted that the Powers press Romania to send troops to Albania. The Frenchman noted (as Sazanov did) that the Romanian government did not seem interested in doing so. Sazanov said that it would be "superfluous" to press the Romanians. Turkhan warned that, if the insurrection triumphed in Albania, Austria and Italy would be constrained to intervene directly, and added that San Giuliano and Berchtold had told him that the two countries were in perfect agreement about Albania. "This agreement," asked Paléologue, somewhat cruelly, "will it include military cooperation?" Turkhan was evasive. The little Albanian's hesitation and reticence left Paléologue with the correct impression that no such assurance had been given.[16]

On July 13, Dr. Wiesner telegraphed from Sarajevo that the *opinion* of influential people in Bosnia was that pro-Serb propaganda there was known and approved of by the Serb government, but he had no evidence of that. There was "sufficient, although scanty" evidence that they tolerated it. He found no proof that the Serb government knew of or aided the murderers. There were "indications" that it was "out of the question." In fact, of course, the assassination plot was hatched in Belgrade with the cooperation of high Serbian military officers.[17] The next day, Berchtold decided to delay sending his ultimatum to Serbia until it was certain that French President Poincaré and Prime Minister Viviani, who were making a state visit to Russia, had boarded ship to leave for home. That was not due to happen until July 23, some nine days away. Berchtold's somewhat amazing reasoning for delay was, (1) so as not to be insulting, (2) to insulate the Czar from the bellicose influence of Poincaré and former Russian foreign minister Izvolski while they might be in a "champagne mood," and (3) the Frenchmen when at sea would have difficulty running their government.[18] In Rome, San Giuliano correctly sensed that Berchtold was up to something, and German ambassador von Flotow reported that the Italian was very pessimistic as to any plans which Berchtold might be hatching.[19]

July 14 was a busy day. Having arrived in Berlin, Turkhan Pasha had an interview with Foreign Minister von Jagow, who said that Germany would not intervene or even pressure Romania regarding Albania. Britain was against it. Therefore, said von Jagow suavely, it was at London that Turkhan must make his case in favor of a *démarche* to Bucharest. The French ambassador reported:

> Turkhan… is not discouraged, but he maintains that Europe has not considered the situation. He asked me to advise Your Excellency [Premier Viviani] how much he is convinced that a démarche at Bucharest appears to him the only way to put an end to the Albanian imbroglio. The replacement of the Prince of Wied with another prince would produce no result, and perhaps worsen things. The only objective to pursue is, in his eyes, to persuade the Albanians that Europe will maintain its creation…if the two Powers [Italy and Austria] intend to each occupy a zone, Turkhan Pasha would not be far from thinking

that Rome dreams of a proposition with a view to the neutrality of Valona.

Throwing the old man a bone, Jagow assured Turkhan that he would continue to caution Greece about advances of the Epirotes. With this less than satisfactory answer, Turkhan left for London that evening.[20]

Meanwhile, Wied was pursuing his own diplomacy with Romania. During July he began to receive regular visits in his study, sometimes for several hours at a time, by a junior member of the Romanian Legation named Ranette. This intimacy with the King caused jealousy not only by other diplomats, but by Palace officials. They refused to even announce him to Wied, leaving this chore to Heaton. The King also caused resentment by bringing Kristo Maxi, a retired Albanian-Romanian banker of doubtful reputation, into his Privy Council. An early supporter of Wied, Mexi also gained daily access to the King while Ranette ruffled feathers by talking to insurgents at Kavaya, some twenty-five miles south of Durazzo. These contacts seem to have paid off somewhat, because around this time Romania sent a second detachment of volunteers and some money. This now made almost a battalion of Romanian soldiers under Wied's command.[21] By July 21, he had 500 Romanian volunteers.[22]

By early July, the nation's somewhat shifty founding father, Ismail Kemal, returned to the scene. As he prepared to board the train at Nice on the French Riviera to return to Albania, the Italian consul came to him with a telegram from San Giuliano which asked for Ismail's opinion on the situation which the Italian considered to be more and more alarming. Ismail went to Rome and conferred with the foreign minister, and the two came to an understanding as to what should be done. He landed at Valona, whereupon he learned that Durazzo was surrounded. He then proceeded to Durazzo (presumably by sea) and had an interview with the King. After conferring with fifteen notables of the district, he told Wied the conclusion which he had reached with San Giuliano and the measures which the notables had decided upon, which were as follows:

- Albania to be divided into three cantons, like Switzerland.
- Wied to dismiss the Cabinet and withdraw.
- The International Control Commission to resume the government.

Wied refused to even discuss the proposals. He impressed the peeved Ismail as having "no proper idea of the state of affairs," and as being oblivious of the exceptional gravity of the moment. Ismail thought Wied seemed incapable of making an observation or putting a question arising from his own personal thought. While Ismail was explaining the different ways that might be adopted to get Wied out of his difficulties, the King never once asked him how he thought they should be put into practice.[23] The next day, Wied received fifteen notables from Valona and summoned all the Albanian chiefs then in Durazzo, as well as Ismail, to the Palace for a meeting. He opened the gathering with a few words in French, explaining why he had called them and inviting them to give their opinions personally on the situation of the country. There was no preliminary discussion by the congregants, as would have been usual in such a situation. Ismail spoke first, although custom dictated that his position required that he should speak last. Wied thanked the men and said that, when he had their remarks translated (sic) and he had studied them, he would inform them of his decision. They waited for several days, but no further communication reached them and they then declared themselves a "Committee of Public Safety." This rival body publicly requested that Wied return government to the International Control Commission. When Ismail's proposals became publicly known, some were so unpopular in Durazzo that he felt compelled to return to Vienna.[24] Ismail later noted bitterly that Wied had "so stupidly wasted" his ten million francs on things like a "court of cassation," when there were no law courts, on school inspectors when there were no schools, and on ambassadors who never left the country.[25]

Despite their doubts, those who had cast their lot with the King could hardly have welcomed the idea of his abdication.

On July 16, two detachments of Romanian volunteers of 250 each were reported to be en route to Durazzo. One Albanian faction greatly valued the Romanian friendship as a counterweight to Serbian, Montenegrin, and Greek influence, while another hoped for a Muslim successor. The German Colonel Schaefer, formerly of the Egyptian Service, who had earlier lobbied the British Foreign Office for an Albanian position, was said to have accepted an important command from Wied and he was expected in Durazzo shortly. This did not solve the King's financial problems, however.

Money was running out. Private negotiations with the rebels at Shiak showed some promise of settlement. They had not pressed their advantage against Valona. But *The Times* of London said that, "Among Europeans outside the Palace universal pessimism reigns regarding the Prince's position." The common verdict from his immediate Palace entourage was believed to be that he must abdicate. However, Wied refused, encouraged by Queen Sophie's "unmitigated enthusiasm for everything Albanian," and her strong opposition to such a move. *The Times* concluded that "his limpet-like policy" was not necessarily condemned to failure, but Albanian and European opinion seemed to be practically unanimous that a European Commission must govern, with or without Wied as titular head.[26] In Vienna, the *Neues Wiener Tagblatt*, which was in close touch with the Ballplatz, reported that "if a miracle does not happen, Prince William's crown can scarcely be saved." They said that, even if his government was overthrown, it would not mean the end of Albanian independence. However, "well informed quarters" regarded events in south Albania as having brought about a "regular collapse," and considered it the business of all Europe to find an exit from the labyrinth. This, at a time when Berchtold was secretly lighting the fuse of his Serbian ultimatum explosive.[27] San Giuliano had sensed something of the danger, and now de Bunsen, Dumaine, and others in Vienna suspected something was up.[28]

330

Meanwhile in Italy, Essad was still plotting against Wied, and San Giuliano was asked by the Albanians to intervene with him to stop it. When the Italian foreign minister told this to the Austrian ambassador, Mérey, the latter smiled and said, "What, you have already shot Colonel Thompson [sic] and you now want the Prince of Wied to disappear!" Mérey did not hide his irritation with Italian conduct in Albania. He had recently told the Russian ambassador in Rome, "The policy of M. Aliotti is detestable. The Italians are all for inducing the Prince of Wied to leave. It is undoubtedly because he shows his confidence in us."[29]

On July 17, the insurgents besieging Durazzo sent a letter to the diplomatic representatives of Britain, France, Italy, and Russia, inviting them to a meeting in Shiak. The German and Austrian ministers were not summoned, presumably because they were perceived as the only remaining adherents of the King. The invitation was refused by the diplomats, but the rebels were invited to meet on a ship. The rebels made no reply. Their spokesmen always seemed to be Serbs, Turks, or Essad's men. Rebel prisoners invariably said that they did not understand what was going on, and that they had been forced to fight because their houses would have been burned down and their fields devastated if they refused to enlist.[30]

An Italian proposal for training a force for Albania ran into problems: Where would the money come from to pay them until the loan was complete? Where would the officers come from? The officers who presumably would be commanding could not leave Scutari to be with them. Recruitment simultaneously with the gendarmerie under the Dutch would complicate matters.[31]

Poor Turkhan was now in London and, on the afternoon of July 17, came to see French ambassador Paul Cambon, repeating the plea which he had made in Berlin. "I have hastened to London," he said,

...because I was told at Berlin that it was at London that the knot [noeud] of the Albanian question was, and I think that is so. Albania is the child of Europe; it is at London where at the meeting of the ambassadors she was given to the world. Europe cannot abandon her; she must make her live or at least aid her to live. Moreover, that is in the European interest, where it has remained since the creation of Albania was considered necessary to maintain the peace between the Powers.

He then described disorder which reigned, massacres, and the progress of the Epirotes.

...if things come to the point of demanding intervention by Austria-Hungary, Albania could not avoid becoming an apple of discord between Austria and Italy. But they could easily, under the threat of a conflict, find a way to reach agreement for a joint occupation by them, for example in neutralizing Valona.

He praised Wied's virtues and said that it would suffice to impress Albanians if Europe sent contingents "as feeble as one likes, 50 men for example," or, Romanian troops could meet the needs of the situation. The main thing was to show that Wied was not abandoned. In a reply which must have made Turkhan grit his teeth, Cambon blithely said that it was unfortunate that Turkhan had come to London before Paris, as Premier Viviani would not be in France upon Turkhan's return, as he was still in Russia with Poincaré. Besides, he added, despite what he was told in Berlin, the hitch was not in London, but in Vienna! It was Vienna that invented Albania to save the peace, said Cambon, while Europe merely realized the Austrian idea. Europe had only one goal or *sine qua non* which Austria, "with more or less grace," accepted: Albania under European control. He said that it was Austria who wished to place immediately at the head of the new state a prince whom she hoped to have dependent upon her. She had never ceased trying to diminish the powers of the International Commission of Control. She was obstinate in her insistence upon unequal shares in the Albanian National Bank and the loan to Wied, and this had delayed matters. The formation of an Albanian armed force under Wied's command depended on solution of those problems. One word from Austria would suffice, he continued: give the Albanian government the money and it could recruit its own army. Anything else was "Utopia" [*utopias*]. He correctly predicted that Romania would only send troops if the Powers did, and if they did—there was no need for Romanians! Germany had already said that she would send none. British attention was concentrated on impending civil war in Ireland, and France was unlikely to do anything in view of its indifference and that of its ally, Russia. Go to Vienna, Cambon urged, and get agreement on the Bank and Loan questions. The other Powers would decide how to help spend the money! Undaunted, Turkhan went to the Foreign Office and spoke with Nicolson and Grey. When Cambon later asked what they had said, Turkhan was forced to confess, "the same thing you did." He packed his bags and left London on the evening of Saturday the 18th and arrived in Paris the next evening. [32]

As if Wied did not have enough trouble, that day in Holland prominent men, including retired generals, publicly and formally petitioned Dutch War Minister Loudon to recall the Dutch Army mission if they could not be assured of the men's safety by aid from the Powers or otherwise. This call was taken up in the Dutch parliament. Loudon had already written such sentiments to Queen Wilhelmina, and the Powers were so informed.[33]

Back in Albania that day, in typically thoughtless fashion, Wied rode out to inspect the Durazzo defences but left behind Heaton, the only one of his suite who had been in the fighting and knew all the positions. Instead, he took with him only some officers and prominent foreign volunteers. While inspecting an artillery position, he got in the middle of a dispute between some of the volunteers and some Dutch gendarmerie officers. The next day German minister von Lucius told Wied's chamberlain, von Trotha, that Wied ought to retire gracefully, before the Powers requested him to do so. Heaton and von Trotha no longer dared repeat such advice to the King and Queen, who now only spoke to them on business. The other courtiers did not help with any work and only seemed ornamental. Nerves were on edge that night as a full dress dinner party for the three foreign admirals was breaking up and heavy shooting near the petroleum magazine was heard, although it proved to be routine.[34]

Vienna was still in a bad humor over Aliotti, "who appears to have been conducting serious intrigues against Austria." In Rome, Austrian ambassador Mérey had been ordered to tell Italy to alter "her whole policy" or their "agreement" could not continue. The message was worded so sharply that San Giuliano was indignant. Zimmermann said that Austria should let Italy occupy Valona, which would become "another heel of Achilles," and there seemed to be some Austrian sympathy for this suggestion. Austria was thought to be considering giving Montenegro compensation if she stayed out of the impending Austrian-Serb war which, by the way, the Bavarian *chargé* in Berlin considered certain. "What the fate of the Principality of Albania would be under all these circumstances can hardly be foreseen today, [the Bavarian wrote]. In the first place, there would be a continuation of the hopeless situation…"[35] On July 18th, Berchtold telegraphed his ambassador in Berlin, Count Szögyény, complaining that Italy, through Aliotti and the Italian press, had for months been abetting the insurgents and undermining Wied so that Italy could grab Albania whenever Austria was involved elsewhere (as it was certainly about to be), and that Italy refused to recall Aliotti or circulate the joint instructions which Berchtold had proposed. Also, while Italy had pressed Germany and Austria to protest the Epirote acts in Greece, it was lukewarm over Albanian-Slav (i.e. Serbian and Montenegrin) disputes. Berchtold wrote, "If in recent weeks we have refrained from speaking more sharply to Rome, it is only from considerations imposed on us by still more pressing questions," meaning the imminent war with Serbia.[36] The fact that Berchtold could spend any time at all on Albanian problems indicates that he was remarkably unconcerned about the danger of a general European war.

Wied was becoming a laughingstock throughout Europe. In Paris, at the *Folies Bergère*, they were singing a ditty, playing on the sounds of the French word for empty, *vide,* and the German pronunciation of Wied ("veed"):

> *Les caisses sont vides* (the treasury is empty)
> *Le trône est Wied* (the throne is Wied)
> *Toute est vide* (everything is empty)
> *Le Prince du vide* (the Prince of empty)[37]

The German Minister in Paris or someone on his staff must have attended the *Folies*, as he reported on the rhyme and the "hopeless situation" which had fastened on Wied the nickname of the "Prince du Vide."[38]

In Albania the night of July 20, the insurgents made a half-hearted movement against Durazzo. For two hours there was heavy firing, principally from the defenders. The correspondent of *The Times* was returning from a visit to Valona at the time, and

> …as our ship swung slowly into the Bay of Durazzo, a magnificent spectacle met our gaze. It was pitch dark night broken by innumerable splashes of brilliant light. In the outer circle of the bay were the larger warships and the sailors aboard, condemned to inactivity, could be seen staring vainly into the night, unable to make out what was passing on shore. Nearer in were the destroyers and torpedo boats. On the deck of one vessel, four imperturbable men were plainly visible, playing cards. Searchlights streamed across the Bay and flashed on the hills, but threw no light on what was passing in the Palace and in the town. Shrapnel flashed continuously in the

335

belts of darkness while the roar of artillery and the crackle of rifle shots mingling with the shrill shouts of the invisible tribal commanders combined to make a species of Armageddon. Soon after midnight the firing ceased as suddenly as it had begun. No one appears to have been hit…At Avlona [Valona], the government is now distributing temporary relief to twelve thousand persons daily. The Epirotes remain in the direction of Ducati at a distance of six hours march…spirited preparations are being made [for defense]. Hills rise above the town; beyond these is a plain intersected for its whole length by a river fordable only at certain points.[39]

Before he left, Ismail Kemal Bey and other notables instigated a resolution from their Valona "Committee of Public Safety" at a meeting of town folk from Valona, Berat, Koritsa, Premeti, Colonia, Argyrocastro, and other towns. The resolution was addressed to Wied and the representatives of most Powers, begging them to dismiss the Cabinet and replace the government entirely by the International Control Commission. It said that only the International Control Commission "can maintain our legitimate sovereign on the throne, assure national unity and territorial integrity, and save from certain death over 100,000 refugees." These refugees were mostly Muslim and seemed to a foreign newspaper correspondent to be devoted to Wied.[40] Edith Durham reported from Valona that the refugees, "burnt out by the Greeks in their recent invasion," still swarmed into that town. Over ten thousand were getting relief "at the rate of two pence [c. 70 cents] per head per day," which barely sufficed for maize (i.e., corn), the cheapest food available. It was organized by a committee appointed by the International Control Commission. Many more were assembled on the hills some hours distant, still supporting themselves with food and livestock they had managed to save, but they would soon need help. They were all in the open, many without even a rug to protect them at night. There were no tents and many children died of exhaustion. There were good doctors on the spot but they needed medicine and equipment. The people came from the mountains where it was "malarious" and excessively hot. Most had lost all that they possessed. Durham estimated that around 50,000 were in the vicinity. "I have never before been faced with such an overwhelming task as that now before us," she wrote. "The dismay of the women when they found I could not supply even one tent, and that bread was all that could be thought of was piteous…they pointed to their bare feet and to the very few bundles they had brought." She asked the readers of *The Times* for donations.[41]

On Sunday, July 19, a secret ministerial council was held at 10 a.m. in Vienna in Berchtold's house, attended by members arriving in ordinary autos instead of official cars so as not to arouse suspicion. The precise terms of the ultimatum to Serbia were there agreed upon and the delivery date was to be 5 p.m. (later changed to 6 p.m.) on Thursday, July 23 "so that after the expiration of the 48 hour time limit…the mobilization orders could be sent out in the night between Saturday and Sunday." (The delivery hour was changed to 6 p.m. to be sure that the French rulers were still at sea). Berchtold said that Berlin was already getting nervous, and the plan had been "leaked out" in Rome.[42] He added, referring to possible annexation of Serbian territory and its effect on the Balkans, that Albania might be given a piece of that country, but was "no dependable factor."[43] The next day, Dr. von Flotow in Rome sent Berlin this account of a conversation of his:

> Marquess di San Giuliano does not on his information regard an attack by Epirotes at Valona as probable. If contrary to expectation an Italian expedition were to become necessary, it would only take place in agreement with Austria…two Italian war ships are lying off Valona. In Brindisi two transport vessels are ready.[44]

The possibility of an Austrian ultimatum to Serbia complicated matters.[45]

Also on July 20, copies of the proposed Austrian ultimatum were sent to the Austrian ambassadors accredited to the major powers, and to the Austrian ministers "at lesser courts," with strict instructions not to deliver them until Friday, July 24, the day after the original was to be delivered to Belgrade. Presumably, this applied to Albania as well. Berchtold did not obtain Franz Josef's approval of the text until July 21, and delayed giving German ambassador von Tschirschky a copy until the 22nd, "since some corrections are still to be made in it," which was a lie.[46]

Disorder in Durazzo was becoming serious. By arrangement of Ekrem Bey Vlora, twelve obsolete Austrian mountain guns arrived on the 20th, and were unpacked and remained in the square with their ammunition for several days. The breech blocks were missing for a while until it was reported to the Palace by telephone that they had been placed in the back of a shed with other materials by mistake. It being the eve of the Muslim holiday of Ramadan, the royal forces who were Muslims began shooting into the air to the consternation of the Europeans, who did not know of the dangerous and senseless custom.[47] Enemy Muslims sent another note, dated the 22nd, to the ministers of the foreign powers in Durazzo, demanding the immediate removal of Wied, whom they described as a bloodthirsty tyrant and lunatic. If their demand was not granted, they said, they would level the town and kill all the inhabitants. Although all the International Control Commission delegates other than the Austrians felt that Wied should constitute the Commission a regency in his place for a while, the threat was ignored and Heaton continued to ride out and inspect the positions of the troops.[48]

Captain Fabius decided that the mountain guns were only fit for defensive purposes and dispersed them over the whole front line. The Austrians, headed by a Captain Heinrich von Clanner, (sent as an "observer" by General Conrad), wanted a

338

battery of their own, and protested to Wied, as if he didn't have enough worries. Wied then inspected all of the artillery positions, whereupon the Austrian Gurschner, untrained in such weapons, said to him, "Your Majesty, this is the worst position I've ever seen in my life." Fabius was present and, when Wied did not reprimand Gurschner, became angry, turned on his heels and went to prepare his resignation, despite de Veer's opposition. Gurschner spent the day in the Palace cellar, presumably pouting.[49]

During his frequent evening visits to the Palace, Admiral Troubridge shared a smoke with Heaton in the garden and acknowledged the seriousness of the King's position, reckoning his only hope to be to leave before being driven out. He shared the wonder that Sophie kept the children at Durazzo during the notorious hot summer malarial season. Palace residents often spent their evenings on the balcony to catch sea breezes to relieve the stifling heat. The admiral expressed a willingness to take them to Romania or anywhere else in the *Defence*.[50]

As early as July 2, Ismail Kemal Bey had spoken to France's minister to Wied, Fontenay, and to their International Control Commission delegate, Krajewski, and said that the government was "non-existent." He said that the "last remedy" was to return power to the International Control Commission. Then Ismail and the Valona Committee of Public Safety sent a telegram urging the same step, which was received in Durazzo in late July and produced a profound impression on the King, following on the heels of Ismail's report to him that there was to be a convention of notables to give their opinion on the subject. When someone urged him to accept the inevitable, Wied demanded, rather desperately, "But what will remain for me then?" ["*mais que me restera-t-il alors?*"]. The reply came:

> What has Your Highness now? The south
> of the country has detached itself, the center is in
> revolt, Scutari is agitated and is only maintained
> by the presence of the international detachments,
> only the city of Durazzo remains. Now, by the

International Control Commission Your Highness
can yet hope to recover your authority over all
Albania.

The King of Romania had sent his minister to Durazzo
before all of the other powers. Minister Burghele, however, did
not become the *doyen* of the little diplomatic corps except in
name. He was a distinguished historian but had not learned the
ropes of diplomacy and did not exercise much influence on
Wied, although he had been in Durazzo since March. He told
Fontenay that, "not having an exact idea yet of the situation, he
hesitated to give advice," and asked whether the proposal to
make Wied the ward of the International Control Commission
was not contrary to the dignity of a sovereign. Fontenay replied
that he didn't think there was time for historical precedents.[51]

In Paris, on July 20, Turkhan repeated his plea for help
and was told that there could be no Russian or individual Power
intervention but that delegates of the International Control
Commission would go to Corfu to urge the Epirotes to accept the
earlier Accord regarding that region. The Albanian Bank would
have to have an Albanian president, one director each from Italy
and Austria, two vice presidents chosen from the Powers, equal
voices for all in the Council of Administration, equal shares in
the Loan, and control of the use of the funds by the ICC.
Turkhan expressed his gratitude for this relatively useless
information and left for Vienna.[52]

In Berlin, which had not yet received the bombshell of
the Austrian ultimatum to Serbia, Albania continued to be a
subject of discussion at the Wilhelmstrasse. Foreign Minister
von Jagow had discussions with both the Austrian and Italian
ambassadors about the problem on July 21. Mérey had told the
German Under-Secretary that Austria wanted Wied to hang on in
Durazzo as his abdication would create "unwelcome
complications in the present position." The Germans were
disinclined to try to tell Wied what to do and they felt that the
disagreements between the Powers and the Albanians over the
organization of the National Bank had resulted in a delay in the

guarantee of his loan advance. This shortage of funds had especially brought Wied to "a precarious position." The Italian ambassador said that, in view of the critical situation, Italy was willing to yield on its demands and hoped that Austria would do the same. Von Jagow again responded in effect that Germany did not care about the Bank either, and only wished the other parties to hurry up and agree before it was too late.[53]

Austrian officials were stiffening their backs in their dealings with Albania and Serbia. The Austrian Finance Minister, Count Leon von Bilinski, said that lack of steadfastness and action by the London Ambassadors' Conference over Scutari and Dibra in 1913 now lead Austria to "reject the repetition of such a spectacle [i.e. a conference] when a unilateral ultimatum had produced results with Serbia a year before."[54] Austria now dominated the Albanian government. In the defense of Durazzo, the Austrians took the lead, even to the point of alienating the German volunteers. Only the Austrian diplomats now had Wied's ear, encouraging him and offering him personal credit. The French minister reported that Austria "places all her bets on the head of the Prince of Wied." When former Ottoman official Sureya bey Vlora asked why Vienna did not take common action with Italy, Berchtold said, "We want to be alone, the fewer the better when one spends a million."[55]

In Berlin on Wednesday, July 22, von Jagow was shown the Austrian ultimatum to Serbia for the first time. He read it that evening and told the Austrian ambassador that it was "too sharp," and demanded too much. He also complained of the Austrian tardiness in sharing it with the Germans.[56] The next day, even as the ultimatum sat in the Austrian Embassy in Russia, waiting to be delivered at the specified time, Czar Nicholai told his finance minister that he thought his foreign minister, Sazanov, was exaggerating the gravity of the situation, and had lost his nerve. The Kaiser had frequently assured the Czar of his sincere desire to safeguard the peace of Europe, he said, and it had always been possible to come to an agreement with him, even in serious cases.[57]

31

A KISS BEFORE DYING

On the fateful day of July 23, at 6 o'clock in the evening, the Austrian ambassador, Baron Giesl, went to the Serbian Foreign Office in Belgrade and handed over the ultimatum, adding that he expected a reply within 48 hours. Prime Minister Pasich was out of town, electioneering. The Serbian finance minister hesitated to accept the proffered paper, so Giesl said, "If you won't take it, I'll leave it on the table." And he did. The ultimatum demanded that Serbia:

- Formally condemn propaganda against the Austrian Monarchy, and suppress it.
- Admit that Serbian officers and functionaries participated in the propaganda.
- Prosecute and suppress such persons.
- Dissolve anti-Austrian groups.
- Eliminate anti-Austrian teaching in schools.
- Discharge from the Army and government hostile persons whom the Austrians would name.
- Permit Austrian agents to investigate Franz Ferdinand's murder and help in carrying out the steps listed above.
- Prosecute the Archduke's murderers.
- Arrest Major Voja Tankovitch and Milan Ciganovitch, implicated in the murder.
- Punish and prevent arms smuggling into Austria-Hungary from Serbia.
- Explain certain anti-Austrian remarks made by Serb officials.[1]

Serbia could have complied. There were precedents. Serbia had in the past formally and publicly disapproved attempts to detach Serb-populated areas from Austria-Hungary. It could have fired the propagandists (as it had promised before) and allowed Austrian agents to help with that. Serbia could have allowed Austrian agents to help investigate the murder. Austria had once let a Serbian magistrate take part in their investigation of an attempt to kill Prince Michael of Serbia. Austria was demanding a secret *bureau de sûreté*, such as France and Germany had permitted Russia to place on their soil to help suppress Russian anarchists. It would "cooperate with the Serbian police and administrative authority."

Serbia did agree to most, but not all of the demands. They would give no guarantee that those behind the plot would be punished and the agitation suppressed. The apparent real reasons for Serbia's failure to fully comply were that it would thereby reveal official relations with the assassins (hardly a worse result than what was already threatened), would end Pan-Serb ambitions, and, perhaps most important, the murderous Black Hand terror society would murder Pasich or the King as they had King Alexander and Queen Draga. They might even add some sadistic refinements. Agreement by Serbia was not, of course, what Berchtold wanted. It would merely have been another hollow diplomatic triumph for Austria, leaving the Serbian problem essentially unresolved.[2] But the world would have had another chance to avoid or delay the fatal collision.

Earlier that day, Romanian minister Take Ionescu was temporarily stopping in London and visited with German Ambassador Prince Lichnowsky, who had known him since Lichnowsky had served as a diplomat in Bucharest. Ionescu told him that, as much as two weeks earlier, Romania had been ready to send a large body of troops to Albania if each of the Great Powers would send even 100 men there. He could not say whether this willingness still existed. He said that he did not believe that the revolutionary movement in Albania was being nurtured either from Serbia or from Greek sources, but rather it had emanated from the Young Turk element, which hoped that in case of new complications something might fall into their laps. He thought that Serbia knew perfectly well that she would not be allowed to go into northern Albania, and she preferred Wied to an Austro-Italian occupation.[3] Presumably Ionescu was referring only to the forces besieging Durazzo, and it seems unlikely that Serbia was as disinterested as he assumed.

The same day, he spoke with the French ambassador in London, making the same assertion regarding a Romanian force if the Powers would send detachments, "even reduced to a few men." Back from his trout fishing, Grey spoke at the House of Commons. Still cautious, he refused to reduce the Scutari garrison but said that he would not object to a *démarche* at Bucharest by all the Powers, asking for the dispatch of Romanian forces.[4] Meanwhile, in Russia that afternoon, Poincaré and Viviani boarded the battleship *France* to return to their country by sea, as Berchtold well knew.[5] By now, the Italian Foreign Ministry was telling the French ambassador that the only solution was for Wied to leave, since the rebels wouldn't negotiate.[6]

Startled by news of Austria's ultimatum, on July 24 the confused Russian Ministerial Council decided "in principle" to a secret partial mobilization of its army. This was approved by the Czar on July 25.[7]

Having received the letter from the insurgents threatening grave consequences if Wied did not leave Durazzo, Wied convoked a meeting with the foreign admirals and reported the danger. He urged the Powers to make a decision on the possibility of landing forces to help, saying that the Bank and militia [*milice*] questions were less urgent. The French foreign Ministry concluded that, as the rebels would not negotiate, the only solution was Wied's departure, but Austria still did not agree.[8]

Seemingly oblivious of the impending European war, at midnight on Saturday, July 25, the Wieds and their suite boarded the *Misurata* to visit loyal Valona, leaving secretly to avoid causing panic in Durazzo. Von Trotha was left behind to hold the fort and protect the children. Due to space restrictions, Heaton and Ekrem Bey Libohova were to bunk in the boat's small sitting room, but Heaton went on deck to a chair due to the heat, and fell asleep. He awakened around 2 a.m., soaked by the

Wied receives the crown, February 21, 1914 (Essad to Sophie's left)

A royal stamp is created

Durazzo Harbor 1914

Festive crowds greet the new king

(L to R) Essad Pasha, Turkhan Pasha, General De Veer

The Palace, Durazzo

Colonel Thomson, Major Kroon, Doctor Reddingius,
General de Veer, Commander Oudemans, and Major Roelfsema

A stroll with the children in Durazzo

Wied and Essad leaving a mosque in Durazzo

Royal gendarmes with machine gun

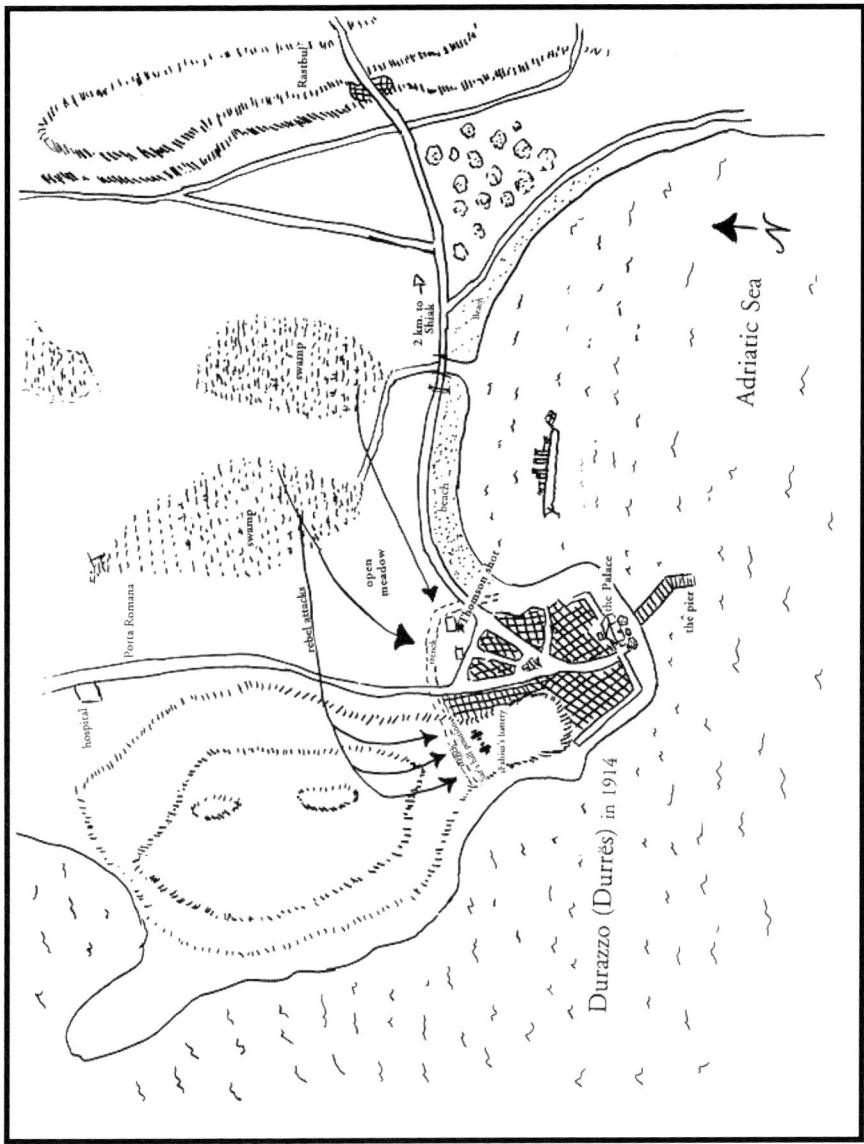

Map of besieged Durazzo

THE CIRCUS OF EUROPE.

Turkey (to Europa, ring-mistress). "INFIRM OF PURPOSE! GIVE ME BACK THE WHIP."

Wied and Major Kroon at Thomson's funeral

Kaiser Wilhelm and Franz Josef

Nikola Pasich, Serbian premier

Wied marches in Thomson's funeral

thick fog as they left the Durazzo harbor. They cruised through the merchant and warships in the bay in the dark. By sunrise, they were close to land again, and, after breakfast, entered Valona harbor. The Gulf of Valona is, at the narrowest point in the Strait of Otranto, only 47 miles from Italy and was the key to the Adriatic. It was thus a place of great interest to Italy. In 1914, there were at Valona about 100 Italian families and three Italian schools.[9] Valona had been the seat of the first government of Albania. It was not a city in any western sense of the word. It was a large unkempt Near-Eastern village situated near the Adriatic, but it had one of the largest and safest harbors in the world.

As the *Misurata* steamed into Valona harbor, on her right lay the rocky island of Saseno, which protects the bay from easterly winds and the open sea. The bay is sheltered on all sides and grey and forbidding hills came right down to it. The harbor was deep, large, and safe for ships. The foreign sloops in the harbor fired a royal salute, which echoed through the hills. As the *Misurata* dropped anchor, a rowboat, manned by oarsmen in scarlet sweaters, rowed the frock-coated governor and deputations, including Orthodox Christian ladies, to the yacht. By the landing stage stood the town commandant, officials and large crowds of enthusiastic Tosks. The American volunteer, Harold Spencer, had been commissioned by Wied to furnish a guard of honor, and it was drawn up, khaki-uniformed, on three sides of the square. Wied complimented them on their smart appearance. The visitors were surprised to see the ubiquitous Dr. Berghausen in the ranks, with sun helmet and Mauser rifle slung over his shoulder, but they managed to ignore him.

The town of Valona lay some mile or so from the port, and had hills forming natural ramparts to protect it. It was a simple town, containing only a few cobblestone streets off the main road, a town hall, an attractive mosque (once a Byzantine church), and a tree-lined square where a monument was later erected to the 1912 declaration of Independence. Down the main road to the port, horse-drawn carriages carried passengers. Most of the houses were built of wood and straw, only a few more comfortable but modest structures being considered the "palaces" of the local nobles. There were no street lights or other city services or utilities.

After landing, the Wieds got into a carriage from which some of the populace unhitched the horses and pulled it down the dusty road and across the marshy plain for the half hour trip to the town. This left the rest of the suite standing in the market square where they were nearly trampled by the mob. Finally, a ramshackle carriage pulled by emaciated horses came by and Ekrem Bey ordered four or five fat nobles out, and the suite entered. The visitors were followed by the population, either on foot or on horseback, through clouds of dust. Covered with that dust, the Wieds arrived at the large Vlora family house, where they were received by Ekrem Bey Vlora and other family members. Larger than the Palace in Durazzo, the house was less elegantly furnished, although there was a painting of Ferid Pasha, the owner's brother, who was once Grand Vizier in Constantinople and was now retired in Egypt. After freshening up, deputations were received who all complained of atrocities by Greek and Epirote bands. Elderly Bektashi Muslim monks told Wied how Greeks had burned their monastery and laid waste the surrounding country. They asked the tall King with the nervous laugh for advice and assistance, which they seemed confident would be forthcoming. Each concluded his audience with the King by saying, "*Rroft Mbreti.*" Captain Ghilardi and other outstanding gendarmes were received. Major Sluys, who had made himself unpopular by friction with local notables and with Harold Spencer, had Spencer forcibly prevented from seeing Wied until Heaton interceded and Wied ordered him admitted. Sluys had called Spencer a liar and a coward, but Heaton, believing the contrary, angrily told Sluys so, and reminded him that, unlike the Dutch officers, Spencer was unpaid. He further promised to write a report of Sluys' behavior, while a crowd outside the gates was cheering constantly and the royal couple had to frequently thank them from the balcony.

A European-style luncheon, personally served by the hosts themselves according to Albanian custom (with no local women present) was followed by a tour of the gaily-decorated town. Wied, in his fancy woolen uniform, and Ekrem, Selim and Heaton, were all on horseback, while Sophie and her two ladies-in-waiting rode in a carriage over the rough road, escorted by six Southern chiefs in national costume and a detachment of Spencer's khaki-clad Tosks. The crowds were so thick and enthusiastic that the visitors had to trot their horses right out of town, where they then encountered refugees who had rushed down from the wooded hills to greet them. The King and Queen visited the refugee camps near Valona which held about 30,000 refugees, who were mostly Muslims from the south who had fled the Greeks. The Wieds were again greeted enthusiastically and a few thousand offered to come to Durazzo to fight the rebels. Unfortunately, there was not enough money to feed and clothe, let alone arm, that many people, so their offer had to be refused.[10]

After a dusty ride back to the house, the traditional fruit syrup over crushed ice was served. Heaton was then taken to the house's "*Haremlik*," where the ladies of the house modestly stayed according to Muslim custom until the deputations left. Albanian Muslim women were only segregated when other Muslim men were present. Well educated and multilingual, they then joined the rest of the visitors. The wife of Wied's *aide de camp*, Selim, was never veiled in the Palace, but had to be when outside or at dinners when Muslim men were present. After tea, the visitors left Valona for the quay, where the King and Queen inspected the excellent Dutch gendarmerie hospital. The *Misurata* weighed anchor at 5 p.m. with everyone more optimistic, arriving at Durazzo early on the 27th.[11]

During the Valona visit, Wied showed no emotion and remained formal, merely bowing to the crowds from Ekrem's balcony. Later, Queen Sophie said that their reception had been wonderful. "It was like awakening from a bad dream," she said, in contrast to all the opposition which they had met from other parts of the country.[12] Edith Durham said of Sophie:

347

The few times I have spoken to her [she] impresses me as a bright young woman, but her only idea is to play Lady Bountiful, distribute flowers, put medals on the wounded and make fancy blouses of native embroidery.[13]

She also liked to take long walks over the Durazzo hills, and wrote "intensely interesting" letters about her experiences to Crown Princess Marie of Romania which cannot, unfortunately, now be found[14]

Only a few hours before the Albanian royal party sailed for Valona, serious events were taking place in Belgrade. At 5:55 that evening, within the time limit, Prime Minister Pasich handed Ambassador Giesl Serbia's reply to the Austrian ultimatum, whereupon Baron Giesl immediately advised that diplomatic relations were severed and proceeded with his staff to catch the 6:30 train for the 10 minute ride across the border.[15]

Berchtold was at Ischl, Franz Josef's favorite retreat, staying at the Hotel Elisabeth, but proceeded to the Emperor's villa when word came, to deliver the fatal news.[16] When Franz Josef signed the mobilization decree he said, "If the Monarchy is to go to Hell now, at least it shall go like a gentleman."[17]

In Berlin, as he doodled sketches of women's faces, von Jagow lied that he had passed to Berchtold a British proposal to mediate the fast-developing Serbian crisis. He had only sent it when he was certain that it would arrive after the time limit in the ultimatum. That evening, Austria ordered mobilization against Serbia.[18]

Modern European wars could not be effectively fought without mobilizations. Even units from the standing professional armies had to be gathered in from their various garrison towns and concentrated, so that they could be transported by rail to the areas where they would fight. By the Twentieth Century all the Great Powers (except, perhaps, Britain) had large numbers of reservists who had to be summoned from civilian life, trained, equipped and concentrated for combat. All of this took varying amounts of time, depending upon the efficiency and planning of the country involved. Some countries, like Germany and France, had efficient plans for speedy mobilizations, while less developed or less efficient countries like Russia or Austria-Hungary notoriously required more time to complete the process. Russian Foreign Minister Sazanov did not know that Austria could not be ready to invade Russia until August 15, at the earliest.[19]

On hearing of Serbia's reply, old Franz Josef, who had reigned through so many wars, seems to have clung to a shred of hope. Although he had the power to stop the proceedings, he passively said, "So it's come! Well, breaking diplomatic relations is not necessarily war." Berchtold assured him that they would only be fighting Serbia, and Franz Josef comforted himself with the remark, "and he ought to know."[20]

In Russia, the government ministers met with the Czar and he approved a "contingent partial mobilization," and secret preparations for general mobilization.[21] The Russian generals had told the frightened Czar that a partial mobilization against only Austria was impossible. The German border had also to be covered, they said, (there being at the time no Polish state as a buffer between the two empires).[22]

Every leader of a great continental Power was now afraid lest his country be defeated due to being late in mobilizing. In London, Grey advised King George V of the concern which Benckendorff had expressed about the crisis. The King wrote in his diary, "It looks as though we are on the verge of a European war caused by sending an ultimatum to Servia [sic] by Austria."[23]

Even though he knew his country was about to go to war with Serbia, Berchtold still had to deal with the Albanian problem, if for no other reason because Albania would have potential strategic value. On July 24, the German, von Tschirschky, spoke with Berchtold and urgently advised him that if he wanted to keep Wied in Albania he had better get the Albanian National Bank question settled at once. In that way funds could be made available to Wied immediately. Berchtold agreed, but said that he had been battling with other Austrian ministers about it and, if the question of the directors of the Bank was solved as Austria and Italy wished, the question of the bank vice presidents would be insignificant.[24]

On Sunday, July 26, the text of the Serbian reply to the Austrian ultimatum was received by the minor officials on duty at the German Foreign Office on the Wilhelmstrasse in Berlin. It had been delayed by the Austrians. Although not accepting all the Austrian demands, it was very conciliatory in tone. Von Jagow did not see it until the next day.[25] At 9:30 a.m. that day, King George received the Kaiser's seafaring brother Prince Heinrich, who had been yachting at Cowes in England and now came to visit his royal cousin at Buckingham Palace. George told him, "The news is very bad. It looks like war in Europe. You had better go back to Germany at once." Heinrich asked, "What will England do?" and the King replied, "I don't know what we shall do. We have no quarrel with anyone and I hope we shall remain neutral." Heinrich believed that George *added* that he thought Britain *would* remain neutral, but that was later controverted.[26]

In Rome, San Giuliano was concerned about the gravity of the quarrel between Italy's Triple Alliance ally, Austria-Hungary, and Serbia. He proposed that Serbia accept the remaining demands "as an obligation to Europe," rather than as a surrender of sovereignty to Austria. That would save face and allow Europe to supervise the situation. Serbian ambassador Michailovitch thought the proposal would be accepted by his government, but it was ignored by the crucial Powers. Paris ignored it, London merely passed it on, and Russia replied evasively, while Berlin accepted. Austria was silent [27] Sir Edward Grey was rusticating in the country again, and Nicolson, with his approval, sent an offer to the other Powers to hold another conference to discuss the crisis.[28]

Meanwhile, the Kaiser, at sea on his annual cruise to cool Norwegian waters, learned of the Austrian ultimatum from a newspaper agency, not from his foreign ministry, making him understandably indignant.[29] On Monday, July 27, Wilhelm returned to Germany from his cruise and went to Potsdam.

Bethmann-Hollweg had sent him a telegram on his train, but intentionally failed to mention Britain's offer to mediate.[30] Bethmann forwarded Grey's mediation offer to Berchtold that evening, but advised him to reject it.[31] That afternoon Conrad told Berchtold that it would be impossible for the foremost Austrian patrol to enter Serbia before August 12, thus dashing Berchtold's hopes for a *fait accompli* which would end the crisis before other Powers could react. Due to Austrian and German delays, the text of the Serbian reply was only sent to the Kaiser's palace at Potsdam at 9 p.m., after he had gone to bed.[32]

32

THE SANDS RUN OUT

By late July, Heaton was inspecting the battle lines at Durazzo twice a day, occasionally forcing lazy Albanian doctors to treat the hundreds of soldiers with malaria, dysentery and other ailments of warfare. Romanian volunteers accompanied the doctors with stretchers and medicine. Queen Sophie organized an Albanian hospital, which was soon filled to capacity, forcing patients to be lodged in private houses in the town. Medals were so highly prized by the Albanians that Wied decided, in order to avoid offense, to award the bronze medals "for gallantry in the field" to *all* the wounded. Consequently, he eventually ran out of the baubles, but also instituted the more prestigious "Order of the Eagle of Albania," to be awarded to those on a list supplied by Heaton. It came with a large star pin created by a jeweler in Vienna.

Hitherto friendly relations between the Palace and the Dutch officers were cooling. After the return from the royal visit to Valona, General de Veer came to visit the King. He was, as was customary, shown to the waiting room next to Heaton's office, where Lamb was apparently also waiting. Heaton took the opportunity to report on Sluys's behavior in Valona and his temptation to put his report on it in writing, whereupon de Veer burst into a tirade, apparently resenting this slur upon one of his men. The two men exchanged heated words. Lamb tried to soothe their tempers, but relations were never the same. Heaton decided that the General was a good man, but inefficient.

The first official notice of Austria's crisis with Serbia to Austria's man in Durazzo, von Löwenthal, seems to have been a telegram dated July 24. It reported that Serbia had been presented the day before with "a number of demands" to be answered within 48 hours. The details of the demands were only sent later, rather casually, on the 27th by way of Austrian Lloyd Line steamer. That same day, the Ballplatz sent a "Circular Decree" to von Löwenthal and other Austrian diplomats, reporting that the Serbian reply was unsatisfactory and that Serbia had mobilized.

As July faded and war clouds gathered over the rest of Europe, the international fleet in Durazzo harbor, Wied's backstop, began to melt away. First, the small Russian cruiser *Askold* left in the dead of night without notice. The commander of the French cruiser said that he presumed it had gone to Brindisi to restock its coal bunkers. A few nights later, the French left just as peremptorily, followed by the British in *H.M.S. Defence* and her escorting destroyer, giving short notice. The German *Breslau* and the several Austrian ships left a few days after that. Only the obsolete Italian ship, *Dandolo*, was left for Wied's protection. Italy did not plan to become embroiled yet in the European war that was brewing up. The Austrian Lloyd steamship service in the Adriatic was discontinued. The Durazzo government had contacted the German armament firm of Erhardt in hopes of buying a longer-range artillery piece with which to bombard the rebels as far away as Shiak or Kavaya, but they were told that the guns were sold out. The irregular Mirdite troops also began to drift away, selling their modern government-issued rifles for five to ten francs apiece. Fabius took the last transport out of Albania before the World War broke out at the end of July, and de Veer was ordered by the Dutch government to return home on August 2. However, he, Kroon, and Mallinckrodt stayed on to try to free the Dutch prisoners captured by the rebels, who were not released until September 19.[1] Street disputes developed between Malissors and sometimes involved gunfire.

Britain ordered Colonel Phillips and the British detachment in Scutari to withdraw to Malta to avoid complications with Montenegro, a Serbian ally. Phillips was ordered on July 30 to hand over his "governorship" of Scutari to the next senior foreign officer. Grey wrote to Lamb:

I presume that Austria and Italy will retain
sufficient naval strength at Durazzo to protect

persons of Prince and of international commission and their staffs, but in the contrary event, you are enjoined to leave Durazzo with your assistant on one of the foreign men-of-war or by Italian or Austrian steamer, as may be most convenient or readily available.

Poor Turkhan had returned to Durazzo from his European peregrinations empty-handed. To add insult to injury, his illiterate black manservant was suddenly arrested as a spy for allegedly signaling the rebels by waving his handkerchief. Very upset, Turkhan secured his release, despite the old man's always suspicious nationalist enemies.[2]

In contrast to the depressing events in Durazzo, Isa Boletin was reported to have left the town the night of July 28, intending to raise the Albanian tribesmen of Serb-occupied Kosovo district against the Serbs. They hoped to recapture Dibra and possibly also Jakova and Ipek while Serbia was preoccupied with its fight with Austria.[3]

On Tuesday, July 28, the Kaiser awakened and read the Serbian reply to Austria for the first time. He was elated. "All reason for war has gone!" he told his *aide de camp*, and went for a horseback ride. He then wrote, "Every reason for war drops away. Giesl [the Austrian ambassador to Serbia] might have remained quietly in Belgrade! On the strength of this I should [i.e. would] not have ordered mobilization!"[4] At ten that morning he wrote von Jagow to the same effect.[5] He was not told that Austria was to declare war that very day. The Potsdam palace telephone was never used for imperial business.[6]

At 11:10 that morning, Austria-Hungary, having ordered home all its diplomatic representatives in Belgrade, was in a quandary as to exactly how to communicate its war declaration to Serbia. This semi-comical problem was solved when it was decided to send a telegram, in French of course, routed through Bucharest, Romania. Back in Germany, Prince Heinrich wrote his imperial brother that King George had said, "We shall try all we can to keep out of this *and shall remain neutral*." (author's

Italics). This somewhat ambiguous report, accurate or not, was interpreted by the Kaiser as a promise of neutrality. "I have the word of a king!" he cried.[7]

In Russia, as a precaution, the timorous Czar signed *two* mobilization orders: one for a general mobilization and one limited to the Austro-Hungarian frontier. These were not to be carried out until final decisions, which would depend on circumstances as they developed.[8] He had been told that even general mobilization did not necessarily mean war.[9]

In London, the Austrian Embassy was already privately discussing with Lichnowsky the possible award of Serbian territory to Bulgaria and Albania following Austria's presumed victory.[10] On July 28, the Kaiser noted that the Austrian naval commander in chief had told the Kaiser's naval *attaché* secretly that Austria and Italy had agreed that Austria would have a free hand in Serbia and Italy would have the same in Albania! If true, it was an odd measure on the part of both countries.[11]

After their lunch at the British Foreign Office on July 29, Grey proposed to Lichnowsky that Austria occupy Belgrade and then halt, whereupon Britain, France, Germany, and Italy would mediate.[12] Otherwise, he said, if France and Germany were drawn into the war, Britain probably would be, also.[13] On that same Wednesday, the 29th, while the Czar was trying in his fumbling way to prevent the situation from spiraling out of control, his foreign minister, Sazanov, received the Czar's partial mobilization order and counseled Paris *not* to favor moderation. He had been advised that Austria had bombarded Belgrade, the Serb capital on the Danube, just across the river from Austro-Hungarian territory. In fact, Serb troops had fired on an Austrian steamer and Austrian batteries then shelled Serb fortifications.[14] Although the Russian-French treaty did not bind either country to mobilize if only Austria did, France reciprocated Russia's bellicosity. Poincaré encouraged the Russians, but Prime Minister Viviani said, "They must avoid fireworks!" Despite this, the French war minister slyly told the Russian military *attaché* that it was proper for Russia to mobilize against Austria, but to keep France in the dark about what they were doing![15]

That afternoon in Russia, German ambassador Pourtalès conveyed Germany's warning that "further continuance" of Russian mobilization would compel Germany to mobilize, and result in a European war. He meant that would occur if Russia mobilized *generally* (i.e. against Germany also), but not if it mobilized only against the Austrian frontier. Sazanov misunderstood.[16] He thought that a partial Russian mobilization would trigger a German one in response. In reality, there was no rush. Everyone knew that Germany would hit France first. Paris urged St. Petersburg to lie and say that their mobilization had stopped.[17]

At 9:40 the night of July 29, Czar Nicholai received Kaiser Wilhelm's telegram stating that he was working toward peace and that military moves would aggravate the situation. The Kaiser accurately predicted that Russian intervention in support of Serbia "...would involve[e] Europe in the most terrible war ever witnessed." Count Fredericks, Nicholai's adjutant, said, "Mobilization means war!" Seized by panic, the Czar replied, "I cannot take the responsibility for such fearful slaughter." He telephoned General Yanoushkevich, his chief of staff, to convert the *general* mobilization back to a partial one, against Austria only. He then sent a telegram to the Kaiser mentioning that military measures for the defense of Serbia had already been "decided" five days earlier. He meant to say, "decided upon," in the sense that they were taken in the abstract, but the Kaiser thought that he meant that mobilization had already been secretly *going on* for five days. Nevertheless, Wilhelm telegraphed Franz Josef to accept the proposal to halt the presumed Austrian advance when it took Belgrade. The Austrian Emperor said, "I am conscious of the import of my decision and have taken it with trust in God's justice."

Early on July 30, German Chancellor Bethmann-Hollweg, having realized the abyss into which Germany had blundered, telegraphed his ambassador in Vienna with a message that must rank as one of the least timely in history. He instructed von Tschirschky that "...we must decline to be dragged by Vienna wantonly into a world conflagration without having any regard paid to our comments…speak to Count Berchtold with great emphasis."[18] Tschirschky breakfasted with Berchtold and read Bethmann's warning to him twice, for emphasis. However, crucially, it did not say that Germany *would refuse to stand by Austria* in a war. Berchtold and General Conrad went to see Franz Josef and Conrad rejected the idea of merely occupying Belgrade (although he had not occupied anything yet). He feared that an early Austrian defeat would encourage other Powers to intervene against Austria. It did not seem to occur to him that an early Austrian victory would have the same result. Berchtold cavalierly said that even Serbian acceptance of the terms would not be enough now. The two officials dickered over what further demands to make, but the more realistic Franz Josef said, "They will not accept."[19] A reassuring "circular" message was sent by Berchtold to von Löwenthal, among others, noting that Austria had been forced to take "purely defensive measures" due to Russian mobilization on its frontier, but that "friendly" talks were continuing.

At 4 o'clock that afternoon, after once cancelling it, the Czar reluctantly ordered a general mobilization. He was under the mistaken impression that Austria would be able to immediately invade Serbia. As we have seen, they were incapable of such a blitzkrieg.[20] Delighted that the Czar's indecision was thwarted, Sazanov telephoned the army chief of staff and told him, "Now you can smash your telephone."

Late on Friday, July 31, Prince Lichnowsky in London telegraphed Prime Minister Asquith (Grey being unavailable), advising that Germany had given Russia an ultimatum to stop mobilizing. At 2 a.m. the next morning, Asquith woke up King George and got him to send a telegram to the Czar, appealing to him to "remove the misapprehension…and to leave still open grounds for negotiation…" On Saturday, August 1, Lichnowsky, who had located Grey, asked him to state the conditions for Britain's neutrality, but the foreign secretary replied that he could make no promises.[21]

As July ended, Durazzo was almost cut off from the greater world. News came only from Austrian official wires and

Italian newspapers, which were notoriously unreliable. The Austrian steamer from Trieste no longer came, cutting off a regular source of quality supplies. Durazzo now had to rely on inferior goods from south Italy. Unofficial word did arrive that Russia and Germany were mobilizing, giving lord chamberlain von Trotha the happy excuse to leave on August 1 with his secretary and five other menservants, all of whom were German Army reservists. This left the Palace with only three indoor menservants, the English butler, Wied's old German valet, the German chef, and Sophie's Arab servant, Hassan. Sami Bey, nominally Trotha's second in command, was lazy and knew nothing of bookkeeping, forcing Heaton to assume his duties. The women servants tried to resign *en masse*, but were dissuaded.[22]

On Saturday, August 1, the Kaiser was dressed in his flamboyant uniform of the Cuirassier Guard Regiment, topped with its silver helmet, surmounted by a golden eagle. With his wife, the Kaiserin, in her claret gown, he rode in an open carriage from Potsdam to the Berlin *Schloss*, or Palace. It was a beautiful day in Berlin. Bethmann and von Jagow had received a telegram which they misinterpreted as Grey's promise that France would remain neutral, with the British guarding the French coast from attack. "That calls for champagne!" cried the Kaiser, clapping his hands. "We must provisionally halt the march towards the West" [i.e. France]. General von Moltke, under protest, telephoned to stop the advance into Luxembourg on the way to France. However, Prime Minister Viviani in Paris, when asked by the German ambassador to confirm France's neutrality (in which case Germany planned to demand control of the cities of Toul and Verdun), replied ominously, "France will have regard to her interests."[23] France promptly then sent her own mobilization order at 3:45 that afternoon, while the Montenegrin parliament declared its support for Serbia despite King Nikola's plea that they show some common sense. He told an Austrian diplomat, "God is my witness. I never willed this war."[24]

The Kaiser was awakened early in Berlin on Sunday, August 2, by his *aide de camp*. Throwing on a military greatcoat over his underclothes, he read a telegram from King George, making it plain that Lichnowsky was mistaken, and that Prince Heinrich's report either had been inaccurate or was no longer valid. Only if Germany remained neutral toward Russia and France would Britain guarantee France's neutrality. The Kaiser then resignedly told the Chief of his General Staff to "do as you wish."[25] He raged, "Grey proves the King a liar...a common cur."[26] Having received a request to receive a personal telegram from Franz Josef, at 10 p.m. that evening Kaiser Wilhelm and his family received its bearer, Ambassador Count Szögyény in the courtyard of the Berlin Palace. The remarks by the Kaiser went something like this:

> Today the Czar telegraphed me that his mobilization "in no way signified war!" I am continually exchanging telegrams in English with the Czar but, to my deepest regret, I have to own that I absolutely cannot understand the present mental state of the Emperor Nicholas. Nor do I know whether the Czar sent his telegrams to me in agreement with his advisors. His present principal advisor is probably the Minister for War, but a decided influence still seems to be wielded by the prayer-healer Rasputin. The Czar's telegram contains perpetual contradictions, and I can to my regret use no other term for them than the word, "lies." No reply has yet been received from Russia to our timed inquiry, but a telegram has arrived from the Czar in which His Majesty assured me that the general mobilization ordered in Russia did not aim at Germany. The reply from Paris contained only empty phrases; but Sir Edward Grey has, with the approval of his Royal master, offered by telegram to guarantee the neutrality of France in the event of war between Germany and Russia [sic]. Of course, I would demand a dead pledge, very precise and hard

conditions from France. I have the impression that France is scared by our mobilization to a very high degree. Under these circumstances, it would be a question of persevering calmly but decidedly in the direction hitherto taken. Above all, I am decided to come to a reckoning with France, and I hope that I will succeed in doing so...[27]

Reviewing the situation privately, he decided that it was all a plot by his dead uncle, British King Edward VII, and his cousin, King George V, whereby "the stupidity and clumsiness of our ally [Austria] has been made a hangman's noose for us."["*wird uns die Dummheit und Ungeschicklichkeit unseres Verbündeten zum Fallstrick gemacht.*"][28] The same day, the Czar declared war.[29]

Winston Churchill, who was part of the British government at the time, later eloquently described these last days of peace:

> When it became increasingly clear to [the German Government] from the reports of the German Ambassador in London, that a general war would find the British Empire ranged with France and Russia,[the Germans] lent themselves to action which a few days earlier would have dispersed the crisis. The Kaiser, now desperately shaken by the imminence of the explosion, and the Czar sincerely clinging to peace, interchanged a series of personal telegrams unique in the story of nations. But neither they, nor their ministers, nor all that Grey might do, could regain control of the purely technical measures and counter measures which the chiefs of armies demanded and took. The first war, between Austria and Serbia, was about a murder. The second war, which absorbed it, was a war between Germany and Russia about precautions. The third and

greatest of all wars, beside which the others were trivial, the war between Germany and France, was merely consequential and happened almost as a matter of form. The German plan for this third war required the invasion of Belgium, and the invasion of Belgium brought the British Empire united to the field. Nothing in human power could break the chain, once it had begun to unroll. A situation had been created where hundreds of officials had only to do their prescribed duty to their respective countries to wreck the world. They did their duty.[30]

But Churchill, who was not, after all unbiased, might have mentioned that Serbia aided the assassins and quibbled over terms for peace; that Russia was more concerned with its prestige in the Balkans than peace; and that France wanted revenge for 1870 and did nothing to restrain its ally. What about Britain? In 1912, when considering British and French discussions of possible naval cooperation in case of war with Germany, Churchill himself said, "Everyone must feel who knows the facts that we have [created] the obligation of an alliance without its advantage and, above all, without its precise definition."[31]

On the same August 2 in Albania, Lamb and de Veer went to Shiak to negotiate for the release of the two Dutch officers who had been captured at Elbasan, but were unsuccessful. That evening, the German and Austrian volunteers who had been fighting for Wied happily packed to leave for their countries after cheering and singing patriotic songs outside the Palace. They had all been decorated with bronze medals by Wied. Their journey to Albania had been a search for adventure so typical of the period, and now their homelands would provide more than enough of that. Wied's chagrin at the loss of their support may be imagined. Reliable and competent soldiers, especially for the artillery, could not be replaced. Holland had mobilized as a defensive measure, resulting in the recall of the invaluable Dutch gendarmerie officers, who took with them more volunteers who were not in the ready reserves of their respective armies. There was little enough to solace the King, but at least the absence of conflicting advice eased tensions somewhat. A Committee of Defence was formed when the Dutch left, made up of a few Austrians, a Romanian officer and a few native chiefs. Heaton wanted to stay with the King, even if Britain mobilized, as he knew his tenure would not be long. Wied telegraphed Grey for such permission through Lamb, and it was granted.

Britain's entry into the war put a serious strain on the remaining relations between Heaton and the royal family. One evening, when alone with Wied on the Palace balcony, Heaton said that the German government had gone mad and had no chance of winning once Britain came into the war. The King did not dispute this, but relations between the two were never the same. While relaxing with other Palace staff in the Oriental Room, Heaton said that Queen Sophie had no more reason to be haughty than he had, as the only reason that his border-raiding Austrian ancestors had not annexed her father's petty principality was the lack of booty to be found there. Unfortunately for Heaton, the Queen was sitting around the corner of the passage with her sewing basket, within easy earshot of his indiscreet boast.

The war accelerated Albanian events in other ways. Albanian bands began to be formed in Durazzo to fight Serbs. The government knew it and did nothing to stop them. The town was still besieged. Every night the rebels fired volleys. Heat, sickness, and desertions reduced the fighting spirit of the loyal forces. Heaton and others, including German Minister von Lucius, openly advised Wied to leave. Heaton, becoming cheeky, even told the King that they should at least drink up the excellent wines in the cellar, leaving what was left "for the next fellow." Wied understandably treated this idea with scorn and refused to give up hope.[32]

The entire International Control Commission met for the last time and belatedly approved the rest of the ten million franc advance to Wied when it was too late to do him much good. The Austrians and Germans urged Wied to leave, as they felt that

Durazzo was undefendable. This left him entirely at the mercy of Italy, which was so far staying out of the European war. Ammunition and food for the troops were running out because Italy had prohibited any supplies, and decreed severe export regulations from Italy. In addition, the "Kosovo people," including Isa Boletin and Hassan Prishtina, had moved away at the suggestion of the Austrians and the Germans to organize a revolt against their new Serbian masters. It was said that Wied had hoped to coordinate any such Albanian rebellion with an Austrian attack on Serbia, since the war between those two countries had begun, but the premature movement of the Kosovans had prevented this. Nevertheless, Wied decided to remain in Durazzo as long as possible. To him, the financial matter was still the most critical point. Austria and Italy were each to make half payment of the advance approved by the International Control Commission, but Italy took advantage of Austria's preoccupation with war and its need to placate Italy, demanding concessions from Albania. These were to take the form of concessions of forest, fishing, and telegraph rights, and the loan was made dependent on those things. Wied bravely refused. Austria also withheld payment to conciliate Italy. The two Powers did agree, however, to pay Wied if he would assure them that Albania would attack the Serbs and invade Serbia, taking advantage of a revolt that would be organized in Kosovo. Wied would not give such assurances because they would violate Albania's neutrality, which had been guaranteed by the Great Powers, a position about which he was not later to be so idealistic. Also, he seems to have perceived that, for the time being, he would be unable to count on active help from Austria due to her "sluggardly mobilization." This inefficiency of the Austrians would have left Albania "at the mercy of all its neighbors just waiting for a good opportunity to divide it up," as Wied later wrote[33]. He later ascribed more noble motives to his refusal to join in the attack upon Serbia:

> ...though I was persuaded, just as all
> Albanians were, that the purely Albanian

territories wrongly…handed over to the Serbians, should be reincorporated with Albania, I was not able to give such assurances in view of the existing circumstances. For thereby Albania would have violated her neutrality, guaranteed by all the Great Powers.[34]

In Berlin on August 9, the wife of the German Prince Blücher, an Englishwoman, visited the massive, fashionable Hotel Esplanade, after which she wrote:

Amongst the faces I saw …were those of Prince and Princess Victor Wied, old acquaintances. He is lame, and is therefore only doing night-watch at the castle [Palace]; his wife is a pretty woman of 23. They are full of anxiety as to his brother's fate, the King of Albania who has been deserted by all foreign powers, and must be absolutely stranded. People here don't seem to have much pity on him. They look upon him as an adventurer forced into the role of a would-be king by his wife's ambition.[35]

By August 11, both the Austrian and Italian governments and banks had refused further money for Wied. His treasury had no cash left and wages had been unpaid for two months, so he ordered Heaton to pay the troops out of his Court funds. Heaton did so reluctantly, as this left barely enough for Palace expenses, and commodities were scarce and "very dear." Wied handed the keys to the safe over to Heaton. There was fear of famine and revolt in Durazzo. At Scutari, only the French and Italian detachments remained, and the French intended to leave if the Montenegrins advanced across the border.[36] Harry Lamb, the British International Control Commission representative, withdrew from Scutari on August 12.[37]

During dinner at the Palace, in the course of a political lecture on the European war which was now getting cranked up,

Queen Sophie said, "Everybody knows that the English soldiers are quite bad." Heaton said nothing and Wied tried to change the subject, looking most uncomfortable. After dinner, when Heaton brought the King his cigar as usual, he asked Wied if he was to take the remark as a hint that he was no longer wanted. He assured the King that he would leave on the next boat if that were the case. Wied was very apologetic and said that it was all a mistake.[38] As he had done so often, he wavered. The foreign diplomats were now unanimous in urging the King to see the handwriting on the wall and leave.[39]

By August 16, Wied was almost ready to throw in the towel. He told Vienna through the Control Commission that he must have an immediate disbursement of part of the promised loan in the form of a million francs, or he could not hold out in Albania any longer. German Minister von Lucius believed that Italy had forbidden export of gold in order to force Wied out and put themselves in. The shore complement of the Italian warship at Durazzo had become around 250 men strong. The Greek minister to Albania, formerly an antagonist to Wied, now was anxious for him to remain and spoke sharply against Italy to von Lucius. He feared that Italy would hang on to Albania and favor the return of Essad Pasha.[40]

In Vienna, Count Forgach of the Ballplatz told ambassador von Tschirschky that Wied's pleas "fall on deaf ears" ["*gegenüber taube ohren*"], and that they had advised the Prince [*Fürsten*] to make peace with the rebels and march against Serbia. Otherwise, he should remember that he was a Prussian officer and return to serve his fatherland.[41]

Wied had decided to send the royal children to Germany with Fraulein von Oidtmann. On August 20, it was decided that Fraulein von Pfuel would go also, and Sophie told her that Heaton would be dismissed. Hearing of this, but not from the King, Heaton followed him to his study after dinner and asked him directly whether it was true. Caught off guard, and true to his nature, Wied evaded the question and said that he was merely considering the possibility as things could not continue as they had been. He said soothingly that, in view of the difference of

Heaton's political opinions from his own, he was certain that Heaton wanted to return to Britain to fight for his native country. Although Heaton had expressed his political opinions about the European war to the King privately, he had always avoided doing so publicly. He told Wied that he was exceedingly sorry if he had offended the King thereby, and that he had done his best for the King. Wied answered half-heartedly that he had been quite satisfied with the Briton, but that it was better for him to leave. Annoyed, Heaton said that he would leave with the ladies and children on the next boat, and went to sulk with other members of the staff in the Oriental Room. After cooling off, however, he returned to Wied and offered to escort the children all the way to Germany. Wied quickly accepted. He was uncertain whether Heaton could get the necessary German and Austrian safe conducts, in view of his enemy alien status in those countries.

The next morning Heaton went to see his friend, German minister Baron von Lucius, who promised him the necessary entry and exit papers, as did the Austrian envoy after consulting his government. As the German valet was gone, he was replaced by an Albanian who had been a bottle washer in a hotel in the United States before returning to his homeland.

On August 22, as Heaton prepared to leave Durazzo, the King called him into his study and presented him with the Order of the Eagle of Albania, with Crossed Swords, the Accession Medal, and a signed photograph of himself in the fancy Albanian uniform. Inscribed on the photo in German was, "In remembrance of joint labors." Wied was charming at this melancholy ceremony, thanked Heaton for all that he had done, and promised to welcome him back in better times. He handed Heaton an excellent reference or "testimonial," giving the war as the reason for their parting. Even Queen Sophie managed to be quite friendly on this occasion. The King gave Heaton a goodly sum of money for traveling expenses and they then had tea, like a couple of Englishmen. After that, Heaton, with the royal children, their two nurses, the ladies-in-waiting, and the chef boarded an Italian ship for the short journey to Bari. The Italian Captain Conte Andreoli, who was sent by Aliotti, escorted them.

As they left, they saw Wied and Sophie waving what must have been a heartbreaking farewell from the Palace balcony.[42]

On August 24, the Muslim insurgents in the southwest sent an ultimatum demanding the surrender of Valona, the departure of Wied, and the hoisting of the Turkish flag. The Valona authorities asked 48 hours to reply.[43] They notified Wied that they could hold out if they had money to procure food and ammunition for the ample manpower which they had. In addition, in their refugee camps there was misery due to food shortages. The rebels, on the other hand, were financially supported by the Serbs and were adequately supplied. Italy may have been helping also. Unexploded shells retrieved in Durazzo were found to be of Italian manufacture.[44] Ironically, Turkey suddenly made propaganda in favor of Wied and his government, and Greece became more friendly. They apparently feared an Italian occupation of Valona and southern Albania.

By the end of August, it was very clear that neither Austria nor Italy was going to keep its financial promises. Austria, Wied's "most loyal support," was now well and truly involved with war against not only Serbia, but also Russia. Wied concluded that the European war would also decide the fate of Albania, and that in the future nothing but dependence upon Germany and Austria would guarantee a free and independent Albania. He was finally forced to the humiliating conclusion that, "at the moment, my country could no longer benefit from my presence." He set September 3 as the date for his departure. When his intention became known, Albanian leaders loyal to him came to implore him urgently to simply move with them to Scutari, and continue the fight from there. He considered their plea, but turned it down. The whole north and east of Albania was, he felt, loyally devoted to him, so that with enough money he could have crushed the rebels in middle Albania. However, as he had learned that the Montenegrins planned to move against Scutari (no longer protected by international forces), and the Serbs planned to occupy the eastern part of Albania, Wied's untrained and unpaid troops could not hope to succeed. They could easily have been cut off from any supplies and starved out.

However, Wied did agree at least that he would not abdicate, thus leaving the door open for his return in better days.[45]

On August 28, the royal children arrived safely in Waldenburg. Heaton had been detained by the German authorities despite his safe conduct pass. They would only allow him to return to Albania. He telegraphed Wied for a recall which would permit him to leave Germany, but apparently von Lucius talked the King out of this, for fear that Heaton would stir up the already pro-British northern tribes against the Austrians.[46]

The International Control Commission, made up of delegates Mehdi, Winchei, Kral, Krajewski, Lamb, Leoni, and Petraiev, were still trying to bring some order out of chaos. On August 31, they went to Shiak to negotiate, but their efforts were undercut when the gendarmes in Durazzo, upon learning that Wied was packing up, complained that he could not leave until he paid their back wages, and they "threatened to make use of their weapons" to enforce their demand. When the Control Commission learned of this, they hastened back to Durazzo.[47] The problem had now become theirs. The same day, further bad news came: Valona had surrendered to the rebels, who immediately hoisted the Turkish flag.[48] To hasten Wied's departure, on September 1 the rebels insolently fired a few shots into the royal palace, which was still guarded by Italian sailors, and demanded that Wied leave immediately.[49] On September 2, Wied summoned the Secretaries and the delegates of the three members of the International Control Commission still in Durazzo (Austria, Italy and France) and, with Turkhan Pasha present, asked them to take over the government during his "temporary" absence from the country. Leoni, the president of the International Control Commission, who was the Italian delegate, replied that they wanted to do so.[50]

The next day Wied issued a public proclamation recounting the difficulties which he had encountered and stating that he thought "…it would be useful that I go to the West for some time."[51] For understatement, this must rank with Emperor Hirohito's remark in August 1945 to his people that "…the war situation has developed not necessarily to Japan's advantage."[52]

Due to the war raging in Europe, it was not possible at once to pack and send to Germany all the royal personal possessions, so the representatives of the Great Powers and the other diplomats in Durazzo promised to seal the Palace and protect its contents. Even the Queen's harp, "so dear to Sophie's heart" had to be left behind.[53] The Palace was locked and the keys entrusted to the Italian minister. Wied and Sophie, along with loyal Turkhan Pasha and several aides, then boarded the *Misurata* and sailed for Venice, where they arrived on September 5. The six month kingdom was over. Albania was no Ruritania, and life there was no operetta.[54]

33

POST MORTEM

Nothing evidenced the effect of the looming war on the policies of Austria and Italy toward Albania so much as their rapid abandonment of interest in its independence. In a letter to the Kaiser which old Emperor Franz Josef drew up as late as July 2, 1914, he surveyed the situation in the Balkans. Turning his attention to Albania, he wrote:

> Some favorable points may certainly be observed. It has been possible to balance the advance of Servia [sic] by the creation of an independent Albanian state, which will after a number of years, when its internal organization is completed, serve as a military factor in the accounts of the Triple Alliance.[1]

As Italy was the third member of the Triple Alliance, both Germany and Austria naturally wanted it to join with them in prosecuting the war. Italy had other ideas. It saw this as a possible opportunity to get the physical foothold in Albania at Valona which had long been coveted. Before the Balkan wars of 1913 had virtually driven Turkey from the Balkans, a treaty between Austria-Hungary and Italy had given either party the right to compensation if the other party occupied Balkan territory. Berchtold now accurately predicted that if he consulted Italy about the war with Serbia, it would ask for Valona in anticipation of Austrian occupation of all or part of Serbia.[2] Austria initially took the position that the treaty had only referred to either party seizing *Turkish* areas in Europe, not parts of new Balkan states. And besides, Austria had recently promised not to *annex* any of Serbia. As Italy continued to withhold a commitment to practical support for the war with Serbia, the Austrians, egged on by the Germans, became more generous with Albania's integrity. The Hungarian Premier, Count Tisza, suggested to Franz Josef that, to avoid complications with Italy and to show others that Austria had no territorial ambitions in Serbia, parts of it should be given to Albania, Bulgaria and Greece after the anticipated victory.[3] At a joint meeting of the Austro-Hungarian government ministers on July 19, the Austrian premier, Count Stürgkh, asked what should be done if Italy took it into her head to seize Valona. Berchtold said that he thought that unlikely, but that Austria would then have to do something similar *"pro forma."*[4] On July 20, Berchtold told the German ambassador that he "could never consent to any transactions on this point."[5] But on July 28, the German ambassador visited Berchtold with a serious message. He had been personally ordered by not only Foreign Minister von Jagow, but Chancellor Bethmann-Hollweg and the Kaiser, to "for God's sake," give in to the Italians to secure their support for the war. Faced with this pressure, Berchtold acquiesced "because we are playing a great game, in which there are serious difficulties to overcome." He also knew that if Valona wasn't yielded, the Italians had their eyes on the Trentino area of the Monarchy itself![6] Unfortunately for Austria-Hungary, once having gotten their way, the Italians decided that they weren't bound to intervene anyway. The Triple Alliance was only defensive, they correctly said, and Serbia hadn't attacked Austria. In fact, it was the other way around. And besides, Italy was irritated at all that "quibbling" which Austria had put them through.[7] Furthermore, incorporating Albanian territories, as Austria suggested, was not in keeping with Italy's historic respect for national states like herself. Perhaps such incorporation was workable for a multi-national empire like the Austro-Hungarian, but not for Italy, he sniffed.[8] In his desperation, Berchtold was even willing to sacrifice Albania to Montenegro in return for that tiny country's neutrality. On July 31, he wired his minister there that, after the war was won, "...eventual wishes of Montenegro in Albania—within the limits of our agreement with Italy—would find most favourable consideration here."[9]

Wied's family had an "I told you so" attitude. His older brother Prince Friedrich zu Wied, wrote on September 6, "As long as possible we tried to dissuade him [from the adventure], feeling that because of his refined decency Willy would be powerless against such conditions."[10] From Venice, Wied and Sophie proceeded to Lugano, Switzerland for a "short vacation," and then traveled on to Germany. His closest Albanian supporters dispersed, some going back to southern Albania, while some went to the north or stayed in Italy. Wied wrote to the Kaiser and requested reinstatement in the German Army, as he had concluded that Albania's independent future depended on the victory of the Central Powers, Germany and Austria. He no doubt also believed that such a victory was his best hope for restoration to the throne. He did not want to sit the war out, as he was, after all, a German Prince and a former German officer with many companions serving on active duty. Count Berchtold supported his decision. Wied's request was granted, and on October 14, 1914, he was assigned as a major on the staff of the Third Regiment of the Guard Uhlans (his former regiment) and on the staff of the Guards Cavalry Division. He left for the front immediately.[11]

No sooner had Wied sailed from Durazzo than a "Senate" consisting of notables, including a Muslim Clerical party and peasants, there adopted resolutions opposing the rule of beys and pashas, restoring the Ottoman flag and the suzerainty of the Sultan of Turkey, and inviting Prince Burhaneddin Efendi, a son of deposed Sultan Abdul Hamid, to become ruler. For good measure, they declared Turkish the official language and, after hoisting the Turkish flag, they recited a Turkish prayer in front of the Palace. The Turkish Prince never showed up.[12] Essad showed up, however, on October 2, with 5,000 or more men from Dibra, Tirana, and Shiak, financed by Italy and armed by Serbia, and took over the Palace. Addressing the crowd from the Palace balcony, he spotted Baron Aliotti, who had also just arrived, and they embraced. Captain Castoldi, Wied's former Italian adviser, also just happened to be present. Wied's supporters and those supporting an independent Albania were thrown into prison. From Germany, Wied sent orders to Durazzo for the return of his possessions to Germany. After a lengthy delay large crates arrived, but they were filled with newspapers, some of the children's toys, and firewood. Essad explained that this was his revenge for the shots which had been fired at his house, and he was simply keeping the rest.[13] With the support of Aliotti and the French member of the Control Commission, Essad actually claimed damages from Wied of a half million marks (about $2,130,000 current U.S. dollars), including expenses for his soldiers. Wied, of course, refused to deal with Essad, who then sold and gave away most of the King's personal belongings, including horses, carriages, silver, the child's rocking horse, art objects, and the like. The Austrian Consul was only able to save a few heirlooms.[14]

By threatening to shoot every member of the "Senate," Essad forced them to name him "President and Premier." The International Control Commission actually recognized him as such on October 4.[15] His ascendancy was short-lived, however. His alliance with Serbia caused a rebellion to break out on November 23, and Durazzo was soon again surrounded by the rebels. Essad was forced, like Wied, to board an Italian ship, whereupon the former chiefs of the rebels sent Wied a telegram. They had the nerve to tell him that they had been deceived by Essad, apologized for their behavior, and asked Wied to return![16] On March 7, 1915, a gala charity performance, sponsored by the "National League of Scutari," was held by the "National Theater" in Scutari, at the Café t'madhe *(sic)* to celebrate the anniversary of Wied's arrival.[17]

In mid-February, 1915, the Provisional Government of Muslims summoned a congress in Elbasan and, amazingly, passed the following resolution:

> Considering the great difficulties the appointment of a prince from the Imperial Ottoman Family as Ruler of Albania meets with, The National Assembly [sic] passes a resolution, in consent with the Imperial Ottoman Government

[by then allied with the Central Powers] to accept a non-Muslim Prince as well, provided that this must be a German prince. It decides to ask Prince Wilhelm—if Germany consents—to accept the Albanian throne again.[18]

It is impossible to tell to what degree this change of attitude was representative of true Albanian sentiment at the time, as opposed to Austrian, German, and Turkish war strategy. However, the later hesitancy of those powers to support Wied's pleas to return lends credence to its authenticity among some former rebels, at least.

When the World War started, the Great Powers (although fighting each other) acquiesced in Greece (then neutral) re-entering "Northern Epirus," as they called it, and this was accomplished on October 26, 1914. Italy occupied Valona "to guarantee Albania's neutrality."[19] By the Pact of London of 1915 between Italy and the British, French, and Russians, Italy was to occupy Valona and its environs, provided that she "should not oppose the partition of the remainder of Albania between Serbia, Montenegro, and Greece."[20] Thus did all the Great Powers, save Austria and Germany, renege on their Declaration of London of 1913 in the interest of wartime expediency. Soon, Italy, Montenegro, and Serbia invaded Albania, taking sections of the country under their control. When Italy (having received the best offer from the Entente) declared war on Austria on May 23, 1915, the Austrians and Germans invaded Albania in response, and were greeted as liberators in most places.[21]

In 1917, after several years to think it over, Wied summarized the conditions which he felt had made his task impossible:

- The lack of an army of any size.
- The International Commission of Control formed a kind of side government in competition with his.

374

- Conflict between the Great Powers hindered agreement on the borders and evacuations.
- Serbia, Montenegro, and Greece constantly upset regions on their borders.
- Foreign money and propaganda were injected.
- Essad had been allowed to remain in the country.
- There was no infrastructure either of civil servants, or physical institutions such as roads, schools, newspapers, railroad or telegraph lines.
- Money was lacking to pay for everything.

He said that religion was not a problem, as all faiths had fought for him. He wrote that "Nothing but the lack of money made it impossible for me to continue..." Wied felt in 1917 that Germany and Austria should make him a huge loan of about 100 million German marks (roughly $23,700,000 in 1914, or $426,600,000 today) on easy terms. "This way [they] would tightly chain Albania to themselves forever." He noted that the customs revenue already yielded five million marks before the Balkan Wars, and he wanted German and Austrian civil servants to supervise it.

In 1917, in retrospect, Wied believed that between his acceptance of the throne and May of 1914, the fear by the Powers of war between themselves made the purpose of Albanian independence and his accession of less interest to them. This was especially true when Austria and Italy had a falling-out and, at the least, were unhelpful with Albania's internal and external threats. In a surprising evaluation of a then current enemy, he had no criticism of the British Foreign Office or its local representatives. On the other hand, he said that Germany had become "decidedly neutral" regarding Albania in the spring of 1914 because of the rivalry between her allies, Italy and Austria, and the desire to keep on good terms with Greece. Wied wrote, in a rather endless sentence:

The Kaiser himself, perhaps under his sister's [the Queen of Greece] and his brother-in-law's influence, had, at any rate, much more interest for the Greek than the Albanian side of the questions which arose, and I learned from reliable sources that his dislike for everything concerning Albania went so far that the Berlin Foreign Office avoided placing before his eyes diplomatic correspondence regarding Albania, fearing to incur His Majesty's ill humour… Under normal circumstances, neither Essad Pasha nor the poor deluded rebels of Shiak would ever have dared to oppose the decisions of united Europe.[22]

Twenty-first century events in Kosovo and Serbia cast doubt on this appraisal of the influence of world opinion on local conflicts.

Why did Wied fail? It has been explained by one historian as follows:

Durazzo was in the area inhabited by the most fanatical Sunni Muslims, many of whom were refugees (or their descendents) from 1878 Bosnia. Albanians hadn't had time to decide their national outlook and character and the groundwork was not prepared for a foreign, Christian prince.[23] Throw in Wied's own *post mortem* (mentioned above) and add the Italian and Serbian meddling, and it becomes apparent that Wilhelm never really had much of a chance. Edith Durham's evaluation of Wied has been widely quoted:

> We may blame Wied for incompetency but only a man of unusual force of character and intimate knowledge of the land could have made headway against the powers combined against him.[24]

There was evidence that Essad was not the chief cause of rebellion against Wied. After Wied's flight in September of

1914, opposition was widespread against Essad in the rest of central Albania outside Durazzo, and it eventually united in what became known as the Union of Kruja, under Haxhi Qerim (Haxi Kerem) and Musa Kasim. This group hoped for either a re-incorporation into the Turkish Empire or for the election of one of the Ottoman princes as King of Albania. The group also attracted many tribal leaders who opposed Essad primarily because he was threatening to construct a central government which might compromise their fiercely defended independence and because his followers did not want a Turkish prince. The Union did not, however, extend its authority into Mati or Dibra.[25]

In February of 1915, Wied's adjutant, Ekrem Bey Libohova, while in Vienna told the Germans that a strong anti-Serb movement had arisen in Albania, with the followers of Essad daily becoming fewer, while those of Wied grew more numerous. However, as Wied was then fighting as part of his old *Garde Kavalleriedivision* in France, the loyal Albanians maintained that it was necessary for him to return to the Balkans and attach himself to the Austrian Army of Archduke Eugen, then in Albania. Wied wrote to Ekrem to instruct him to sound out the Ballplatz on their view of the plan. Ekrem discussed it with General Consul Rappaport, the Austrian departmental chief for Albania, and division chief Count Forgach, who were both quite enthusiastic. Ekrem, prompted by Wied, asked the German foreign office to recommend the plan to the Kaiser, but the Germans said that they must first consult the Austrians formally, and asked Wied to send a written request. Ekrem balked at this, indicating that Wied was unsure of his status, but agreed to write to Wied.[26]

On February 24, 1915, Wied wrote to the Kaiser, requesting assignment to the staff of the supreme command of the Austrian Army scheduled to fight Serbia in the spring of 1915. The Austrian Army, despite Conrad's bellicose appetite, had been forced to defer invasion of Serbia so as to first fight the Russians. Wied explained to the Kaiser that he had promised the Albanians, who had remained loyal, to return as soon as he could, and he wanted to keep his word. As the sea was blocked by the Entente's ships, he wanted to return by land by way of Serbia. Austria had "enthusiastically" consented to his plan. The government again said that it would defer to Austria. However, in March of 1915, the impending war between Austria and Italy (the Italians having sold themselves for Entente promises of other people's territory) prevented an offensive against Serbia for the time being. In reply to Wied's letter, the Kaiser commissioned a rather curt reply in which he reminded Wied that his wish of six months earlier to rejoin the German Army had been granted, that conditions in the Albanian and Serbian areas were unsettled, and that "...German princes, so long as fit for service, have their place in the German Army for the duration of the war."[27]

When the Austrian offensive was finally agreed upon, Wied contacted the Austrians again, but found them less enthusiastic than before. They gave him no reason. He assumed that it was because they "did not know my untiring loyalty toward the Austro-Hungarian Empire." When Serbia and most of Albania were eventually completely occupied by them, the Austrians actually tried to stop all written and telegraphic communication between Albania and Wied by censorship. They also tried to prevent both written and personal contact between Wied and expatriate Albanians in Austria-Hungary and Bulgaria, but they failed. By now, Wied's portrait circulated widely in Albania.[28] He had been busy by other means to maintain his tenuous contact with his adopted country. He named as his court jeweler Williband Kluge of Berlin, who created for him the Order of the Black Eagle and the Enthronement Medal, which he awarded a number of times between 1915 and 1922,[29]

In March of 1915, shortly after the Kaiser's negative message, Wied received this disappointing letter from the German foreign minister:

> 20 March, 1915
> His Highness Wilhelm zu Wied
> Very esteemed Prince!

My best thanks for your kind lines of the 13th which reached me yesterday. I assume that, in the meanwhile, an answer to your letter to H.M. the Emperor has been received. I will try to let the letter to the Control Commission in Durazzo reach its destination.

It is difficult to speak on the situation in Albania *qua* State Secretary; I ask, therefore, that the following be considered my private understanding.

In the present maelstrom of world crisis, the Albanian state, as it has been conceived by the London Conference, will be submerged. What will later be formed or created is difficult to predict. The policy of Italy is obscure (Aliotti seems first of all to want only to comply with your wishes), but it has appeared at times that they favor Essad to a certain degree or want to make use of him. [Italy was then still neutral].

To keep you as a combatant should be welcome to the Vienna lords; but will they, in the final analysis, carry the match through to the end for you?

Since your rule in Durazzo has, for the time being, been ended by the world war, I would (in case you might be considering a return) await the unfolding of events, since all the necessary conditions and elements for reconquest are missing.

I repeat again, however, that I am not, as State Secretary, to give any advice at this time and therefore speak only from the standpoint of private political observations.

Jagow[30]

It must have come as a bit of a shock and humiliation to Wied to learn that, despite his abandonment of all pretense at neutrality, he could not count on the support of Austria and Germany in his desire to resume the throne.

In May of 1915, as Italy entered the war against Austria and Germany, the *New York Times* reported that Wied had, at his request, been transferred to the staff of the German Army to be sent against Italy.[31]

During the war, the Germans kept tabs on the activities of expatriate Albanians. Old Turkhan Pasha was relatively inactive politically, living a retired life and drawing no Turkish pension since he had become an Albanian citizen. The Germans believed that he would be sympathetic to their cause if they followed a pro-Albanian policy. Dr. Michael Tortoulis, one of Wied's former ministers, lived in Lausanne, Switzerland, but spent three weeks with Wied in 1915, and was very optimistic that Wied would return to Albania. Wied reportedly told him, "We will have Albania again!" Faik Bey Konitza, a nobleman from southern Albania, also lived in Lausanne, but had a more hostile attitude toward Germany. Highly educated, he had lived in England and America and had been a loyal supporter of Wied. His brother, Mehmed Bey Konitza, tried to agitate the southern Albanians into signing a declaration that they wanted Greece to occupy south Albania, and such a paper was sent to Venizelos.

In Berne, Switzerland, in 1915, an Albanian named Djèvad Merouche Bey met with a German agent and put forth a proposal of his "political friends," whereby (1) Wied would march with the Austrian and German armies against the Serbs in Albania, (2) Wied would be acknowledged as king (*könig*) of Albania by Germany and Turkey, (3) the Turkish Sultan, in his capacity as Caliph (religious leader of all Muslims) would name a Grand Mufti (local Muslim religious leader), and publish a declaration in the Istanbul official gazette that Wied, King of Albania, as a man of the Central Powers allied with Turkey, was to be respected and obeyed by all Muslims. Once this was done, Merouche Bey promised, he and his friends would see that Albania would be entirely in the service of the Central Powers. He further agreed to the proposal of Austrian Consul von Para to send a commission from Corfu to Albania to lead a national movement.[32]

Ahmed Zogu, leader of the loyal Mati tribe (and himself later King of Albania, 1928-1939), who had served with the Austrians during their war with the Serbs, in February, 1916 took Durazzo and "raised the National flag in our Prince's Palace,"[33] as he reported. A message in French was sent to Wied in Waldenburg from Elbasan on March 7, 1916, reporting an enthusiastic celebration there of the second anniversary of his arrival in Albania.[34] Zogu prepared for a national congress and organized demonstrations of loyalty to Wied in Durazzo, but in early March, 1917, the Austrians came and prohibited political assemblies for the duration of the war. Austria's allies, the Turks, wanted this because by then they hoped to get Albania back somehow.[35]

An interesting indication that Queen Sophie may have indulged in a bit of cloak-and-dagger espionage on her own is evidenced by a secret telegram to the German foreign office from their ambassador in Berne on April 18, 1916. Baron von Romberg reported that an Albanian from Scutari named "Jake Nn. Guga" was offering his "service for the collection of information of a political nature" from Albanians residing in Paris, Corfu, etc. He had been an interpreter-secretary for the American tobacco company, Lorillard, in Serbia, and asserted that he could travel unhindered to Paris because of his passport. He gave as references his uncle, Pietro Dotmassei in Trieste, and Nocolo Grata and Peter Kakerigi, both ostensibly in Sophie's service.[36]

In October of 1916 Austria, and Turkey led by Enver Pasha, were having discussions about the future of Albania. Enver offered to have Turkey influence the Muslim Albanians in favor of the Central Powers and stated his readiness to furnish a Muslim prince for Albania. Austria was suspicious and opposed this, as well as the proposal floating about that Prince Cyril, the second son of Czar Ferdinand of Bulgaria (another Austrian ally), be made King of Albania. Austria was no more anxious for

Bulgaria to reach the Adriatic than it had been for Serbia to do so.

Faced with Austrian opposition, Enver disclaimed any selfish interest by Turkey in Albania, but he said that he had information that Austria was using south Slav troops to occupy Albania, and that this and their policies were alienating the population. The people were complaining that Albanian schools had been closed and Latin calligraphy required, etc. It was understood, of course, that gold would be required to influence affairs.[37]

The Bulgarians soon disclaimed any intention to place Prince Cyril on the Albanian throne and simply urged Austria to keep Italy from getting any foothold there.[38]

In January of 1917, the Austrian command published a declaration to the Albanian people, assuring them that they had come as liberators and friends, and not as conquerors. It said that their desire was to give Albania "a well-ordered administration," and train up their people to "actually exercize the right to autonomy." When that was possible, Austria would "begin the formation of Albanian self-government" [*Selbstverwaltung*].[39] This language hardly suggested that Austria was interested in the return of Wied.

Meanwhile, the Italians, who had by now occupied Valona, were spreading the word that Wied had no intention of returning to Albania. However, in Germany the *Dresdener Anzeiger* newspaper reported "from reliable sources" that Wied was still considered the lawful ruler and, as soon as the war was ended, would assist in giving the country a rebirth [*geburt*]. Queen Sophie often resided in Waldenburg and Wechselburg with her Schönberg relatives, accompanied by two Albanian *kavasses* [guards] whom she allowed to address her as "Majesty."[*Majestät*][40]

Some time before the end of January, 1917, Wied composed a lengthy memoir or essay regarding his Albanian adventure and his evaluation of the situation as it stood. This *Denkschrift über Albanien* (Memoir or Note upon Albania) was semi-candid and naturally self-serving. It also expressed Wied's

382

assertion that Albania was better off in the camp of the Central Powers. In what would seem to be an unusually public move, a copy was sent to the *Dresdener Anzeiger* where it was published on January 30, 1917, and to all the kings, princes and grand dukes of the German Empire in August of 1917, the latter receiving a transmittal letter reading much as follows:

> I ask Your Royal Highness…to carefully peruse the [enclosed] so that the promotion of my case will be crowned with fairness, and Germany will also remain true to the lawful claim to the name of one of the protectors of independent little states.[41]

The attitude of the Kaiser, as German Emperor, was naturally awaited by the addressees as well as by Wied. In July of 1917, Wied had begun writing more urgent letters to persons whom he thought could help him. On July 14, he wrote from Waldenburg to the Grand Duke of Baden that he had only left Albania temporarily [*vorübergehend*], and that he then

> …perceived that the salvation of my country [sic] lay only in close connection with the Central Powers, and arranged to put myself in the service of the German Emperor…the sympathy of my Albanians [is] always upon the side of Germany and her allies and Austria-Hungary in this war…I and my people have taken an active part on the side of the alliance in the struggle against the common enemy…[and reinstatement of an independent Albania] under my government, and certainly, with the nature of their ethnographic and economic conditions, it would only be an act of justice to enlarge their borders appropriately…

He signed himself both "Prince of Albania" [*Fürst von Albanien*] and "Prince of Wied" [*Prinz zu Wied*], seemingly inconsistent with both his German status and his claimed Albanian kingship. The reference to enlarged borders no doubt included Kosovo, the sacrifice which the Powers had made to Serbia in 1913.[42]

On July 20, 1917, Wied wrote a similar letter to the new German Chancellor, Dr. Michaelis, expressing his confidence that Germany would recognize his rights and asking that the Kaiser be presented with the matter. He pointed out that it would be to the interest of Germany and Austria to have Albania beholden to them. He asked also that Germany agree to his early return to Albania or, at least acknowledgment of his title and a promise of Albanian representation at any peace conference. Similar letters went to the Austrian, Turkish, and Bulgarian foreign ministers.[43]

As may be imagined, Wied's requests were not entirely welcome after three years of world war, with no end in sight. Perhaps a typical response within Germany was from the King of Saxony, Sophie's homeland, who was said to have read the screed with interest. But no reply could be sent until the German foreign minister, von Kühlmann, decided by what *title* Wied should be addressed. This seemingly petty question was a matter of some political importance, as it might imply recognition or refusal of Wied's claim and bind future decisions about the region.[44]

The Auswärtiges Amt let it be known that they were addressing him as "Prince [*Fürst*] Wilhelm zu Wied, Prince of Albania." A telephone call from Baron Werner von Grunau, the Foreign Office representative in the Kaiser's suite, advised that the Kaiser had not answered Wied's letter at all.[45] In Vienna, Count Ottokar Czernin was now Austro-Hungarian Foreign Minister. He frankly told German ambassador Count Wedel that he wanted to avoid hurting Wied, but he did not want to give him a written answer, either. He wanted to also avoid acknowledging Wied's claims and obligating the Austrian government by addressing him as "Prince of Albania." It seemed to Czernin that

Wied's missive and the *Denkschrift* were "positively naïve," and his desire to return to the throne "hardly feasible...in practice."[46] In the event, the Austrian ambassador in Berlin, Prince Gottfried Hohenlohe, was advised that the new Austrian emperor, Karl (Franz Josef having finally died in November, 1916), had read Wied's writings and merely authorized thanks, as Austria could not make commitments which might tie her hands at any peace conference.[47]

Finally, on September 14, 1917, in a letter addressed to "Prinzen Wilhelm zu Wied, Fürsten von Albanien" at Waldenburg, the German foreign office confirmed that they had delivered his letter to the Kaiser, but

> ...the Government is not, to their regret, in a position to comply with Your Highness's expressed wishes, as the future form of Albania must remain reserved for the peace conference. This understanding... is shared by the Austro-Hungarian Government.[48]

The Central Powers might, however, have been wise to use any residual goodwill in Albania towards Wied. In late October, 1917, German Consul Dr. Eiswalt in Sarajevo, relying on Turkish sources, reported that the Catholic Albanians, long cultivated by Austria, had developed a pronounced anti-Austrian bias during the Austrian occupation under Archduke Max. On the other hand, Wied still had adherents and might have been well-received on his return. A traveler to Albania had quipped, "Wied is no Coburg [like Czar Ferdinand of Bulgaria], he is no bright boy [*heller kopf*], but he is a soldier and still better than the Hapsburger!"[49]

The new Austrian Emperor and King of Hungary, Karl, had a seemingly inexhaustible supply of counts within the Monarchy from which to draw his advisers. He had chosen Count Ottokar Czernin as his new foreign minister. Czernin was a "gifted dilettante," but lazy, vain, arrogant, and unpredictable. A Bohemian (literally) aristocrat like Berchtold, he even resembled him somewhat, but seemed to share the new Emperor's belief that an Austrian peace initiative was needed.[50]

On November 7, 1917, Count Czernin was in Berlin and met with Wied. The chief topic was a possible declaration of war by Albania against the Entente Powers. The allies, Italy and France, now had troops in the Balkans and the Russian Revolution (at that moment being taken over by the Bolsheviks) had led to armistice negotiations between Germany, Austria, and Russia which looked promising. Cessation of the war with Russia would mean freeing thousands of Central Powers troops to fight on other fronts. Wied also raised the possibility of Albania taking part in any later peace conference, with either him or his agents representing the country. He reminded that, although he was serving in the German Army, and numerous Albanian volunteers were in the Austrian forces, Albania was still technically neutral! Czernin expressed reservations about Albania sitting at a peace conference for the same reason: it had already been decided that only belligerent powers would participate. Czernin said that he would discuss the matter with the Germans, and urged Wied to discuss it with German foreign minister von Kühlmann. Wied did meet with that minister the same day to discuss the matter and Kühlmann said that any declaration of war should come not only from Wied, but also from notables and representatives of the country. Wied replied that this would be no problem and predicted that the Albanians would rally around him. Von Kühlmann then hedged, and promised to consider the matter "more closely," and have a "full exchange of views with Vienna."

Having still received no affirmative reply, Wied composed in Waldenburg an emotional, lengthy memorandum to the new German Chancellor, Count von Hertling, which he transmitted on December 13. He reminded the Chancellor of his discussions with Czernin and von Kühlmann, and estimated that 80,000 to 100,000 Albanians would be available for war service if Albania declared war and peace was made with Russia. He pointed out that the Albanians were accustomed to the climate and terrain and "...hardened by nature, bold, brave and hardy," and thus good soldier material. They had already won praise as volunteer battalions with the Austrian Army, and he proposed that German and Austrian officers would lead them and that there would be "conscription of all able-bodied Albanians." This, he wrote, would bind the sentiments of the Albanians to the Central Powers. He pledged to never allow an enemy of theirs to control the Adriatic through Albania.

Wied pointedly reminded Hertling of public statements which the German Chancellor and the Austrian Prime Minister, Ritter von Seidler, had made acknowledging the right of peoples to decide upon their governments. Hertling had told the Reichstag of Germany's recognition of the right of self-determination of the people of Poland, Kurland [part of Latvia] and Lithuania, so how then could they do less for Albania? Even German-occupied Belgium, Wied noted, had been promised restoration of its status, and Poles had always actually hated Germans, as he knew. He felt that a battle, in which Albanians would help expel the Italians and French from Valona and southern Albania, would unify the nation as the Franco-Prussian War had unified Germany in 1870-71. It would also help them look toward "wider future borders... as wide as the... population allows."

In summary, he affirmed that Albania could be a dam against unlawful Slav and Greek expansion in the Balkans, and act as a bridge between Germany, Austria and Turkey.[51] The reaction to this plea can perhaps be best demonstrated by the following despatch from the German ambassador in Vienna to the Chancellor:

Vienna, the 29th December 1917

The government here has a corresponding writing received from the Prince Wilhelm zu Wied, but intend preliminarily not to answer it at all, since no answer is directly called for and entering into the question of an Albanian declaration of war would acknowledge the

387

competence of the Prince, which one would like at the present moment to avoid.

As for the rest, the demonstration of the Prince's belief in the dispositions of the Albanians is considered optimistic. Austro-Hungarian civil servants and officers presently in Albania express their consideration that the Prince has almost no support and influence there, [and] were there still a single Albanian there standing in his service, it would be to get his bread and obviously deluded.

Wedel[52]

The Austrians believed that Wied had been deceived by some Albanians who had come to Vienna to plead their case, but who had not even been received at the Ballplatz. Wied tried to communicate with the Austrians through a young German, Count Solms-Wildenfels, and even sought an audience with Emperor Karl. This request was, as the German ambassador put it, "handled in a courteous, dilatory fashion."[53]

German-Austrian negotiations with the Bolsheviks resulted in peace on the eastern front in February 1918, and this apparently made it easier for Wied to get leave from his military duties so as to visit Waldenburg, where he wrote that the political situation had so changed that "...the work for my home country [i.e. Albania] is taking my whole attention."[54] He was excited, no doubt, by the cheers of Albanian expatriates such as Pandele Evanghele, who claimed to be president of the Albanian colony in Bucharest, Romania, which had been occupied by the Central Powers since December of 1916. On March 7, 1918, Evanghele cabled "King Wilhelm I of Albania" a fawning expression of "eternal submission and true love," begging him to return "as soon as possible, surrounded by all of us who live in foreign lands, to our homeland."[55] Spurred by such support (real or artificial), he sat down that very day and dispatched a letter to the Kaiser, signing himself merely, "Wilhelm, Fürst von Albanien." In the letter he reminded the emperor that he had served three and one-half years on the staff of the German Guard Cavalry

Regiment as both a German Prince and officer, discharging his duty to both his "old fatherland" and Albania. He begged to respond to the call of his Albanians to lead them in arms against the Italians and to reinforce the Austrian front in Albania with an army of at least 50,000 men. According to "extremely reliable information" from Albania, he wrote, by far the largest majority still supported him and fervently awaited his return. Therefore, he begged to be released from his command of the Guard Cavalry staff so that he could devote himself completely to his Balkan plans. A copy of the plea was forwarded by the Kaiser's staff to Chancellor Count Hertling for his advice.[56]

As no favorable answer was forthcoming, Wied became more frantic and insistent. When General Freiherr von Marschall, Chief of the Kaiser's Military Cabinet, wrote to ask Wied what the Austrians thought of his request, he was forced to reply on March 28 that negotiations with them were "not yet concluded." Regardless of that, he wrote, he wanted to be relieved of his command so as to be able to keep his promises to his Albanian subjects "and the preservation of my personal honor thereby." He sensed that his people, despite their loyalty to the Central Powers, were in danger of being parceled out to other countries.[57]

Apparently sympathetic, Marschall spoke to the Foreign Office representatives attached to the Kaiser's suite, and said that he could not refuse Wied's request to relieve him from duty for the duration of the war, and asked the Foreign Office to discuss the matter with him.[58] The Foreign Office approved of Wied's resignation and his plan to raise an army, provided that the Austrian military headquarters approved.[59] When Wied asked for a German passport, it created something of a diplomatic stir. The new Austrian foreign minister (another count!) Burian pointed out the implications of granting a German passport to a man claiming to be the sovereign of another country. Nevertheless, should the Germans grant such a request, Burian asked that it be marked, "For travel to Austria-Hungary and allied countries," using his old title of "Prince of Wied."[60] Wied complained bitterly to the German Foreign Office that the

Austrians in Albania were suppressing all demonstrations in his favor and that all letters addressed to him by his loyal followers were confiscated in Vienna. Somewhat inconsistently, he also asserted that the March 7 anniversary of his arrival and his March 26 birthday were always celebrated, and that his picture hung "everywhere, even in the smallest cottage." The Germans remained evasive and merely observed that the general peace settlement would also decide Albania's fate. At that time, Germany was making her final "big push" on the Western Front, hoping to knock out the British and French armies before starvation in Germany and floods of American troops could turn the tide against her.[61]

While Wied was thus occupied, he also had to deal with somewhat bizarre press publicity involving himself. First, he had to deny a German newspaper report in March of 1918 that he was being considered to replace the King of Romania, which country had been almost completely conquered by Germany. Because of his patronage by the Romanian royal family in securing the (albeit illusory) Albanian throne, and his wife's close connections with them, he tried to inform the *Dresdener Anzeiger* that it was an "idle invention." He had not the remotest thought of abandoning his Albanian quest.[62] The prevailing mindset of implanting kings on foreign thrones was not yet the anachronism it would soon become.

More grotesque still was a story emanating from England, Germany's bitter enemy. In January and February of 1918, an obscure London Magazine published articles written anonymously by Harold Sherwood Spencer, the American who had fought bravely as a volunteer for Wied's government in Albania in 1914. The articles stated that Britain was having a hard time winning the war because the Germans possessed a "Black Book," containing the names of 47,000 prominent British subjects who were being blackmailed because of their perverted sexual proclivities. The book allegedly included not only the former British Prime Minister, Asquith, but also the judge who would eventually try the libel case resulting from the article! One of the persons mentioned in the article sued the publisher,

Pemberton Billing, a Member of Parliament, for criminal libel. A woman by the name of Eileen Villiers testified at the trial that she had seen the Black Book in Wied's possession at some time after 1913. Spencer, now a captain in the British Royal Flying Corps, testified that he had been *aide de camp* to Wied and that German agents were using the book to degrade the morals of the British. The trial degenerated into a circus when Spencer began to discourse on diseased clitorises and similar theories, and Lord Alfred Douglas (Oscar Wilde's famous lover) vented his spleen irrelevantly on poor, dead Oscar. Both men had to be ejected from the court, but this did not prevent the jury from acquitting the publisher. Spencer, however, was later locked up as a lunatic. Once again, truth proved far stranger than fiction.[63]

When news of these sensational allegations reached wartime Germany, Wied was forced to inform the German newspapers that Spencer was never his *aide de camp* or adjutant, which was true. He also denied that Spencer had been in the service of his government in any capacity, which was not quite true, and he denied that he had ever heard of any such Black Book, which was probably true.[64]

By late August of 1918, German resistance on the Western Front was collapsing and even the Kaiser and his generals sensed that they must soon sue for peace.[65] Despite that, on August 29 Wied favored Foreign Office Secretary of State von Hintze, who was attached to the Kaiser's suite, with a "strictly confidential," lengthy, impassioned jeremiad reviewing his situation. He alleged that Austria had recognized his Albanian claims in the winter of 1914/1915 and agreed in early 1915 that he could share in the offensive against Serbia. But since the war with Italy broke out in the spring of 1915 and Count Burian became Austrian Foreign Minister for the first time, the Austrians had changed their tune. When he wrote to Count Czernin, the Austrians had even refused to answer in writing, sending subordinates to deliver oral replies. Wied refused to accept this insult and forbade the ambassador, Prince Hohenlohe, to address him as "Prince Wied." He demanded to be addressed as "Prince of Albania," as he signed himself. After his conversations with Czernin and von Kühlmann in November of 1917, he got no reply until Vienna sent an unofficial "gentleman" who told him that it was not desired that Albania participate in the war "as a state." Despite Austrian obstruction and censorship, he wrote, he had received oral and written reports from Albania painting an accurate picture of the situation there: although originally greeted as liberators, two and one half years of Austrian occupation had made them hated. Any disloyalty to Wied was probably fomented by von Kral, now the civil governor, and by pro-Italian and pro-Essad elements. Despite proposals to put Archduke Max on the Albanian throne, he felt that the people only wanted Wied. Albania had prospered during the war to the extent that streets, bridges, and light railroads had been built by the combatants and much money had come into the country. Many merchants had become millionaires. Wied also asserted that the country contained a wealth of first-rate anthracite coal mines, perfect for coal-burning ships. Perhaps for this reason, he had found sympathy only in naval circles, who were concerned about Entente control of the port of Valona. Neither the Albanians, Turkey, nor Bulgaria wanted Austria to control Albania, and this made a perfect opening, he felt, for Germany to profit from the situation, especially with a German Prince on the throne. Besides, Austria-Hungary had neither the means nor the capacity to profit from Albanian trade and industry. If even the conquered Romanian dynasty was allowed to remain, and German troops sustained the new state in the Balkans and Ukraine, why not Albania as well? He knew that he had made mistakes, but he was better prepared now. Austria-Hungary was dissolving into various nation-states and Slavs, the enemies of the Albanians, were becoming powerful. Albania could be a dam against their spread, and "Germany's sentry and lookout" in the Mediterranean and the Balkans.[66]

Of course, these matters were soon out of the hands of the Kaiser and his government. He was forced to go into exile in Holland, and the new German government was forced to sign an armistice in November of 1918, which was virtually a surrender.

Wied was now only another ex-officer of a defeated army, living in a newly-proclaimed republic.

34

AN EXILE IN HIS OWN COUNTRY

With the World War ended by an armistice, Austria-Hungary dissolved, and Italy one of the victorious allies, an Albanian national assembly was convened in Durazzo on Christmas Day, 1918, under the auspices of Italy. It soon selected a provisional government headed by loyal old Turkhan Pasha Premeti, which included a number of Wied's old associates, including Prenk Bib Doda, Mehmed Bey Konitza, Sami Bey Vrioni, and Dr. Michael Tortoulis. This government, in turn, appointed Turkhan Pasha, Mehmed Bey and others to be Albanian delegates to the Paris Peace Conference, which was to convene in January, 1919.[1] The appointments were not without controversy, however. The *Journal de Genève* (Geneva) reported, via its Athens bureau, that certain Albanian circles were indignant that Turkhan and Mehmed presumed to represent Albania, since Turkhan was thought to have been close to the Germans and Turks during the war. Also, he received a small pension of 700 francs (now about $2,400) a month from the account of the "Princess of Wied" via the Turkish ambassador to Germany. He was also alleged to report monthly to the Princess. Konitza was accused of being the "faithful instrument of Germany and Austria" in Albania during the war, and of receiving 1,500 francs (today around $5,100) during the war, to go to Athens to make arrangements with King Constantine, before that monarch was forced out by the Entente as pro-German.[2] Apparently these false reports were Greek propaganda or the work of anti-Italian Albanians in Greece, if not honest mistakes. Mehmed Bey Konitza had been Albanian representative in London during the war.[3]

In April, 1919, Akif Pasha Elbasani (a seemingly honest but not able Wied minister), who was considered the leading Albanian politician at the time, told a British Foreign Office official that he and many others wished to return to Wied's rule.

Many were loyal and sympathetic to Wied, he said, as "an unfortunate man who was driven from the land by foreign intrigues."[4]

In January 1920, a group of Albanian leaders, including Ahmed Zogu, Akif Pasha of Elbasan, and Eshref Frasheri, formed a congress which declared the principality in abeyance and constructed a "High Council of Regency." It was composed of one member from each of Albania's four religious communities: Bektashi, Sunni, Catholic, and Orthodox. A Monsignor Bumci, a northerner, was the Catholic regent. The regents felt that Wied had hopelessly compromised himself by fighting in the German army during the war, as the victorious Allies would certainly object to his return. They also realized that the expenses of a royal court were beyond Albania's capabilities. They felt Wied would be "the powerless axis of unlimited intrigue."[5]

Wied requested the peace conference in Paris in 1919 to recognize his right to return but, unsurprisingly, this was "met with indifference."[6] Released from the German army, he, like many other suddenly unemployed princelings, must have been concerned for his modest fortune while the country was wracked with disorder and revolution. In January of 1920, he apparently arranged to have family jewels combined with those of other wealthy Germans and flown to Sweden for safety. The jewels were sent to a "Doctor Engineer" Karl von Stockhausen and Countess Anna zu Wildenfels, wife of his friend, the Count. Unfortunately, the Swedish authorities seized the jewels as smuggled goods, and began a prosecution against the good doctor and the Countess. Once again, Wied's affairs made headlines to his embarrassment and a minor diplomatic problem for the new German Republic. Stockhausen and the Countess defended themselves in the Swedish court by claiming the rights of a foreign sovereign to immunity since, they said, the jewels belonged to the Prince of Albania. The Swedes scratched their heads and had their embassy in Berlin inquire of the German government (1) whether Wied had abdicated and reverted to being a German, (2) whether Wied had been effectively deposed by the purported Albanian Parliament on September 28, 1914, when it elected a Turkish Prince, and (3), what rights would Wied have to the jewels under German law if he was still Prince?[7] Apparently the Auswärtiges Amt had asked Wied whether he had abdicated and he denied that he had done so. They then so informed the Swedish Embassy and pointed out that, since the war began they had no representation in Albania and so no accurate information about its government. Moreover, Germany had no law about sovereign immunity other than generally-accepted international law.[8] In the event, the Swedish court found the defendants not guilty of smuggling, and the jewels were released.[9]

Wied was still hoping to return to the vacant Albanian throne. Living in upper Bavaria, he confided to a confidant that it was his duty to satisfy his people's desire for his return and, to that end, negotiations had already begun with the finally victorious Serbs. He claimed that they were now actually sympathetic to his plan! The chief problem, he said, was the old one: money. But apparently he was prepared to pledge the Albanian coal, copper, and zinc deposits, as well as the customs and water power rights, to whomever would lend him the money. He was going to attempt to obtain a ten million dollar loan from an American concern in return for a "monopoly concession to establish motion picture theaters and produce films." Even certain titles such as "confidential commercial advisor" to Wied were on offer.[10]

In the summer of 1923, the Albanian-American Bishop, Fan Noli, and a committee in Vienna which included Akif Pasha (who had been named one of the "Regents" for Albania by the assembly after the war), Hassan Prishtina, Zia Dibra and Irfan Bey hoped to take power and appoint a foreign ruler, even "possibly Prince Wied." Noli was a republican, but the Nationalists favored a constitutional monarchy and many still professed loyalty to Wied. In January, 1925, Ahmed Zogu, former Wied loyalist, was elected President.[11] His ambitions and Wied's Central Powers record ended Wied's possibility of a restoration. By March, 1924, the royalists looked abroad,

396

approaching several European princes, titled men, and an English Anglophile, as well as some millionaires and industrialists.[12] Until the monarchy was formally abolished by the Parliament on January 17, 1925, imaginative speculations about candidates for the throne were received. Some stories had a basis in unofficial initiatives by enterprising emigrants. Most politicians in Albania supported a monarchy, and Zogu acquiesced in an approach to John, the British eighth Duke of Atholl, who wisely declined upon the advice of his Foreign Office. The vacant throne became an international joke in August of 1923, when the London *Evening News* carried the front page headline, "Wanted, a King: English Country Gentleman Preferred—apply to the Government of Albania." The Prime Minister of Albania received over seventy applications, most from suburban London, including those from a ballet teacher and a dentist.[13]

When Zogu changed the constitution and was proclaimed "King Zog" in August, 1928, Wied issued a formal protest from Berlin, although he acknowledged that a free referendum on his return was currently impossible. He only awaited "the right moment" to return, he said. The Wieds had settled near Munich, living modestly at 21 Schnellwittchenstrasse, with Wied even driving his own car. They regularly visited Sophie's Rumanian family castle and estate, *Fantanele*, near Bacau, some 150 miles north of Bucharest. Wied enjoyed hunting there. In June of 1931, Wied went to The Hague, where he visited the bigger-than-life caped statue of his champion, Colonel Thomson. He was photographed by the local newspapers, hat in hand, in his double-breasted suit and bow tie, standing below the colonel's statue. He clipped the article out and mailed it, with a note in poor Albanian, to a friend. It eventually found its way to the Albanian archives.[14] Until 1928, Wied continued to hold an Albanian passport, but when Zog became King, the passport was not renewed, so the Prince begged one from Liechtenstein.[15]

In May, 1935, Wied was graciously invited by King Carol II of Romania to the conference of the Balkan Pact in Bucharest, although Albania was not even a party to the pact. He was given the usual royal honors, but was put up at a modest, six shilling a day (c. $25 today) room in a busy commercial hotel. He usually dressed in brown tweeds, looking healthy and athletic. He claimed that he had never lost touch with the Albanians, and especially admired the mountaineers of the north and south as "fearless, independent men of unswerving loyalty and attachment." "If my people want me, I will go back at any time."[16] The call never came. Some thought that King Zog, without a son, might make Wied or Wied's son his heir, but that was not to be, either.

Sophie died at *Fantanele* in 1936. Wied lived another nine years, also dying in Romania, near Sinaia, in the chaotic last days of World War II, while that country was under virtual Soviet Russian occupation.[17]

His old arch-enemy, Essad Pasha, had long since met his end, having been shot to death in Paris in the summer of 1920 by an Albanian student.[18]

Perhaps it can be fairly said of Wied, in summary, that apart from a spectacular and strife-filled year in which he was the toy of the Great Powers, his life took the same course which it would have followed if he had never heard of Albania. But during his brief time in Albania, he had truly been a prisoner-- of brutal circumstances beyond his control, and of his own indecision.

The world of princes, barons and counts (if not quite of kings and queens) is gone. They were human, and certainly no more virtuous or intelligent than today's rulers. But their superficial glitter made the world a more colorful place for a long time.

35

POSTSCRIPT

It seems clear now, as it should have been even in 1914, that Wied had little or no chance to succeed in the chaotic land to which his naïveté and his wife's ambition had sent him. Even had he been a remarkable man in the mold of the Albanian hero, Skanderbeg, there were too many odds against him. Even had the World War not taken the last shred of practical support from him, the task of a foreign prince planted in a badly divided, hopelessly backward land would have been virtually impossible. He was lucky not to have shared Mexican Emperor Maximilian's fate.

This last attempt at an "Anthony Hope" Ruritanian romance was turned by reality into a humiliating near-tragedy for all the world to see. But, after all, Wied lived out the rest of his life much as would have been expected of a simple man of modest talents, an army officer and a retired gentleman. His fate, albeit on a more modest scale, was not so different from that of the Kaiser, Emperor Karl, and countless other monarchs. Kaiser Wilhelm spent the next 22 years cooped up in a chateau in Holland, while poor Emperor Karl, after failing twice even to reclaim Hungary, died of pneumonia at his exile on the island of Madeira within a very few years.

NOTES

INTRODUCTION

[1] The hero spoke fluent German and, as all the novel's characters have German names, and as the native tongue of most European monarchs was German, that was perhaps an excusable slip.

[2] Frederick Morton, *Thunder at Twilight* (New York: Charles Scribners Sons. 1989) p. 84

[3] "Balkan" is an old Turkish word which means mountain or very high land. (Stephen Bonsal, *Suitors and Suppliants: The Little Nations at Versailles* (New York: Prentice Hall, Inc., 1946) Chapter V., p.69.

[4] John Kenrick, "The Merry Widow 101. History of a Hit Part II." Musicals 101.com.

[5] *Ibid.*

[6] Fritz Jüdtmann, *Mayerling: The Facts Behind the Legend* (London: George Harrap & Co., 1971); *The* (Memphis) *Commercial Appeal*, December 26, 1992; In 1992 the girl's body was reported stolen from her grave. Rudolf's mother was from a notoriously crazy royal family.

[7] Barbara Tuchman, *The Proud Tower* (New York: The MacMillan Co., 1966) pp. 212, 213.

[8] "*Prinz, Fürst, Principe*," etc.: in German, "*Hoheit*," or "*Durchlaucht*;" in French, "*Altesse.*"

[9] Lord Frederic Hamilton, *The Vanquished Pomps of Yesterday* (New York: George H Doran Co., 1921) p. 51.

[10] Anthony Sampson, *Anatomy of Britain* (London: Hodder & Stoughton. 1966) p. 11.

[11] James W. Gerard, *Face to Face with Kaiserism* (New York: George H. Doran Co., 1918) p. 206.

[12] George J. Adler, compiler, *German-English Dictionary* (New York: D. Appleton & Co., 1902) p. 215.

[13] Virginia Cowles, *1913 An End and a Beginning* (New York: Harper & Row, 1968) p. 163.

[14] George M. Thomson, *The Twelve Days* (New York: G.P. Putman's Sons, 1964) p. 34.

[15] *Alfred Rappaport Ritter Von Arbengau*, http://www.austro-hungarian-army.co.uk/biog/rappaport.htm.

[16] Investiture with a fiefdom made them *zu* as well as *von*. Frederic Morton , *Thunder at Twilight* (New York: Charles Scribner's Sons, 1989) p. 29.

[17] James W. Gerard, *My Four Years in Germany* (New York: George H. Doran Co., 1917) p. 121.

[18] Lord Frederic Hamilton*, p. 51.

[19] Cowles, pp. 61, 79; David Fromkin, *Europe's Last Summer* (New York: Alfred A. Knopf, 2004) p. 176; *"The Outlook, A Weekly Newspaper," Vol. 81 Sep.-Dec. 1905*, p. 1011.

[20] Encyclopedia Britannica, 5th Edition, Volume 20, "Spain", p. 1100; Infanta Eulalia of Spain, Court Life From Within (New York: Dodd Mead & Co., 1915) pp. 49, 50.
[21] The "Great Powers" were usually considered to consist of Britain, France, Russia, and Austria. After 1871 Germany and Italy were, by tacit consent, admitted to the club.
[22] Stephane Groueff, Crown of Thorns (Lanham: Madison Books, 1987) pp. 24, 25.
[23] The (London) Times (London) November 6, 1913, p.7.
[24] Chedomille Mijatovich, A Royal Tragedy (New York: Dodd, Mead & Co., 1907) pp. 193- 204;Francis Yeats-Brown, Bloody Years (New York: The Viking Press, 1932) p.71n1.
[25] Mijatovich, pp. 206-208; Rebecca West, Black Lamb and Grey Falcon, (New York: The Viking Press, 1943) p. 11; André Gerolymatos, The Balkan Wars (New York: Basic Books, 2002) p. 23; Frederick Palmer, With My Own Eyes, (Indianapolis: The Bobbs-Merrill Co., 1932) p. 233.
[26] Sir Sidney Lee, King Edward VII, Vol. II (New York: The MacMillian Co., 1927) pp. 270-273.
[27] Infanta Eulalia, pp. 50, 51.

A WORD ABOUT WORDS

[1] "Pound Sterling," Wikipedia, the free Encyclopedia; http://en.wikpedia.org/wiki/pound_sterling, p.3; "Turkey," The Encyclopedia Britannica (11th Edition), p.441. (online facsimile).
[2] Franz Werfel, The Forty Days of Musa Dagh (New York: The Modern Library, 1934) p. 821; H. P. Willmott, World War I, (New York: Darling Kindersley Publishing, Inc., 2006) p. 304; Encyclopedia Britannica (1961 Edition) "Turkey" p. 595.

PRELUDE, THE BACKGROUND STORY

[1] Edith Durham, Twenty Years of Balkan Tangle (London: George Allen & Unwin, 1920) p. 179.
[2] Tullio Irace, With the Italians in Tripoli (London: John Marney, 1912) pp. 1-9.
[3] André Gerolymatos, The Balkan Wars (New York: Basic Books, 2002), p. 210.
[4] J. Swire, Albania The Rise of a Kingdom (London: Williams & Norgate Ltd., 1929) p. 101.
[5] Gerolymatos, p. 224.
[6] Charles Homer Haskins and Robert Howard Lord, Some Problems of the Peace Conference (Cambridge: Harvard University Press, 1920), p. 278.
[7] Swire, King Zog's Albania, p. 235; Tomes, p 150.
[8] Ferdinand Schevill, A History of the Balkans (New York: Dorset Press, 1991) p. 473.
[9] Harry F. Young, Prince Lichnowsky and the Great War (Athens: University of Georgia Press. 1977) p. 61.
[10] Gerolymatos, p. 228; The Encyclopedia Britannica, 5th edition, Vol. 2, p. 991.

1 – ALBANIA, THE SETTING

[1] Gervase Belfeld, Introduction to Duncan Heaton-Armstrong, The Six Month Kingdom (London: I.B. Taurus, 2005) p. xiii.
[2] Isa Boletini, http://en.wikipedia.org/wiki/Isa_Boletini, 12/13/2006.

[3] *Encyclopedia Britannica*, "Albania", pp. 510, 511; D.R. Oakley-Hill, *An Englishman in Albania* (London: The Centre for Albanian Studies, 2002, pp. 3-14.

[4] *The (London) Times*, March 4, 1914, p. 5

[5] Edith Durham, the English expert, said that the correct word was "Maltsor." *The (London) Times*, August 25, 1913, p. 6

[6] P.N. Pipinelis, *Europe and the Albanian Question,* (Chicago: Argonaut Inc., 1963) p. 29.

[7] Jason Hunter Tomes, *King Zog of* Albania (New York: New York University Press, 2003) p. 8.

[8] Tomes, p. 12; Swire, *Rise of a Kingdom*, pp. 5-22.

[9] Tomes, p. 13

[10] *Ibid.,* p. 15

[11] Swire, *Rise of a Kingdom*, pp. 30, 37.

[12] *Ibid.,* p. 45; Tomes, p. 9.

[13] Swire, p. 37.

[14] *Ibid.,* p. 45; *The (London) Times*, January 17, 1914, p. 7.

[15] *Ibid.,* pp. 58, 66.

[16] *Ibid.,* p. 67.

[17] *Ibid.,* p. 67.

[18] Misha Glenny, *The Balkans* (New York: Penguin Books, 2001) p. 415.

[19] Tomes, p. 10.

[20] Belfield, p. vi.

[21] *Ibid.,* pp. 160, 162.

[22] Durham, *Balkan Tangle*, p. 182.

[23] *The (London) Times*, April 29, 1914, p. 7.

[24] John D. Treadway, *The Falcon and the Eagle* (West Lafayette: Purdue University Press, 1983) pp. 67, 686.

[25] Encyclopedia Britannica (Encyclopedia Britannica Supplement to the 13th Edition, 1926, Vol. I, "Albania") p. 86.

[26] Tomes, p. 7.

[27] Gorrit T. A. Goslinga, *The Dutch in* Albania (Rome: Szêjzat (Le Pleiadi), 1972) p. 52.

[28] Tomes, p. 7; Owen Pearson, *Albania and King Zog* (London: I.B. Taurus, 2004) p. xiii.

[29] *The (London) Times,* August 14, 1913, p. 6.

[30] *The (London) Times*, March 20, 1914, p. 5.

[31] Swire, Rise of a Kingdom, p. 166.

[32] Tomes, pp. 54, 55; Wied, p. 63.

[33] *The (London) Times*, August 14, 1913, p. 6.

[34] Pipinelis, p. 11; *The (London) Times*, March 12, 1914, p.4.

[35] Tomes, *King Zog*, p. 79.

[36] Swire, pg. 187.

[37] Durham, *High Albania*, p. 28.

2 – SOME ROYALTY AND CAST OF CHARACTERS

[1] *The (London) Times*, Jan. 7, 8, 1914, pp. 7,5; Swire, *Rise*, p. 186; Goslinga, pp. 20, 21.

[2] Kenneth Rose, *King George V* (New York: Alfred A. Knoph, 1984) p. 361.

[3] Margot Asquith, *An Autobiography* Volume III (New York: George H. Doran Co., 1922) p. 162.

[4] Burton J. Hendrick, *The Life and Letters of Walter H. Page* (Garden City: Doubleday, Page & Co., 1925) p. 155.

[5] Young, p. 56.

[6] Hendrick, pp. 155, 313.

[7] Virginia Cowles, *1913* (New York: Harper & Rowe, 1968) p. 39; Emil Ludwig, *July '14* (G.P. Putnam's Sons, 1929), p. 142.

[8] Ludwig, *July '14*, p. 142.

[9] William Jannen,Jr., *The Lions of July* (Novato: Presidio Press, 1996) pp. 50,51.

[10] Rose, p. 89.

[11] George M. Thomson, *The Twelve Days* (New York: G.P. Putnam's Sons, 1964) p.91.

[12] Julia Nicolson, *The Perfect Summer* (New York: Grove Press, 2006) pp. 51. 52.

[13] Viscount Grey of Falloden, *Twenty Five Years* (New York: Frederick A. Stokes Co., 1925) pp. 259, 264.

[14] Grey, p. 266.

[15] Cowles, p. 143; Ludwig Reiners, *The Lamps Went Out in Europe* (New York, Pantheon, 1955) p. 61.

[16] Joseph Redlich, *Emperor Francis Joseph of Austria* (New York: The Macmillan Co., 1929) p. 512.

[17] Cowles, p. 144

[18] Winston S. Churchill, *The World Crisis. The Eastern Front* (New York: Charles Scribner's Sons, 1931) p. 52.

[19] Charles Tansill, *America Goes to War* (Boston: Little Brown & Co., 1938) p. 30, n. 83.

[20] FirstWorldWar.com—*Who's Who*, "Leopold von Berchtold," September 24, 2005.

[21] Emil Ludwig, *July '14*, p. 42.

[22] John D. Treadway, p. 98.

[23] Thomson, p. 41.

[24] Winston Churchill, p. 28.

[25] Vladimir Dedijer, *The Road to Sarajevo* (New York: Simon & Schuster, 1966) pp. 131, 132.

[26] *Franz Ferdinand The Proprietor*,http://www.btinternet.com,/~j.pasteur/Proprietor.html.

[27] Ludwig Reiners, p. 76; Frederic Morton, *Thunder at Twilight* (New York: Charles Scriber's Sons, 1989) pp. 33, 34.

[28] James Gerard, *Face to Face with Kaiserism*, p. 165.

[29] Cowles, p. 61.

[30] James Gerard, *Face to Face with Kaiserism*, p. 20.

[31] Edward, Duke of Windsor, *A King's Story* (New York: G. P. Putnam's Sons, 1951) pp. 101, 102; James W. Gerard, *My Four Years in Germany* (New York: George H. Doran Co., 1917) p. 52.

[32] *Ibid.*, p. 312.

[33] John Van der Kiste, *Kings of the Hellenes* (Phoenix Mill: Alan Sutton Publishing, 1994) pp. 66, 67.

[34] Ann Topham, *Memories of the Kaiser's Court* (New York: Dodd Mead & Co., 1914) p . 278.

[35] *Ibid.*, p. 288.

[36] *Ibid.*, p. 278. start an index
[37] Viktoria Louise of Prussia, *The Kaiser's Daughter* (Englewood Cliffs: Prentice-Hall inc., 1977) p. 3; Gerard, *My Four Years*, p. 199.
[38] Bernhard von Bülow, *Memoirs. 1897-1903* (London: Putnam, 1931) pp. 135, 136.
[39] Ludwig Reiners, *The Lamps Went Out in Europe* (New York: Pantheon, 1955) p. 51.
[40] The Kaiser called him, affectionately, "Lanky Theo" (Morton, p. 278.)
[41] Gerard, *Face to Face*, p. 34; *My Four Years*, pp. 37, 327.
[42] Emil Ludwig, *July '14*, p. 66.
[43] Gerard, *Face to Face*, p. 34; Thomson, p. 119.
[44] Hendrick, p. 296.
[45] Young, p. 60; Gerard, *My Four Years*, p. 138.
[46] Gerard, *My Four Years*, p. 423.
[47] Sir Edward Grey, p. 283.
[48] Count Johann Bernstorff, *Memoirs of Count Bernstorff* (New York: 1936), p. 162.
[49] Robert K. Massie, *Nicholas and Alexandra* (New York: Atheneum, 1967) pp. 264, 265.
[50] Thomson, p. 64.
[51] Harold Nicolson, *King George V* (New York: Doubleday & Co., 1953) p. 203, n. 2.
[52] Nicolson, p. 63.
[53] Massie, pp. 228-233.
[54] Ivor Porter, *Michael of Romania* (Stroud: Sutton Publishing Ltd, 2005) p. 2; Arturo E. Beéche-Bravo, *H.M. King Michael I of Romania, A Tribute* (Falköping: Rosvall Royal Books, 2001) p. 10.
[55] *Ibid.*
[56] *Time*, November 10, 1939, p.40.
[57] Lee, p. 16.
[58] Hannah Pakula, *The Last Romantic* (New York: Simon & Schuster, 1984) pp. 79, 80; Queen Marie, *The Story of My Life* (New York, Charles Scribner's Sons, 1934) p. 368.
[59] *American Heritage,* Vol. XIV, April 1953, pp. 43-65.
[60] Blanche Roosevelt, *Elisabeth of Rumania* (London: Chapman & Hall) pp. 1-25.
[61] Pakula, pp. 100, 101.
[62] Roosevelt, p. 8.
[63] *The Lady's Realm, An Illustrated Monthly Magazine*, Vol. IV, May, 1898; Vols. I and III, 1896 (London: Hutchison & Co.)
[64] Belfield, in Heaton, *The Six Month Kingdom*, p. xii.
[65] *The Lady's Realm*, Vol. I, p. 648.
[66] *The Lady's Realm,* Vol. II (London, Hutchinson & Co., 1897) p. 657.
[67] Queen Marie of Romania, *The Story of My Life* (New York: Charles Scribner's Sons, 1934) p. 247.
[68] Rebecca West, *Black Lamb and Grey* Falcon (New York: Viking Press, 1943) p. 12.
[69] *Ibid.,* pp. 367, 568, 570.
[70] Ludwig, p. 94; *Encyclopedia Britannica*, Vol. 17, "Nikola Pasich," p. 365.
[71] Ludwig Reiners, *The Lamps Went Out in Europe* (New York: Pantheon Books, 1955) p. 105.
[72] Sidney B. Fay, *The Origins of the World* War, 2nd Edition (New York: The Macmillan Co., 1930) p. 446.
[73] Treadway, p. 1.

[74] Treadway, p. 2.

[75] West, p. 1052.

[76] Treadway, p. 18.

[77] Grand Duke Alexander, *Once a Grand Duke* (Garden City: Garden City Publishing Co., 1932) p. 160.

[78] Edith Durham, *Twenty Years of Balkan Tangle*, p. 211.

[79] Treadway, pp. 99, 101; West, p. 1054.

[80] Swire, p. 159.

[81] William L. Shirer, *The Collapse of the Third Republic*, Vol. I, (New York: Simon & Schuster, 1969) p. 115.

[82] Fay, Vol. I, pp. 434, 435.

[83] Queen Marie of Rumania, p. 256.

[84] Christopher Buyers, 4dw.net/RoyalArk/Albania/wied.htm; Belfield, p. xi; *The (London) Times*, November 24, 1913, p.7.

[85] Marshall B. Davidson, "Carl Bodman's Unspoiled West," *American Heritage Magazine, Vol. XIV, No. 3,* April, 1963, p. 43,

[86] Queen Marie, *Story*, p. 505.

[87] Belfield, p. xxix.

[88] Szinyei-Merse, p. 68.

[89] Wilhelm II, *The Kaiser's Memoirs* (New York: Harper & Bros., 1922) p. 166; Queen Marie, *Story*, pp. 542, 543.

[90] *The (London) Times,* April 28, 1914, p. 7.

[91] Queen Marie, *Story,* p. 543.

[92] Wikipedia, http://de.wikipedia.org/wiki/Sophie_von_Sch%B6nburg-Waldenburg, 7/8/07.

[93] Queen Marie, *Story,* p. 542.

[94] Theo Aronson, *Crowns in Conflict* (Manchester: Salem House, 1986) pp. 41-46.

[95] Galeazzo Ciano, *The Ciano Diaries 1939-1943* (New York: Doubleday & Co., 1946) p. 64.

[96] *Enclycopedia Britannica Vol. 19*, (1961) *"Antonio di San Giuliano",* p. 946; Irace, p. 184.

[97] *Encyclopedia Britannica, Vol. 23,* (1961) "Eleutherios Venizelos", p. 68; Van der Kiste, p. 70.

[98] Swire, *Rise*, pp. 57, 58.

[99] Durham, *High Albania*, 2000 reprint of 1909 edition, pp. 334-344; Swire, *Rise*, p. 84.

[100] Edith Durham, *Albania and the Albanians, Selected Articles and Letters 1903-1944* (London: Centre for Albanian Studies, 2001) p. 28.

[101] Swire, *Zog*, p. 104.

[102] Stephan Bonsal, *Suitors and Suppliants: The Little Nations at Versailles* (New York: Prentice Hall, Inc., 1946) p. 83.

[103] Swire, *Zog*, pp. 92, 93.

[104] Bonsal, p. 206.

[105] Durham, *Balkan Tangle*, p. 181.

[106] Swire, *Zog*, p. 79.

[107] Francis Yeats-Brown, *Bloody Years* (New York: The Viking Press, 1932) pp 61,62.

[108] Pearson, pp. 2, 64. Heaton, pp. 14, 15. 175.

[109] Joyce Carey, *Memoir of the Bobotes* (London: Phoenix Press, 2000) p. 155.

[110] Heaton, pp. 14, 15, 175.

[111] Pearson, pp. 42, 43.

[112] Prince Wilhelm zu Wied, *Denkschrift uber Albanien*, 1917, manuscript reprint, pp. 10, 11.

[113] Bonsal, p. 74.

[114] Swire, pp. 78, 79; Dr. Gezim Alpion, *"Baron Franz Nopsca and his Ambition for the Albanian Throne"*, *BESA Journal*, Vol. 6, No. 3, Summer, 2002, pp. 25-32.

[115] Swire, p. 90.

[116] Swire, pp. 118, 119.

[117] G.P. Gooch and Harold Temperley, editors, *British Documents on the Origins of the War, 1898-1914, Vol., X, Pt. I,* (London: H.M.S.O., 1934) abbreviated hereinafter as B. D., Sir. F. Elliott to Sir Edward Grey, February 22, 1914, p. 63.

[118] German Foreign Ministry Archives, 1867-1920, "Albania, die Fürstliche Familie," 1913-1920 (U.S. National Archives, Reel 3, T-137, Frames 298-511), hereinafter G. D., Nadolny to General Staff, July 28, 1918.

[119] Swire, *Rise*, p. 200.

[120] Albanian Archives, Tirana, Albania, December 12, 1913; Heaton, p. 141.

[121] Heaton, pp. 26, 138.

[122] Tomes, p. 50.

[123] Belfield, pp. xxi-xxiii.

[124] Goslinga, pp. 11, 12, 13, 15, 24, 36, 37.

[125] Goslinga, p. 12.

[126] Belfield, p. 30; Karl Kautsky, *Outbreak of the World War, German Documents Collected by Karl Kautsky* (New York: Oxford University Press, 1924) pp. 102, 103,(hereinafter *Kautsky*); Wilhelm zu Wied, p. 21.

[127] Luigi Albertini, *The Origins of the War of 1914* (Oxford: Oxford University Press, 1952) Vol. I, p. 526.

[128] Wied, p. 22.

[129] Albertini, *Vol. I, p. 526.*

[130] Spirit of Albania; "Edith Durham", www.geocities.com/SpiritofAlbania/edith.htm.

[131] Johnathan E. Helmreich, *Contemporary Review, May 1993, "The Serbs: A Warning from a Past Contributor"*, p. 10; Harvey Hodgkinson, Introduction, M. Edith Durham, *Albania and the Albanians, Selected Articles and Letters 1903-1944* (London: Centre for Albanian Studies, 2001) pp. i-xx.

[132] John Hodgson, Introduction, *High Albania* by Edith Durham (London: Phoenix Press, 1985) p. xv.

3 – OTTOMAN ALBANIA

[1] Luigi Albertini, *The Origins of the War of 1914, Volume 1* (Oxford University Press, 1952) p. 524.

[2] P.N. Pipinelis, p. 24.

[3] John Hodgson, *Introduction, High Albania,* by Edith Durham (London, Phoenix Press, 2000), p. xi.

[4] Edith Durham, *High Albania*, pp. 9, 10.

407

[5] *Ibid.*, p. 318.

[6] *Ibid.*, p. 327.

[7] Oakley-Hill, p. 24; Durham, *High Albania*, et sec., *p. 25.*

[8] Tomes, p. 11.

[9] *Ibid.*; Swire, *Rise*, pp. 23-27.

[10] Swire, *Rise*, p. 79.

[11] Swire, *Rise*, pp. 58, 59.

[12] Tomes, pp. 9, 24, 25.

[13] Swire, p. 52.

[14] *Ibid.*, p. 71.

[15] *Ibid.*, p. 77.

[16] *Ibid.*, p. 78.

[17] *Ibid.*, p. 79.

[18] *Ibid.*, p. 86.

[19] Tomes, *Zog,* pp. 18, 19.

[20] Pipinelis, pp. 27, 28.

[21] *Ibid.*

[22] J. Swire, *King Zog's Albania* (New York: Liveright Publishing Co., 1937) p. 243.

4 –THE LONDON CONFERENCE

[1] Churchill, pp. 50, 51.

[2] Morton, p. 88.

[3] West, p. 341.

[4] Churchill, pp. 51, 52.

[5] Owen Pearson, *Albania and King Zog* (London: I. B. Taurus, 2004) p. 6.

[6] Pearson, p. 20.

[7] *Ibid.*, p. 14.

[8] *Ibid.*, p. 29.

[9] Swire, p. 132.

[10] *Ibid.*, p. 145.

[11] Treadway, p. 111.

[12] Swire, *Rise*, p. 134.

[13] *Ibid.*; Treadway, p. 114.

[14] Treadway, p. 118.

[15] *Ibid.*, p. 143.

[16] *Ibid.* p. 144.

[17] *Ibid.*, p. 119.

[18] *Ibid.*, p. 120.

[19] *Ibid.*, p. 127.

[20] Pearson, p. 30, 31.

[21] Alex Dragnich and Slavko Todorovich, *Prelude to World War I: Balkan Wars and Serbo-Albanian Relations* (srpska-mreza.com/bookstore/kosovo5.htm, p.8.

[22] *Pearson* p. 32.

[23] Ismail Kemal Bey, *The Memoirs of Ismail Kemal Bey*, (London: Constable & Co., 1920) pp. 371-373.

[24] Swire, p. 183; Later King Fuad of Egypt.

[25] Ismail Kemal Bey, pp. 374, 375.

[26] Pearson, p. 31.

[27] *Ibid.*

[28] Swire, *Rise*, p.145.

[29] *Ibid.*

[30] *Ibid.*

[31] Fay, p. 442.

[32] Treadway, p. 121.

[33] Roderick McLean, *Royalty and Diplomacy in Europe* (Cambridge: Cambridge University Press, 2001) p. 66.

[34] Dragnich and Todorovich, pp. 5, 6.

[35] Robert K. Massie, *Dreadnought* (New York: Random House, 1991) p. 838.

[36] Lavender Cassels, The Archduke and the Assassin (New York: Stein & Day, 1985) p. 136.

[37] Churchill , p. 57.

[38] Young, pp. 54, 55.

[39] Hew Strachan, *The First World War, Vol. I, To Arms* (Oxford: Oxford University Press, 2001) pp. 55. 56. A krone was worth about $0.20 in 1912.

[40] Churchill, p. 58.

[41] Ferdinand Schevill, *A History of the Balkans* (New York: Dorset Press, 1991), p. 473.

[42] Grey, p. 252.

[43] Zara Steiner, *The Foreign Office and Foreign Polic*y, 1898-1914 (Cambridge: Cambridge University Press, 1969) p. 10.

[44] R. Bruce Lockhart, *British Agent* (New York: G. P. Putnam's Sons, 1933) p. 44; Grey, *Twenty-Five Years*, Vol. II, p. 238.

[45] Hendrick, p. 345.

[46] Fay, Vol. I, pp. 335, 341, 434, 442; Janne, p. 63; W. Bruce Lincoln, *In War's Dark Shadow* (New York: The Dial Press, 1983) p. 411.

[47] Grey, p. 253; Young, p. 34.

[48] *Ibid.*

[49] Fay, p. 442; Young, pp. 55, 56.

[50] Churchill, p. 57.

[51] Young, p. 6.

[52] Grey, p. 257.

[53] Treadwell, p. 129.

[54] Cowles, p. 37; Mitchell Garnett and James Godfrey, *Europe Since 1815* (New York: Appleton Century Crofts, 1947) p. 516; Nicholson, p. 213.

[55] Grey, p. 256.

[56] *Encyclopedia Britannica*, Vol. 10, 1961, ed., "Grey of Falloden", p 864.

[57] Young, pp. 4, 24, 28.

[58] *Ibid.*, pp. 49, 50.

[59] Rose, pp. 89, 90.

[60] *Ibid.*, p. 51; Grey, p. 265.

[61] Young, p. 49.

[62] Grey, Vol. II, p. 261.

[63] *Ibid.,*, p. 256.

[64] *Ibid.*, p. 257.

[65] Swire, *Rise*, p. xvii; Treadway, p. 130; Goslinga, p. 5.

[66] Goslinga, p. 6.

[67] Young, p. 63.

[68] Grey, p. 266.

[69] Young, pp. 67, 68.

[70] Swire, *Rise*, p. 147; Mehmed Bey Konitza, Rassik Dino, and Philip Nogga.

[71] Tomes, p. 19.

[72] Dragnich & Todorovich,*op.cit.*,pp. 13, 14.

[73] Pyrrhus J. Ruches, *Albania's Captives* (Chicago: Argonaut Inc., 1965) p.73.

[74] Strachan, p. 52.

[75] Lamar Cecil, *Wilhelm II*, Vol. 2, (Chapel Hill: The University of North Carolina Press, 1996) p. 188.

[76] Immanuel Geiss, *July, 1914* (New York: Charles Scribners Sons, 1967*)*, p. 44.

5 – 1913

[1] Kaiser to Czar, January 13, 1913, Isaac Don Levine, ed. *Letters from the Kaiser to the Czar*, (New York: Frederick A. Stokes, Co., 1920) p. 255.

[2] Cowles, p. 127.

[3] *Ibid.*

[4] *Ibid.*, p. 99.

[5] B. D., Vol. X, Part II (London: H.M.S.O., 1938), Rodd to Grey, January 6, 1913, p. 659.

[6] Shirer, p. 115.

[7] Shirer., p. 115.

[8] Pearson, p. 38.

[9] *The[London] Times*, January 30, 1913, p. 7

[10] Morton, p. 37.

[11] Pearson, p. 38.

[12] Cowles, p. 138.

[13] Morton, p. 39.

[14] Immanuel Geiss, *July 1914* (New York: Charles Scribner's Sons, 1967) pp. 43-45.

[15] Levine, p. 257.

[16] Pearson, p. 39; Gerolymatos, p. 223.

[17] Grey. P. 200.

[18] Fromkin, p. 88.

[19] Giles MacDonogh, *The Last Kaiser* (New York: St. Martin's Press, 2000) p. 140.

[20] Erich Raeder, *Grand Admiral* (Da Capo Press, 1960) p. 33.

[21] The Lady's Realm, An Illustrated Monthly Magazine (Vol. IV, May-October 1898), p. 175.

[22] Pearson, p. 39, *The (London) Times* , August 14, 1913, p. 6.

[23] Young, p. 61.

[24] Sir Rennell Rodd, *Social and Diplomatic Memories1902-1919*, Chapter VII Rome 1912-1913, (London: Edward Arnold & Co., 1925) p. 223.

[25] Treadway, pp. 135, 136.

[26] Swire, *Rise*, pp. 157-159.

[27] Nicolson, *King George*, p. 214.

[28] Cowles, p. 38.

[29] Grey, p. 259.

[30] *Ibid.,* p. 260.

[31] Helmreich, p. 332.

[32] Pearson, p. 40.
[33] *Ibid.,* pp. 40, 41.
[34] Helmreich, *The Serbs.*
[35] Treadway, p. 137.
[36] R. J. Crampton, *The Hollow Détente* (London: George Prior Publishers, 1979) p. 90.
[37] Pearson, p. 41.
[38] Pipinelis, pp. 49, 50.
[39] Pearson, p. 41.
[40] Treadway, p. 143.
[41] Carey, pp. 155, 156.
[42] Treadway, p. 142.
[43] Pearson, p. 42; Treadway, p. 144.
[44] Treadway, p. 145.
[45] Grey, p. 261.
[46] Dragnich & Todorovich, pp. 10, 11.
[47] Dimitrije Popovic, *Borba za narodno ujedingenje, 1909-1914*, Belgrade 1936, pp. 100, 102, cited in Dragnich and Todorovich, p. 9.
[48] Popovic, as cited in Dragnich and Todorovich, p. 103.

6 – WAR CLOUDS OVER SCUTARI

[1] Treadway, pp. 146, 147.
[2] *Ibid.,* p. 150.
[3] *Ibid.,* p. 151.
[4] *Ibid.,* p. 152.
[5] *Ibid.*
[6] Shirer, p. 115.
[7] Pearson, p. 42.
[8] Helmreich, p. 332.
[9] Treadway, pp. 155, 156.
[10] Pearson, p. 43.
[11] Swire, *Rise*, p. 179.
[12] George W. Gawrych, *The Crescent and the Eagle* (London: I. B. Taurus, 2006) p. 101.
[13] B. D. , Vol. X, Pt. II, Captain High Watson to Sir Edward Goschen, May 12, 1913, p. 699.
[14] Herbert A. Gibbons, *The New Map of Europe* (New York: The Century Co., 1914), pp. 360-365.
[15] Helmreich, p. 332.
[16] D. D., Paul Cambon (London) to Doumergue, May 28, 1914, No. 296.
[17] *L'Illustration*, June 14, 1913, p. 566.
[18] *Ibid.*
[19] Grey, p. 257.
[20] Pearson, p. 38.
[21] Virginia Cowles, p. 39.
[22] Swire, *Rise*, p. 173.
[23] Swire, *Rise*, p. xviii.
[24] Pearson, p. 43.

[25] *Ibid.,* p. 44.
[26] Alexander Baltzy and A. Williams Salomore, editors, *Readings in 20th Century European History* (New York: Appleton-Century-Crofts, Inc., 1950) p. 39.
[27] D. D., Sir Edward Grey to Sir F. Cartwright, July 4, 1913, Number 137, [31230].
[28] B. D., Vol. IX, p. 949n.
[29] Helmreich, p. 332.
[30] Swire, *Rise*, p. 173; Pearson, p. 44.
[31] B. D., p. 949n.
[32] Goslinga, p. 8.
[33] Goslinga, p. 8.
[34] *The (London) Times,* August 1, 1913, p. 7.
[35] Pearson, p. 45.
[36] Grey, pp. 256, 463.
[37] *The (London) Times,* December 5, 1913, p. 7.
[38] Helmreich, p. 333.
[39] Pearson, p. 46; *The (London) Times*, August 13, 1913, p. 20.
[40] Grey, p. 262.
[41] Grey, p.262.
[42] Tomes, Zog, p. 21.
[43] Young. p. 61.
[44] Grey, pp. 262, 264.
[45] Nicolson, *King George V*, p. 214.

7 - THE SEARCH FOR A KING

[1] Crampton, p. 119; *Wikipedia*, "Duke of Urach".
[2] Swire, *Rise*, p. 183.
[3] Crampton, pp. 119, 211 n53.
[4] Swire, *Rise*, p. 13.
[5] Marie, *Story*, p. 426.
[6] *The (London) Times,* January 7, 1914, p. 7.
[7] Albertini, *Vol. I*, p. 526.
[8] Sir Francis Bertie to Sir Edward Grey, February 3, 1913, F. O. 371/1789 No. 5182; Wikipedia, "Fuad I of Egypt"; William Stadiem, *Too Rich* (New York: Carroll & Graf Publishers, 1991) p. 103.
[9] British National Archives, Documents on Ahmed Fuad, February 4, 1913, No. 57821/5309.
[10] Sir Edward Grey to Sir Gerard Lowther, F. O. 371/1789, No. 5182.
[11] "*Kongresi Sqiptar I Triestes Vitit* 1913, http://ragovapress.blog.com/1803574/. translated by Suela Lesaj.
[12] Crampton, p. 211, n53.
[13] Christian Schmitz, , "*Fürst Wilhelm Prinz zu Wied in Internationalen Pressedarstellungen* (Maschinenschriftliche Magisterarbeit" [Baccalaureate thesis], (Universität Bochum, Germany 1991) p. 15.
[14] Infanta Eulalia, *Court Life*, pp. 71-76.
[15] Sir Francis Bertie to Sir Edward Grey, March 28, 1913, No. 155.
[16] *Ibid.*
[17] *Le Figaro*, March 21, 1913.

[18] *Le Figaro*, March 21, 1913; Edward Berenson, *The Trial of Madame Caillaux* (New York: The Notable Trials Library, 1995) pp. 238, 239.

[19] *Le Figaro*, April 28, 1913.

[20] F. O., 371/1806.

[21] Swire, *Rise*, pp. 147, 148.

[22] Dr. Gezim Alpion, quoting Baron Franz Nopcsa in "Baron Franz Nopcsa and His Ambition for the Albanian Throne," *BESA Journal*, Summer 2006, Vol. 6, No. 3, pp. 327-345.

[23] Schmitz, p. 13.

[24] Marie, *My Life*, p. 426; Tomes, p. 76.

[25] Schmitz, p. 13, n. 122; Tomes, p. 756.

[26] Tomes, p. 23.

[27] *Le Figaro*, April 28, 1913.

[28] Sir Francis Bertie to Sir Edward Grey, April 28, 1913, No. 217.

[29] British National Archives, *Documents on Ahmed Fuad, Duc de Montpensier and Edith Durham*, 1913, 1914, Minute, April 30, 1913, No. 19 781.

[30] Wikipedia, "Ferdinand d'Orleans (1884-1924)"

[31] Pearson, p. 42.

[32] Schmitz, p. 15.

[33] Wied, Friedrich Wilhelm zu Wied und Heinz Schwarz, *Wilhelm Fürst von Albanien, Prinz zu Wied*, (Wied website, 2006) p. 5.

[34] Geoffrey Bocca, *Kings Without Thrones* (New York: The Dial Press, 1959) p. 233.

[35] Schmitz, p. 16.

[36] Ismail Kemal Bey, p. 375.

[37] *Ibid.*, pp. 379, 380; Belfield in Heaton, p. xiii.

[38] Belfield, in Heaton, p. xiii.

[39] Pearson, p. 50; Marie, *Story*, p. 542.

[40] Gooch & Temperley, B, D., Vol. X, Pt. I.

[41] E. T. S. Dugdale, editor, *German Diplomatic Documents 1871-1914* Vol. IV (New York: Harper & Brothers, 1931), pp. 188, 189.

[42] Donald Hunt, "Sidelights on the Prussian Guard"; *Tradition, The Journal of the International Society of Military Collectors*, No. 60 (c. 1971) pp. 26, 33.

[43] *The New York Times*, December 14, 1913.

[44] Wied & Schwarz website, p. 4.

[45] Schmitz, p. 16.

[46] *Ibid.*, p. 17.

[47] Marie, *My Life*, p. 541.

[48] *Ibid.*

[49] Crampton, p. 119; Marie, *My Life*, p. 550; Marie, *Ordeal*, p. 51; Encyclopedia Britannica, Vol. 14, 1968 ed., Titu Maiorescu, p. 649.

[50] B. D., Barclay to Grey, Oct. 13, 1913, Vol. X, Part 1.

[51] Crampton, p. 119.

[52] *Ibid.*

[53] *The (London) Times*, Oct. 4, 1913, p. 5.

[54] Swire, *Rise*, p. 183.

[55] Schmitz, p. 17.

[56] Crampton, p. 119.

[57] Swire, *Rise*, p. 183.

[58] Crampton, p. 119.

[59] B. D., Vol. X, Part 1, October 30, 1913, p. 55, Barclay to Grey, notes by Nicolson.
[60] *Ibid.,* p.59, Barclay to Grey, notes by Nicolson.
[61] Schmitz, p. 18.
[62] *The (London) Times*, November 24, 1913, p. 7; Pearson, p. 50; Belfield in Heaton, p. xiii; Ismail Kemal, p. 380.
[63] Crampton, p. 154.
[64] B. D., Vol. X, Pt. 1, p. 81.
[65] *Ibid.*
[66] *Ibid.,* p. 83.
[67] *Ibid.,* p. 85.
[68] Wied and Schwarz, p. 7.
[69] B. D., Vol. X, Pt 1, Goschen to Grey, Dec. 2, 1913, p. 71; *The (London) Times,* December 5, 1913, p. 7.
[70] Schmitz, p. 18.
[71] B. D., Vol. X, Pt. 1, Goschen to Grey, Dec. 15, 1913, p. 79.
[72] *Ibid.,* Dec. 20, 1913, p. 80.
[73] A French Franc was equal to about 20 U. S. cents.
[74] Crampton, p. 155.
[75] B. D., Vol. X, Pt. 1, Buchanan to Grey, Dec, 26, 1913, p. 86.
[76] Crampton, p. 155.
[77] Schmitz, p. 18.
[78] *The Illustrated London News*, March 7, 1914, p. 1.
[79] *The New York Times*, Dec. 14, 1913.

8 – THE POT BOILS

[1] Goslinga, p. 10.
[2] *The (London) Times,* Sept, 2, 1913, p. 5.
[3] *Ibid.,* Sept. 19, 1913, p. 5.
[4] Georgina Howell, *Gertrude Bell, Queen of the Desert, Shaper of Nations* (New York: Farrar Straus & Giroux, 2006) pp. 129-140.
[5] Charles Doughty-Wylie, Letters to Gertrude Bell, 1913 (University of Newcastle, England, Gertrude Bell Collection.)
[6] Doughty to Bell (n. d.)
[7] *Ibid.,* Sept. 3.1913.
[8] *The (London) Times*, Sept. 23, 1913, p. 5.
[9] Swire, *Rise*, p. 169; *The* (London) *Times*, Nov. 18, 1913, p. 5.
[10] Fay, p. 455.
[11] Goslinga, pp. 10, 11.
[12] Crampton, p. 211, n. 45; Swire, *Rise*, p. 174; Goslinga, p. 6; www.worldstatesmen.org/Albania.htm.
[13] Swire, *Rise*, p. 182.
[14] Pearson, pp. 46.
[15] *The (London) Times*, Jan. 17, 1914, p. 5.
[16] Carnegie Endowment for International Peace, 1914 Report, The Other Balkan Wars (Washington: 1993 reprint) pp. 1, 6.
[17] Swire, *Rise*, p. 176; *The (London) Times*, Sept. 25, 1913, p. 5.
[18] *The (London) Times*, August 25, 1913, p. 6.
[19] Swire, *Rise*, pp. 175, 176.

[20] Fay, Vol. I, Chargé Kühlmann to Bethmann, Sept. 24, 1913, p. 466.

[21] *The New York Times*, September 23, 1913, p. 4.

[22] Pearson, pp. 47, 48.

[23] *Ibid.;* Vladimir Dedijer, p. 155.

[24] Doughty to Bell, Sept. 22, 1913; Swire, *Rise*, p. 169.

[25] *Ibid.*

[26] Doughty to Bell, Sept. 25, 1913.

[27] *Ibid.*, Sept. 29, 1913.

[28] *Ibid.*, Oct. 6, 1913.

[29] Dedijer, p. 156.

[30] *The (London) Times*, Oct. 1-2, 1913, p. 5.

[31] *Ibid.*, Oct. 14, 1913, p. 5.

[32] Morton, p. 114.

[33] Doughty to Bell, Oct. 9, 1913.

[34] Pipinelis, pp. 56, 57.

[35] Charles Haskins and Robert Lord, *Some Problems of the Peace Conference* (Cambridge, Harvard University Press, 1920) p. 278.

[36] Swire, *King Zog*, p. 235; Tomes, p.150.

[37] Fay. p. 465.

[38] Ruches, p. 77; Pearson, p. 49.

[39] *The (London) Times*, September 2, 1913, p. 5.

[40] Fay, Vol. I, p. 459..

[41] Ruches, pp. 75, 76.

[42] Swire, *Rise*, p. 171.

[43] Doughty to Bell, October 12(?), 1913.

[44] Crampton, p. 130

[45] *Ibid.*

[46] Helmreich, *Diplomacy*, p. 418.

[47] Fay, Vol. I, pp. 472, 473.

[48] *Ibid.*, p. 469.

[49] Churchill, p. 69.

[50] Fay, Vol. I, pp. 466-473.

[51] *Ibid.*, p. 472, n. 208.

9 – ULTIMATUM

[1] Fay, p. 23.

[2] Morton, p. 126.

[3] Fritz Fischer, *War of Illusions*, (New York: W. W. Norton & Co., Inc., 1975) p. 220.

[4] Swire, *Rise*, p. 179.

[5] Fay, p. 474.

[6] Treadway, p. 162; Pearson, p. 49; Swire, *Rise*, p. 179.

[7] Fay, p.474.

[8] Steiner, p. 146.

[9] Morton, p. 126.

[10] *Ibid.*

[11] Churchill, p. 58.

[12] Strachan, p. 59; Dedijer, p. 158.

[13] Fritz Fischer, pp. 220-223.

10 – SETTING THE BOUNDARIES

[1] Helmreich, p. 420.
[2] *The (London) Times*, October 28, 1913; Marie, *Story*, p. 276.
[3] Crampton, p. 128.
[4] Doughty to Bell, Oct. 31, 1913,
[5] Crampton, p. 159.
[6] *The (London) Times*, November 18, 1913, p. 7.
[7] Doughty to Bell, Nov. 21, 1913.
[8] Pipinelis, p. 57.
[9] Doughty to Bell, Nov. 23, 1913.
[10] Pearson, p. 50; Swire, *Rise*, pp. 171, 172.
[11] Crampton, pp. 127-130.
[12] Doughty to Bell, December 19, 1913.
[13] *Ibid.,* December 23, 1913.
[14] Stephen Constant, *Foxy Ferdinand* (New York: Franklin Watts, 1980) p. 289.
[15] Mark Sullivan, *Our Times, 1900-1925*, Vol. IV (New York: Charles Scribners Sons, 1932) p. 434.

11 – PREPARATIONS

[1] Belfield, p. 178; Goslinga, p. 12.
[2] *Ibid.,* p. 17.
[3] *Ibid.*
[4] Goslinga, p. 52; Heaton, p. 95
[5] Heaton, p. 95.
[6] Pipinelis, pp. 12, 13; B. D., Gooch & Temperley, p. 58.
[7] G. D., Grey to von Kühlmann, Dec. 15, 1913.
[8] B. D., Rodd to Grey, Vol. X, pt. 1, Dec. 31, 1913, p. 90.
[9] Pipinelis, p. 11.
[10] G. D., Waldhausen to Bethmann, December 17, 1913.
[11] Heaton, p. 141; A. A., Nicolo Martinaj to Prenk Bib Doda, Dec. 12, 1913.
[12] B. D., Vol. X, pt. 1, de Bunsen to Grey, p. 84.
[13] Crampton, p. 211, n. 45.
[14] Jules Witcover, Sabotage at Black Tom (Chapel Hill: Algonquin Books, 1989), pp. 236, 316.
[15] Nadolny to Bethmann Hollweg, Nov. 23, 1913, quoted in Wied, *Denkschrift*, Appendix II.
[16] Pearson, p. 51; *The (London) Times*, Nov. 29, 1913, p. 7.
[17] *Ibid.,* Nov. 28, 1913, p. 7.
[18] *Ibid.,* Jan. 7, 1914, p 7.
[19] Belfield in Heaton, pp. xxi, xxviii, xix; Heaton, p. 1.
[20] Heaton, p. 2.
[21] *Ibid.,* p. xxv.

[1] *The (London) Times*, Jan. 7, 8, 1914, pp. 7,5; Swire, *Rise*, p. 186; Goslinga, pp. 20, 21.

[2] *The (London) Times*, Jan. 17, 1914, p. 5.

[3] Nadolny to Bethmann-Hollweg, January 16, 1914, quoted in Wied's *Denkschrift*, Appendix III, p. 69.

[4] Belfield in Heaton, pp. xiv, xv.

[5] *The New York Times*, March 8, 1914, Section III, p. 1.

[6] B. N. A., William Schaefer to Sir Ralph Paget, Jan. 12 to 16, 1914; Claud Russell to William Schaefer, Feb. 2, 1914, F.O. 371/1892.

[7] Wied, pp 15, 16.

[8] Morton, pp. 162, 163.

[9] Gerard, *My Four Years*, p. 52; Louis Ferdinand, *The Rebel Prince* (Chicago: Henry Regnery Co., 1952) p. 234; Hunt, p. 33.

[10] Gerard, *My Four Years*, p. 251.

[11] Princess Viktoria Louise, p. 83.

[12] Wilhelm II, p. 164.

[13] Ancient Greek ruling council of aristocrats.

[14] Wilhelm II, pp. 165-169.

[15] Heaton, pp. 2, 3.

[16] Crampton, p. 157.

[17] Bernd Fisher, p. 8.

[18] D. D., Barrère (Rome) to Doumergue, *3e, Serie Tome IX* (Jan. – 16 Mar, 1914) No. 67, Jan. 12, 1914.

[19] D. D., Manneville, Chargé (Berlin) to Doumergue, *3e Serie, Tome IX*, Jan. 13, 1914, No. 67.

[20] B. D., De Bunsen to Nicolson, Jan. 16, 1914, Vol. X, pt. 1, p. 90.

[21] Crampton, p. 156.

[22] *Ibid.*

[23] *The New York Times*, Mar. 8, 1914.

[24] *The (London) Times*, Jan. 19, 1914, p. 7.

[25] B. D., Lamb to Crowe, Jan, 17, 1914, Vol. X, pt, 1, pp. 92, 93; Swire, *Rise*, p. 128.

[26] Swire, *Zog*, p. 19.

[27] Heaton, pp. 3-5.

[28] *Ibid.*

[29] *The New York TImes*, Jan. 6, 1914, p. 1.

[30] B. D., Jan. 20, 1914, Vol. X, pt. 1, p. 94.

[31] *The (London) Times*, Jan. 22, 1914, p. 7.

[32] B. D., Jan. 21, 1914, Vol. X, pt. 1, p. 95.

[33] B. D., Lamb to Grey, Jan. 22, 1914, Vol. X, pt. 1, p. 96; Crampton, p. 155.

[34] Swire, *Rise*, pp. 186, 187.

[35] *The (London) Times*, Jan. 24, 1914, p. 7.

[36] *Ibid.*, Jan. 29, 1914, p. 5; worth about $0.044 in 1894, its value fluctuated. *Lexic.us/definition of/pilasters* October 23, 2008.

[37] G. D., German Foreign Office note, unsigned, Jan. 2, 1914.

[38] G. D., State Secretary of Reichschatzamt to Auswärtiges Amt, January 26, 1914.

[39] D. D., Blondel to Doumergue, *3e Serie, Tome IX*, January 28, 1914, no. 19.180.

[40] Goslinga, p. 48, (apparently quoting Buchberger.)

[41] G. D., Pourtalès to Auswärtiges Amt, January 27, 1914.

[42] *The (London) Times*, January 28, 1914, p.6.

[43] G. D., Flotow to Auswärtiges Amt, January 29, 1914.

[44] *The (London) Times*, January 30, 1914, p. 5.

[45] *Ibid.,* February 2, 1914, p. 5.

[46] *Ibid.,* February 6, 1914, p. 5.

[47] G. D., von Tschirschky to Foreign Office, February ?, 1914; Crampton, p. 156.

[48] B. D., Vol. X, pt. 1, p 97.

[49] Heaton, p. 6.

[50] A franc was apparently worth about 20 cents U.S.; Wied, *Denkschrift*, Appendix IX.

[51] Wied, Appendix IV, p.74; Swire, Rise, p.194.

[52] G. D., Feb. 7, 1914, unsigned copy of letter to Wied.

[53] Durham, *Letters*, pp. 58, 59; Swire, *Rise*, p. 173.

[54] *The New York Times*, May 31, 1914, Sec. III, p. 3.

13 – THE TRAVELING PRINCE

[1] D. D., *Tome IX* (1 Jan. – 16 Mar. 1914) No. 239, Doumergue to Cambon in London, Feb. 7, 1914.

[2] D. D., *Tome IX*, Doumergue to all French Ambassadors, Feb. 8, 1914, No. 242.

[3] Crampton, p. 155.

[4] *The (London) Times*, Feb. 9, 1914, p. 5.

[5] *Ibid.*

[6] *Ibid.*, Feb. 11, 1914, p. 5.

[7] D. D., *Tome X* (1 Jan. – 16 Mar. 1914) No. 337, Barrère (Rome) to Doumergue, Feb. 20, 1914.

[8] *The (London) Times*, Feb. 11, 1914, p. 5.

[9] G. D., Flotow to Berlin, Feb. 11, 1914.

[10] *The (London) Times*, Feb. 12, 1914, p. 5.

[11] Rodd, Ch. VII (Internet Sept. 25, 2000) p. 15.

[12] *The (London) Times*, Feb. 12, 1914, p. 7; Feb. 11, 1914, p.5

[13] *Ibid.,* Feb. 14, 1914, p. 7,

[14] G. D., Flotow to Berlin, Feb. 11, 1914.

[15] G. D., Millberg?, Royal Prussian Minister in Rome to Bethmann-Hollweg, Feb. 11, 1914.

[16] B. D., Vol X, pt. 1, Feb. 12, 1914, p. 99.

[17] *The (London) Times*, Feb. 13, 1914, p.5.

[18] *Ibid.,* Feb. 11, 1914, p. 5.

[19] *Ibid.,* Feb. 13, 1914, p. 5.

[20] B. D., Vol. X, Pt. 1, Feb. 12, 1914, p. 99.

[21] G. D., von Tschirschky to Berlin, February 14, 1914; Heaton, pp. 7, 8; *The (London) Times*, Feb. 14, 1914, p. 7; *The (London) Times*, Feb. 16, 1914, p. 7; Heaton, p. 6.

[22] Ruches, p. 81; *The (London) Times*, Feb. 14, 1914, p. 7.

[23] *Ibid.,* Feb. 16, 1914, p. 7

[24] *Ibid.,* Feb. 18, 1914, p. 8.

[25] G. D., German Embassy, Rome (signature illegible) to Berlin, Feb. 17, 1914.

[26] *The (London) Times*, Feb. 19, 1914, p. 7; B. D., Vol. X, Pt. 1, Grey to Goschen and King George, Feb. 18, 1914, pp. 100, 101; Heaton, p. 8; G. D., Lichnowsky to Foreign Office, Feb. 19, 1914.

[27] *The (London) Times*, Feb. 20, 1914, p. 7.

[28] *Ibid.,* Feb. 20, 1914, p. 7.

[29] Heaton, p. 9; *The (London) Times*, Feb. 29, 1914, pp. 5, 7; *The (London) Times*, Feb. 21, 1914, p. 7; B. D., Vol. X, Pt. 1, George Grahame to Grey, Feb. 20, 1914, p. 102; G. D., Schoen to Bethmann-Hollweg, Feb. 20, 1914.

[30] *The New York Times*, Jan. 7, 1922, May 19, 1913, Nov. 29, 1912.

[31] *Ibid.,* Jan, 7, 1922.

[32] Heaton, p. 9.

[33] B. D., Vol. X, Pt. 1, Grey to Bertie, Feb. 19, 1914, p. 101.

[34] B. D., Vol. X, Pt. 1, Grey to Bertie, Mar. 4, 1914, p. 105.

14 – THE CEREMONY

[1] *The (London) Times*, Feb. 23, 1914, pp. 5, 7; Feb. 22, 1914, p. 7; *The New York Times*, Feb. 22, 1914, Sec. III, p. 2; Heaton, pp. 12-14; G. D., (initialed "St. S.") May 29, 1914; D. D., Dumaine (Vienna) to Doumergue, Feb. 22, 1914, No. 343; Friedrich Wilhelm zu Wied und Heinz Schwarz, *Wilhelm Fürst von Albanien, Prinz zu Wied*, (Wied website), 20060, pp. 1, 7.

15 – BEWARE OF GREEKS

[1] B. D., Vol. X, Pt. 1, Sir F. Elliot to Grey, Feb. 22, 1914, p. 103.

[2] *The (London) Times*, Feb. 23, 1914, p. 7.

[3] G. D., Goschen to von Jagow, Feb. 24, 1914.

[4] *The (London) Times*, Feb. 26, 1914, p. 7.

[5] G. D., Szögyény to Wied, (undated).

[6] Heaton, pp. 9, 10.

[7] *The (London) Times*, Feb. 7, 1914, p. 7.

[8] Ruches, p. 80.

[9] *The (London) Times*, Feb. 27, 1914, p. 7; Feb. 26, 1914, p. 5; Ruches, p. 82.

[10] *The (London) Times*, Feb. 27, 1914, p. 7; Feb. 26, 1914, p. 5; Ruches, p. 82.

[11] *The (London) Times*, Mar. 2, 1914, p. 5.

[12] Ruches, p. 84.

[13] G. D., Winckel to Auswärtiges Amt, Feb. 26, 1914.

[14] G. D., Pourtalès to Auswärtiges Amt, Feb. 28, 1914; Heaton, pp. 10, 11, 175, n5; *The (London) Times*, Mar. 2, 1914, p. 5.

[15] B. D., Vol. X, Pt. 1, p. 104.

[16] Ruches, p. 81.

[17] *The (London) Times*, Mar. 3, 1914, p. 5.

[18] *Ibid.*

[19] Wied, pp. 50, 51.

[20] *Ibid.,* pp. 1-14.

[21] *Ibid.,* p. 16.

[22] *The (London) Times*, Mar. 11, 1914, p. 7; Mar. 12, 1914, p. 5.

[23] *Ibid.,* Mar. 11, 1914, p. 7; Mar. 12, 1914, p. 5.

[24] Edith Durham, Albania and the Albanians, p. 28.

[25] Swire, *Zog*, p. 104.

[26] D. D., *Tome X*, Descas (Belgrade) to Doumergue, Jun. 1, 1914, No. 317.

[27] B. D., Vol. X, Pt. 1, Grey to Elliot, Mar. 2, 1914, p. 105.

[28] Ruches, p. 83.

[29] *Ibid.,* pp. 86, 87.

[30] *Ibid.,* pp. 86, 87.

[31] *The (London) Times*, Mar. 4, 1914, p. 5.

[32] Ruches, pp. 88, 89.

[33] B. D., Vol. X, Pt. 1, Elliot to Grey, Mar. 5, 1914, p. 108.

[34] Ruches, p. 88.

[35] *The (London) Times*, Feb. 26, 1914, p. 5.

16 – TRIESTE

[1] *The (London) Times*, Mar. 6, 1914, Heaton, pp. 16, 17.

[2] Belfield in Heaton, p. xxiv.

[3] Heaton, pp. 16-18.

[4] *The (London) Times*, Mar. 9, 1914, pl 8.

[5] *Ibid.,* Mar. 6, 1914, p. 5.

17 – ARRIVAL

[1] The (London) Times, February 12, 1914, p.7; March 19, 1914, p.7; May 20, 1914, p.7; June 16, 1914, p. 7; Heaton, pp. 18-22; de Szinyei-Mrese, pp. 151,156,161; Tomes, pp. 116,117; Oakley-Hill, pp. 4,6,9; B. D. Vol X, Pt 1, Lamb to Grey, March 7, 1914, p. 107

[2] Oakley-Hill, p.11.

[3] Robert D. Ball and Paul Peters, Military Medals & Orders of the United States and Europe (Atglen: Schiffer Military/Aviation History, 1994) p 9.

[4] Morton, p. 164.

[5] Heaton, pp. 18-22, 33,79-87; Belfield in Heaton, pp. xxvi, xxviii, xxix; *The (London) Times*, Feb. 12, 1914, p. 7, Mar. 19, 1914, p. 7, May 20, 1914, p. 7; Ismail Kemal Bey, pp. 380-382; Durham, *Albania and the Albanians*, pp. 58, 59; Morton, p. 163; Oakley-Hill, p. 3.

18 – THE SHORT HONEYMOON

[1] Heaton, p. 25.

[2] *Ibid.,* pp. 33, 34.

[3] *The (London) Times*, Apr. 29, 1914, p. 7; Sturdza spelled his name as Burghelea in his book, *Suicide*, p.13.

[4] Heaton, p. 30.

[5] D. D., *Tome IX*, Krajewski (delegate) to Doumergue, Mar. 9, 1914, No. 424.

[6] Heaton, p. 31.

[7] G. D., Schneider to Foreign Office, Mar. 9, 1914.

[8] Wied, p. 17.

[9] B. D., Vol. X, Pt. 1, Elliot to Grey, Mar. 8, 1914, p. 108.

[10] *The (London) Times*, March 12, 1914, p. 5; Goslinga, p. 24.

[11] Ruches, p. 88; Goslinga, pp. 24, 25.

[12] A.D. Freizi to Wied, March 11, 12, 1914; De Veer to Princely Chancellery, Mar. 15, 1914.

[13] *The (London) Times*, Mar. 14, 1914, p. 7.

[14] Swire, *Rise*, p. 200.

[15] *Ibid.*, p. 201.

[16] G. D., unsigned report (Warburg?) to Berlin, Mar. 17, 1914; Swire, *Rise*, p. 200; B. D., Vol. X, Pt. 1, Lamb to Grey, Mar. 17, 1914, p. 111; Belfield in Heaton, p. 32; Pearson, pp. 60, 61; *The (London) Times*, Mar. 19, 1914, p. 7, Mar. 20, 1914, p. 5; Durham, *Letters*, p. 58.

[17] *Ibid.*, Mar. 18, 1914, p. 59.

[18] G. D., Commission Minutes, Mar. 19, 1914.

[19] G. D., Turkhan Pasha to Mehdi Bey, Mar. 31, 1914.

[20] *The (London) Times*, Mar. 23, 1914, p. 7.

[21] Ruches, pp. 89, 90.

[22] Goslinga, p. 46.

[23] *Ibid.*, p. 48.

[24] *The (London) Times*, Apr. 6, 1914, p. 7.

[25] Ruches, p. 78.

[26] Swire, *Rise*, p. 202, 203.

[27] A gold coin, worth 20 francs, containing 5.80 grams of gold, *Wikipedia, Napoleon (coin)*.

[28] *The (London) Times*, Mar. 23, 1914, p. 7.

[29] Heaton, p. 31, *The (London) Times*, Mar. 31, 1914, p. 7.

[30] *Ibid.*, Mar, 14, 1914, p. 7; Mar. 30, 1914, p. 7; Swire, *Rise*, pp. 203-205; D. D. Vol. X, Nos. 22, 38, Krajewski to Doumergue, Mar. 24, 1914.

[31] Morton, p. 169.

[32] D. D., Vol. X, No. 1, Krajewski (Valona ICC) to Doumergue, Mar. 17, 1914; Goslinga, p. 24.

[33] *The (London) Times*, Mar. 30, 1914, p 7; Mar. 31, 1914, p. 7; D. D., Vol. X, Nos. 22, 38, Krajewski to Doumergue, Mar. 24, 1914; *The (London) Times*, Apr. 9. 1914, p. 7.

[34] Wied, p.18; D. D., 3e Serie, Tome X, 17 Mar. – 23 July, 1914) Paris: Imprimerie Nationale, 1926) Krajewski to Doumergue, Apr. 6, 1914, No, 81; Swire, *Rise*, p. 238; *The (London) Times*, Apr. 16, 1914, p 7.

[35] *Ibid.*, Apr 6, 1914, p 7; Apr, 8, 1914, p. 7; Heaton, p. 34; Goslinga, p. 25.

[36] Wied, p. 18.

[37] *The (London) Times*, April 6, 1914, p 7.

[38] Redlich, p. 521.

[39] B. D., Vol. X, Part II, Rodd, (Rome) to Grey, Mar. 30, 1914, p. 643.

[40] D. D., *Tome X*, No. 47, Cambon (Berlin) to Doumergue, Mar. 30, 1914.

[41] B. D. Vol. X, Part I, Apr, 14, 1914, de Bunsen to Grey, p. 112.

[42] Laurence Lafore, *The Long Fuse* (Philadelphia: J. P. Lippincott, Co., 1965) p. 193.

[43] Goslinga, p. 25.

[44] *The (London) Times*, April 9, 1914, p. 7.

[45] G. D., von Treutler to Berlin, April 6, 1914.

[46] *Ibid.*, Zimmerman to von Treutler, April 9, 1914.

[47] *Ibid.*, Nadolny to Bethmann Hollweg, April 10, 1914.

[48] Cecil, p. 197.

[49] *The (London) Times*, April 8, 1914, p. 7; *The (London) Times*, April 10, 1914, p. 7.

[50] A. D., telegram to Wied, April 8, 1914; Swire, *Rise*, p. 269.

[51] *The (London) Times*, April 14, 1914, p. 7; April 6, 1914, p 7.

[52] *Ibid.*, April 14, 1914, p. 7.

[53] Wied, p. 23.

[54] 10 kilometre zone; G. D., Vol X, Pt. I, pp. 92, 93, Lamb to Grey, Jan. 17, 1914, Rodd to Grey, Apr. 21, 1914, p. 112.

[55] *The (London) Times*, April 11, 1914, p. 7; Swire, *Rise*, p. 186.

[56] *The (London) Times*, April 20, 1914, p. 7.

[57] *Ibid.*, April 25, 1914, p. 7.

[58] B. D., Vol. X, Part I, Grey to Bertie, May, 5, 1914, pp. 114, 115.

[59] Morton, p. 172.

[60] The (London) Times, April 28, 1914, p.7.

[61] *Ibid.*, April 14, 1914, p. 7.

[62] Morton, pp. 175, 176.

[63] Heaton, pp. 37, 38.

[64] *Ibid.*, p. 36.

[65] *Ibid.*, pp. 36, 37.

[66] *The (London) Times*, April 16, 1914, p. 7; April 20, 1194, p. 7

[67] B. D., Vol. X, Part II, p. 780; Sir George Buchanan to Sir Edward Grey; F. O. 15312/15312/14/38, No. 100.

[68] *The (London) Times*, April 18, 1914, p. 7.

[69] *Ibid.*, April 20, 1914, p. 7.

[70] B. D., Vol. X, Part I, Sir Rennell Rodd to Grey, April 12, 1914, p. 112.

[71] *The (London) Times*, April 28, 1914, p. 7.

[72] *Ibid.*

[73] Quote from *L'Illustration* June 14, 1913, p.566.

[74] Heaton, p. 43; de Jessen, *L'Illustration,* June 14, 1913, p. 566.

[75] Heaton, pp. 40-43.

[76] Swire, *King Zog*, p. 202.

[77] Heaton, pp. 43-45.

[78] *Ibid.*, pp. 38, 39.

[79] *The (London) Times*, May 4, 1914, p. 7

[80] *Ibid.*, May 8, 1914, p. 7; Swire, *Rise*, pp. 221, 222,

[81] Goslinga, p. 26.

[82] *The (London) Times*, May 4, 1914, p. 7.

[83] G. D., Nadolny to Foreign Office, May 4, 1914.

[84] *Ibid.*, Nadolny to Bethmann, April 6, 1914.

[85] *Ibid.*, Warburg to Bethmann, May 15, 1914.

[86] D. D. *3e, Serie Tome X*, Doumergue to de Fontenay, May 19, 1914, No. 251.

[87] Ruches, p. 91.

[88] Goslinga, p. 26.

[89] *Ibid.*, p. 27.

[90] Belfield in Heaton, p. xxv.

[91] Morton, p. 208.

[92] Heaton, pp. 47-49, Swire, *Rise*, p. 204.

[93] Wied, p. 18; *The (London) Times*, May 21, 1914, p. 7.

[94] Swire, *King Zog*, p. 155.

[95] *The (London) Times*, May 13, 1914, p. 7.

[96] *Ibid.,* May 14, 1914, p. 7.
[97] Goslinga, p. 29.
[98] *Ibid.,* pp. 51, 52.
[99] Belfield in Heaton, p. xxv.
[100] Ruches, p. 94.

19 – THE PLOT THICKENS

[1] *The (London) Times,* May 28, 1914; Swire, *Rise,* pp. 210, 211; Pipinelis, p. 31.
[2] Heaton, pp. 51-56.
[3] Swire, *Rise,* p. 207; Heaton, pp. 64-66.
[4] Wied, p. 18; *The (London) Times,* May 28, 1914, p. 7.
[5] Goslinga, p. 30.
[6] *The (London) Times,* May 28, 1914, p. 7.
[7] Heaton, pp. 60, 61; Swire, *Rise,* p. 207.
[8] Goslinga, p. 30.
[9] Swire, *Rise,* p. 207.
[10] Heaton, pp. 60, 61; *The (London) Times,* May 28, 1914, p. 7; Wied, pp. 19, 20.
[11] Goslinga, p. 30.
[12] Heaton, p. 61.
[13] *Ibid.,* pp. 64-66.
[14] B. D., Vol. X, Pt. 1, Lamb to Grey, May 19, 1914, pp. 115, 116.
[15] *The (London) Times,* May 29, 1914, p. 7.
[16] Swire, *Rise,* p. 208.
[17] *Ibid.*
[18] B. D., Vol. X, Pt. 1, Lamb to Grey, May 19, 1914, pp. 115, 116; Heaton, p. 61; D. D., *Tome X,* Krajewski to Doumergue, May 19, 1914, no. 251.
[19] Goslinga, p. 30.
[20] B. D., Vol. X, Pt. I, Lamb to Grey, May 19, 1914, pp. 115, 116.
[21] Heaton, pp. 64-66; *The (London) Times,* May 29, 1914, p. 7.
[22] *Ibid.*
[23] *Ibid.,* May 20, 1914, p. 7.
[24] Heaton, pp. 64-66; Wied, p. 18.
[25] Heaton, pp. 64-66.
[26] Swire, *Rise,* p. 208.
[27] Wied, p. 19.
[28] *Ibid.*
[29] Bonsal, p. 71.

20 – AFTERMATH

[1] Goslinga, p. 30.
[2] *Ibid.*
[3] Heaton, pp. 66-69; *The (London) Times,* May 21, 1914, p. 7.
[4] *Ibid;* Goslinga, p. 32.
[5] *The New York Times,* May 22, 1914, p.8.
[6] *The (London) Times,* May 20, 1914, p.7; Dedijer, p. 119.
[7] *The (London) Times,* May 22, 1914, p. 7.

[8] Belfield in Heaton, p. xxvi.
[9] *Ibid.*, p. xxxvii.
[10] B. D., Vol. X, Pt. I, Grey to Lamb, May 20, 1914, p. 116.
[11] *The (London) Times*, May 22, 1914, p. 7.
[12] West, p. 243.
[13] B. D., Vol. X, Pt. II, Goschen to Nicolson, May 23, 1914, p. 793.
[14] *Ibid.,* Vol. X, Pt. II, Goschen to Grey, May 22, 1914, p. 793.

21 – COMPLICATIONS

[1] Goslinga, p. 32; Heaton, pp. 70, 71; Swire, *Rise*, p. 212.
[2] Goslinga, p. 33.
[3] *Ibid.*
[4] Swire, *Rise*, p. 212.
[5] *Ibid.,* p. 210.
[6] Heaton, pp. 72-74, 78.
[7] B. D., Vol. X, Pt. I, Lamb to Grey, May 22, 1914, p. 117.
[8] *The (London) Times*, May 27, 1914, p. 7.

22 – DISGRACE

[1] D. D., *Tome X*, Krajewski to Doumergue, May 25, 1914, No. 280.
[2] *The (London) Times*, June 1, 1914, p. 7; Heaton, pp. 79-81.
[3] Wied, pp. 9, 10; Heaton, pp. 79-81.
[4] Wied, p. 9.
[5] Heaton, pp, 79-81; Goslinga, p. 34; D. D., *Tome X,* Krajewski to Doumergue, May 25, 1914, No. 280.
[6] Goslinga, p. 34.
[7] Heaton, pp. 79-81; D. D., *Tome X,* Krajewski to Doumergue, May 25, 1914, No. 280.
[8] *The (London) Times*, May 25, 1914, p. 7.
[9] Heaton, p. 81.
[10] Goslinga, p. 34.

23 – PICKING UP THE PIECES

[1] Goslinga, p. 34.
[2] Heaton, pp. 82-85.
[3] D. D., *Tome X*, Fontenay to Doumergue, June 1, 1914, No. 320.
[4] *Ibid.,* Fontenay (Durazzo) to Doumergue, May 28, 1914, No. 299.
[5] B. D., Vol. X, Pt. I, Grey to Lamb, May 25, 1914, p. 116.
[6] Crampton, p. 158.
[7] *The (London) Times*, May 26, 1914, p. 7; May 27, 1914, p. 7.
[8] D. D., Tome X, Krajewski to Doumergue, May 25, 1914, No. 280.
[9] *Ibid.,* No. 281.
[10] *The (London) Times*, May 28, 1914, p. 7.
[11] Heaton, pp. 86, 87.
[12] G. D., Nadolny to Bethmann, May 29, 1914; Swire, *Rise*, p. 209; Heaton, p. 87.
[13] *Ibid.,* p. 89.
[14] D. D., Tome X, Fontenay to Doumergue, May 29, 1914, Nos. 301, 303.

[15] G. D., Flotow to Bethmann, May 28, 1914.

[16] Goslinga, p. 34.

[17] *Ibid.,* pp. 37, 38.

[18] *Ibid.,* p. 38.

[19] *Ibid.*

[20] *The (London) Times*, June 1, 1914, p. 7.

[21] D. D., *Tome X,* De Manneville to Doumergue, May 30, 1914, No. 308.

[22] *The (London) Times*, May 29, 1914, p. 8.

[23] *Ibid.,* June 2, 1914, p. 7.

[24] *The (London) Times*, May 28, 1914, p.7.

[25] Swire, *Rise*, p. 210.

24 – FRICTION

[1] Belfield in Heaton, p. xxiv.

[2] *Ibid.,* p. xxv.

[3] *The (London) Times*, June 1, 1914, p. 7.

[4] G. D., Nadolny to Berlin, June 3, 1914.

[5] *Ibid.,* Nadolny to Von Jagow, June 3, 1914.

[6] *Ibid.,* (U. St. S.) = *Unter Staats Secretar?* June 15, 1914.

[7] Rappaport, *Arbengau.*

25 – INTRIGUE AND STRATEGIES

[1] Heaton, p. 91.

[2] *The (London) Times*, June 4, 1914, p. 7.

[3] *Ibid.,* June 5, 1914, p. 7.

[4] *Ibid.,* June 8, 1914, p. 7.

[5] Wied, p. 21.

[6] Heaton, pp. 92-94; Goslinga, p. 41; *The (London) Times*, June 26, 1914, p. 7.

[7] In the 1937 and 1952 films of *The Prisoner of Zenda*, the picaresque villain, Rupert of Hentzau, makes a very similar escape.

[8] Heaton, pp. 92-94; Goslinga, p. 41; *The (London) Times*, June 8, 1914, p. 7; Wied, p. 21.

[9] Goslinga, p. 41; Rodd, p. 10; Swire, *Rise*, p. 217.

[10] *The (London) Times*, June 8, 1914, p. 7.

[11] Wied, p. 22.

[12] *The (London) Times*, June 11, 1914, p.7.

[13] Heaton, p. 92.

[14] *The (London) Times*, June 6, 1914, p. 7.

[15] Heaton, pp. 126-128.

[16] *The (London) Times*, July 17, 1914, p. 7; Belfield in Heaton, p. 180.

[17] *The (London) Times*, July 16, 1914, p. 7; Belfield in Heaton, p. 177.

[18] In an interview with the English paper, he managed to offend both the British and the Germans.

[19] Hendrick, pp. 291-293.

[20] Swire, *Rise*, p.217.

[21] B. D., Vol. X, Pt. 1, Grey to Rodd, June 4, 1914, pp. 118, 119.

[22] Crampton, p. 158.

[23] Albertini, Vol. I., pp. 525, 526.

[24] *Ibid.*, p. 526.

[25] B. D., Vol. X, Pt. 1, Goschen to Grey, June 5, 1914, p. 120.

[26] In which a prominent politician's wife killed a newspaper editor.

[27] Hendrick, p. 297.

[28] Lafore, p. 184.

[29] G. D., Pourtalès to Bethmann-Hollweg, June 6, 914.

[30] *Ibid.*, von Tschirschky to Bethmann-Hollweg, June 7, 1914.

[31] *Ibid.*, von Schoen to Bethmann-Hollweg, June 11, 1914.

[32] *Ibid.*, (Unsigned-probably von Flotow) to Bethmann-Hollweg, June 11, 1914.

[33] *The (London) Times*, June 11, 1914, p.7.

[34] Albertini, Vol. I., p. 526.

[35] *Ibid.*

[36] B. D., Vol. X, Pt. 1, Grey to Lamb, June 13, 1914, p. 120; Swire, *Rise*, pp. 217-218.

[37] D. D., *Tome X*, Beguin Billecocq (Vice Consul Scutari) to Bourgeois (Foreign Minister), June 11, 1914, No. 351.

[38] *Ibid.*, Fontenay to Viviani, June 26, 1914, No. 443.

[39] *The (London) Times*, June 12 and 15, 1914, p. 7.

[40] *Ibid.*, July 14, 1914, p. 7.

[41] *Ibid.*, June, 13, 1917, p. 7.

[42] Lafore, p. 184.

[43] Fromkin, p. 101.

[44] Dedijer, p. 158.

26 – THE DEATH OF THE KING'S CHAMPION

[1] The paper had different categories of correspondents: "Special," "Our Own," etc.

[2] Account of the events of June 15 is gleaned from: Goslinga, pp. 36, 45; Heaton, pp. 99-101, 104, 105; *The (London) Times*, June 18, 1914, July 8, 1914, p. 7.

[3] Wied, p. 22.

[4] *The (London) Times*, June 16, 1914, pp. 7, 8.

[5] *The New York Times*, June 23, 1914, p. 5.

[6] Goslinga, pp. 36, 45; Heaton, pp. 99-101, 104, 105; *The (London) Times*, June 18, 1914, p. 7, July 8, 1914, p. 7.

[7] Heaton, pp. 106, 107; *The (London) Times*, June 18, 1914, p. 7; Goslinga, pp. 45, 46; B. D. Vol. X, Pt. I, Lamb to Grey, June 13, 1914, (note), p. 120.

[8] *The (London) Times*, June 18, 1914, p. 7; Heaton, p.p. 106, 107.

27 – FALSE HOPES

[1] B. D., Vol. X, Pt. 1, Grey to Lamb, June 13, 1914, pg. 120 (note).

[2] *Ibid.*, Lamb to Grey, June 16, 1914, p. 121.

[3] Belfield in Heaton, p. xxxiv.

[4] B. D., Vol. X, Pt. 1, Crowe to Lamb, June 17, 1914, p. 121.

[5] D. D., *Tome X*, Fontenay to Viviani (F. M.), June 17, 1914, No. 396.

[6] *Ibid.*, Fontenay to Viviani, June 19, 1914, No. 411.

[7] *Ibid.,* Fontenay (Durazzo) to Viviani (Foreign Minister), June 17, 1914, No. 391; Dumaine to Viviani, same date, No. 395.

[8] Heaton, pp. 111-117.

[9] Belfield in Heaton, p. xxviii.

[10] *The (London) Times,* June 19, 1914, p. 7.

[11] D. D., *Tome X,* Fontenay to Viviani, June 19, 1914, No. 411.

[12] A title for well educated and well known Muslim scholars or priests and religious leaders, named for the semi-mythical 12th Century Turkish character, Nesreddin Hodja. "Transwicki: Hodja," from Wiktionary, 31 August, 2007.

[13] *The (London) Times,* June 22, 1914, p. 7.

[14] Heaton, pp. 118-120.

[15] *The (London) Times,* June 23, 1914, p. 7.

[16] B.N.A. Letter, Edith Durham to "Mr. Nevinson", June 23, 1914, F. O. 371 18 96.

[17] Heaton, p. 120; Belfield in Heaton, pp. xviii, xxx, xxix.

[18] Belfield in Heaton, p. xxx.

[19] Heaton, p. 120.

[20] D. D., *Tome X,* Dumaine (Vienna) to Viviani, June 22, 1914, No. 427.

[21] B. D., Vol. X, Pt. 1, Rodd to Grey, June 23m 1914, p. 123.

[22] Grey, p. 293.

[23] Goslinga, p.41.

[24] *The (London) Times,* June 25, 1914, p. 7.

[25] *Ibid.,* June 27, 1914 and June 29, 1914, pp.7; Wied, *Denkschrift,* p. 22.

[26] Heaton,p.122.

[27] *The (London) Times,* June 25, 1914, p.7.

[28] B. D. Vol. X, Pt. 1, de Bunsen to Grey, June 26, 1914, p. 124.

[29] D. D. *Tome X,* Fontenay to Viviani, June 28, 1914, No. 449.

[30] Pipinelis, p. 61.

[31] Heaton, pp. 57, 121.

[32] Fischer, p.407.

[33] *The New York Times,* June 28, 1914, Section II, p.1.

[34] Heaton, pp. 137,138; Goslinga, pp. 48, 49.

[35] D. D. *Tome X,* Fontenay to Viviani, June 26, 1914, No. 443.

[36] B. D., Rodd to Grey, Vol. X, Pt. 1, June 22, 1914, p. 125; Grey to Lamb and Phillips, June 25, 1914, p. 125.

[37] Maurice Baumont,*The Fall of the Kaiser* (London: George Allen & Unwin, Ltd., 1931) p. 247.

[38] Wied, p. 23.

[39] *The (London) Times,* June 29, 1914, p.7; July 8, 1914, p. 7; *The New York Times,* June 26, 1914, Sec. II, p.1.

[40] *The (London) Times,* July 17, p.7; Swire, *Rise,* pp. 221,222.

[41] *Ibid.,* pp. 223-227.

28 - ANOTHER ROYAL MURDER

[1] Churchill, pp. 62, 64.

[2] Redlich, p. 521.

[3] Thomson, p.63.

[4] Emil Ludwig, *Wilhelm Hohenzollern* (New York: G. P. Putnam's Sons, 1927, p.433.

[5] Churchill, p.67.

[6] Joachim von Kurenberg, *The Kaiser* (New York: Simon and Schuster, 1955) p. 291.

[7] Ludwig, *July '14*, p.41.

[8] *Ibid.,* p.49.

[9] *The (London) Times*, July 1, 1914, p.7.

[10] D. D. *Tome X*, Fontenay to Viviani, June 28, 1914, No. 449.

[11] *Ibid.,* Descos to Viviani, June 30, 1914, No. 468.

29 – THE POT SIMMERS

[1] Churchill, p.66.

[2] *Ibid.,* p. 68.

[3] Kautsky, No. 11, von Tschirschky to Bethmann, July 2, 1914, p.65; Albertini, p. 131.

[4] Pipinelis, p. 61.

[5] Belfield in Heaton, p. xxvi.

[6] *Ibid.,* p. xxvii.

[7] D. D. Barrère to Viviani, July 1, 1914, No. 468.

[8] Pipinelis, p. 13.

[9] *The (London) Times*, July 4, 1914, p. 7

[10] *Ibid.,* July 11, 1914, p.7.

[11] *Ibid.,* July 14, 1914, p.7.

[12] *Ibid.,* July 14, 1914, p. 7, July 13, 1914, p.7.

[13] *The New York Times*, July 4, 1914, p. 1.

[14] Churchill, p. 71.

[15] Reiners, p. 119.

[16] Churchill, p. 72.

[17] Fay, Vol. II, p. 203; Churchill, p.75.

[18] Churchill, p.73.

[19] *Ibid.*

[20] B. D., Vol. X, Pt.1, Grey to Akers-Douglas, July 21, 1914, p.127.

[21] Churchill, pp. 76, 77.

[22] *Ibid.,* p.77.

[23] *Ibid.,* p.79; Fay, Vol. II, pp. 230-233.

[24] Churchill, p. 80.

[25] *Ibid.,* pp. 80, 81.

30 – THE SHADOWS DARKEN

[1] *The (London) Times*, July 9, 1914, p.7.

[2] *Ibid.,* July 10, 1914, p. 7.

[3] *Ibid.,* July 7, 1914, p.7.

[4] A. Nekludoff (translation by Alexandra Paget), *Diplomatic Reminiscences* (New York: E.P. Dutton & Co., 1920), pp. 338,339.

[5] B. D., Vol. X, Pt. 1, Lamb to Grey, July 11, 1914, pp.126, 127, 128; D. D. *3e Serie, Tome X*, Fontenay to Viviani, July 11, 1914, No. 496; *The (London) Times*, July 15, 1914, p. 7; Wied, p. 23; Heaton, p. 138.

[6] Belfield in Heaton, p. xxix.

[7] D. D., *3e. Serie, Tome X*, Blondel to Viviani, July 10, 1914, No. 490.

[8] Kautsky, von Waldburg to Bethmann, July 11, 1914, No. 41, pp. 102, 103.

[9] *The (London) Times*, July 11, 1914, p.7

[10] *Ibid.,* July 13, 1914, p.7.

[11] Goslinga, p. 49; *The (London) Times* July 15, 1914, p.7.

[12] D. D., *3e Serie, Tome X*, Deville to Viviani, July 15, 1914, No. 518.

[13] *The (London) Times*, July 15, 1914, p. 7.

[14] *Ibid.,* July 16, 1914, p. 7.

[15] Fay, Vol. II, p. 236.

[16] D. D., *3e Serie, Tome X*, Paléologue to Viviani, July 11, 1914, No. 495.

[17] Fay, Vol. II, pp. 236,239; Dedijer, p. 418.

[18] Fay, Vol. II, p. 240.

[19] *Ibid.,* p. 256.

[20] D. D., *3e Serie, Tome X*, Cambon to Viviani, July 14, 1914, No. 509.

[21] Heaton, pp. 140,141.

[22] D. D., *Tome X*, Fontenay to Bienvenu-Martin, July 21, 1914, No. 549.

[23] Swire, *Rise*, pp. 227,228; Ismail Kemal, p. 384.

[24] Ismail Kemal, p. 384; Swire, *Rise*, p.228.

[25] Ismail Kemal, pp. 379-383.

[26] *The (London) Times*, July 18, 1914, p.7.

[27] *Ibid.,* July 17, 1914, p. 7.

[28] Fay, Vol. II, pp. 245-248.

[29] D. D., *3e Serie, Tome X*, Barrère to Bienvenu-Martin (Foreign Minister *pro tempore*), No. 520.

[30] *The (London) Times*, July 20, 1914, p.7; Wied, pp. 23, 24.

[31] D. D., *3e Serie, Tome X,* Bienvenu-Martin) to all French diplomats, July 17, 1914, No. 525.

[32] *Ibid.,* Cambon to Viviani, July 17, 1914, No. 526.

[33] Goslinga, p. 49.

[34] Heaton, p. 142.

[35] Kautsky, von Schoen to Bavarian President of Ministerial Consul, July 18, 1914, No. 386, p.618.

[36] Albertini, Vol. I, p.527.

[37] von Kurenberg, p. 271.

[38] Kautsky, *Supplement IV*, No. 2, von Schoen to Bavarian Prime Minister, July 18, 1914, Report 386, p. 620.

[39] *The (London) Times*, July 21, 1914, p. 7.

[40] *Ibid.*

[41] *The (London) Times*, July 30, 1914, p. 7.

[42] Fay, Vol. II, pp. 249, 250.

[43] *Ibid.,* pp. 250, 251.

[44] Albertini, Vol. II, p.252.

[45] *Ibid.,* Vol. I, p. 527.

[46] Fay, Vol. II, p. 252.

[47] Heaton, pp. 143, 144.

[48] *Ibid.,* pp. 144, 145; B. D., Vol. X, Pt.1, Lamb to Grey, July 23, 1914, p. 127.

[49] Goslinga, p. 49.

[50] Heaton, pp. 144,145.

[51] D. D., *Tome X*, Fontenay to Bienvenu-Martin, July 21, 1914, No. 549.

[52] *Ibid.,* Bienvenu-Martin to main French embassies, July 20, 1914.

[53] G. D., Von Jagow to von Tschirschky, July 21, 1914.
[54] Fay, Vol. I, p. 474.
[55] D. D., *Tome X*, Fontenay to Bienvenu-Martin, July 23, 1914, No. 568; George Gawrych, *The Crescent and the Eagle*, (London: I.B. Tauris, 2006), p. 35.
[56] Fay, Vol. II, p. 265.
[57] Catrine Clay, *King, Kaiser, Tsar* (New York: Walker & Co., 2006), p. 306.

31 – A KISS BEFORE DYING

[1] Fay, Vol. II, pp. 271-273.
[2] Reiners, pp. 62, 118; *Austrian Red Book* (London: George Allen & Unwin, Ltd., 1919) Vol. 2, No. 38, Count Berchtold to Count Szapary, July 25, 1914, p. 30; No. 73, Count Szapary to Count Berchtold, July 27, 1914, p.133.
[3] Kautsky, Lichnowsky to Berlin, July 23, 1914, p. 167.
[4] D. D. *Tome X*, Bienvenu-Martin to all embassies, July 23, 1914, No. 562; Morton, p. 307.
[5] *Ibid.*, p.302.
[6] D. D. *3e Serie, (1911-1914) Tome XI*, Barrère to Bienvenu-Martin, July 24, 1914, No. 14.
[7] Fay, Vol. II, p.298.
[8] D. D. *(1871-1914) 3e Serie (1911-1914), Tome XI*, de Fontenay to Bienvenu-Martin, July 24, 1914, no. 10; Barrère to Bienvenu-Martin, same date, No.14.
[9] Oakley-Hill, p. 33.
[10] Wied, p.24.
[11] Swire, *Zog's Albania*, pp. 65, 66, 151, 155; Szinyei-Mrese, pp. 151, 156, 161; Oakley-Hill, p. 33; *The New York Times*, March 8, 1914, p.1.
[12] V.P. Kennedy, quoted in *Albania and the Albanians, Selected Articles and Letters 1903-1944* (London: Centre for Albanian Studies, 2001), page 252.
[13] Belfield, p.xxix.
[14] Heaton, p. 32; Marie, *Story*, p.543; after inquiry by the author in 2008, both the Romanian Archives and Marie's grandson, King Michael, deny knowledge of the letters.
[15] Reiners, p. 121; another source places the train time at 6:30, Thomson, pp. 77,78; see *Austrian Red Book*) Vol. 2, No. 2, Count Berchtold to Baron von Giesl, July 24, 1914, p. 2.
[16] Thomson, p.78.
[17] Ludwig, p. 242.
[18] Reiners, p. 121.
[19] *Ibid.*, p 127.
[20] *Ibid.*, p. 122.
[21] Fay, Vol. II, pp. 306,314.
[22] Bruce Lincoln, *In War's Dark Shadow* (New York: The Dial Press, 1983), pp. 430; 431; Fay, Vol. II, pp. 303,304,315,316; Reiners, p. 136.
[23] Clay, p. 305.
[24] G. D., Von Tschirschky to Bethmann-Hollweg, July 25, 1914.
[25] Thomson, p. 85.
[26] *Ibid.*
[27] Reiners, p. 128.

[28] Thomson, p. 86.
[29] Fay, Vol. II, p. 266.
[30] Thomson, p. 99.
[31] *Ibid,* pp. 101,102.
[32] *Ibid.;* Reiners, pp. 121,130.

32 - THE SANDS RUN OUT

[1] Goslinga, p. 50.
[2] Heaton, pp. 158-160; According to *The (London) Times* of July 30, The French cruiser *Edgar Quinet* left the morning of July 29; B. D. Vol. X, Pt. 1, Grey to Lamb, July 30, 1914, p. 128; *Austrian Red Book*, Berchtold to von Löwenthal, July 24,27, 1914, Vol. 1, No. 31, pp. 76,77; Vol. 2, July 31, 1914, No. 79, p. 140.
[3] *The (London) Times*, July 30, 1914, p. 7.
[4] Thomson, p.103.
[5] Reiners, p. 131.
[6] Thomson, p. 104.
[7] *Ibid.,* pp. 106,114; Kautsky, Heinrich to the Kaiser, July 28, 1914, p. 238.
[8] Thomson, p. 105.
[9] Reiners, pp. 137-139, 143-151.
[10] *Ibid.,* p.132.
[11] Kautsky, note by Wilhelm, July 28, 1914, to No. 328, p. 293.
[12] Thomson, p.114.
[13] *Ibid.,* p. 115.
[14] Reiners, pp. 134, 135.
[15] Thomson, pp. 121, 132.
[16] Reiners, pp. 135, 136.
[17] *Ibid.,* pp. 141,142.
[18] Thomson, p. 124.
[19] Reiners, p. 138.
[20] *Ibid.,* p.136.
[21] *Ibid.,* pp. 137-139, 143-151; Kautsky, Kaiser to Czar, July 29, 1914, No. 359, p.315; *Austrian Red Book*, Vol. 3, Circular Manifesto to certain Austrian embassies and missions, July 31, 1914, No. 78, pp. 68, 69.
[22] Heaton, pp. 160-167.
[23] Thomson, pp, 151-154.
[24] *Ibid.,* p. 160.
[25] *Ibid.,* p. 161.
[26] *Ibid.,* p. 115.
[27] *Austrian Red Book*, Vol. 3, No. 105, Count Szögyény to Count Berchtold, August 2, 1914, p.95.
[28] Fay, Vol. II, p. 223, n. 53.
[29] Clay, p. 312.
[30] Churchill, p. 82.
[31] Thomson, p. 89.
[32] Heaton, pp. 164, 160-167; Wied, p. 25.
[33] Wied, p. 26.
[34] Swire, *Rise*, p. 230.

[35] Evelyn, Princess Blücher, *An English Wife in Berlin* (New York: E.P. Dutton & Co., 1920) p. 7.

[36] *The (London) Times*, August 11, 1914, p.5; Wied, pp. 27, 28.

[37] B. D. Vol X, Pt. 1, footnote, Lamb to Grey, July 23, 1914, p. 127.

[38] Heaton, pp. 164, 165.

[39] L. S. Stavrianos, *The Balkans Since 1453* (New York: Holt Rineheart & Winston, 1958) p. 511.

[40] G. D., von Lucius to Auswärtiges Amt, August 16, 1914. He called the complement the *besatzung.*

[41] G. D., Tschirschky to Auswärtiges Amt, August 20, 1914.

[42] Heaton, pp. 168, 169.

[43] *The (London) Times*, August 26, 1914, p. 7.

[44] Wied, pp. 27, 28.

[45] *Ibid.,* pp. 27, 28; Heaton, pp. 170-172; 181.

[46] *Ibid.,* p. 171.

[47] Ruches, p. 94.

[48] Wied, pp. 27, 28; Heaton, pp. 170-172, 181.

[49] Belfield in Heaton, p. 181.

[50] Wied, p. 28

[51] *Ibid.,* Appendix VII.

[52] David Bergamini, *Japan's Imperial Conspiracy* (New York: William Morrow & Co. Inc, 1971) p. 100.

[53] Marie, *The Story of My Life*, p. 543.

[54] B. D. Vol. X, Pt. 1, footnote from Lamb to Grey, July 23, 1914, p. 127.

33 – POST MORTEM

[1] *Austrian Red Book*, Vol. 1, No. 1, Franz Joseph to Wilhelm, July 2, 1914, p. 1.

[2] *Ibid.,* No. 3, Discourse between Count Berchtold and the German ambassador, July 3, 1914.

[3] *Ibid.,* No. 12, Relation of the Hungarian Premier, Count Tisza, July 8, 1914.

[4] *Ibid.,* No. 26, Council of Ministers for Common Affairs, July 19, 1914, P. 56.

[5] *Ibid.,* No. 35, Discourse between Count Berchtold and the German ambassador, July 20, 1914, p.83.

[6] *Ibid.,* Vol. 2, No. 87, Count Berchtold to the Imp. and Roy. Ambassadors in Rome and Berlin, July 28, 1914, p. 148.

[7] *Ibid.,* Vol. 3, No. 88, Mérey to Count Berchtold, August 1, 1914, p. 82.

[8] *Ibid.,* No. 127, Mérey to Count Berchtold, August 4, 1914, p. 113.

[9] *Ibid.,* No. 76., Count Berchtold to Minister Otto in Cetinje, July 31, 1914, p.66.

[10] Wied and Schwarz, p.5.

[11] Wied, p.29.

[12] Ruches, p.94; Wied, p.30.

[13] Heaton, pp. 170-172, 181; B. D. Vol. X, Pt. 1, footnote on Lamb to Grey, July 23, 1914, p. 127; Ruches, p. 94; *The New York Times*, September 4, 1914, p. 1; *The New York Times*, October 5, 1914, p.1.

[14] Wied, pp. 31, 32.

[15] Ruches, p. 94; Fischer, *King Zog*, p.12.

[16] Wied, p. 33.

[17] A. A., Theater Kombtaar souvenir program.

[18] Wied, p. 34.

[19] Swire, *King Zog*, p. 154.

[20] *Ibid.*

[21] Wied, pp. 35, 36.

[22] *Ibid.,* pp. 52, 63: Swire, *Rise*, pp. 196,197.

[23] Belfield, p. xxxv.

[24] Durham, quoted in Fischer, *King Zog*, p. 11.

[25] Fischer, *King Zog*, p. 12; Wied, p. 30.

[26] G. D., unsigned report February 27, 1915(?); *"Alfred Rappaport Ritter von Arbengau,"* http://www.Austro-hungarian-army.co.uk/biog/Rappaport.htm.

[27] Wied, pp. 38-40; G. D., unsigned communication to Wied, March 13, 1915.

[28] *Ibid.,* pp. 38-40.

[29] "Alfred Rappaport…"

[30] G. D., Jagow to Wied, March 20, 1915.

[31] *The New York Times*, May 25, 1915, p. 1.

[32] G. D., Jacoby (Berne) to Bethmann-Hollweg, December 14, 1915; Heaton, p.25.

[33] Fischer, *King Zog*, p. 18.

[34] G. D., unsigned message to Wied, March 7, 1916.

[35] Swire, *Zog's Albania.*, p. 92.

[36] G. D., von Romberg to Auswärtiges Amt, April 16, 1916.

[37] *Ibid.,* Lossow to Grand Headquarters Political Department, October 2, 1916.

[38] *Ibid.,*, von Massow to Auswärtiges Amt, December 29, 1916.

[39] Wied, p. 82, quoting the *Dresdener Anzeiger* of January 30, 1917.

[40] G. D., Royal Prussian ambassador (Dresden) to Bethmann-Hollweg, June 9, 1917.

[41] *Ibid.,* Delegation of Baden, verbal note, August 17, 1917.

[42] *Ibid.,* Wied to Baden, July 14, 1917.

[43] *Ibid.,* Wied to Michaelis, July 20, 1917.

[44] *Ibid.,* Portern to von Kühlmann, August 18, 1917.

[45] *Ibid.,* State Secretary to Saxon Legation, August 25, 1917; Cecil, p. 287.

[46] G. D., Wedel to Michaelis, August 19, 1917.

[47] *Ibid.,* copy of Ballplatz to Hohenlohe, August 17, 1917.

[48] *Ibid.,* Auswärtiges Amt (signature illegible), to Wied, September 14, 1917.

[49] *Ibid.,* Eiswalt to Michaelis, October 26, 1917.

[50] Gordon Brook-Shepherd, *The Last Habsburg* (New York: Weybright and Talley, 1968), pp. 57, 58.

[51] G. D., Wied to Hertling, December 13, 1917; Wied, p. 45.

[52] G. D., Wedel to Hertling, December 29, 1917.

[53] *Ibid.,* Wedel to Auswärtiges Amt, January 31, 1918.

[54] *Ibid.,* Wied to the Kaiser, March 7, 1918.

[55] *Ibid.,* Evanghele to Wied, March 7, 1918.

[56] *Ibid.,* Wied to the Kaiser, March 10, 1918.

[57] *Ibid.,* Wied to Marschall, March 28, 1918; Wied to von Hintze, August 29, 1918.

[58] *Ibid.,* (illegible) to Hertling, March 31, 1918.

[59] *Ibid.,* State Secretary to Grunau, March---1918.

[60] *Ibid.,* Stelberg to Auswärtiges Amt, May 10, 1918; Wied to von Hintze, August 29, 1918.

[61] *Ibid.,* Rosenberg Memorandum, May 31, 1918.

[62] *Ibid.,* copy from *Neue Prüssische Zeitung*, March 18, 1918.

[63] Pat Barker, *The Eye in the Door* (New York: A Plume Book, 1995), pp. 278-281, 152-154; Julian Burnside, "*R.V. Pemberton Billing—The Black Book Case*", http://www.users.bigpond.com/burnside/pembertonbilling.htm.
[64] *The New York Times*, July 1, 1918.
[65] Giles Macdonagh, *The Last Kaiser* (New York: St. Martin's Press, 2000), p. 398.
[66] G. D., Wied to von Hintze, August 29, 1918.

34 – AN EXILE IN HIS OWN COUNTRY

[1] Swire, *Rise*, p. 285.
[2] G. D., undated newspaper clipping c. 1919.
[3] Pearson, p. 117; Swire, *Rise*, p. 257.
[4] Belfield, *Six Months*, p. xviii; Heaton, p. 87.
[5] Fischer, *King Zog*, p. 19.
[6] Raymond Hutchings, *Historical Dictionary of Albania* (Scarecrow Press: 1976), p. 240.
[7] G. D., Auswärtiges Amt verbal note, January 7, 1920.
[8] *Ibid.,* von Honiel to Swedish Embassy, January 7, 1920.
[9] *The New York Times*, May 19, 1920.
[10] G. D., Teck of Prussian Legation to *Auswärtiges Amt*, February 10, 1920.
[11] Fischer, *King Zog*, p.65.
[12] Swire, *King Zog's Albania*, p.15.
[13] Tomes, p. 75.
[14] Belfield, p. xxix; A.A., *Haagsche Courant*, June 13, 1931, Letter, September 20, 1931 to Pater Joannes Shlaken.
[15] Swire, *King Zog's Albania*, p. 202; A. A. Letter, Wied to Pater Joannes Shlaken, September 20, 1931.
[16] Belfield, p. xxix.
[17] *Ibid.,* p. xix.
[18] Tomes, pp. 41.

BIBLIOGRAPHY

PRINTED WORKS

Adler, George J., compiler, *German-English Dictionary* (New York: D. Appleton & Co., 1902)

Albertini, Luigi, *The Origins of the War of 1914*, Vol. 2, (Oxford: Oxford University Press, 1952)

Alexander, Grand Duke, *Once a Grand Duke*, (Garden City: Garden City Publishing Co., 1932)

Aronson, Theo, *Crowns in Conflict* (Manchester: Salem House, 1986)

Asquith, Margot, *An Autobiography, Vol. III* (New York: H. Doran Co., 1922)

Asprey, Robert, *The Panther's Feast* (New York: Carroll & Graf Publishers, 1959)

Ball, Robert and Peters, Paul, *Military Medals, Decorations & Orders* (Atglen: Schiffer Military/Aviation History, 1994)

Baltzy, Alexander and Salomore A. Williams, editors, *Readings in 20th Century European History* (New York: Appleton-Century-Crofts, Inc., 1950)

Bassett, Richard, *Balkan House* (London: John Murray, 1990)

Baumont, Maurice, *The Fall of the Kaiser* (London: George Allen & Unwin, Ltd., 1931)

Beéche-Bravo, Arturo, *H. M. King Michael of Romania, A Tribute* (Falkoping: Rosvall Royal Books, 2001)

Berenson, Edward, *The Trial of Madame Caillaux* (New York: The Notable Trials Library, 1995)

Bergamini, David, *Japan's Imperial Conspiracy* (New York: William Morrow & Co. Inc, 1971)

Bernstorff, Count Johann., *Memoirs of Count Bernstorff* (New York: Random House, 1936)

Blücher, Princess Evelyn, *An English Wife in Berlin* (New York: E. P. Dutton & Co., 1920)

Bocca, Geoffrey, *Kings Without Thrones* (New York: The Dial Press, 1959)

Bonsal, Stephan, *Suitors and Suppliants: The Little Nations at Versailles,* (New York: Prentice Hall, Inc., 1946)

Brook-Shepherd, Gordon, *Archduke of Sarajevo* (Boston: Little, Brown & Co., 1984)

Bülow, Bernhard von, *Memoirs* (London: G. P. Putnam, 1930)

Carey, Joyce, *Memoir of the Bobotes* (London: Phoenix Press, 2000)

Carnegie Endowment for International Peace, *The Other Balkan Wars, 1914 Report*, Introduction by George F. Kennan (Washington: 1993 Reprint)

Cassels, Lavender, *The Archduke and the Assassin* (New York: Stein & Day, 1985)

Cecil, Lamar, *Wilhelm II, Vol. 2* (Chapel Hill: The University of North Carolina Press, 1996)

Chekrezi, Constantine A., *Albania Past and Present* (New York: Arno Press and New York Times, 1919)

Churchill, Winston S., *The World Crisis, The Eastern Front* (New York: Charles Scribner's Sons, 1931)

Ciano, Galeazzo, *The Ciano Diaries 1939-1943* (New York: Doubleday & Co., 1946)

Clay, Catrine, *King, Kaiser, Tsar* (Walker & Co, 2006)

Constant, Stephen, *Foxy Ferdinand* (New York: Franklin Watts, 1980)

Cowles, Virginia, *1913 An End and a Beginning* (New York: Harper & Row, 1967)

Crampton, R. J., *The Hollow Détente* (London: George Prior Publishers, 1979)

Curley, Jr., J. P., *Monarchs in Waiting* (New York: Dodd Mead & Co., 1973)

Dedijer, Vladimir, *The Road to Sarajevo* (New York: Simon & Schuster, 1966)

Devere-Summers, Anthony, *War and the Royal Houses of Europe* (London: Arms & Armour, 1990)

Dugdale, E. T. S., editor, *German Diplomatic Documents 1871-1914 Vol. IV* (New York: Harper & Brothers, 1931)

436

Durham, M. Edith, *Albania and the Albanians, Selected Articles and Letters 1903-1944* (London, Centre for Albanian Studies, 2001)

Durham, M. Edith, *High Albania* (London: Edward Arnold, 1909) 2000 reprint with Introduction by John Hodgson

Durham, M. Edith, *The Struggle for Scutari* (London: Edward Arnold, 1914)

Durham, M. Edith, *Twenty Years of Balkan Tangle* (London: George Allen & Unwin, 1920)

Edward, Duke of Windsor, *A King's Story* (New York: G. P. Putnam's Sons, 1951)

Encyclopedia Britannica, Vol. 14, 1968 ed., "Titu Majorescu."

Eulalia, Infanta of Spain, *Court Life From Within* (New York: Dodd, Mead & Co., 1915)

Fay, Sidney B., *The Origins of the World War (2nd Edition)* (New York: The Macmillan Co., 1930)

Ferdinand, Louis, *The Rebel Prince* (Chicago: Henry Regnery Co., 1952)

Figuier,Louis, *Le Savant du Foyer*(Paris: Librairie de L. Hachette et Cie., 1870)

Fischer, Bernd Jurgen, *King Zog and the Struggle for Stability in Albania* (New York: East European Monographs distributed by Columbia University Press, 1984)

Fischer, Fritz, *War of Illusions* (New York: W. W. Norton & Co. Inc., 1975)

Fromkin, David, *Europe's Last Summer* (New York: Alfred A. Knopf, 2004)

Garnett, Mitchell and Godfrey, James L., *Europe Since 1815* (New York: Appleton-Century Crofts, 1947)

Gawrych, George W., *The Crescent and the Eagle* (London: I. B. Taurus, 2006)

Geiss, Immanuel, *July, 1914* (New York: Charles Scribner's Sons, 1967)

Gerard, James W., *Face to Face With Kaiserism* (New York, George H. Doran, Co., 1918)

Gerard, James W., *My Four Years in Germany* (New York: George H. Doran, Co., 1917)

Gerolymatos, André, *The Balkan Wars* (New York: Basic Books, 2002)

Gewehr, Wesley, *The Rise of Nationalism in the Balkans 1800-1930*, (Archon Books, 1931)

Gibbons, Herbert A., *The New Map of Europe* (New York: The Century Co., 1914)

Gilbert, Martin, *Winston S. Churchill, Vol. III, The Challenge of War* (Norwalk, Easton Press, 1971)

Glenny, Misha, *The Balkans, Nationalism War, and the Great Powers* (New York: Penguin Books, 2001)

Goslinga, Gorrit T. A., *The Dutch in Albania* (Rome: Szêjzat (Le Pleiadi), 1972)

Grey, Viscount of Fallodon, *Twenty-Five Years* (New York: Frederick A. Stokes, Co., 1925)

Groueff, Stephane, *Crown of Thorns* (Lanham: Madison Books, 1987)

Hamilton, Lord Frederic, *The Vanished Pomps of Yesterday* (New York: George H. Doran Co., 1921)

Haskins, Charles Homer & Lord, Robert, *Some Problems of the Peace* (Cambridge: Harvard University Press, 1920)

Heaton-Armstrong, Duncan, *The Six Month Kingdom*, Introduction by Gervase Belfield (London: I. B. Taurus, 2005)

Helmreich, Ernest C., *Diplomacy of the Balkan Wars 1912-1913* (Cambridge: Harvard University Press, 1938)

Hendrick, Burton J., *The Life and Letters of Walter H. Page* (Garden City: Doubleday, 1925)

Herbert, Aubrey, *Ben Kendim* (New York: G. P. Putnam's Sons, Ltd., 1925)

Howell, Georgina, *Gertrude Bell, Queen of the Desert, Shaper of Nations* (New York: Farrar Straus & Giroux, 2006)

Hutchings, Raymond, *Historical Dictionary of Albania* (Scarecrow Press, 1976)

Irace, Tullio, *With the Italians in Tripoli* (London: John Marney, 1912)

Jannen, William J., *The Lions of July* (Novato: Presidio Press, 1996)

Jüdtmann, Fritz, *Mayerling: The Facts Behind the Legend* (London: George Harrap & Co., 1971)

Kaplan, Robert, *Balkan Ghosts* (New York: St. Martin's Press, 1993)

Kautsky, Karl, editor, *Outbreak of the World War, German Documents Collected by Karl Kautsky* (New York: Oxford University Press, 1924)

Kemal, Ismail Bey, *The Memoirs of Ismail Kemal Bey* (London: Constable & Co., Ltd., 1920)

Kinross, Lord, *Atatürk* (New York: William Morrow & Co., 1965)

Konitza, Faik, *Albania, The Rock Garden of Southeastern Europe* (Boston: Vatra, 1957)

Kurenberg, Joachim von, *The Kaiser* (New York: Simon & Schuster, 1955)

Lafore, Laurence, *The Long Fuse* (Philadelphia: J. P. Lippincott, Co., 1965)

Lee, Sir Sidney, *King Edward VII, Vol. II* (New York: The Macmillan Co., 1927)

Levine, Isaac Don, editor, *Letters from the Kaiser to the Czar* (New York: Frederick A. Stokes, 1920)

Lichnowsky, Karl, *Heading for the Abyss* (London: Constable, 1928)

Lincoln, W. Bruce, *In War's Dark Shadow* (New York: The Dial Press, 1983)

Lockhart, R. H. Bruce, *British Agent* (New York: G. P. Putnam's Sons, 1933)

Louis Ferdinand, Prince, *The Rebel Prince* (Chicago: Henry Regnery Co., 1952)

Ludwig, Emil, *July '14* (New York: G.P. Putnam's Sons, 1929)

Ludwig, Emil, *Wilhelm Hohenzollern* (New York: G.P. Putnam's Sons, 1927)

MacDonogh, Giles, *The Last Kaiser* (New York: St. Martin's Press, 2000)

Marie of Roumaina, *Ordeal, The Story of My Life* (New York: Charles Scribner's Sons, 1935)

Marie of Roumaina, *The Story of My Life* (New York: Charles Scribner's Sons, 1934)

Massie, Robert K., *Castles of Steel* (New York: Random House, 2003)

Massie, Robert K., *Dreadnaught* (New York: Random House, 1991)

Massie, Robert K., *Nicholas and Alexandra* (New York: Atheneum, 1967)

Massie, Robert K., *The Last Courts of Europe* (New York: The Vendome Press, 1981)

McLean, Roderick, *Royalty and Diplomacy in Europe* (Cambridge: Cambridge University Press, 2001)

Mijatovich, Chedomille, *A Royal Tragedy* (New York: Dodd, Mead & Co., 1907)

Miller, William, *The Ottoman Empire and its Successors. 1801-1927* (Cambridge: The University Press, 1927)

Morton, Frederic, *Thunder at Twilight* (New York: Charles Scribner's Sons, 1989)

Nekludoff, A., *Diplomatic Reminiscences* (Translation by Alexandra Paget) (New York: E. P. Dutton Co., 1920)

Nicolson, Harold, *King George V* (New York: Doubleday & Co., 1953)

Nicolson, Julia, *The Perfect Summer* (New York: Grove Press, 2006)

Oakley-Hill, D. R., *An Englishman in Albania* (London: I. Taurus, 2002)

Pakula, Hannah, *The Last Romantic* (New York: Simon & Schuster, 1984)

Palmer, Frederick, *With My Own Eyes* (Indianapolis: The Bobbs-Merrill Co., 1932)

Pearson, Owen, *Albania and King Zog* (London: I. B. Taurus, 2004)

Pipinelis, P. N., *Europe and the Albanian Question* (Chicago: Argonaut Inc., 1963)

Peacock, Wadham, *Cutting Out the New Kingdom* (New York: D. Appleton & Co., 1914)

Pope-Hennessy, James, *Queen Mary* (New York: Alfred A. Knoph, 1960)

Porch, Douglas, *The French Secret Services* (New York: Farrar Straus & Giroux, 1995)

Porter, Ivor, *Michael of Romania* (Stroud: Sutton Publishing, Ltd., 2005)

Raeder, Erich, *Grand Admiral* (Da Capo Press, 1960)

Redlich, Joseph, *Emperor Francis Joseph of Austria* (New York: The Macmillan Co., 1929)

Reiners, Ludwig, *The Lamps Went Out in Europe* (New York: Pantheon, 1955)

Rodd, Sir J. Rennell, *Social and Diplomatic Memories* (London: Edward Arnold & Co., 1925)

Rohl, John, editor, *1914: Delusion or Design?* (New York: St. Martin's Press, 1973)

Roosevelt, Blanche, *Elisabeth of Rumania* (London: Chapman & Hall, 1891)

Rose, Kenneth, *King George V* (New York: Alfred A. Knoph, 1984)

Ruches, Pyrrhus J., *Albania's Captives* (Chicago: Argonaut Inc., 1964)

Sampson, Anthony, *The Anatomy of Britain* (London: Hodder & Stoughton, 1966)

Schevill, Ferdinand, *A History of the Balkans*, (New York: Dorset Press, 1991)

Schmitz, Christian, *Fürst Wilhelm Prinz zu Wied in Internationalen Pressedarstellungen* (Maschinenschriftliche Magisterarbeit: Universität Bochum, 1991)

Shirer, William L., *The Collapse of the Third Republic* (New York: Simon & Schuster, 1969)

Smith, Alison J., *A View of the Spree* (New York: The John Day Co., 1962)

Stadiem, William, *Too Rich* (New York: Carroll & Graf Publishers, 1991)

Stavrianos, L. S., *The Balkans Since 1453* (New York: Holt Rineheart & Winston, 1958)

Steiner, Zara S., *The Foreign Office & Foreign Policy* (Cambridge: Cambridge University Press, 1969)

Strachan, Hew, *The First World War, Vol. I, To Arms* (Oxford: Oxford University Press, 2001)

Sturdza, Prince Michel, *The Suicide of Europe* (Boston: Western Islands, 1968)

Sullivan, Mark, *Our Times Volume IV* (New York: Charles Scribner Sons, 1932)

Sulzberger, C. L., *The Fall of Eagles* (New York: Crown Publishers, 1977)

Swire, J., *Albania, The Rise of a Kingdom* (London: Williams & Norgate, Ltd., 1929)

Swire, J., *King Zog's Albania* (New York: Liveright Publishing Co., 1937)

Szinyei-Mrese, Antoinette de, *Ten Years, Ten Months, Ten Days* (London: Hutchinson & Co., 1940)

Tansill, Charles C., *America Goes to War* (Boston: Little Brown & Co., 1938)

Taylor, Edmond, *The Fall of the Dynasties* (Garden City: Doubleday & Co., 1963)

Thomson, George M., *The Twelve Days* (New York: G. P. Putnam's Sons, 1964)

Tomes, Jason, *King Zog of Albania* (New York: New York University Press, 2003)

Topham, Anne, *Memoirs of the Kaiser's Court* (New York: Dodd Mead & Co., 1914)

Treadway, John D., *The Falcon & The Eagle* (West Lafayette: Purdue University Press, 1983)

Tuchman, Barbara, *The Proud Tower* (New York: The Macmillan Co., 1966)

Van der Kiste, John, *Kings of the Hellenes* (Phoenix Mill: Alan Sutton Publishing, 1994)

Vickers, Miranda *The Albanians. A Modern History* (London: I. B. Taurus, 1995)

Viktoria Louise, Princess, *The Kaiser's Daughter* (Englewood Cliffs: Prentice-Hall Inc., 1977)

Werfel, Franz, *The Forty Days of Musa Dagh* (New York: The Modern Library, 1934)

West, Rebecca, *Black Lamb and Grey Falcon* (New York: Viking Press, 1943)

Wied, Wilhelm zu, *Denkschrift über Albanien, 1917* (Manuscript reprint; 2005 Translation by Christine Arnold)

Wilhelm, II, *The Kaiser's Memoirs* (New York: Harper & Bros., 1922)

Wilmott, H. P., *World War I* (New York: Darling Kindersley Publishing, Inc., 2006)

Wilson, Lawrence, *The Incredible Kaiser* (New York: A. S. Barnes & Co., 1963)

Yeats-Brown, Francis, *Bloody Years - A Decade of Plot and Counter Plot by the Golden Horn* (New York: The Viking Press, 1932)

Young, Harry F., *Prince Lichnowsky and the Great War* (Athens: University of Georgia Press, 1977)

PERIODICALS

Alpion, Gezim, *Baron Franz Nopcsa and His Ambition for the Albanian Throne, BESA Journal, Vol. 6, No. 3,* Summer 2002.

Alpion, Dr. Gezim, Baron Franz Nopcsa...", quoting Nopcsa in Robert Elsie's "The Viennese Scholar Who Almost Became King of Albania, *East European Quarterly*, XXXIII, No. 3, September 1999, pp. 327-345.

Davidson, Marshall B., "Carl Bodman's Unspoiled West*",* *American Heritage Magazine, Vol. XIV, No. 3.,* April 1963.

Helmreich, Jonathan, "The Serbs: A Warning From a Past Contributor", *Contemporary Review,* May 1993.

Hunt, Donald, "Sidelights on the Prussian Guard"; *Tradition, The Journal of the International Society of Military Collectors,* No. 60 (c. 1971)

The Illustrated London News, March 7, 1914.

L'Illustration (Paris), June 14, 1913.

The Lady's Realm, An Illustrated Monthly Magazine, Vols. I – IV, November 1896 – October 1898. (London: Hutchinson & Co.)

Le Figaro (Paris), March 21, 1913.

The National Board for Historical Service, *The Establishment of the Principality of Albania, 1912-1913* (Washington: Government Printing Office 1918).

The New York Times, 1913, 1914, passim; February 15, 2007.passim means 'here and there'

The Outlook, A Weekly Newspaper, Vol. 81, September – December 1905 (New York: Outlook Co.)

Punch, February 25, 1914; June 3, 1914.

The Times (London) 1913-1914, *passim.*

DOCUMENTS

Albanian Archives, Tirana, Albania, (abbreviated herein as A. A.)

Austrian Redbook, Official Files Pertaining to Pre-War History (3 Vols.) (London: George Allen & Unwin Ltd., 1920)

British Documents on the Origins of the War, 1898-1914, Vols. IX, X, edited by G. P. Gooch and Harold Temperley (London: H. M. S. O., 1934) (abbreviated herein as B. D.)

British National Archives, *Documents on Ahmed Fuad, Duke de Montspensier, Edith Durham, et al,* 1913, 1914, FO/371/1892. (B.N.A. herein)

Documents Diplomatiques Français, 3e Serie, Tomes X, XI, 1911-1914 (Paris: Imprimerie Nationale, 1926) (abbreviated herein as D. D.) Doughty-Wylie, *Charles, Letters to Gertrude Bell,* 1913 (University of Newcastle, England, Gertrude Bell Collection, herein abbreviated "Newcastle")

German Foreign Ministry Archives, 1867-1920, *Albania, Die Fürstliche Familie, 1913-1920* (U.S. National Archives, Reel 3, T-137, frames 298-511) (G. D. herein)

German Documents collected by Karl Kautsky, *Outbreak of the World War*, edited by Max Montgelas and Walter

444

Schücking (New York: Oxford University Press, 1924 (herein known as Kautsky)

WEBSITE ARTICLES

Aubrey Herbert, wikipedia,
 http://www.answers.com/topic/aubrey-herbert.
Buyers, Christopher, 4dwnet/RoyalArk/Albania/wied.htm.
Dragnich, Alex and Todorovich, Slavko, *Prelude to World War I: Balkan Wars and Serbo-Albanian Relations* (http://www.srpska-mreza.com/bookstore/kosovo/kosovo5.htm
The Duc de Montpensier and the Throne of Albania,
 http://heraldica.org/topics/france.pacte1909.htm
Edith Durham, http://www.geocities.com/spiritofalbania/dith.htm
Highness, http://en.wikipedia.org/wiki/Highness
Isa Boletini, http://en.wikipedia.org.wiki/Isa_Boletini,
 12/13/2006
Kendrick, John, *The Merry Widow: History of a Hit*,
 Musicals101.com, 11/18/2005
Mindaugas II of Lithuania,
 http://en.wikipedia.org/wiki.Wilhelm_von_Urach
Odegard, Mark, *Noble, Princely, Royal, and Imperial Titles,*
 http://www.heraldica.org/topics/odegard/titlefaq.htm.
Rappaport, Alfred, *Ritter von Arbengau,* http://www.austro-hungarian-army.co.uk/biog/rappaport.htm.
Reitweiser, William Addams, *Mediatized*,
 http://members.aol.com/eurostamm/
Mediatize.html, January 1998.
Wied, Friedrich Wilhelm zu und Schwarz, Heinz, *Wilhelm Fürst von Albanien, Prinz zu Wied*, (Wied website, 2006).

PHOTOGRAPHS

Photographs of Albania from the Netherlands Institute of Military History or Albania National Archives, Tirana, Albania.

INDEX

Durazzo, xxxix, 5-6, 8, 37, 39, 52, 56, 60, 74, 82, 87, 159, 168, 194-195, 216, 220, 224, 226, 239, 252, 257, 275, 285, 335, 357, 373, 376

Durazzo, Bishop of, 171, 179

Durazzo, Marchese, 202, 242

Durchlaucht, 31, 166

Durham, Edith, xxxvii, 8, 42-43, 45, 64, 76, 115, 118, 144, 174, 198, 221, 242. 278. 285, 299-301, 323, 325, 336-337, 347, 376

Eagle of Albania, Order of, 200, 352

Eccleston Square, 12-13, 75

Edgar Quinet, cruiser, 297

Edward VII, King of Britain, xxv, 21, 24

Egypt, xxxvii, 96, 152, 210, 346

Eifel, 25

Eiswalt, Dr., 385

Ekrem Bey Libohova, 161, 201, 211, 238, 246, 259, 274, 287, 344, 377

Ekrem Bey Vlora, 160-161, 180, 225, 338, 346-347

Elbasan, 8, 47, 112, 117, 142, 148, 185, 187, 214, 237, 253, 275-276, 303, 361, 373, 381

Elbasani, xxviii

Electors, xvii

Elena, Queen of Italy, 29, 33

Elisabeth, Empress, xxi, 14, 18, 71, 311

Elisabeth, Queen of Romania, 24-25, 32-33, 102-103

Elizabeth II, Queen of Britain, x

Elliott, Sir Francis, 172, 182, 205, 235

Elyseé Palace, 176

Enthronement Medal, 378

Enver Pasha, 381

Epirus, 2, 8, 184, 189, 325

Epirus, Northern, xxxix, 114, 162, 167, 172-173, 175, 184, 189, 206-207, 212, 215, 374

Epirus, Relief Fund, British, 221

Erbprinz, 31

Ersek (Colonia), 190, 208, 212, 221, 231-232, 336

Esebeck, Baron, 144

Eshref Frasheri, 395

Essad Pasha Toptani, 36-37, 41, 47, 68, 70, 76-78, 83, 86-89, 102, 110, 115, 128, 140, 146, 148-149, 159-160, 162, 164, 170-173, 179-180, 184, 186, 188, 196-197, 202, 206, 210, 212, 214-215, 217, 228, 230, 234-235, 238-

Fry, C.B., 95
Fuad, Ahmed, King of
    Egypt, 55, 95-97, 103
Fürst, xvi, 31
fustanella, 2, 197

Galli, Signor, 114, 288
Garde du Corps, 31
Garde-Uhlan Regiment, 105
Garibaldi, Giuseppe, 42, 51
Gazette, Cologne, 107, 143
Gazi, Ahmed Muhtar Pasha,
    84
Gendarmerie, 123, 133, 150,
    185, 187-188, 208, 212-
    213, 217, 233, 240, 255,
    266, 272, 289, 316, 333,
    368
George I, King of Greece,
    xxii, 19, 34
George V, King of Britain,
    10-11, 22, 61, 74, 93, 95,
    100, 173-174, 349-350,
    357, 359
George VI, x, xi
George Karageorgevich,
    Prince of Serbia, 28, 302
German Empire, xviii, xl,
    204, 270, 349, 356, 375,
    392
Germeni, Themosticles, 213
Germeses, Thesistakli, 221
Ghani, Toptani, 36

Ghegs, 2, 46
Ghermanos, Bishop, 214

Ghica, Prince Albert, 95,
    101
Ghilardi, Leon, 190, 234,
    277-278, 346
Giesl, Baron, 53, 342, 348,
    354
Giolitti, Giovanni, 34, 73,
    168
Gioni, Marco, 272, 290,
    295-296
Gjakove (Jacova, Djakova),
    354
Glouster, H.M.S., 190, 193-
    194
Goremykin, Ivan, 23
Goschen, Sir Edward, 108-
    110, 136, 182-183, 248-
    249, 280
Graf, xvi
Grammos, Mount, 226
Gramosta District, 283
Grand Vizier, 3, 72
Granet, Colonel, 223
Graphic, 111
Grata, Nicolo, 381
Graz (Austria), 273
Grecophones, 7
Greece, xix, xx, 54, 64, 82,
    88, 91-92, 116-117, 173,
    182, 208, 216, 220, 233,
    365, 367, 374
Grenadier, xii
Grey, Sir Edward, 11-12, 58,
    60, 70, 73-76, 78, 81-82,
    88, 90-93, 96, 104, 107-
    110, 116, 122, 125-126,
    131, 137, 158, 161-162,

165, 174-175, 178, 189,
223, 247, 253, 261-262,
278-279, 292, 302, 306,
309, 310, 315, 318, 333,
344, 349, 350, 353, 355,
357

Groningen, 291

Gruda, 205, 222-223

Grunau, Baron Werner von,
384

Guga, Jake nn., 381

Gumpenberg, Baron von,
251, 253

Gurakuchi, Louis, 100, 301

Gurshner, William, 305, 339

Gustav, Adolf VI, of
Sweden, x

Gycas, 95, 101

Haakon VII, King of
Norway, x, xix

Habsburg, 5

Hague, The, 397

Hamdi Rebeiki, sheik, 283,
290

Hamid Bey Toptani, 86-87,
291

Hamilton, Lord John, 173-
174

Harrach, Count, 225

Hassan (servant), 358

Hassan Bey Prishtina, 39,
138, 210, 363, 396

Hassan Riza Bey (Hussein
Reza), 37, 68, 88

Hassler, Herr, 288

Haxhi (Haxi), Qerim
(Kerim),, 377

Heaton-Armstrong, Duncan,
ix, 40, 143-144, 158,
165, 171, 192, 196, 198,
200-201, 211, 214, 225-
226, 228-229, 231, 235,
237-238, 240, 242, 245,
247, 252, 256, 267, 269,
286, 288, 301, 303, 305,
315, 328, 334, 339, 344,
346, 352, 358, 362, 364-
366, 368

Heaton-Armstrong, Jack,
272, 275, 276, 297, 315

Heinrich, Prince of Prussia,
350, 354, 359

Helmreich, Counselor, 165

Herbert, Aubrey, 64, 152,
221, 224, 308-309

Hertling, Count von, 386,
389

Herzegovina, freighter, 290,
298, 305

Hierolochoi, 120, 213

Hilmi Pasha, 8

Himira (Khimira), 216

Hintze, von, Secretary, 391

Hodjas, 298, 320

Hoif Reitschule, 172

Hofburg, 14

Hoheitz, 31, 166

Hohenlohe, Prince Gottfried,
192, 385

Hohenzollern, xx

Hohenzollern-Sigmaringen,
23

456

Hohenzollern-Sigmaringen, Prince Karl, 23, 95, 97
Hohenzollern, yacht, 71, 215, 312, 317
Holland, 40, 91, 333, 397
Holy Roman Empire, xvii
Hope, Anthony, xi, xiii, 234, 399
Hornborstel, attaché, 242
Hospital, British, 300, 323
Hotel Elisabeth, 348
Hoti, 205, 222-223
Hoyos, Count Alexander, 52, 318
Huchnite, 226
Hungary, 123, 226
Hussar, xii

Ibrahim, Captain, 267
Ifran Bey, 396
Imperial, Hotel, 171
Imperali, Marquess, 62
International Boundary Commission, 112, 118-119, 129, 131, 146, 222-223, 235
International Control Commission, 90-92, 105, 108, 114, 123, 143, 162-164, 174-176, 185-186, 193, 197, 202, 206-207, 209, 213, 215, 217, 231, 233, 235, 259, 261, 269, 272, 313, 323-324, 329, 338, 340, 362, 368, 373
Ionescu, Take, 103, 106, 152, 272, 318, 343-344

Ipek, 223, 354
Ippen, Chief, 165
Isa Boletin, 36, 47, 51, 93, 100, 117, 160, 245, 274, 290, 295-296, 354, 363
Ischl, 305, 348
Ishmi, 276, 320
Islam (n.f.n.), 221
Ismail Kemal Bey Vlora, 38, 47-48, 54, 63, 72, 88-89, 95, 97, 99, 102, 107-109, 160-163, 188, 206, 210, 265, 328, 336, 339
Ismet (Izzat, Izzet) Pasha, 95, 146, 149, 162
Istanbul, xxxvi
Isvolski, Alexander, 135, 177, 327
Italy, 49, 53, 56, 74, 82, 97, 106, 125, 131, 167, 219-220, 267, 270, 279, 316, 334, 345, 370, 374, 378, 380

Jacova (Djakova, Gjakove), 354
Jäger, xii
Jagow, Gottlieb von, 22, 67, 103, 106, 108-109, 122, 182, 248-249, 327-328, 340-341, 354, 371, 379
Janina, (Jannina), 1, 40, 47, 58, 70
Johantho, M. de, 101
Joslyn Art Museum, 32
Journal de Genève, 394
Jovanovich, Y.M., 303

458

Melek Bey Frasheri, 251
Mellan, 221
Mensdorff, Count, 61-63,
74-75, 165
Mérey, Count Kajetan, 170,
225, 235, 331, 334, 340
Merry Widow, The, xi
Mexi, Kristo, 39, 138-139,
160, 313, 328
Mexico, xxi
Michael, Prince of Serbia,
343
Michaelis, Georg, 384
Michaelovich, Ambassador,
350
Midhat Bey Frasheri, 221,
263
Militia, (Millice), 344
Ministerium des Äussern, 16
Miramare, 225
Mirdita, 2-3, 45-47, 147,
188
Mirdita, Abbot of, 193
Mirdites, 34-35, 188, 210,
250-251, 272, 276, 286,
289, 294, 296, 300, 353
Mischich, Colonel, xxv
Misurata, ship, 214, 255-
259, 265, 344-345
Mohammed, Belil, 221
Moltedo, Captain, 238, 273
Moltke, Helmuth von, 69,
234, 271, 358
Mon Repo, 178, 180
Monastir, 1, 112-113, 119
Montenegro, xii, xix, xxi,
xxvi, xxxviii, 5, 6, 37,

43, 47, 50, 53, 55, 63-64,
73, 76-78, 79, 86, 88,
115, 222, 334, 353, 358,
367, 371, 374
Montpensier, Duke of, 97-
102
Moore, Arthur, 287, 300
Morava, Mount, 233
Moritz, von Schaumburg-
Lippe, 95, 101
Morocco, xxxvi, xxxvii,
166, 177
Mufid Bey Libhova, 39,
115, 120, 134, 146, 160,
162, 217, 239, 242, 246,
258, 263, 274, 320, 323
Mufti, Grand, 380
Muhammad V, Sultan, 50
Mujuskovic, Lazar, 64
Munich, 397
Muricchio, Lt. Colonel, 213,
238, 273
Musa Kuasim (Kasim), 237,
268, 377
Muslims, 7, 46, 86, 204-205,
220, 347, 376
Mustafa Bey, 184
Mustafa Ndroga (Broka),
237, 268

Nadolny, Dr. Rudolf, 114,
139-140, 143, 147, 152,
219-220, 232-233, 241-
242, 270
Napoleon I, xvii, xix
Napoleon III, xix, 14
Napoleon, Prince, 96

Napoleons (coins), 8, 214
Nardella, composer, 197
National Zeitung, 190
Nazim, Pasha Grand Vizier, 97
Nebel, Reporter, 173
Neues Palais, 105, 317
Neues Weiner Tagblatt, 330
NeuWied am Rhein, 25, 31, 32, 146, 178-180
Nice, France, 38
Nicholai II, Czar of Russia, 22, 24, 66, 70-71, 185, 227, 237, 281, 341, 349, 355-357, 360
Nicolic, Andra, 64
Nicolson, Sir Arthur, 73-74, 76, 97, 108, 318, 333, 350
Nieder Alt Wied, 24
Nikola, King of Montenegro, 29-30, 35, 43, 50-53, 72-74, 77-78, 81-82, 302, 358
Nogga, Phillip, 103, 138, 160, 258, 263, 267, 304
Noord Brabant. cruiser
Nopca, Franz, 100
Norakovic, Stojan, 64
Norway, xix, 91, 350

Ober Alt Wied, 24
Ogran, 221
Oidtmann, Fraulein von, 161, 364
Olga, Queen, 19
Orleans, Duke of, xiii

Orosh, 117, 147, 210
Orthodox Christians, 7, 86, 138, 186, 190, 395
Osman Bali, 37
Österreichische Rundshau, 103
Otranto, Strait of, 345
Otto, King of Bavaria, xxi
Otto, King of Greece, 111
Ottoman Empire, xix, xxxvi, 44, 47, 207

Paar, Count, 311
Pact of London, 1915
Palace, the (Durazzo), 160-161, 198-200, 234, 243, 246, 291, 339, 369, 372, 381
Palèologue, Maurice, 326
Papoulis, Anastasios, 189-190
Para, von, Consul, 380
Paris, 11, 96, 101, 176, 333, 335, 340, 381, 398
Paris Peace Conference, 394-395
Pasha, xxviii, 4, 35
Pasich, Nichola, 28, 54, 56, 66, 78-79, 118, 311, 343, 348
Paul, King of Greece, x
Pearson, Owen, ix
Peles, Castle, 324
Permeti, 208
Petar I, Karageorgevich, King of Serbia, xxv,

462

xxvi, 27-29, 115, 302-303

Petraiev, Aleksander, 213, 368

Petrovich, Commissioner, 114

Petrovich, General Laza, xxiii, xxiv

Pfuel, Fraulein von, 161, 181, 214

Phillips, Colonel George Fraser, 8, 141, 147, 162-163, 187, 202, 205, 222-223, 227, 248, 266, 269, 297, 302-303, 306, 353

Piaster, (Turkish), xxviii

Pichon, Stephen, 125

Pimodan, Count, 250, 275-276, 297, 301

Plamenc, Petar, 30, 83

plis, 2, 36

Pocketbook of Counts, A, xvi

Pogradets, 212

Poincaré, Raymond, 12, 30, 52, 59-60, 68, 82, 176, 327, 332, 344, 355

Poland, 387

Pompey, 194

Popovich, Jovo, 73, 76, 81

Porta Romana, 195, 285, 298

Portugal, xxi

Potsdam, 33, 103-105, 143, 160, 166, 312, 317, 350, 351, 354

Pound sterling, xxviii

Pourtalès, 175, 185-186, 281, 355

Premeti, 221, 336

Premeti, Turkhan Pasha, 39, 134, 188, 208-210, 212, 215-216, 226, 229, 233, 235, 246, 248, 263-265, 281, 286, 299, 313, 315, 320, 324, 326-328, 331-332, 340, 354, 368-369, 380, 394

Prenk Bib Doda, 34-35, 41, 45, 47, 139, 147, 162, 182, 188, 210, 224, 227, 247, 250, 263, 271-272, 275, 297, 298-299, 301, 306, 394

Prinz, 31

Prishtina, Hassan Bey, 39, 138, 210, 363, 396

Prizren, 115, 123, 223

Protocol of London, 72

Provisional Government of 1912-1914, 38, 64, 83, 87, 89, 91, 95, 99, 108, 115, 146, 150, 163, 271

Provisional Government of 1915, 373

Prussia, xviii, 31

Puglia, launch, 233

Punch, 19, 85

Quai d'Orsay, 176, 233

Quamil (Kamil) Haxifeza

Quirinale Palace, 33, 168, 170

Rainier, Prince of Monaco, x
Ranette, M., 201, 328
Rappaport, Alfred, 271, 377
Rastbul, (Raspul), 229, 245, 250, 252, 273, 285, 291, 295, 298
Red Crescent, 77
Red Cross, 77, 112, 295
Red Star, 295
Reddingius, Tiddo, 134, 287, 304
Refugees, 310, 347
Regency, 395-396
Regina Elena, ship, 231
Reich, xviii
Reichstag, 21, 163, 387
Reimers, Hendrik G.A., 134, 305
Reiter, xvi
Reshan, 226
Revenue, 8
Rhin, Hotel du, 176
Rhineland, xviii, 24, 103
Ritz Hotel, 173
Riviera, French
Rjetsch, 186
Rodd, Sir Rennell, 67, 77, 168, 218, 301
Roelfsema, Lucas, 133-134, 228, 231, 239, 245, 251, 253, 287, 300
Roman Catholics, 7, 46, 188, 203, 247, 267, 385, 395
Romania, xix, xxxvi, xxxix, 53, 103, 125, 167, 208, 220, 232, 286, 324, 328, 330, 333, 343, 390
Romanian War of 1877-1878, 26
Romberg, Baron von, 381
Rome, 40, 167, 172, 188, 235, 254, 279
Rossi, (n.f.n.), 221
Rudolf, Crown Prince, xiii, 14, 71, 311
"Ruritania", xi, 234, 369, 399
Russia, xxxviii, xl, 47, 56, 60, 73, 76, 165, 184, 220, 281, 321, 324, 344, 349, 361, 386
Russo-Turkish War, xxi, 84

Salandra, Antonio, 34, 44
Salic Law, xxvii
Salonika, xxxix, 78, 113, 196
Salvari, Miltiades, 180
Sami Bey Vrioni, 201, 225, 256, 267, 358, 394
San Giovanni di Madua, 8, 52, 62, 85-86, 140, 194
San Giuliano, Antonio, 34, 42, 52-53, 64, 73, 92, 106-108, 164, 168-169, 172, 225, 227, 254, 262, 264, 274, 279, 282, 288-289, 301, 315-316, 326-328, 330-331, 337, 350

Santi Quaranta, 83, 85, 191, 213, 216, 221, 233

234-235, 237, 242, 250,
255, 264, 276, 283, 300,
372
Tisza, Count Istvan, 123,
314, 318, 371
Tomes, Jason ix
Tomjenovic, Officer, 239
Toptani, Abdi Bey, 138,
230, 263
Toptani Clan, 229
Toptani, Vehid Bey, 70
Tosks, 2, 4, 197, 345, 347
Totleben, Count, 185
Tourtoulis, Doctor Michael,
182, 210, 227, 263, 380,
394
Trautmansdorff, Count Carl,
159
Trent (Trentino), 219, 371
Trentino (Trent), 219, 371
Tribuna, 246
Trieste, 39, 73, 97, 100, 110,
190, 192, 288, 358
Trieste Stock Exchange, 288
Trifari, Admiral, 258
Triple Alliance (Central
Powers), xxxix, 49, 103,
132, 173, 206-207, 212,
281, 284, 306, 350, 370-
371, 380
Triple Entente, 106, 114,
132, 212, 281, 355, 374,
378
Tripoli, xxxviii, 253
Tripolitania, xxxvii, 38
Trotha, Commandant von,
161, 168, 193, 196, 198,

201, 211, 225, 228, 231,
245-246, 253, 256, 260,
266, 275, 289, 298, 334,
344, 358
Troubridge, Admiral Ernest,
74, 300, 339
Tsale, Pandeli, 221
Tsarskoe Selo (also
Czarskoe), 185
Tschirschky, von, Count
Heinrich, 89, 103, 139,
164, 171, 312, 314-315,
318, 338, 349, 357
Tsouras, Major, 324
Tunisia, xxxvii
Turin, Count of, 95, 101
Turkey, 35, 52, 58, 60, 88,
188, 210, 367, 370
Turkhan Pasha Premeti, 39,
134, 188, 208-210, 212,
215-216, 226, 229, 233,
235, 246, 248, 263-265,
281, 286, 299, 313, 315,
320, 324, 326-328, 331-
332, 340, 354, 368-369,
380, 394

Uhlan, 31, 155
Uhlan Regiment, Third
Guard, 53, 105, 155,
157, 372
Umberto, King of Italy, xxi
Union of Kruja, 377
United States, 53, 116
Urach, von, Duke (Prince)
of, 95, 97, 101, 134, 215,
265

266, 275, 289, 298, 334,
344, 358
von Tschirschky, Count
Heinrich, 89, 103, 139,
164, 171, 312, 314-315,
318, 338, 349, 357
von Urach, Duke (Prince)
of, 95, 97, 101, 134, 215,
265
von Waldburg zu Wolfegg,
Count, 324
von Wiesner, Friedrich, 326
Vranya, Serbia, 302
Vironi, 5
Vrioni, Sami Bey, 201, 225,
256, 267, 358, 394
Vukotich, Janko, 30

Waldburg zu Wolfegg,
Count, 324
Waldenburg. 181, 192, 368,
381, 383, 385, 388
Walford, William, 253
Walsh, Sir Arthur, 173
Wat Marasch, 148
Watson, Captain Hugh, 83
Wedel, Ambassador, 384,
388
West Yorkshire Regiment,
8, 141, 223
Wied, Archbishop Count
Hermann zu, 24
Wied-Neuwied, xviii, 32
Wied, Crown Prince Carol
Victor, 214

Wied, Prince Alexander
Philip Maximillian, 24,
32
Wied, Prince Friedrich zu,
109, 372
Wied, Prince Victor, zu, 31,
102, 106, 109, 179, 364
Wied, Princes of, 24
Wied, Princess Pauline, 109
Wied-Runkel, 32
Wied, Wilhelm zu (Fifth
Prince), 181
Wied, Wilhelm zu, Prince
(King) of Albania, 31,
3791, 96, 102-103, 105,
153, 165, 179, 321-322,
329, 339, 363, 365-368,
372, 397, [title; 281,
384, 389, 391]
Weiner Bank Verein, 115,
172, 212
Wiesner, Dr. Friedrich von,
326
Wilhelm II, Kaiser, xxvi, 16-
17, 20-21, 23, 34, 52, 57,
59-60, 63, 66-71, 74, 83-
85, 113, 118, 124, 126,
154-155, 215, 218-220,
227, 262-263, 278-280,
284, 289, 306, 311, 317-
318, 324, 350, 354-356,
358-360, 378, 392, 399
Wilhelmina, Princess of the
Netherlands, 31
Wilhelmina, Queen of the
Netherlands, 31, 91, 112,
114, 333

471